Families of the World

FAMILIES

OF THE WORLD

Family Life at the Close of the Twentieth Century

VOLUME 1
THE AMERICAS AND THE CARIBBEAN

Hélène Tremblay

Translated by Hilary and Paul Childs-Adams

Script editor Pat Capon

FARRAR, STRAUS AND GIROUX

New York

Copyright © 1988 by Famo Ltd.
Translation copyright © 1988 by
Hilary and Paul Childs-Adams
All rights reserved
Printed in Hong Kong by South China Printing Co.
Designed by Helen Barrow
First edition, 1988

Library of Congress Cataloging-in-Publication Data
Tremblay, Hélène.
[Familles du monde. English]
Families of the world: family life at the close of the 20th
century / Hélène Tremblay; translated by Hilary and Paul
Childs-Adams; script editor, Pat Capon.—1st ed.
p. cm.
Translation of: Familles du monde.
Contents: v. 1.The Americas and the Caribbean.
1. Family—Cross-cultural studies. 2. Family—History—20th
century. I. Capon, Pat. II. Title.
HQ518.T6813 1988   306.8′5—dc19   88-7106

Credits

CARTOGRAPHY AND GRAPHICS
Barbara Mullin,
Department of Geology and Geography,
Hunter College, New York City

RESEARCH ASSISTANT
Noemie Terzian

With the assistance, on the Amazon statistics, of
Dr. Nancy Flower, assistant professor,
Department of Anthropology,
Hunter College, New York City

PHOTO EDITOR
Lauren Stockbower

Acknowledgments

All the help I have received has been of great importance, but everyone who has given me support will understand why I am thanking my friend Jean Tetrault first. For the last twenty years, his presence in my life has provided me with a world vision and, in doing so, has permitted the concept of this book to come to life.

AND

The support of the following institutions has been essential:
The Canadian International Development Agency (CIDA)
The United Nations Children's Fund (UNICEF)
United Nations Development Programme (UNDP)
Canada Save the Children
United Nations Photographs & Exhibit Section
United Nations Fund for Population Activities (UNFPA)
The correspondents of the Third World Press Agency (IPS)
The Samuel & Saidye Bronfman Foundation, Montreal
United Nations Department of Public Information (DPI)
Le Musée de l'Homme, Paris
Pathé Kodak, France
The Olympus Corporation, Consumer Products Group, USA.
DHL Worldwide

BUT

So many people have helped me on a personal basis, including all those friends who knew how to stay silent when I was preparing myself for this new life. A special word has to be said for those who listened, fed, sheltered me while I was searching for the means to achieve my goal: Chantal, Annick, Dietrich, Lolette, Ariele, François, Elizabeth, Christiane, Charles, Lise, Gisele, Gaetan, and my father.

Special and deep-felt gratitude to Henri Crepeau, whose initial financial generosity allowed my first step into this great adventure.

WITH

A special acknowledgment to those who, in every country, accompanied me patiently in my search for the family. With great emotion, I think of those who so kindly opened their doors to let me into the warmth of their homes and honored me with their friendship: THE FAMILIES.

Preface

by JEAN GUIART
Professor at the National Museum of Natural History
Director of the Ethnological Laboratory and Institute
Le Musée de l'Homme, Paris

Hélène Tremblay has created, with an original and ethnographically impeccable approach, a document that enables the reader to understand the everyday lives of people in all parts of the world. Although we have a vague idea that some of them enjoy affluence, while the vast majority live in poverty, comparisons always rely on figures which mean little to anyone. Here the facts speak for themselves, sometimes in stark cruelty. The privileged prosperity of people in the West—when they have jobs—and the varying degrees of poverty of the rest of the world are strikingly apparent in these photo-essays, without a single superfluous word.

We have become accustomed to violence on television and to photographs depicting groups of people in the grip of famine, in the final stages before death. We know nothing of the conditions of everyday life among the peoples of the tropical Third World, most of whom live in vast conurbations lacking the most essential public services. From time to time there are reports in the media of armed revolt by young people in various parts of the world: the reports never mention the conditions of frustration in which they have grown up or the daily miracles, verging on martyrdom, of the mothers and elder sisters who support their inevitably large families and somehow never despair.

I find Hélène Tremblay's approach very satisfying. She begins with the photographs and supplements them with text. This enables her to succeed at what ought to be the ambition of every ethnographer, although so many fail, even when they are able to persuade their publishers to be generous with illustrations, since they have not succeeded in ridding themselves of the idea that the picture is there to illustrate the text. Photographs, however, say far more than words, conveying a vision that is both general and personal as well as information of unparalleled accuracy, even though the best professional scholars have hitherto failed to adapt to them. In individual collections and public archives lie hundreds of thousands of unused photographs containing the answers to specific questions, which have remained unanswered because no one has ever attempted to organize and make systematic and scientific use of this potential source of information. The experts have not been trained to do this and pour scorn on the very idea: Hélène Tremblay, however, points the way with a sure touch.

Everyday life is never more than the very stuff of existence, the quintessence of life and labor under every clime and in every civilization. It is so close to us that we are often incapable of describing it, devoting ourselves instead to analyzing institutions that fascinate by virtue of their strangeness and their exoticism. Even the most famous ethnologists have failed to put their finger on the pulse of the everyday life of the men, women, and children whose existence provides the foundation for their theoretical analysis. Only Margaret Mead had the spark of genius to evoke, albeit only in descriptive terms, the details of the environment and the thousands of elements and actions that make up life, every day, day after day, and that seem so obvious that they are ultimately over-looked and forgotten.

I regret that no member of my scientific staff had the idea for this book. Hélène Tremblay presents herself and her concept without false modesty, in the full conviction that she is right. And she is.

I hope this book will provide ample food for thought and will prove as enriching an experience for its readers as it has been for me as I have followed its progress from its inception. It is a book I would have liked to have written myself.

Table of Contents

Introduction

In the autumn of 1981, I had the idea of writing *Families of the World*, and only now, seven years later, comes the publication of the first volume. What I naïvely thought would be a four-year project became a vision that will most likely take a lifetime. Today, having visited sixty countries and lived with more than eighty families, I have finally begun to approach my dream.

In 1981 I was a television producer and had been working in the communication field for eight years. In this industry I had all the means of modern communication at my fingertips, but I found myself wondering why it was that in an age in which communication takes place at the touch of a button, the world's residents had not yet met. During my own travels, I would encounter children, their mothers and fathers; our eyes would meet, full of curiosity about each other. At home, I would lie awake at night and try to imagine myself in another country, but I was too ignorant to let my imagination drift; I wanted to meet the people of the world face to face. How does one discover the world short of spending a lifetime traveling and having access to thousands of books? I realized that people all over the world have one thing in common: family life.

The idea of a book on family life took root deep inside me; I willingly left everything behind in order to pursue it. I had to go, so that I could never say, "One day I had an idea, but . . ." The very thing that in my early teens I had promised myself never to do.

Now that I have finished this first volume, it is clear to me that my approach was the right one. I believe that if every family on earth had access to this book, the world would truly meet for the first time. What better way to foster awareness, understanding, and tolerance.

The day in the life of each family portrayed in this book is a faithful description of people and events, a composite of a three-day stay with them between May 1983 and October 1985. In order to adequately document the living conditions of my hosts, I spent at least two weeks in every country. "What adventures you must have had," people often exclaim, and I have had a few. The minute I was left alone with the Yanomami in Amazonia, the whole tribe, women, children, and men, started to undress me. They were naked and were curious to see if my body was like theirs. I had to stand there and wait for the tribe to finish its investigation. It was an awkward moment, but I was not worried.

For some reason, they thought that my nudity was extremely funny, and everyone had a great time. But I suppose that if a naked person came into your house, you might feel like dressing him, too.

I was more worried the night I was abandoned by my guide in the Andes. Bolivia was the first country I visited. My guide did not speak very good English, and my Spanish was still not very good. The guide left but seemed to promise to return. He never did. I spent the night in a little mud house, but I did not really sleep. I have never learned to be afraid, but that night I wondered whether it would not be wise for me to become better acquainted with that emotion. The next day I found my way back alone across the mountain trails, asking myself if this dream of mine was really a good idea after all.

It was. Often we are scared because of our prejudice. People in every country that I have visited have welcomed me. Often the doors that were opened to me were no more than splintered pieces of wood, but that did not make the families any less generous. In Mexico, Pascuala decided that I was her godmother. She announced it all over the village. I wish that I could really be one and visit her mountain home more often. In Honduras, I shared Martha's bed and its fleas and lice. But the confidence and warmth we exchanged when the little girl snuggled up to me was worth the days of itching I endured.

Coming suddenly into these people's lives was often awkward. To put down my bags and say, "Well, just act as if I'm not there," is asking an awful lot. But I have spent many intimate moments with these mothers, sharing the long hours necessary for cooking, laundry, and other daily tasks; lining up beside them and their families on the floor to sleep or sharing their only bedroom. I was welcomed like a sister, and when I left, the families often said, "It's like you've always been here." I remember how heartbreaking it was to hold the grandmother of La Praesita in my arms as she sobbed. She was in her eighties, and I thought she might have seen herself in me and mourned the young adventurous woman that she had once dreamt of being.

But I had to leave. I have 160 countries to visit and other friends to make. Each country is an adventure, an adventure of the heart, of the emotions experienced while sharing intimately with people. Every day teaches me something new, and this is where I get my energy and resolve.

I hope that readers can share my passion and experience this exciting endeavor for themselves. I hope that this book will help parents open their children's eyes to the other people in the world. I hope that students will better understand the inequalities between the developed and the developing world, and that men and women will gain a sense of solidarity when they see how many, like them, fight the same battle every day: to keep their children alive and raise them with dignity.

A very ambitious project, I have often been told. Why is that so? It is so simple to say, "Mr. and Mrs. Smith, I want to introduce you to Mr. and Mrs. Gonzáles . . . and their family."

South America

AMAZONIA

THE YANOMAMI FAMILY

Carlos, age 25(1)
Mother, 21 (2)
Older Son, 7 (3)
Younger Son, 4 (4)
Baby Son, 18 months (5)

° This family's ages are approximate, as the Yanomami
have no notion of measured time.

SHABONO PABLO TELI
April 5

Predawn: Long before sunrise the biting cold awakens the residents of the Pablo Teli *shabono* (communal house). The fires that were rekindled over and over during the night are now no more than glowing embers. Languidly, arms reach out from hammocks to revive the flames. There are fifteen fires in this *shabono* and each one represents a family. Now comes the sound of adults clearing their throats, blowing their noses, and spitting on the beaten earth. At one fire, Baby Son is crying as he struggles to open his eyelids which are sealed with crust from an infection caused by flies. From their hammock, Mother plucks a few bananas hanging over her head and throws them on the coals along with some palm leaves stuffed with nutmeats. Breakfast will soon be ready.

Mother is the third wife of Carlos, one of the *shabono*'s leaders. Except for Carlos, who was given his name by Protestant missionaries, the rest of the tribe do not use the names given to them at birth. These names are sacred and forbidden. People address each other by familial relationship. The Yanomami are very simple communal people. Gentle, lovable, quick to laughter, they seem closer to our primate ancestors than any other Amazonian tribe. Their lives consist of procuring food and lying back in their hammocks to chat with one another. A well-meaning outsider thought to motivate the tribe by giving them machetes, but that only enabled the Yanomami to get their food faster and spend more time at play.

After feeding her children, Mother joins the other women on their way to fish. They travel swiftly in single file, woven baskets suspended on their backs and their unweaned babies perched inside. They follow the trail across the savanna and plunge into the jungle. Older Son follows with some of the other children.

Mother's husband, Carlos, is off hunting with the other men, taking advantage of the final days of the dry season. A born leader, Carlos is respected for his courage and his skill as a hunter.

Carlos' first wife lives in another *shabono* with their two children. He cast her out for infidelity. His second wife is sterile and lives at her mother's fire, where Carlos still supports her. Mother is the youngest sister of the second wife and has borne Carlos three children. Carlos' strength and courage enable him to support his three wives, his family, and his in-laws.

Grandfather leaves for one of the *shabono*'s three *conucos* (gardens). There is no hierarchy in the Yanomami household, but the elderly are respected and are sought after for their experience and their advice, As is his custom, Grandfather carries his spear to protect himself from animals or an enemy from another *shabono*. He picks bananas from the garden, and while he is there, burns the trunks of trees that were chopped down recently. By pushing back the forest, he uncovers enough soil to plant banana saplings. In the other *conucos*, there is a little manioc and enough cotton to weave the hammocks.

Deep in the forest, the women split up into smaller groups. Mother sets off with two young girls. One of them has just reached puberty and, although pregnant, she runs and skips along like a child. After more than an hour's walk across steep hillsides along an almost invisible path, they reach the edge of a stream. They delve into the water, submerging their baskets and dredging them along the bottom to catch squirming little shrimps and small crabs. The first catch of shrimps is for them, and they gorge themselves. This delicacy cannot wait.

Like all Yanomami babies, Baby Son is a true acrobat. In a sling made of bark, he clings to his mother as she climbs over trees and branches caught in the middle of the stream. He greedily eats the little shrimps she offers him. Full and satisfied, he falls asleep rocked by his mother's movement. From time to time, Older Son stops fishing to pick wild fruits from the banks, look into a bird's nest, and explore his surroundings.

Yanomami of all ages know the forest up to a distance of two days' walk in all directions from their *shabono*.

Midday: In the garden, the heat has become unbearable. Grandfather departs heavily laden. With relief he returns to the cool jungle, where the sun, blocked by gigantic trees, never reaches the forest floor. At home, Grandmother crouches near the fire, surrounded by the children who chose to remain there. She offers a dry old breast to one of her grandsons to pacify him. Even though he is more than three years old, he is just recently weaned. His mother and father and their new baby have gone hunting together, and he is upset. Grandmother smiles patiently. She knows that this push out of infancy is rough for him. Grandparents care for all the small children and make room in their narrow hammocks for those in need of a little affection. Dozens of times a day the two old people suck the children's toes to remove the tiny parasitic fleas that burrow in the flesh and cause unbearable itching.

In midafternoon, Grandmother gets up to go and fill gourds at the river and look for firewood in the forest. Her body and her legs, made muscular by walking and working, still bear heavy loads easily. Only her skin, wasted by parasitic illnesses, reveals her age.

The Yanomami are unaware of measured time, but habit, intuition, and intimacy with nature enable the women who separated in the morning to meet on the way home. Along the way, they also gather fruits and nuts that catch their eyes. They stop in a small clearing to wrap their harvest in banana leaves. Back at the *shabono*, Mother puts each small package into a basket hanging above the family hammocks. She and Carlos have only to stretch out their hands to put them in the fire. Both men and women cook: it requires little skill and no utensils.

Upon their arrival at the *shabono*, some women and children jump into the nearby river to cool off. They do not wash themselves. Their scalps and bodies, stained by soil, ashes, and bodily waste, will never be clean.

Early evening: The family is reunited around the grandparents' fire. Mother's sister, her husband, and their baby come back empty-handed from hunting but bring wild honey and fruit that they have found on their way home. Yanomami men and women are forbidden to make love in the *shabono* and often use hunting as an excuse to be together. The two travelers discuss their bad luck. The *shabono* has stayed in place for too long now, and the group has exhausted the game and fish in their area. The Yanomami are seminomadic and every several years they build a new *shabono* on virgin land that must be at least a two-day journey away from other *shabonos*.

On her son-in-law's return, Grandmother leaves the fire. It is forbidden for them to meet face to face and to speak. This taboo derives from a myth about a love affair between a man and his mother-in-law. This myth is probably a preventive measure, for Yanomami women marry and bear children so young that they are often desirable to their daughters' husbands. The son-in-law sits in his hammock, with his baby in his arms, feeding him mashed banana. Yanomami fathers always take time to care for their children and play with them.

Night falls. Piled in the hammocks, the family stuff themselves with fruit, honey, and shrimp. It is clear that Carlos will not return from hunting tonight, so Grandfather will stay at his daughter's fire to protect her family.

Mother stacks wood next to her hammock to fuel the fire during the night. Grandfather and the few men left block and camouflage the entrance to the *shabono* with small tree trunks balanced on top of each other. From the outside it is impossible to distinguish the opening from the rest of the enclosure. Enemies are unlikely to find it, and even if they do, they will wake the inhabitants with the noise they will make trying to force their way in.

The children fall asleep lying on top of the adults. They feel warmer sharing the small hammocks on these cold nights, and legs and arms dangle close to the fire. In the gathering dusk, one or two old men can still be heard philosophizing about life, but eventually the lack of an audience sends them off to sleep. One of Mother's sisters sits on the ground next to her fire. She is menstruating and is thus considered unclean. Her hammock is forbidden to her. She spends the night catching and eating the fleas that jump from hammock to hammock.

The shabono is a circular, half-covered building with an open courtyard in the center where children play and festive occasions are celebrated

Under the shabono's roof, there are fifteen fire sites. Around each one there are three hammocks marking each family unit. The community constitutes a relatively autonomous social unit

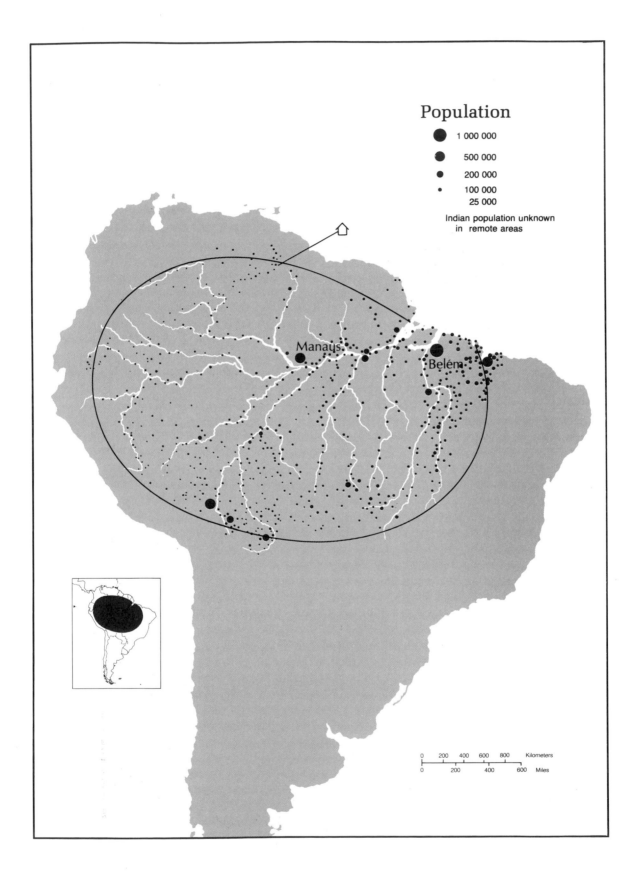

Population

- ● 1 000 000
- ● 500 000
- ● 200 000
- · 100 000
- 25 000

Indian population unknown
in remote areas

Manaus

Belém

| 0 | 200 | 400 | 600 | 800 | Kilometers |
| 0 | 200 | 400 | 600 | Miles |

AMAZONIA*

THE NAME:[38] The river, and eventually the region, got the name Amazon from the account of the chronicler Friar Gaspar de Carvajal, who accompanied the Spanish conquistador Francisco de Orellana on the first expedition from Peru to the mouth of the river in 1541–42. Among other adventures, Carvajal reported that the Spanish were attacked by "women warriors," whom he called Amazons after the women warriors of the Greek myth.

AREA:[39] 6,288,000 sq. km. (2,427,810 sq. mi.)
Distribution by country:[40]
    Brazil: 3,560,000 sq. km. (1,374,524 sq. mi.) 54% of national territory
    Bolivia: 520,000 sq. km. (200,773 sq. mi.) 47%
    Colombia: 309,000 sq. km. (119,306 sq. mi.) 27%
    Ecuador: 138,000 sq. km. (53,282 sq. mi.) 27%
    Peru: 785,000 sq. km. (303,090 sq. mi.) 61%
    Venezuela: 175,750 sq. km. (67,857 sq. mi.) 19%
    Guyana: 156,750 sq. km. (60,522 sq. mi.) 73%
    Suriname: 163,309 sq. km. (63,054 sq. mi.) 90%
    French Guiana: 86,450 sq. km. (33,379 sq. mi.) 90%

WATER:[41] The Amazon River is 6,264 km. (3,892 mi.) from source to mouth; it contains 50% of all flowing water in the world and drains 40% of South America. It has more than 1,000 tributaries, 17 of which are more than 1,600 km. (994 mi.) in length. Ocean shipping can go up as far as Iquitos in Peru, 3,680 km. (2,287 mi.) from the river's mouth.

VEGETAL DISTRIBUTION[42]
    Tropical rain forest: 1,710,000 sq. km. (660,235 sq. mi.)
    Seasonal semi-evergreen forest: 2,710,000 sq. km. (1,046,337 sq. mi.)
    Savanna: 390,000 sq. km. (150,580 sq. mi.)
Annual rate of forest clearing:
    15,000 sq. km. (5,791 sq. mi.) per year
    Total cleared by 1980 (Brazil and Colombia only): 113.181 sq. km. (43,699 sq. mi.)

CLIMATE:[43] Average temperature: 26° C. (78° F.). Variation between the hottest and coolest month is seldom more than 5° C. (39° F.)
    Precipitation: 1,500–4,000 mm. (58.5–156 inches)

TOTAL POPULATION:[44] 4,841,000

NATIVE GROUPS PER COUNTRY: Indians are a small minority in most countries, and a very small minority in Amazonia. The population consists mainly of white settlers who have migrated from more densely populated regions and is concentrated chiefly in areas of rapid economic development.

BOLIVIA[45]
    Total pop. Bolivian Amazon: 911,566 (1976)
    Indian pop.: 120,000–130,000 (1.8%–2.2% tribal Indians in department of Beni).

BRAZIL[46]
    Total pop. Brazilian Amazon: 11,750,000 (1980)
    Indigenous pop.: 2% (estimate)
    State and territories include: Amazonas, Pará, Amapá, Acre, Roraima, Rondonia, Maranhão, and Mato Grosso
    41% urban (Belém, Santiago)
    Some major Indian groups in Brazil:
    Tukanoans: 11,554 (also in Colombia)
    Makuxi: 14,497
    Yanomamo: 9,000 (approx.) (8,500 in Venezuela)
    Tikuna: 17,528
    Kayapo: 2,740
    Xavante: 4,593

COLOMBIA[47]
    Total pop. Colombian Amazon: 298,000 (1972)
    Some major Indian groups in Colombia: Witoto, Tukanoans, Cubeo, Maku

ECUADOR[48]
    Total Ecuadorian Amazon: 173,000 (1974)
    Indian pop.: 36,000–51,000
    Some major Indian groups in Ecuador:
    Jungle Quechua: 25,000–35,000
    Jivaroan: 10,000–15,000
    Cofán: 297
    Waorani: 500
    Siona and Secoya: 347

GUYANA[49]
    Indian pop. 37,000 (approx.) (1981) (4% of total pop.)
    Some major Indian groups in Guyana:
    Warau
    Wapishana
    Macusi: 4,500
    Waiwai: 2,300

* See p. 272 for Amazonia sources, which do not correspond to the citation format for the rest of this book.

FRENCH GUIANA: 1,000–2,000 (of total 63,000) (1981)[50]

PERU[51]
Total pop. Peruvian Amazon: 739,000
Indian pop.: 220,000 (approx.) (2.5 times the native Indian pop. of Brazil)
Some major Indian groups in Peru:
Lowland Quechua: 35,000
Campa: 28,000
Aguaruna: 25,000
Cocama-Cocamilla: 21,000
Machinguenga: 12,000

SURINAME[52]
Indian pop.: 10,500 (approx.) (1980)
Some major Indian groups in Suriname:
Trio, Waiyana

VENEZUELA[53]
Total pop. Venezuelan Amazon: 413,400 (1971)
Indian pop.: 40,000 (approx.)
Some major Indian groups in Venezuela (1972):
Warao: 15,000 (partly in Guyana)
Panare: 1,708
Piaroa: 1,886
Ye'cuana: 1,200
Pemon: 2,700
Yanomamo: 8,500

SOCIAL INDICATORS FOR BRAZILIAN AMAZON[54]
Life expectancy: 48 years (1970)
Infant mortality: 124/1000 children up to one year (1970)
Doctors per 10,000 pop.: 3.0 (1970)
Illiteracy rate of labor force: 52%
Per capita GNP: 194 U.S.$ (1970)

LANGUAGE: Besides the national languages, many indigenous groups have their own. The principal lowland linguistic groups are Carib, Tupi, Arawak, Panoan, and Ge. Other languages, such as Yanomama, are isolated and do not belong to any of these major groups.

ECONOMIC ACTIVITIES
Petroleum: Peru, Venezuela, Bolivia
Mining: Brazil
Cattle: Brazil, Venezuela, Bolivia
Timber: Brazil, Peru
Extractive products (latex, Brazil nuts): Brazil, Peru
Plantation crops (coffee, rice, sugarcane, rubber, guarana, cocoa, etc.): Brazil, Peru, Ecuador, Venezuela

THE YANOMAMO[55]

MEANING: "People of our tribe"
The Yanomamo are divided into four language groups, of which the Yanomami are one.

TERRITORY
177,000 sq. km. (68,340 sq. mi.) of tropical rain forest along the border between Brazil and Venezuela. Their socioeconomic system is based on extensive areas of land.

The Yanomami practice a type of intermittent nomadism. Their agricultural system and their hunting and fishing require regeneration of fauna and flora. (The indigenous population is the best caretaker for the preservation of the ecosystem of the region.)

Rivers passing through their territory: Orinoco, Padamo, Ocamo, Mavac, Manaviche

HISTORY
Until recently one of the largest unacculturated groups of indigenous people in South America, the Yanomamo, in contrast to many societies in South America, appeared to have escaped the ravages of earlier centuries. Until recently they were able to live successfully in relative isolation, their traditional culture intact. That isolation has been shattered. In the early 1970s Brazil built a federal highway through Yanomamo territory. In 1973, a measles epidemic decimated fourteen Yanomamo villages. Missionaries want to save their souls; anthropologists want to study their bodies, minds, and behavior; prospectors searching for gold, settlers, national and multinational corporations want their land. The outcome of the onslaught is far from certain.

POPULATION
Brazil: 8,000 dispersed in 150 villages
Venezuela: 8,500 dispersed in 120 villages
Between 1950 and 1983 they lost an estimated 25% of their population, which is presently decreasing at the rate of 0.5% per year.
50% can expect to reach the age of 15 years. For those that reach this age, there is an additional life expectancy of 20 years.
21.7% of population is more than 30 years old; 7% more than 50 years old.

DENSITY: 0.11 pers./sq. km. to 0.16 pers./sq. km.

HABITAT: A village consists of one communal house called a *shabono*. All villages maintain frequent contacts for the exchange of goods and marriage alliances.

ACTIVITIES (or SUBSISTENCE)

Hunting, fishing, gathering, agriculture (plantains are the staple crop). They spend 4 to 6 hours a day on subsistence activities. The rest of the day is spent talking and resting.

FAMILY

Fertility: Average of 8 live births per woman, but of these, only 3 survive to maturity.

Crude death rate: 44%

Polygamy is accepted if the man can feed the children, the women, and their parents.

HEALTH

They believe that illnesses are caused by *hekuras* (bad spirits) that act in some independent way or are sent by their enemies.

ARGENTINA

THE CATOIRA FAMILY

César José Catoira, age 42 (1)
Nora Elva Catoira, 40 (2)
César Pablo Catoira, 17 (3)
Rubén Darío, 13 (4)
Alejandra Elisabeth, 12 (5)
Claudia Noemi, 10 (6)

1 dog

CORDOBA
June 20

5:15. The alarm clock rings, rings, and keeps on ringing as if the idea were to wake up the whole world! Everyone, that is, except César Catoira, for whom the alarm is intended and who pretends not to hear. Finally, shaking off his sleep, César exposes his lumbering body to the cold and damp that permeate his house and dresses quickly. A twenty-minute drive, half an hour to drink a cup of coffee and chat with his co-workers, and he clocks in at six-thirty.

For the past twenty years, César has worked as a garage mechanic for EPEC, Argentina's national electric company. The privilege of a regular salary, the good fortune of never having been without a job, and a lot of perseverance have enabled him to build, with his own hands, his five-room brick house. It has taken him twelve years, and it still isn't completely finished.

When they were first married and with their first child, César and Nora's house was a single room with a kitchen. Another boy was born, then a girl, and then another. César had to add two bedrooms and a bathroom. Now he has built yet another room on the flat roof so his growing sons and daughters can sleep separately. Part of his next paycheck will go to buy a bed and the boys will move in at the end of the month. Finally, thirteen-year-old Rubén will be able to play his drums to his heart's content without disturbing the rest of the family. Since his salary does not always cover all expenses, César repairs cars for people in the neighborhood in the evening. His garage is next to the house.

7:00. Rubén jumps out of bed, dresses, grabs a piece of fruit, and exits noisily, slamming the door behind him, heedless of the rest of the family who are still in bed. In fifteen minutes he will be sitting in class.

Sometimes Nora stays in bed until ten o'clock, but today is washday and she has to get up. She makes coffee and goes out into the yard to start the washing machine. The machine is more than fifteen years old, so Nora rinses and wrings out the clothes by hand before hanging them outside on the line. Afterward, she rouses her daughters. Alejandra and Claudia have no classes until the afternoon, but their morning's schedule is full. After coffee and a slice of bread and jam, they have to tidy the rooms, sweep the house, shower, wash their hair, and eat lunch. Alejandra is taking a hairdressing course on Saturdays and is going to practice on her mother this morning.

11:00. His sisters are in the shower when César Pablo emerges, dragging his feet nonchalantly. He turns on the television while waiting for his mother to serve him breakfast. This year he developed peritonitis and underwent surgery, missing most of his senior year. He is not prepared for the year-end exams and spends his days hanging around the neighborhood with some unemployed friends. César Pablo talks about becoming a lawyer but makes no effort to complete his education. His mother is a firm believer in success through education and plans to ask the college to let César Pablo enroll as an auditor. But she is exasperated with her son. "If César wants to be a lawyer, he'd better get moving," she says.

Her hair in curlers, Nora stands in front of the stove preparing lunch for her family. She cooks different things for everyone, and they all eat at different times. The first sitting is for the girls, the second for the boys, and the last for her husband. Nora doesn't question catering to each member of her family. To her this is what being a mother means, and she goes about her tasks good-naturedly and calmly. "I don't understand how these women manage when they go out to work," she says.

1:00. After eating their lunch, the girls put their school aprons on over their jeans and sweaters. They attend private school, as their father maintains they get a better education there. As soon as his sisters leave, Rubén arrives, sits down at the table, and waits to be served. Afterward, he goes off to downtown Córdoba, where he is taking a course at the Conservatory of Music two days a week. These are his favorite afternoons. Rubén is a cheerful and outgoing teenager. He loves his drums and intends to be a musician.

Nora and César Pablo have their lunch in front of the television, which turns out soap operas from morning till night. César's buddies arrive and drag him out of his chair. Now Nora can enjoy her shows in peace and quiet.

3:30. César José comes home from work. Another arrival, another meal to heat and serve. After eating, her husband trots quietly off to bed for a nap while Nora cleans up the kitchen. Then she starts ironing the clothes that have dried in the morning sun and wind.

6:00. The family gathers around the table for the traditional *mate* tea. Friends drop by, as they do every evening, and everyone joins in the animated discussion. The Catoiras are a relaxed, casual family, and their openness and friendliness make their home a favorite of the neighborhood. Nora turns down the television's sound but doesn't switch the set off. She fills the gourd with the herb and hot water and passes it around. Then she clears off a corner of the table so that the children can do their homework, in the midst of all the noise.

After his siesta, César retires to the garage to work on a neighbor's car. When he has finished, he showers and rejoins the family. There is nothing he likes more than these daily meetings in the kitchen. Today there will even be a little concert, with Rubén playing the drums, César Pablo the accordion, and a friend the guitar. Inspired by the irresistible music, César and Nora begin to dance a tango, the real Argentine tango, danced to immutable rules which they have mastered to perfection.

9:30. Nora is cooking again. Standing next to her stove, she cuts up herbs and tomatoes and heats them in the oil to make sauce for noodles. Argentina's famous beef, considered the world's best, is a luxury item for the Catoiras. *Asados* (grilled steaks) are only for weekends. The custom is to dine late, and dinner won't be served for another hour. As she does almost every evening, Nora adds another place setting or two for friends who drop by. In its corner, the television continues its endless litany of soap operas.

12:00. Rubén, who shares the pullout bed in the kitchen with his brother, is exhausted. He takes refuge in his parents' bed while waiting for the family and their friends to leave. Nora bravely starts to wash up and put things away, while the men discuss unemployment. "Maybe we should leave Córdoba and look for work in the South," the young people speculate. But the South is cold and far away from their families. If they wait, maybe the new government will do something. But it's late; their question will remain unanswered tonight.

1:00. After a final wipe with the sponge, Nora sets the fearsome alarm clock and climbs into bed. The lights go out, and the dog, who has slept all day, wakes up. He will spend the night by the front door, but his barking will not disturb the sleep of the Catoira family.

It took César twelve years of steady work and a lot of perseverance to build his house. Soon the boys will move into their own room on the roof

As they do every evening, friends drop in on the family for the traditional mate. Inspired by the music, César sweeps Nora up in a tango

ARGENTINA*

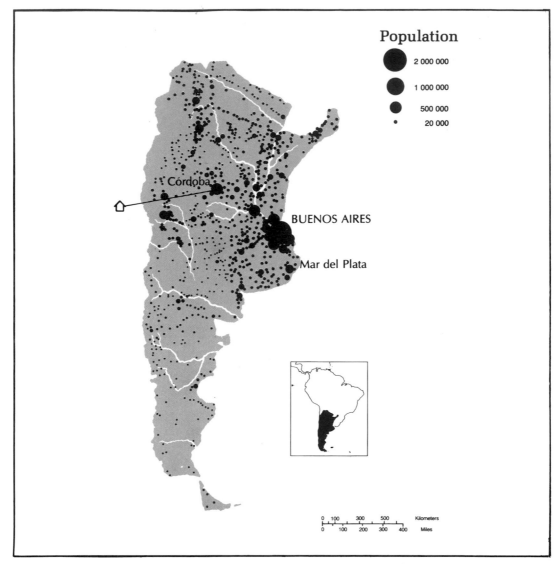

Population

2 000 000

1 000 000

500 000

20 000

Córdoba

BUENOS AIRES

Mar del Plata

| 0 | 100 | 300 | 500 | Kilometers |
| 0 | 100 | 200 | 300 | 400 | Miles |

THE NAME: From Latin *argentum,* meaning "silver." For the Spaniards, it was the road to the silver mines in Bolivia

THE PEOPLE: The Argentinians

GEOGRAPHY
West and southwest: Andes mountain ranges
South: Patagonia (semi-desert)
Northwest: Gran Chaco—vast subtropical lowlands and rain forest
Northeast: Mesopotamia
  Max. altitude: 6,960 m. (22,835 ft.) (Mt. Aconcagua)
Area: 2,780,889 sq. km. (1,073,340 sq. mi.)

° See p. 270 for Source Notes.

Density: 11 pers./sq. km. (28 pers./sq. mi.) (1986)
Arable land: 13% (1987)
Forest: 22%
Climate: Warm. Temperate over the pampas, where rainfall occurs at all seasons but diminishes toward the west.
  In the north and west, the climate is more arid, with high summer temperatures, while in the extreme south it is dry, but much cooler.

CAPITAL: Buenos Aires, pop. 2,908,000 (1980)

LANGUAGE: Spanish

RELIGION: Majority Catholic

POPULATION: Total: 30,600,000 (1985)
    Annual growth: 1.6% (489,600) (1980–85)
    Doubling time: 44 yrs.
    Urban: 85% (1985) (est. for year 2000: 89%)
    Rural: 15%

AGE GROUPS: (1980)
    12% less than 5 yrs.
    30% less than 15
    39% less than 20
    29% from 20 to 39
    21% from 40 to 59
    12% 60 yrs. and over

ETHNIC GROUPS
    White: 85%
    Mestizo, Indian, and other: 15%

HISTORY
    Originally inhabited by various nomadic Indians in the south and agriculturalist Indians in the north
    1501–2: Discovery of the Río de la Plata by Amerigo Vespucci
    1520–25: Arrival of Magellan and Cabot
    1536: Establishment of Buenos Aires by Pedro de Mendoza
    1541: Asunción becomes first permanent settlement
    Until 1776: Part of the Viceroyalty of Peru
    After 1776: Part of the Viceroyalty of the Río de la Plata
    May 25, 1810: Political autonomy of Buenos Aires
    July 9, 1816: Independence from Spain of the United Provinces of the Río de la Plata
    1853: Adoption of constitution
    1880–1916: Oligarchy
    1930: Military coup replaces civilian rule
    1945–55: Juan Perón's dictatorship
    1973: Perón reelected president
    1976–1983: Military in power
    1982: Loses Falklands (Malvinas) War to the British
    1983: Return to democracy

FAMILY
Marital status, for population 15 yrs. and older: (1980)
    Single: 28%
    Married: 52%
    Common-law: 7%
    Widowed: 11%
    Divorce is illegal.
Female head of household: 19% (1979 est.)
Fertility rate: 3.3 (1985)
Births out of wedlock: 27% (1979)
Teenage births: 13% (1979)
Contraception: 74% (1984)
Government's position on family planning: Considers the level of fertility to be satisfactory; current policy is to maintain it at its current level.

SOCIAL INDICATORS
Life expectancy: 72 yrs. (male: 67; female: 73) (1985)
Infant mortality: 35/1,000 births (1985)

Crude birth rate: 24/1,000 pop. (1985)
Crude death rate: 9/1,000
Health:
    Access to health services: 70% (urban: 80%; rural: 21%)
    Births attended by trained health personnel: no data†

HOUSING
Persons per household: 3.9 (1980)
Electricity: 6% without (1980)
Access to safe water: 63% (urban: 72%; rural: 17%) (1983)
Source of water: (1980)
    Piped inside: 73%
    Piped outside: 13%
    Not piped: 14%
Toilet facilities: (1980)
    Flush: 96%
Building materials: (1980)
    Concrete: 75%
    Wood: 11%
    Adobe: 2%
    Other: 12%
    Buildings considered precarious: 8%

EDUCATION
Literacy: 94% (male: 94%; female: 94%) (1980)
Gross enrollment ratio: (1985)
    First level: 108% (completing in 1980–84: 66%)
    Second: 70%
    Third: 36%
Educational attainment, for population 25 yrs. +: (1980)
    None: 7%
    First level: incomplete: 33% (complete: 33%)
    Second: entered: 20%
    Third: 6%

ECONOMIC ACTIVITY
Economically active population: 38% (male: 55%; female: 20% (1985)
Agriculture: 13% act. pop.; 14% of GDP
Mines: 4% act. pop.; 9% of GDP
Industry: 24% act. pop.; 22% of GDP
Services: 59% act. pop.; 55% of GDP
Per capita GNP: 2,130 U.S.$ (1985)
Population in absolute poverty: (1977–84)
    Urban: 30%
    Rural: 35%
National currency/per U.S.$: 601.81 pesos (1985)
Principal resources:
    Cereals: wheat, corn, soybeans; Cattle

COMMUNICATIONS
Radio:
    Transmitters: 202 (1979)
    Receivers: 16,000,000—540/1,000 pop. (1983)
Television:
    Transmitters: 75 (1977)
    Receivers: 5,910,000—199/1,000 pop. (1983)

† Indicates either that no data exist or that the government of the country in question has not made the information available.

BOLIVIA

THE QUISPE MAMANI FAMILY*

Jaime Mamani, age 39 (1)
Felipa Quispe, 36 (2)
Tiburcio Mamani Quispe, 16 (3)
Antonia, 11 (4)
Reynaldo, 7 (5)
Alejandro, 4 (6)

50 sheep
40 alpacas
2 pigs
1 cow   2 dogs
2 rabbits   1 cat

° Most South Americans have two surnames. The first reflects their father's and the second their mother's. When a woman marries, her husband's paternal name replaces her mother's name. The children's first surname will be their father's, their second their mother's.

QUISIHUYO
May 12

6:30. Despite the rooster's insistent crowing, the Quispe Mamani family do not throw back their heavy alpaca wool blankets. The province of Gamacho is on an isolated plateau of the Andes Mountains 4,600 meters (15,092 feet) above sea level. At night the temperatures plunge below freezing. Pulling on the petticoats that she left at the foot of the bed last night, Felipa leaves the tiny family bedroom, which barely contains three beds and a small table. She crosses the yard to the outbuilding that serves as a kitchen. She glances across the homestead, which contains within its stone walls her in-laws' home, the family livestock, and two large storehouses for the sheep and alpaca wool, grain, and potatoes. In the kitchen, Felipa crouches before the hearth, a simple pile of stones, and, using a wooden taper, lights the *taka*, a fuel made of sheep dung.

A few minutes later, her husband, Jaime, rises and walks quickly across the high plateau. Today he will cook for agricultural engineers from the capital who are studying the conditions for raising sheep and alpacas. It took them six hours of driving up a rough jeep trail to reach the province of Gamacho. The dry stubbly grass that the sheep and alpacas eat is about the only vegetation that thrives at this high altitude, and the animals' wool is the family's primary means of support. Today, Jaime has an opportunity to earn some extra money. Jaime's family and those of his two brothers, twelve people in all, share a five-hectare farm (a *minifundio*) which their father left them. Some of the land is used for growing oats for the livestock, but they plant potatoes on most of it.

7:00. Tiburcio drinks his tea sitting at his mother's side next to the hearth. Then he fills his *llicla* (a square piece of woven cloth worn around the shoulders and knotted against the body) with boiled *chuños* and sets out for school. *Chuños* are potatoes that have been frozen during the cold nights and dried in the burning midday sun. The family's diet consists exclusively of *chuños*, eaten either in soup or boiled and eaten cold.

It will take Tiburcio over an hour to get to school. On his way, he takes the alpaca herd far out into the vast, sweeping landscape of the high plateau. This year, the dry season is long, and grass is hard to come by. The alpacas must be led farther and farther away. As he passes near a stream, Tiburcio washes his hands and feet. Every morning his teacher checks his pupils for cleanliness. Tiburcio makes every effort to please his teacher, as he dreams of one day becoming one himself.

Tiburcio's sister, Antonia, does not go to school. In fact, only one of Tiburcio's eighty schoolmates is a girl. School is considered useless for Aymara Indian girls. They marry and have children early. Before marriage, there is a period called *serviñacu*, one year in which they live with their prospective husbands on a trial basis to see if they are compatible. Antonia expects that she will be married within three years and will spend that time learning household duties. Now she feeds the two pigs and two rabbits, before going behind the house to lay out the frozen potatoes in the sun to dry. Then she will prepare the midday meal.

9:00. Felipa and her two sisters-in-law go into the field to gather potatoes. Seven-year-old Reynaldo follows them, leading the cow and guiding the sheep. He is in charge of the flock. He ties the cow to a post. The short grass around it will soon be devoured, so during the day he will move it several times. Next March, when Reynaldo starts school, Alejandro, the youngest, will take over the task.

Sheltered from the wind behind stone walls, the women dig up the potatoes one by one with hoes and toss them into their *lliclas*. The pigs follow them, rooting through the earth with their snouts to make sure nothing has been left behind. Reynaldo keeps a watchful eye on the pigs and throws stones at them if they dare to overtake the women.

12:00. Antonia brings her mother and aunts their food. She spreads out a *llicla* and arranges the meal: boiled *chuños*. The peasant women straighten their backs, their hands on their haunches, and relax. They are very happy to sit down for a while. As they eat lunch, they chat among themselves. Felipa bursts out laughing at one of her sisters-in-law, whose joyous temperament is very much a rarity among the Indians of the high plateau. The harsh life in this corner of the world offers little reason for gaiety. Two years ago Felipa had to send her newborn daughter to distant relatives because she could not feed the child. "It was just one mouth too many," she says. But at this moment the three women seem to forget the hardship they endure.

2:00. Before going back to work, Felipa takes some coca from a pouch hanging from her skirt and passes a few leaves to each woman. Chewing coca leaves (the plant from which cocaine is made) will give the women energy to continue their work. Coca relieves pain, banishes hunger, and overcomes fatigue. Chewing coca is a routine part of daily life, and the Indians are unaware that it diminishes their life expectancy. Antonia joins the women in the fields. In two weeks the *chuño* harvest will be over. Then it will be time to cut the oats, which are turning golden in the meadows. Work continues at the same pace until nightfall.

6:00. The sun has set behind the hill. The *chuños* that have been dug up in the course of the day are laid on a blanket outside and covered with oat straw. Tomorrow, Antonia will lay them in the burning midday sun. Each day they will become smaller, blacker, and more wrinkled until, in six days, they will be completely dry and ready to be stored stacked with the sheep and alpaca wool in the locked storehouse where the year's stockpile is kept.

Tiburcio appears at the crest of the hill, herding before him the alpacas, which he has collected on his way home from school. The sheep and the cow come home with Reynaldo. The cold is chilling; in the kitchen, one by one, the family draws near to the fire. Once again Felipa sits in front of the hearth to prepare the evening meal. Near her

Antonia peels little black *chuños*, which, when plunged into boiling water, return to their original consistency. After making the rounds of the enclosures and checking on the animals, Jaime comes back to join the family. They can hardly be seen in the light of the glimmering coals. Felipa and Jaime's family enjoy a quiet intimacy, and their conversation is muted and gentle.

In the bedroom, father and eldest son eat by flickering candlelight, seated on the edge of the beds with their noses practically in their plates. It is always the same food, but they eat with gusto. Tiburcio recounts the details of the daily football game the students play with their teachers during lunch recess. Jaime listens attentively to his son. He is proud of him. Tiburcio is the first person in the family to have access to education. Alejandro enters the room and steps over his father and brother, burying himself under the warm alpaca blankets without even taking off his *chullo* (a woven hat that covers the ears). He is asleep immediately.

7:30. Felipa and Antonia stay in the kitchen, and their conversation becomes more animated. They are planning their Saturday, when they spin the wool from their animals to weave blankets and ponchos to sell in the small market of Quisihuyo. Since the days of the Incas, the elaborate woven patterns of the Indian clothes and their distinctive hats have had special meaning. The patterns and colors reflect everything from social standing to marital status to town of origin. Nowadays, many clothes are factory-made and the individual identity of the designs has been lost, but here, far away from the capital, the women still weave their traditional family patterns using natural dyes.

9:00. Felipa and Antonia leave the kitchen fire and join the men in the bedroom. They stand on their beds to take off several layers of clothing, leaving on the warmest for the night. The only one with her own bed, Antonia hugs her cat against her for warmth. The American evangelical movement has made its way up here, and each family member prays aloud. Then all is quiet. But Felipa also prays to Pachama—the goddess of the land and fertility—for enough potatoes to last until the next harvest.

The paternal inheritance. A minifundio, five hectares of land for three families (twelve people in all), planted almost entirely with potatoes

At lunchtime one can eat in the fields under a burning sun, but in the evening the temperature drops below freezing. Then the family draws near the fire

BOLIVIA

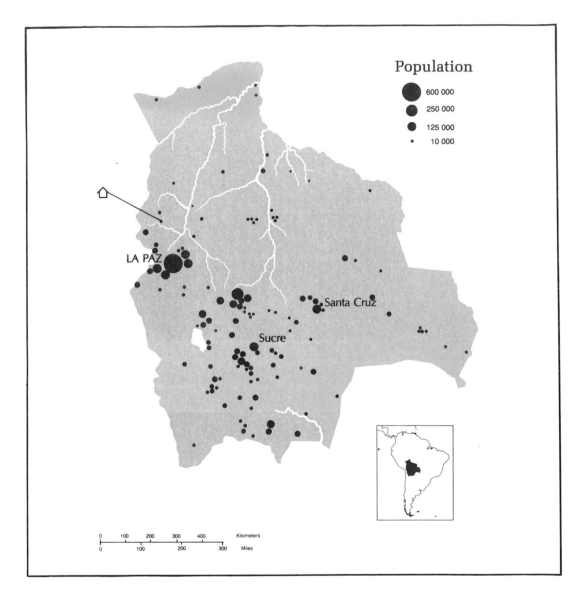

Population

- 600 000
- 250 000
- 125 000
- 10 000

LA PAZ

Santa Cruz

Sucre

```
0   100  200  300  400      Kilometers
0        100       200      300    Miles
```

THE NAME: From the name of "the Liberator,"
  Simón Bolívar

THE PEOPLE: The Bolivians

GEOGRAPHY
  To the west, the Altiplano—a bleak plateau
    bordered by two ranges of the Andes Mountains;
    the world's highest inhabited regions
  The *yungas*—the eastern mountain slopes and
    valleys
  The Amazon-Chaco lowlands
  Max. altitude: 6,755 m. (22,162 ft.) (Mt. Tocorpuri)
Area: 1,098,581 sq. km. (424,164 sq. mi.)

Density: 5.6 pers./sq. km. (14 pers./sq. mi.) (1986)
Arable land: 3% (1987)
Forest: 51%
Climate: Ranges from humid and tropical in the
    northern and eastern lowlands to cool and cold in
    the Andes Mountains above 3,500 m.
    Most rain falls between November and March.
    The aridity accentuates toward the east.

CAPITAL: La Paz, pop. 881,404 (1982)

LANGUAGE: Spanish, Quechua, Aymara (official)
    55% of the people do not speak Spanish; 32%
    speak only Spanish.

RELIGION
Majority Catholic
Cult worship widespread

POPULATION: Total: 6,400,000 (1985)
Annual growth: 2.7% (172,000) (1980–85)
Doubling time: 27 yrs.
Urban: 48% (1984) (est. for year 2000: 52%)
Rural: 52%

AGE GROUPS: (1980)
17% less than 5 yrs.
43% less than 15
53% less than 20
28% from 20 to 39
14% from 40 to 59
5% 60 yrs. and over

ETHNIC GROUPS:
Indian: 60% (est.)
Mestizo: 32%
White and other: 8%

HISTORY
100 B.C.–1200: Tiahuanaco civilization
1200–1500: Aymara and Inca cultures
1532: Spanish colonization
1776: Attached to the Viceroyalty of the Río del
  Plata
August 6, 1825: Independence
1884: Loses access to the Pacific Ocean in a war
  with Chile
1903: Cedes Acre to Brazil
1932–35: Discovery of oil
  Paraguay claims territory after Chaco War
1952: Bolivian national revolution
1982: Civilian government elected

FAMILY
Marital status, for population 12 yrs. and older: (1976)
Single: 29%
Married: 59%
Widowed: 10%
Divorced: 2%
Female head of household: no data
Fertility rate: 6.3 (1985)
Births out of wedlock: no data
Teenage births: 11% (1977)
Contraception: 26% (1984)
Government's position on family planning: After
  census of 1976, the government adopted a policy to
  increase population size. It involved direct
  intervention in the field of fertility, and family-
  planning clinics were closed.

SOCIAL INDICATORS
Life expectancy: 52 yrs. (male: 49; female: 54) (1985)
Infant mortality: 127/1,000 births (1985)

Crude birth rate: 43/1,000 pop. (1985)
Crude death rate: 15/1,000
Health:
Access to health services: 23% (1980–85)
Births attended by trained health personnel: no
  data

HOUSING
Persons per household: 4.3 (1976)
Electricity: 66% without (1976)
Access to safe water: 43% (urban: 78%; rural: 12%)
  (1983)
Source of water: (1976)
Piped inside: 11%
Piped outside: 28%
Not piped: 61%
Toilet facilities: (1976)
Flush: 12%
Other: 9%
None: 78%
Building materials: (1976)
Adobe: 57%
Other: 43%

EDUCATION
Literacy: 63% (male: 76%; female: 51%) (1976)
Gross enrollment ratio: (1984)
First level: 91% (completing in 1980–84: male:
  62%; female: 72%)
Second: 37%
Third: 16%
Educational attainment, for population 25 yrs. +:
  (1976)
None: 49%
First level: incomplete: 29%
Second: entered: 11%
Third: 5%

ECONOMIC ACTIVITY
Economically active population: 31% (male: 48%;
  female: 14%) (1985)
Agriculture: 50% act. pop.; 17% of GDP
Mines: 10% act. pop.; 20% of GDP
Industry: 14% act. pop.; 7% of GDP
Services: 26% act. pop.; 56% of GDP
Per capita GNP: 470 U.S.$ (1985)
Population in absolute poverty: (1975)
Rural: 85%
National currency/per U.S.$: 2,314 pesos (1985)
Principal resource: Natural gas

COMMUNICATIONS
Radio:
Transmitters: 184 (1981)
Receivers: 3,500,000—575/1,000 pop. (1983)
Television:
Transmitters: no data
Receivers: 386,000—64/1,000 pop. (1983)

BRAZIL

THE MARIANO DE SOUZA CALDAS FAMILY

Moises de Souza Caldas, age 36 (1)
Eleci Mariano de Souza Caldas, 39 (2)
Samuel Mariano de Souza Caldas, 17 (absent)
Elieu, 15 (3)
Marilda, 13 (4)
Lauro Antonio, 12 (5)
Luciane, 10 (6)
Silvando, 8 (7)
Simone, 4 (8)
Ivone, 4 (9)
Ione, 3 (10)
Uiles, 22 months (11)

1 pig	*1 cat*
3 chickens	*1 horse*
2 dogs	*1 mule*

GURIRI
December 24

5:45. The dawn light has difficulty piercing the fog that hangs over the dirt road and the abandoned fields. But Eleci, more courageous than the dawn, rises without hesitation to make coffee. Her husband, Moises, gently pushes his sleeping son Uiles and gets out of bed. He moves the baby's crib, which is blocking the doorway, slides into the tiny kitchen between the table and the bench, and heads for the well at the bottom of the yard. The well is shallow, and the water he pulls up in the bucket is salty. He showers and rinses his mouth. The morning silence is now broken by the tinny sound of samba music coming from the radio Eleci has switched on.

Moises goes to the barbed-wire enclosure to milk the cows he keeps for a restaurant owner in town. He has little hope of earning much from the job. With inflation running at 200 percent and rising every day, milk has become a luxury, and the town wholesaler is buying less. Moises hopes that the garbage will yield some treasures. After milking he will spend all morning combing the dumps. He is able to sell the glass bottles, metal scraps, and paper to the recycling plants. He also finds food for the sow and wood for the kitchen fire. The slightest item has value. Nevertheless, Moises prefers to be offered a day's work on the land and waits for someone to employ him.

Last year the de Souzas were so poor that they could no longer pay their rent and found themselves in the street. The prefecture authorities assigned them a little plot of land and gave them what they needed to build a mud shack. At first Eleci hoped that life there would be less miserable. She was disillusioned when the garbagemen arrived to unload their trucks fifty meters from the house. The place soon became a regular dump and the smell is appalling. The wind scatters all sorts of garbage in the fields, and the house is infested with flies. "I've heard that flies spread disease," worries Eleci, afraid for the children's health. She is homesick for the quiet countryside of Minas Gerais and her family there. But here the city is close by, and medical services and schools are available. In addition, Moises and the boys can earn some money.

6:30. The children stretch and straighten out of the fetal position. It is hard to get up, even though the old mattresses and mats spread on the floor of the three tiny rooms are less than comfortable. They freshen their faces in a bowl of cold water and pounce on their breakfast of hot milk with sugar and dry biscuits, which they eat sitting in a row on the bench in the yard. Two children have already left home. The eldest, Samuel, works in construction and rents a room from his boss. Their daughter Marilda left at the age of twelve to live with her boyfriend's family.

Elieu is the only child helping the family financially. An apprentice mason, he is working on the extension of one of the resorts for Brazil's jet set that are taking over the coastline. As Elieu leaves the house to catch the bus that will take him to work, Lauro Antonio mounts the horse and little Silvando scrambles on top of the mule to drive the cows to the pasture.

10:30. Eleci finishes sweeping the cement-slab floor while her youngest children play in a little hut they have built. Dark gray clouds hover in the midmorning sky. "It always rains at Christmas," observes Eleci. She sits on a stool, her back against the doorframe, sorting black beans and throwing them into the water boiling on the wood fire. When she has enough money, she buys kerosene but uses it only for cooking quick meals.

11:30. Moises returns from the beach of Rasa, a couple of miles across the fields, where he has bought fresh fish from the fishermen. Beans, rice, and fish form the family's daily diet. Eleci cooks everything for lunch and they eat the leftovers for supper. "The garbage truck is coming! The truck is coming!" cries one of the children outside. Except for Eleci, everyone in the family rushes toward the dump as their neighbors come running across the fields. Lauro and Luciane have brought the cart onto which their father can pile the fruits of their search.

1:30. Eleci sends one of the children to tell Moises that lunch is ready. Crammed in the kitchen, the children and their parents eat ravenously in silence. After the meal, Moises leaves for the fifteen-minute walk to catch a bus to Cabo Frio. He hopes to collect the wages owed to him for a job he did three months ago. In Eleci's mind it's just a convenient excuse to join the crowds of men packed in the cafés for a drink or two on Christmas Eve. She knows better than to expect him back soon.

Eleci sits down for a breather and stretches her swollen legs. She has suffered from varicose veins since her third pregnancy and after each birth has begged the doctors to give her a tubal ligation and put an end to her suffering. In Brazil there are few social services for the poor, and no doctor wanted to treat her for free. But this time, she will have her wish. This pregnancy, her eleventh not counting three miscarriages, will be the last. One doctor has agreed to operate without charge, since a twelfth could be fatal.

"This will be another girl," Eleci says, patting her stomach. "I prefer boys—they bring home their pay, and they take care of you when you're old. Girls, like Marilda, you raise them up and just when they can help you they go off with a man."

Just then a neighbor comes by with the message that Marilda won't be arriving until Boxing Day. Moises will be even angrier with his daughter. He has never accepted her departure from the house and has not spoken with her since. Eleci is more tolerant and doesn't agree with her husband. "Why make a scene? Marilda is in love, and what can you do about love?" she asks him.

3:00. A second garbage truck appears. With their father gone, the children are free to search the garbage for new toys. Lauro finds some boards and builds a shelter for the three chickens. The girls have found a complete doll's tea set and start playing tea. But games are mixed with responsibilities, and the little housekeepers must bring drinking water from the public tap installed in the middle of the fields about a ten-minute walk from the house. They return in Indian file, each with a little plastic bucket filled to the brim. They deposit the water in front of Eleci and return to playing house.

4:30. Elieu, back from work, washes himself in the shed and searches in the cupboard for some clothes to go dancing. Before dressing, he lies down for a few minutes next to his little brother, who is sleeping in the house's only bed.

"The more children there are, the more work," says Eleci. However, she smiles finally as she watches Lauro and Silvando return with the cows.

6:30. The leftovers consumed, the children stay outside despite the fine rain to enjoy the long summer evening. These children, who have played quietly all day, seem, like children all over the world, to fear the onset of night. They grow wilder, run, climb onto the hillocks and shout, as if to warn the earth that they'll still be here tomorrow. But Eleci has only to appear in the doorway to put an end to their frantic activity.

8:30. Elieu leaves the house trailing a cloud of cologne. Eleci follows his white silhouette until it disappears, but her eyes never leave the road. She wonders if Moises will come home this Christmas Eve, or if he'll stay in the city. Before, there were meetings at the church. Eleci liked that; it gave her a chance to meet people. But her husband had an argument with the minister and since then she has been deprived of her only entertainment.

Tired of waiting, Eleci slowly turns her misshapen body toward the interior of the house. Seven children need her to fall asleep. Seven children who have never celebrated Christmas Eve, and their mother, who has forgotten.

At first Eleci hoped that life there would be less miserable. She was disillusioned when the garbagemen arrived to unload their trucks fifty meters from the house

When they have enough money, they buy kerosene, but Eleci saves it for quick meals

BRAZIL

THE DA COSTA SOUZA FAMILY

Pedro Leôncio de Souza, age 50 (1)
Terezinha da Costa Souza, 47 (2)
Maria Lúcia da Costa Souza, 25 (3)
Vera Lúcia, 24 (4)
Maria do Rosário, 23 (5)
Francisco Eudes, 22 (6)
Benedita (Bene), 18 (7)
Benilda, 16 (8)
Francisca Lêda, 11 (9)
Antônia Alice (Tânia), 13 (10)
Raimunda, 10 (11)

1 duck
2 chickens
1 pig

ROCINHA
August 12

As she does every morning, Terezinha da Costa Souza gets out of bed and sticks her head in the next room, where her eight daughters are sprawled pell-mell in the three bunk beds that fill up the six-square-meter room. She shakes her daughter Benilda, the easiest to awaken, who noisily gives the signal to her three sisters who are going to school. Today, twenty-five-year-old Maria Lúcia gets up as well. She is a night student and works afternoons at the community's day-care center. Her sister Benedita works there in the morning. This morning, Maria Lúcia is taking her mother's place at a parents' meeting in her sisters' school. She has coffee with her father before he goes to work.

6:30. Pedro Leôncio opens the door and is greeted by the violent August winds that rip through Rio de Janeiro. The bay is already drenched in sunlight, and the skyscrapers' gleaming whiteness is in sharp contrast to Rocinha's terra cotta. Rocinha, Rio's most populous *favela* (slum), clings to the slope of a steep mountainside. Poised over the gardens of Rio's wealthy, the shanties overlook bays of breathtaking beauty. Only a splendid curtain of green dotted with the blue water of swimming pools separates the two extremes of Brazilian society. The irony that the least privileged have the best view has not been lost on the real estate developers, who would love to "relocate" the *favelas*. There are 600,000 *favelas* in Brazil. One third of the population of Rio de Janeiro lives in these shantytowns. The poorest of the poor, they have come from the interior of the country in the hope of a better life.

Pedro Leôncio joins the workers leaving for the city center as they walk single file down the dirt lanes to the road where they will catch the bus. A carpenter, Pedro is working on a luxurious villa. He treasures and shows with pride the photos of his work given to him by his employer.

His son Francisco Eudes and daughters Vera and Maria do Rosário also make the descent. Unlike his father, Eudes has no skill and works as an office messenger. Like most of the women in Rocinha, Vera and Maria are maids. These children do not take much pride in their work. Indeed, it often makes them feel envious of those who are better off. Yet they know they are fortunate to be employed.

8:30. The *favela* is oddly quiet in the morning. The students have made their way through the sewers and the garbage to their schools. The workers are gone and their young children are at the day-care center. Terezinha finally has a moment to herself and begins to sing. She is happy living here. Her husband, Pedro, is homesick for Ceará, the region in the Northeast where they came from. "We were even poorer there," Terezinha says. "And so alone. Four of my children died because there was no doctor." Terezinha and Benilda have both been sick recently, and Terezinha is sure they would be dead if they still lived in Ceará. She listens to the sound of the washing snapping in the wind in front of the house. This "curtain" disappears only in the evenings and on Sunday, when the little ninety-square-meter house is revealed in all its glory. It is blue and one of the prettiest in all Rocinha. It took Pedro six years to build it, carrying the bricks up the mountain piece by piece on his back. The da Costa Souzas have the added luxury of blue stucco because their five older children who work have helped them.

9:00. Maria Lúcia returns from her meeting at school. She is very passionate about the community and has registered her concern over the shortage of schools and the fact that the underpaid teachers often fail to show up. Since her mother's illness, Maria Lúcia manages the household. She is tireless. She shops, cleans, and pays the bills. Today she cleans the oil drums in which the family's water supply is stored. The water is delivered weekly to those who can afford it. Those who can't must go to the public tap halfway down the mountain. The construction of a water tank up on the mountaintop is still in the project phase: it has been promised "soon" for far too long.

11:00. Four pots are simmering on the stove: black beans, rice, chicken, and potatoes. Terezinha still does the cooking, and everything is ready when the girls come home from school at noon. A friend drops in with her baby and Terezinha generously asks her to join them for lunch. In the absence of table and chairs, everyone finds a place to stand and eat.

2:00. It's Tânia's turn to clean up the kitchen. So Terezinha sits down at the sewing machine to finish a quilt she intends to sell. She leaves the door open so she can invite her friends to drop in for a chat. Raimunda, Francisca, and Benilda play in front of the house with friends, babysitting for the women who are busy fetching water and doing the laundry. Benedita is off to a meeting to prepare for vaccination day. Like Maria Lúcia, she also participates intensely in the social life of their community.

4:30. Vera is the first one home from the city. She has brought a friend and her two children, one of whom is sick. They are taking him to visit the old healer who lives on top of the mountain. The healer will simply bless the child in front of a wall of idols and say an ancient prayer, but the two women are convinced that this is necessary for his well-being. While they respect medical technology, many Brazilians cannot bring themselves to ignore old beliefs.

5:00. The traffic in Rua 1 picks up. It's quitting time and the men return heavily laden with sacks of stones, bricks, sand, and, of course, buckets of water. There's always a water shortage in Rocinha, and nobody would think of coming back empty-handed.

The meal stretches over the whole evening as the family trickles in from work and off to school. Maria Lúcia returns from yet another meeting,

this time about the day-care canteen and its supply problems. As soon as she has eaten, she leaves for her evening courses. Eudes and Maria do Rosário will meet her there directly from work. They are all finishing high school. But Maria Lúcia has no great expectations of going to the university. "I'm twenty-five already," she says. "I just want a job that will get me out of Rocinha."

7:00. Terezinha takes a chair outside and leans it against the fence. She rests her tired legs while she talks to the students at the day-care center. In the evenings, the center turns into a primary school. The place is filled with people of all ages. Vera is one of them. Unlike her brother and sisters, she refused for years to go to school but has finally realized that a better education will get her a better job. She will be twenty-four when she completes her second year of school in December. A lot of the illiterate students are over twenty, and it is very hard for them to settle down in this school designed for small children. Terezinha abandons her post when the classes begin.

8:30. Pedro comes home from work. He sits on the kitchen steps and eats his dinner. Despite his large family, he has no company. Terezinha and Raimunda are already asleep. Benilda sits on the bed with her school books on her knees. In the bathroom, Tânia showers with a bucket of water. Pedro goes in to lie beside his wife and watch TV.

10:00. The television sets are still on in both rooms, but even *Louco Amor*, the most popular soap opera, can't keep everyone from falling asleep. When she comes home, Vera switches off the television sets, sits down with a plate of rice, and waits up for her brother and sisters.

11:30. The pots of rice and beans have been scraped clean by the time Eudes climbs into his bed between the bathroom and the kitchen. Vera and Maria Lúcia are the last ones to grab a blanket from the pile in the corner of the room. They each push and nudge their way onto an already occupied bed, lying head to foot with their sleeping bedmates.

This "curtain" of drying clothes disappears only in the evening and on Sunday, when the little house is revealed in all its glory. It is blue and one of the prettiest in all Rocinha

In the absence of table and chairs, everyone finds a place to eat

BRAZIL

THE ARATANHA FAMILY

Pedro Aratanha, age 30 (1)
Efigenia Aratanha, 30 (2)
Pedrinho Aratanha, 3 (3)
Carola, 18 months (4)

2 birds

RIO
February 10

5:45. Pedro Aratanha gets out of bed quickly without waking his wife. Adjusting his blue officer's uniform, he leaves very early to avoid the traffic jams, but it still takes him three-quarters of an hour on his motorcycle to drive to Navy headquarters in the city center. Following in his father's footsteps, Pedro is a Navy doctor. Once or twice a week he has night duty. He loves his profession, although he dislikes having to spend four months a year at sea on board a troop transport and being away from his young family.

6:30. Three-year-old Pedrinho follows his mother everywhere, but regretfully Efigenia has no time for him. A shower, a glass of milk, and she is running toward her car. Maria, the new maid, takes Pedrinho in her arms and makes a fuss over him so that he will stop crying.

As she drives past the bus stop, Efigenia sighs in relief. She's grateful for her new car. It saves her half an hour every morning, and being able to listen to news and music makes the forty-minute commute bearable. Efigenia is a doctor, like her husband, and a part-time pediatrician at the Naval Hospital. As with most of Brazil's young middle-class women, Efigenia has finished her education and embarked on a career. She is lucky that her job allows her to be home by early afternoon.

7:30. Maria makes the children's breakfast, their "special," a mixture of high-protein cereals invented by their grandfather. The supply is replenished whenever they spend the weekend with Pedro's parents by the sea. While Maria cleans the house, Pedrinho tries to keep his little sister amused. Carola is a nervous, excitable child and often needs soothing. A little more patience and they will soon be able to run to their heart's content on the playground. The Aratanhas live in one of Brazil's suburban high rises. These residential complexes provide many luxuries for young middle-class families. Even the smallest apartment has a maid's room (the pool of domestic labor is vast and affordable) and there are football fields, tennis courts, party rooms, a gym, and a sauna—all fenced in and patrolled twenty-four hours a day.

Pedrinho and Carola are hungry, and before they take the bus to the day-care center, they wolf down a plate of chicken and peas that Maria reheats according to Efigenia's instructions. Every ten days a woman comes to make a variety of delicacies and stores them in the freezer. This solution satisfies everyone, especially Efigenia, who gains a few hours of freedom without having to worry about the abysmal quality of the maid's cooking.

1:00. Efigenia parks the car close to the shopping center to run errands and perhaps pick up some clothes for the children, one of her favorite chores. Although a working couple, Efigenia and Pedro are very doting parents. Well informed about child rearing, they send their children to a progressive day-care center. Efigenia is able to allow herself some free time in the afternoon without guilt. Today she stops by the beauty salon to have her legs waxed.

4:00. Efigenia arrives at the apartment complex gate just as the day-care bus stops at the guardhouse. The children see their mother and jump up and down on their seat in excitement. Efigenia covers them with kisses and leads them to the playground, where Maria is waiting with the toys.

5:30. Pedro parks his motorcycle in the garage behind his wife's car. He goes quickly up to the apartment, slips into a bathing suit, joins his family by the pool, and dives luxuriously into the welcoming water. All around him, groups of children are playing. Their parents survey them proudly, comfortable in the knowledge that their offspring will not know hardship.

When the elevator stops at the eighth floor of Building 4, Pedrinho and Carola stumble out, exhausted. Pedro immediately takes a shower, and Efigenia brings him the two children, who are delighted to share the water with their father. The house rings with shouts of laughter.

Efigenia takes her turn in the bathroom. Pedro dresses the children in shorts and T-shirts. The nights are too hot to wear anything more. The family gathers in the living room while Maria prepares the children's dinner. They sold the couch last week, so they all sit on the floor. The Aratanhas are moving soon to Recife, a city in the North, as Pedro's career requires him to spend two years stationed away from his hometown. Efigenia should have no problem finding a new job. Doctors are always needed.

The toy box is turned over, and Pedro is assembling a racetrack for Pedrinho. It is hard to tell who is enjoying himself more. Carola is having fun naming all the objects her mother points at; she is proud of her vocabulary.

Efigenia, who grew up with four brothers and sisters, used to dream of a family of five children. But after Carola was born, she realized that her two children require an enormous amount of attention and energy on her part. With Pedro's agreement, she had a tubal ligation, and they do not regret their decision. The past three years have been full ones: their marriage after graduation, two babies one after the other, and setting up a household and pursuing their careers.

7:00. Pedro sits down at the table with his two children. He feeds Carola while watching Pedrinho amuse himself by building little mountains out of the rice, beans, and vegetables on his plate. He's not hungry. His father insists, and Pedrinho begins to cry. Carola is also having trouble finishing her meal and decides to add her voice to her brother's. The family's tranquillity is definitely shattered. Efigenia takes Carola in her arms. Another warm shower will calm her down. After searching for Carola's favorite doll, Pedro tucks the children into their cribs, kisses them good night, and leaves as Efigenia prepares to read them a bedtime story.

8:30. Tranquillity reigns again. Pedro and Efigenia can now eat their dinner. The evening meal is always simple: croissants, cheese, fruit, and hot chocolate. Maria finishes the washing-up, wishes them good night, and retires to her little room adjacent to the kitchen. Efigenia hopes that Maria will not leave them, as all her predecessors have done. In the suburbs it is difficult to keep domestic servants; most prefer to be able to return to their families in the *favelas* at night.

10:00. Efigenia carefully lays out the clothes the children will need for tomorrow. The thought that the alarm clock will go off at dawn is enough to convince Efigenia and Pedro that it is bedtime. They both like to go to bed early.

Everything is provided for the well-being of young families: football fields, tennis courts, party rooms, a gym, and a sauna—all fenced in and patrolled twenty-four hours a day

The past three years have been full ones: their marriage just after graduation, two babies one after the other and setting up a household and pursuing their careers

BRAZIL

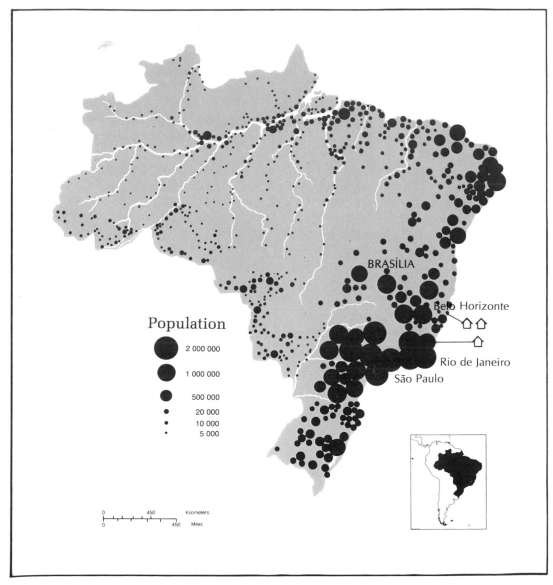

Population

- 2 000 000
- 1 000 000
- 500 000
- 20 000
- 10 000
- 5 000

BRASÍLIA

Belo Horizonte

Rio de Janeiro

São Paulo

THE NAME: From the timber *brasil*, the country's renowned dye wood

THE PEOPLE: The Brazilians

GEOGRAPHY
North: Amazon Basin and the arid Nordeste region
West-central: plateau of Mato Grosso and plains of Pantanal
East-central: hills of the coastal lowlands and interior plateaus
Southeast: coastal mountain range
South: Brazilian highland plateau
  Max. altitude: 3,014 m. (9,888 ft.) (Pico da Neblina)

Area: 8,511,965 sq. km. (3,286,488 sq. mi.)
Density: 16 pers./sq. km. (41 pers./sq. mi.) (1986)
Arable land: 9% (1987)
Forest: 66%
Climate: Varies from hot and wet in the tropical rain forest of the Amazon Basin to temperate in the savanna grasslands of the central and southern uplands, which have warm summers and mild winters.

CAPITAL: Brasília, pop. 1,176,908 (1980)

LANGUAGE: Portuguese

RELIGION
Majority Catholic

The practice of numerous Afro-Brazilian spiritualist religions is widespread, especially Macumba and its most important sects, Candomble and Umbande.

POPULATION: Total—135,600,000 (1980)
Annual growth: 2.2% (2,983,200) (1980–85)
Doubling time: 33 yrs.
Urban: 73% (1985) (est. for year 2000: 79%)
Rural: 27%

AGE GROUPS: (1982)
14% less than 5 yrs.
38% less than 15
49% less than 20
30% from 20 to 39
15% from 40 to 59
6% 60 yrs. and over

ETHNIC GROUPS
White: 60%
Mixed: 33%
Black: 7%

HISTORY
5000 B.C.: Populated by the Tupi-Guarani Indians
1493: Pope Alexander VI gives the Portuguese all land west of the Cape Verde Islands
1500: Discovery by the Portuguese
1630: Portuguese colonization
1789: Rebellion against Portuguese rule
1815: Brazil becomes a kingdom
September 7, 1822: Independence
Brazil becomes an empire until 1880
1888: Abolition of slavery
1889: Proclamation of the republic
1979: After a succession of dictatorships, military government moves toward democracy

FAMILY
Marital status, for population 15 yrs and older: (1980)
Married: 50%
Single: 30%
Consensually married: 7%
Widowed: 8%
Separated: 4%
Female head of household: no data
Fertility rate: 3.6 (1985)
Births out of wedlock: no data
Teenage births: 13% (1981)
Contraception: 50%
Government's position on family planning: Has indicated awareness of its responsibility to provide information and access to family planning to those who voluntarily choose to plan their families.

SOCIAL INDICATORS
Life expectancy: 64 yrs. (male: 61; female: 67) (1985)
The average age varies; it can be up to 10 years less in the northeast.

Infant mortality: 63/1,000 births (1985)
Crude birth rate: 30/1,000 pop. (1985)
Crude death rate: 8/1,000
Health:
Access to health services: no data
Births attended by trained health personnel: 73% (1984)

HOUSING
Persons per household: 4.2 (1982)
Electricity: 33% without (1980)
Access to safe water: 76% (urban: 86%; rural: 53%) (1983)
Source of water: (1980)
Piped: 53%
Not piped: 47%
Toilet facilities: (1980)
Flush: 42%
Other: 33%
None: 23%
Building materials: no data

EDUCATION
Literacy: 74% (male: 76%; female: 73%) (1980)
Gross enrollment ratio: (1983–85)
First level: 104% (completing in 1980–84: 20%)
Second: 35%
Third: 11%
Children 7–17 yrs. who study only: 58% (1984); who study and work: 14%
46% of the children 7 to 10 years old from families living on one minimum salary have never been to school.
Educational attainment, for population 25 yrs. +: (1980)
None: 33%
First level: incomplete: 50% (complete: 5%)
Second: entered: 7%
Third: 5%

ECONOMIC ACTIVITY
Economically active population: 49% (male: 72%; female: 27%) (1980)
Agriculture: 30% act. pop.; 16% of GDP
Mines: 4% act. pop.; 4% of GDP
Industry: 20% act. pop.; 28% of GDP
Services: 46% act. pop.; 52% of GDP
Per capita GNP: 1,640 U.S.$ (1985)
Population in absolute poverty: no data
National currency/per U.S.$: 6,200 cruzeiros (1985)
Principal resources:
Soybeans, coffee, meat
Second-largest exporter of iron ore
Third-largest exporter of gold

COMMUNICATIONS
Radio:
Transmitters: 1,818 (1983)
Receivers: 50,000,000—386/1,000 pop. (1983)
Television:
Transmitters: 137 (1983)
Receivers: 16,500,000—127/1,000 pop. (1983)

CHILE

THE FERNÁNDEZ FAMILY

Juan Esliver Fernández, age 42 (1)
Elisabeth Ramírez de Fernández, 42 (2)
Patricia Inadina Ramírez Fernández, 21 (3)
Jexica del Pilar, 13 (4)
Javier Esliver, 11 (5)
Ruth Elisabeth, 9 (6)

3 dogs
2 cats
8 chickens

TALCAHUANO
June 1

7:30. Elisabeth has slept through the alarm again and rushes out of her room to wake up her children. This happens often during the weeks her husband, Juan, works a late shift at Armco, a huge American multinational company that produces parts for the mining industry. In the kitchen, she lights the charcoal fire in the brazier to warm the cold June air and grill toast. Then she puts the milk and water on the gas stove to boil and, for the second time, dashes into the children's bedroom. No one has stirred. "Get up now!" she orders. Patricia, Javier, and Jexica obey. Ruth, the *guagua* (baby), exploits the privilege of the youngest and has her bowl of hot milk in bed.

With only fifteen minutes to spare, Elisabeth and her eldest daughter, Patricia, corral the three students. In minutes their shoes are brushed, white school aprons donned, and shiny black hair combed and plaited. As the children wolf down their tea and toast, Elisabeth once more writes a note to the teacher to excuse their lateness. Then she walks them to the corner to see them across the wide paved boulevard that connects the suburb of Talcahuano to the city of Concepción. Car and bus drivers in Chile are merciless.

When Elisabeth returns she finds Patricia in the middle of a large-scale cleaning operation. She has stacked the furniture in a corner and is attacking the wooden floor with steel wool before she sweeps and waxes it. This daughter from a first marriage cannot find a job and so shares the daily chores with her mother.

8:30. Elisabeth installs herself behind the counter of the tiny shop attached to the yellow concrete house. She and her daughters supplement their budget by selling a bit of everything imaginable: fruits, vegetables, bread, milk, and cigarettes. On these cold mornings, Elisabeth lights the charcoal brazier behind the counter to keep her feet warm. She takes out her knitting and waits for customers. The shop is open seven days a week, but the flow of customers has dwindled, since many factories have closed and more shops like hers have opened.

9:30. Juan wakes to the sound of Patricia moving furniture. He likes these relaxed mornings and takes a leisurely tour of his property, inspecting his tiny backyard and chicken coop with the same satisfaction as a lord surveying his manor. Life is treating him well. His factory is working to capacity, and in spite of the poor economic climate, his family is faring far better than their many unemployed customers. Juan and Elisabeth give their thanks to God every day. They are among the growing numbers of Latin Americans who have converted from Catholicism to American evangelism. Hungry, Juan stoops to pat the dog and enters the store to call his wife. Elisabeth takes a brioche from the shelf and goes to cook some eggs for her husband. Finished with her cleaning, Patricia picks up her mother's knitting and takes over in the shop.

10:30. Juan and Elisabeth leave for the market to replenish their store supplies. With unemployment so rampant in Chile, their customers have less and less money and restrict their purchases to the bare minimum. The Fernándezes must be careful to stock their shop with items within the range of their customers' budgets. They go separately down the long, perfumed aisles inquiring about prices, comparing and buying the cheapest items. The two of them are home an hour later in time for the children's return.

As soon as they walk in the door, the children hang up their aprons and school bags, kiss their parents, and disappear into their room. These are well-behaved children, and their parents place their obedience and their education above everything else. The most important thing in Juan and Elisabeth's life is to prepare their children for a career. "School is the only way to do that," says Juan.

2:00. Lunch is the main meal of the day. Everyone except Patricia, who is minding the store, gathers around the table in the dining room, which today is warmed by a ray of sunshine. They savor the warmth. This year they have not been able to afford to use the gas heater that sits in a corner of the living room, and any day now the interminable cold and rainy season will begin. Elisabeth won't sit down to eat until all have finished their soup and been served the black beans.

After lunch Juan kisses his wife goodbye and leaves for the factory. His faithful old Peugeot will get him there just in time for his three o'clock shift. Javier dons his soccer uniform and disappears with a group of friends. He practices twice a week in single-minded pursuit of his dream of becoming a professional soccer player.

Jexica takes over the store, as she does every afternoon. The neighbors drop in to buy a little and chat, not daring to complain about their fate. There is in everyone the fear of being branded subversive. Jexica's friends hang out here, listening to the radio and gossiping for a while before taking their books out and doing their homework on the store's counter. Patricia has gone into Concepción to apply for a secretarial job. She is one of many applicants and is losing hope. Elisabeth has no illusions. "Our children go to school, but what good is it to them when there's no work?"

Lying dreamily in the sunshine in her parents' room, Ruth watches television. Any soap opera will do. Ruth's only real interest these days is her Thursday ballet classes; she dreams of being a prima ballerina.

Elisabeth keeps a few chickens in the yard, fattening them up for festive occasions. She throws them the scraps from the meal through the kitchen window. Then she puts on a sweater for her daily visit to her aging mother.

6:00. Jexica locks the store; she will go to church with her mother for the evening service. Dinner will not be served until much later, and now the family has *las once* (the Chilean early supper) of toast and avocado. While their mother and sister are at church, Ruth and Javier do their homework around the kitchen table, helped by Patricia, who finishes a piece of crochet work while watching *Dallas* on the black-and-white kitchen TV. The family cats lie at their feet, stealing some warmth from the charcoal brazier Javier has slid under the table.

Later on, as Elisabeth prepares the evening soup, the children lay out their gym clothes for the next day. Gym is their favorite class, and they are meticulous about their appearance on gym days.

10:30. The last meal of the day is a casual affair. Each person eats when he or she feels like it, warming their stomachs before sliding under the cold damp covers. Their beds lying side by side, Ruth, Javier, and Jexica converse quietly before falling asleep.

11:30. Elisabeth has waited up for Juan. While she serves him his soup, they recount the events of the day. Juan inquires anxiously about Patricia's interview. "There is no way of knowing yet," answers Elisabeth. The couple's faith in God and in education is tested every day, when all they see ahead is hard times. But still they give their thanks to God and ask him to bless their children—one who dreams of soccer, another of ballet, and especially the oldest, whose dreams are being quickly supplanted by a harsh reality.

Juan drives his faithful old Peugeot to the factory where he works

They savor the warmth of the ray of sunshine. This year the family cannot afford to use the gas heater, and any day now the interminable cold and rainy season will begin

CHILE

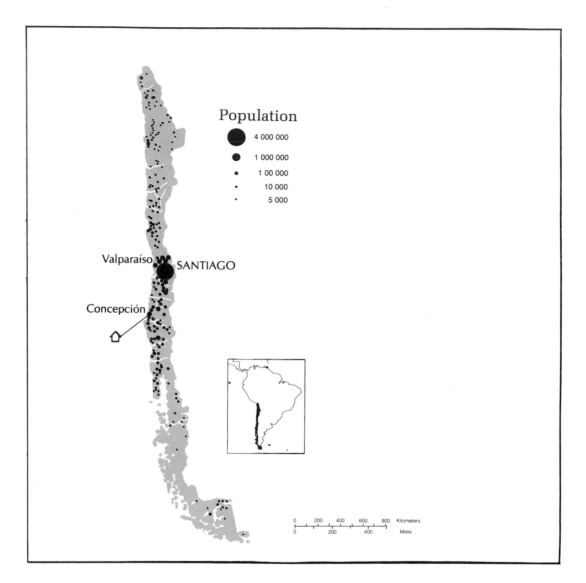

Population

- 4 000 000
- 1 000 000
- 1 00 000
- 10 000
- 5 000

Valparaíso   SANTIAGO

Concepción

| 0 | 200 | 400 | 600 | 800 | Kilometers |
| 0 | | 200 | | 400 | Miles |

THE NAME: From Aymara, meaning "there where the earth ends"

THE PEOPLE: The Chileans

GEOGRAPHY: Three parallel regions running from north to south
East: Chilean Andes
Center: intermediate depression (*pampa central*)
West: coastal cordillera
South: lakes and fjords
    Max. altitude: 6,880 m. (22,572 ft.) (Ojos del Salado)
Area: 756,626 sq. km. (292,135 sq. mi.)

Density: 16 pers./sq. km. (40 pers./sq. mi.) (1986)
Arable land: 7% (1987)
Forest: 20%
Climate: Ranges from extreme aridity in the north through a Mediterranean climate in the center, where winters are wet and summers dry, to a cool temperate zone in the south, with rain at all seasons. In the extreme south, conditions are very wet and stormy.

CAPITAL: Santiago, pop. 4,067,047 (1985 est.)

LANGUAGE: Spanish (official)
    The Araucanians speak Mapuche.

RELIGION
Catholic: 81% (1970)
Protestant: 6%
Other: 2%
Unknown: 11%

POPULATION: Total—12,000,000 (1985)
Annual growth: 1.6% (192,000) (1980–85)
Doubling time: 44 yrs.
Urban: 84% (1985) (est. for year 2000: 89%)
Rural: 16%

AGE GROUPS: (1983)
11% less than 5 yrs.
32% less than 15
42% less than 20
33% from 20 to 39
17% from 40 to 59
8% 60 yrs. and over

ETHNIC GROUPS
Mestizo: 65%
White: 30%
Indian: 3%
Other: 2%

HISTORY
Inhabited by the Araucan Indians
1536: The Spanish arrive, led by Diego de Almagro
1561–1810: Part of the Viceroyalty of Peru
September 18, 1810: Independence
1879–84: Expands territory by winning war against Peru and Bolivia
1891–1970: Succession of governments and political turmoil
1970: Election of Salvador Allende Gossens, the first Marxist to be elected in a free democratic election
Since 1973: Military dictatorship of General Augusto Pinochet

FAMILY
Marital status, for population 15 yrs. and older: (1982)
Single: 33.3%
Married: 51.5%
Consensually married: 2.4%
Widowed: 9.6%
Separated from husband or partner: 3.3%
Divorce is illegal.
Female head of household: no data
Fertility rate: 2.5 (1985)
Births out of wedlock: no data
Teenage births: 17% (1980)
Contraception: 43% (1984)
Government's position on family planning: Considers a significant increase in population essential, but it is not the responsibility of the state to increase or reduce rates of population growth, and decisions regarding family size should be freely made by the family unit. The state supports information and education to "dignify and encourage motherhood."

SOCIAL INDICATORS
Life expectancy: 70 yrs. (male: 67; female: 73) (1985)
Infant mortality: 19/1,000 births (1985)
Crude birth rate: 22/1,000 pop. (1985)
Crude death rate: 7/1,000
Health:
Access to health services: no data
Births attended by trained health personnel: 95% (1984)

HOUSING
Persons per household: 5 (1985)
Electricity: 25% without (1970)
Access to safe water: 85% (urban: 100%; rural: 18%) (1983)
Source of water: (1970)
Piped inside: 62%
Piped outside: 19%
Without: 19%
Toilet facilities: (1970)
Flush: 51%
Other: 46%
None: 3%
Building materials: (1970)
Brick: 64%
Wood: 33%

EDUCATION
Literacy: 94% (1983)
Gross enrollment ratio: (1984)
First level: 107%
Second: 65%
Third: 15%
Educational attainment, for population 15 yrs. +: (1979)
None: 10%
First level: 58%
Second: 30%
Third: 4%

ECONOMIC ACTIVITY
Economically active population: 33% (male: 47%; female: 20%) (1984)
Agriculture: 19% act. pop.; 9% of GDP
Mines: 7% act. pop.; 15% of GDP
Industry: 14% act. pop.; 18% of GDP
Services: 60% act. pop.; 58% of GDP
Per capita GNP: 1,430 U.S.$ (1985)
Population in absolute poverty: (1985)
Urban: 27%
Rural: 55%
National currency/per U.S.$: 161.08 pesos (1985)
Principal resources: World's leading producer of copper

COMMUNICATIONS
Radio:
Transmitters: 109 (1979)
Receivers: 3,550,000—304/1,000 pop. (1983)
Television:
Transmitters: no data
Receivers: 1,350,000—166/1,000 pop. (1983)

COLOMBIA

THE GONZALES FAMILY

Gabriel Gonzales, age 33 (1)
Teresa Gutieng de Gonzales, 33 (2)
María Jenne Gonzales, 13 (3)
John Walter, 11 (4)
Viena Milena, 7 (5)
Alvaro Santo Fino, 3 (6)

1 dog
1 cat
chickens

NEIVA
October 26

6:30. The Gonzales family is jolted by salsa music blaring from the clock-radio. It's time to rise and shine!

Eleven-year-old John Walter gets up and goes outside to the garden to continue his dream, while his parents wake up to reality under a stream of cold water from the shower. Moments later Gabriel is starting up his motorcycle. "See you soon, *mi amor*," says Teresa, kissing him goodbye. At the end of the street, he turns left into Calle 14, which will take him to the center of Neiva. The city nestles in the valley beneath the dramatic, ever-changing Colombian sky, dwarfed by the encircling mountains that reach up to capture the clouds in their myriad shades of gray.

Gabriel drives toward the center of town, instinctively avoiding the potholes in the dirt. He comes to a halt in front of a pile of cement in the Cambulos neighborhood and jumps off his motorcycle to greet his father-in-law and two nephews. A mason, Gabriel is self-employed—like 50 percent of Colombia's work force—and he still has three months of work ahead of him. So far, he's been lucky enough to land a succession of contracts, enough even to share with his family.

"*Mi amor!*" His mother's voice breaks into John Walter's dream and he begins his first chore of the day: cleaning the cage and feeding the chickens they have been fattening for almost two months. In two weeks' time Teresa will be able to sell them in the market. The money helps. Gabriel makes slightly more than minimum wage but has no job security or money set aside in case of illness.

"*Mi amor!*" Again comes Teresa's loving reminder that María Jenne has chores of her own. She pulls the garden hose from the back of the house to the front, watering the patio, a few plants, the hundred square feet of grass, and the mango tree as she goes. Then she sweeps away the layer of sand that settles every day inside the house.

8:00. "*Mi amor!*" Teresa commands again. Viena Milena waits till she is told to get up. She is a little lazy, which annoys her elder sister, Jenne, but doesn't bother her at all. She moves at her own pace, making a brief attempt at tidying up the children's room, and then finishing the homework she abandoned last night.

Gabriel is extending the house where they have lived for the last ten years. The sand is already piled in the yard. The first money they can spare will go for bricks and cement. When they were first married, they lived at Gabriel's mother's house, where their first children were born. As soon as they had scraped a little money together, they bought a lot and began to build. Now their two daughters want their own room, and the living room is no longer big enough for the constant stream of friends dropping by. Part of the garden will have to be sacrificed and two of the fruit trees chopped down.

Teresa leaves her kitchen briefly to shop at the grocery store on the corner. A few minutes later, her refrain of "*Mis amores*" is well understood. A breakfast of tortillas, omelettes, and hot chocolate beckons the children to the shade of the plum tree. Little Alvaro sets his plate of food next to John Walter's. He has been with the Gonzales family for only ten days. His mother is very ill and can no longer look after her children. Like many women in Colombia, she is on her own. Teresa, who found her afternoons unoccupied once all her children were in school, asked the authorities for permission to take him in. Alvaro very quickly became one of the family and has thrived on their love and attention. His favorite is John Walter, whom he follows everywhere, even to the children's bathroom, which Gabriel recently built.

10:30. John Walter cuts some banana leaves from the tree. He's going to dress up as an Indian for

Halloween. Now he has everything he needs but the feathers. In the background the radio blares away—a never-ending cascade of salsa. Always the same, it seems, but not for Teresa, who hums along with every new tune.

In the yard, Alvaro grits his teeth as Jenne pours the first bowlful of cold water on his head. "*Mi amor*, let me soap you! Let me rinse you off! Alvaro, *mi amor!* You're as shiny as a new penny!"

11:30. Standing in the corridor, Jenne gulps down her soup. She looks lovely in her white uniform, her hair tied neatly back. She wants very much to be tall and waits for the school bus standing straight and proud in front of the house.

12:00. Gabriel and his nephews arrive for lunch. The sun has moved overhead and they take their places at the table beneath the avocado tree. The nephews pay for their food, providing another small addition to Teresa's budget. For lunch: soup, rice, boiled beef, and salad. For the children sitting in the yard there is soup and a bowl of rice. If there is any meat left over when the men are finished, the children will have a taste.

1:00. The children have left for school and Teresa is alone with little Alvaro. It's time for *Ronda de Piedra*, her favorite soap opera. She sits on the couch in the living room and lights up a cigarette, sharing for half an hour another world with characters she has known for over a year. It means nothing to Alvaro. He falls asleep.

The salsa starts up again. Teresa returns to her kitchen and cleans up before the flies can swarm into the house. Next comes the inevitable daily ritual of washing the clothes in the cement basin in the yard.

Her friend and neighbor stops by to chat and to have some *tinto*, Colombia's justly famous coffee. She is a twenty-year-old orphan with six brothers and sisters to raise. The two women discuss the death of a neighbor in a car accident. His young widow is expecting a child very soon, and they worry about her future. Tonight, the whole neighborhood will join the grieving family to say a rosary for the dead man.

5:30. The children come home from school. "*Buenas noches, mis amores!*" their mother calls from the kitchen. It's Milena's turn to tend to the chickens. John Walter is reunited with his Indian costume, and Alvaro is reunited with John Walter. Half an hour later, Gabriel and Jenne arrive on the motorcycle. In the time it takes Gabriel to shower, the rice and fried bananas are set out, then quickly devoured. The evening can begin.

Gabriel goes to pick up some used pieces of wood that he has been given to build the two new bedrooms. When he returns, he sits down with his family and friends on his front-yard brick wall. Across the street, their neighbors have brought out their chairs. They share the latest gossip as they watch the passersby. This is a moment of glory for the pretty girls who preen themselves, attracting admiring glances as they stroll toward the grocery store on the pretext of buying a Coke.

8:30. The street empties. Teresa and Gabriel go and pray for the soul of their young neighbor. The narrow street nearby is blocked with cars, and a large crowd gathers. On the front steps and inside the yard, the family keeps its vigil until tomorrow's funeral. People draw near to the dead man in his glass-covered coffin, his eyes open so that his life will renew itself in his unborn child. The house is overflowing with people as the prayers begin.

When Teresa and Gabriel come home, the children are in bed. Teresa makes popcorn while Gabriel walks to the corner to buy some Coke. They switch the television on to watch a soap opera together.

11:00. "Come, *mi amor!*" Teresa tugs her drowsy husband's arm. The couple share the last task of the day: cleaning the cage and feeding the chickens. Before he goes to bed, Gabriel brings his motorcycle into the living room and locks and bars the door. "*Buenas noches, mi amor.*"

At night family and friends perch on their front wall sharing the latest gossip as they watch the pretty girls who preen themselves on their stroll to the grocery store on the pretext of buying a Coke

For the children sitting in the yard there is soup and a bowl of rice. If there is any meat left over when the men are finished, the children will have a taste

COLOMBIA

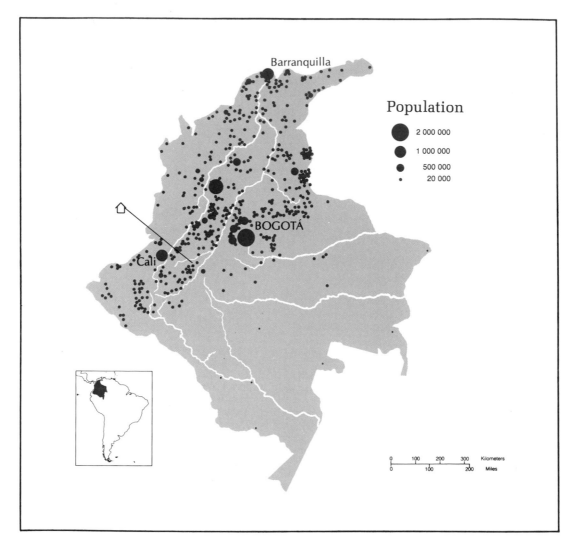

THE NAME: Given by Simón Bolívar in honor of Christopher Columbus

THE PEOPLE: The Colombians

GEOGRAPHY
Flat coastal areas broken by the high Sierra Nevada de Santa Marta mountain range
Central highlands and sparsely settled eastern plains (*llanos*), drained by tributaries of the Orinoco and Amazon rivers
Max. altitude: 5,800 m. (19,000 ft.) (Pico Colón)
Area: 1,138,914 sq. km. (439,737 sq. mi.)
Density: 25 pers./sq. km. (65 pers./sq. mi.) (1986)
Arable land: 5% (1987)
Forest: 44%

Climate: Conditions vary with altitude, from tropical heat on the coast and the eastern plains to cool, springlike weather with frequent light rains in the highlands, where the dry seasons are from December to February and June to August.

CAPITAL: Bogotá, pop. 4,169,000 (1983 est.)

LANGUAGE: Spanish

RELIGION: Majority Catholic

POPULATION: Total—28,700,000 (1985)
Annual growth: 2.1% (602,700) (1980–85)
Doubling time: 33 yrs.
Urban: no data
Rural: no data

AGE GROUPS: (1980)
12% less than 5 yrs.
36% less than 15
48% less than 20
32% from 20 to 39
14% from 40 to 59
6% 60 yrs. and over

ETHNIC GROUPS
White: 20%
Mestizo: 58%
Mulatto: 14%
Black: 4%
Indian: 1%
Zambo (mixed black and Indian): 3%

HISTORY
Originally inhabited by the Chibchas
1499: Discovery by Alonso de Ojeda
1525: Founding of first city, Santa Marta, by Rodrigo de Bastidas
1559: Part of the Viceroyalty of Peru
1718: Part of the Viceroyalty of New Grenada
July 20, 1810: Independence
1819–30: Part of the Republic of the Gran Colombia
1899–1903: "Thousand Days' War"; separation from Panama
1958: Liberal and Conservative pact goes into effect with election of liberal president

FAMILY
Marital status, for population 15 yrs. and older: (1985)
Married: 38%
Common-law: 15%
Widowed: 5%
Separated from husband or partner: 4%
Divorce is illegal.
Female head of household: 16% (1980 est.)
Fertility rate: 3.8 (1985)
Births out of wedlock: no data
Teenage births: no data
Contraception: 55% (1984)
Government's position on family planning: Considers levels and trends of population growth and fertility satisfactory. It supports family planning as an important component of its maternal and child health program but not with specific demographic goals.

SOCIAL INDICATORS
Life expectancy: 64 yrs. (male: 62; female: 66) (1985)
Infant mortality: 48/1,000 births (1985)
Crude birth rate: 30/1,000 pop. (1985)
Crude death rate: 8/1,000

HEALTH
Access to health services: 75% (1980–83)
Births attended by trained health personnel: 51% (1984)

HOUSING
Persons per household: 5.4 (1985)
Electricity: 22% without (1985)
Access to safe water: 81% (urban: 84%; rural: 20%) (1984)
Source of water: (1985)
Piped inside: 71%
Wells: 11%
River: 15%
Other: 3%
Toilet facilities: (1985)
Flush: 70%
Latrine: 7%
None: 23%
Building materials: (1985)
Cement, brick: 67%
Adobe or dirt: 17%
Wood: 16%

EDUCATION
Literacy: 85% (male: 86%; female: 84%) (1981)
Gross enrollment ratio: (1985)
First level: 117% (completing in 1978: 37%)
Second: 50%
Third: 13%
Educational attainment, for population 20 yrs. +: (1973)
None: 22%
First level: incomplete: 56%
Second: entered: 18%
Third: 3%

ECONOMIC ACTIVITY
Economically active population: 49% (male; female: no data)
Agriculture: 26% act. pop.; 26% of GDP
Mines: 7% act. pop.; 10% of GDP
Industry: 14% act. pop.; 22% of GDP
Services: 53% act. pop.; 42% of GDP
Per capita GNP: 1,320 U.S.$ (1985)
Population in absolute poverty:
Urban: 34% (197–84)
Living on minimum salary (10,000 pesos) or less: 51% (1980)
Without salary: 13% (1980)
National currency/per U.S.$: 142.31 pesos (1985)
Principal resources: Coffee, sugar

COMMUNICATIONS
Radio:
Transmitters: no data
Receivers: 3,650,000—133/1,000 pop. (1983)
Television:
Transmitters: 49
Receivers: 2,700,000—98/1,000 pop. (1983)

ECUADOR

THE MUÑIZ REGAS FAMILY

Hugo Ilario Muñiz García, age 38 (1)
Paula del Jesús Regas Quemez, 31 (2)
María de Lourdes Muñiz Regas, 15 (absent)
Marcella Lucrecia, 13 (absent)
Petita del Jesús, 11 (3)
Tarlin Yennes, 8 (4)

8 chickens
1 sow
1 donkey
1 cat

LA UNIÓN
October 10

It's pitch black outside the bamboo house of the Muñiz Regas family, but Hugo gets up abruptly and runs to the door. It's the same thing every night. Wild donkeys come from the hills to ravage the family corn patch in front of the house. Hugo chases them away with a stick and returns to his mat, but the donkey brays are now replaced by a chorus of roosters. In spite of the concert the household goes back to sleep. Finally the roosters do the same.

5:00. All the roosters of Ecuador can now shout themselves hoarse. There's no mistaking the dawning day. The birds are singing. The fowl come down from the trees, the pig gives out a last snore, and the chickens cry hungrily. Hugo leaves for the coffee plantation where he works. He will eat breakfast there.

Hugo is a coffee producer himself but has suffered many setbacks in the last two years: drought one year, floods the next. His two hectares have produced only five bags of coffee this year instead of the usual forty. After this bad harvest, most of the other peasants left their remote mountain villages and went to the city in search of work, but Hugo preferred to stay and take a job in a big neighboring plantation. He weeds the rows of coffee bushes and gets paid 60 sucres (90 cents, U.S.) a day plus two meals.

Through the wall of cane that separates the bedroom from the kitchen, Paula can be seen moving about. Using a hollow reed, she blows into the coals to rekindle the kitchen fire. The wood stove consists of an earthenware pot enclosed in a large wooden box with a cane lattice veneer.

6:00. Tarlin arrives from his grandparents' house next door. He's been sleeping there since he was five, to keep the old couple company. He picks up his school notebooks and stretches out on the ground on the straw mat next to his sleeping sister. Petita opens her eyes and, without getting up, reaches out for her notebook. The two children finish their homework in companionable silence.

The children vacate the floor of the bedroom for that of the kitchen. Breakfast is ready: a cup of water with coffee extract added, a bowl of rice, a piece of salt-pork fat, and on the side, instead of bread, *verde asada*, green banana cooked over a wood fire.

7:20. Grandmother calls out the time from her doorstep. Petita and Tarlin don their uniforms, swipe an orange from the tree, and leave for the ten-minute walk to La Unión. The village is comprised of half a dozen buildings surrounding a large field that doubles as a soccer field and a schoolyard. The biggest house in the village is that of Señor Valez, owner of the coffee plantation where Hugo works and director of the peasant coffee cooperative. Valez is the most important man in the village, and everything that is needed is usually supplied by him. He sells the men rum when they play cards and shoot pool at his house and is the village butcher as well. On Wednesday, peasants bring their pigs to be slaughtered. On Sundays, they bring their cows. Mr. Valez sells the meat and takes a commission, of course.

The primary school, next door to Valez's house, has only three teachers for its six classes. Petita will graduate this year. Next year, if possible, she will leave to attend high school in Jipijapa. Her sisters, María and Marcella, already attend and live with their aunt. Although the school is free, the uniforms are not and the Muñiz Regas family cannot even afford that expense this year. Her future in their hands, Petita patiently awaits her parents' decision.

8:00. Time to do the laundry. Two years ago, the men dug a large hole in the ground between Paula's mother's house, her brother's, and her own to catch rainwater. Paula walks to the hole and crouches on a flat rock with a bucket and soap beside her. With great gusto, she begins her battle against dirt. Finished, she sits on the rungs of the ladder in front of her door to catch her breath. The chickens and the sow come running, and Paula throws rice down for the hen. She shoos away the greedy sow.

Now for a brief visit with her mother-in-law. Paula feels a bit lonely these days with her daughters and most of her neighbors gone to the city. She sets off down the overgrown road, once the only bus route to the village, now a boulevard for the peasants' farm animals. Last winter, rain washed out the road and now the bus takes an hour-and-a-half detour and still drops one off a four-hour walk away. María and Marcella can barely manage to come home on weekends. The road takes Paula past the village school, where she hears the children rehearsing a song for tomorrow's "Miss Unión" festival, and leads her back into the jungle toward her in-laws'. Their large bamboo house is filled to capacity. Three of her sisters-in-law live there with their husbands and children. Paula lived there too when she was first married, but very soon afterward her father helped the young couple build their own house next to his.

11:00. On her return, Paula's mother immediately steps over the fence separating their houses to have a chat while Paula begins to make a lunch of *chicharrones* (banana fried in pork fat), rice, and minuscule morsels of beef. Mother and daughter are very close and spend as much time as they can together. Paula throws the scraps and cooking water through the kitchen window, below which the pig delightedly wallows in the mud. The children, who have only a half day of school, return home.

After lunch Tarlin goes down the road to his cousin's to play. Petita lies on the wooden bed to start her homework, but she falls asleep. Hugo returns from work and takes a nap in the hammock in the front room.

3:00. Petita wakes up and goes out to pick wild fruits with her friends. Paula takes her place on the bed and reads the newspaper brought back by her brother from the city. As she reads, she listens to the conversations that drift through the thin walls as peasants pass in front of the house. The walls are so thin she can even talk with her mother from where she is, and the two women often converse this way.

Hugo gets up, grabs his machete, and disappears into the forest in back of the house. He is clearing a piece of land to cultivate rice. Each afternoon he works there a few hours. Hugo is a courageous, hardworking, and responsible man who has not let his recent misfortune dishearten him. But Paula's spirit is tested even further when she walks to the nearby spring to fetch water and notices their own donkey in the middle of the vegetable garden. He has already destroyed most of it and now it must be replanted. The donkey gets a thorough beating and is tied to a tree in the yard.

5:00. From each house around La Unión comes the sound of women blowing their reeds to start the evening fires. In the Muñiz Regas yard, the rooster and his hens climb up the ladder and settle into their tree. Petita brings the pig into the pen beneath the house as Hugo and Tarlin wait for their meal. Night falls.

Paula serves Hugo his meal in the front room, which is her husband's domain. Lit by a candle, the table is the only piece of furniture in the house besides the bed and the hammock. Paula kneels on the kitchen floor with her children. This custom does not bother her. Light falls from a single candle onto the plates on their knees. Their faces remain in the shadows as they talk quietly.

The dishes are left until tomorrow. There is not enough light and the candle must be used sparingly. It is time for bed. Tarlin returns to his grandmother's house. Petita spreads her mat at the foot of her parents' wooden bed. Hugo and Paula slide underneath the mosquito netting. They are soon asleep. The night belongs to the crickets.

Paula throws the scraps and dishwater out the window. Underneath, the pig delightedly wallows in the mud

The walls are so thin that Paula can converse from her bed with her mother, who lives next door

ECUADOR

QUITO

Guayaquil

Cuenca

Population

● 1 000 000

● 250 000

● 50 000

· 10 000

| 0 | 50 | 100 | 150 | Kilometers |
| 0 | 20 | 60 | 100 | Miles |

THE NAME: From Spanish, meaning "middle of the world." Named by a scientific expedition which discovered the geodesic line in the country.

THE PEOPLE: The Ecuadorians

GEOGRAPHY
  Coastal lowland on the Pacific
  Andes Mountains separated by high valleys
  In the east, the mountain foothills and plains of the Amazon Basin
  The Galápagos Islands are part of the national territory
  Max. altitude: 6,310 m. (20,556 ft.) (Chimparazo) and the world's highest active volcano: 5,896 m. (19,300 ft.) (Cotopaxi)

Area: 283,561 sq. km. (109,483 sq. mi.)
Density: 33 pers./sq. km. (84 pers./sq. mi.) (1986)
Arable land: 9% (1987)
Forest: 50%
Climate: Ranges from the tropical rain forest on the coast and in the eastern region to the tropical grasslands of the central valley and the permanent snowfields of the Andes.

CAPITAL: Quito, pop. 1,003,875 (1984 est.)

LANGUAGE: Spanish (official)
  Majority of Indians speak Quechua.

RELIGION: Majority Catholic

POPULATION: Total—9,400,000 (1985)
    Annual growth: 2.9% (272,600) (1980–85)
    Doubling time: 25 yrs.
    Urban: 52% (1985) (est. for year 2000: 61%)
    Rural: 48%

AGE GROUPS: (1982)
    15% less than 5 yrs.
    42% less than 15
    53% less than 20
    29% from 20 to 39
    13% from 40 to 59
    6% 60 yrs. and over

ETHNIC GROUPS
    Indian: 40%
    Mestizo: 40%
    White: 10%
    Black: 5%
    Other: 5%

HISTORY
    Originally inhabited by various Indian tribes
      (Quitos, Caraque)
    1534: Fall of the Incas to Spanish conquistadors
    Until 1740: Member of the Viceroyalty of Peru,
      under the name Kingdom of Quito
    1740–1809: Part of the Viceroyalty of New Grenada
    August 10, 1809: Proclamation of independence
    1809–22: War of independence
      Becomes part of Greater Colombia (a
      confederation consisting of Ecuador, Panama,
      Colombia, and Venezuela constituted under the
      leadership of Simón Bolívar)
    May 13, 1830: Becomes a sovereign state
    1941: Peru seizes the Amazon area
    1979: Return to democracy after seven years of
      military rule

FAMILY
Marital status, for population 12 yrs. and older: (1982)
    Single: 36%
    Married: 38%
    Common-law: 14%
    Widowed: 5%
    Separated from husband or partner: 2%
    Divorced: 1%
Female head of household: no data
Fertility rate: 4.8 (1985)
Births out of wedlock: no data
Teenage births: 13% (1978)
Contraception: 40% (1984)
Government's position on family planning: Supports
    responsible parenthood and appropriate education
    for the advancement of the family. It has not
    expressed a view on the levels of fertility. However,
    the government directly supports a family-planning
    program intended to improve maternal and child
    health and family well-being.

SOCIAL INDICATORS
Life expectancy: 65 yrs. (male: 63; female: 67)
    (1985)
Infant mortality: 66/1,000 births (1985)

Crude birth rate: 36/1,000 pop. (1985)
Crude death rate: 8/1,000
Health:
    Access to health services: 18% (1980–83)
    Births attended by trained health personnel:
      26% (1984)

HOUSING
Persons per household: 5 (1985)
Electricity: 37% without (1982)
Access to safe water: 59% (urban: 98%; rural: 21%)
    (1983)
Source of water: (1982)
    Piped inside: 45%
    Piped outside: 7%
    Well or spring: 20%
    River or stream: 14%
    Distribution cart: 11%
Toilet facilities: (1982)
    Flush: 47%
    Latrine: 13%
    None: 40%
Building materials: (1982)
    Cane: 34%
    Adobe: 29%
    Concrete: 24%
    Wood: 9%

EDUCATION
Literacy: 80% (male: 84%; female: 76%) (1982)
Gross enrollment ratio: (1984)
    First level: 114% (completing in 1980–84: 62%)
    Second: 55%
    Third: 32%
Educational attainment, for population 25 yrs. +:
    (1982)
    None: 25%
    First level: incomplete: 17% (complete: 34%)
    Second: entered: 0%
    Third: 8%

ECONOMIC ACTIVITY
Economically active population: 29% (male: 46%;
    female: 12%) (1982)
Agriculture: 48% act. pop.; 12% of GDP
Mines: 3% act. pop.; 18% of GDP
Industry: 14% act. pop.; 21% of GDP
Services: 35% act. pop.; 49% of GDP
Per capita GNP: 1,160 U.S.$ (1985)
Population in absolute poverty: (1980–82)
    Urban: 40%
    Rural: 65%
National currency/per U.S.$: 69.56 sucres (1985)
Principal resources:
    Petroleum
    Bananas, coffee

COMMUNICATIONS
Radio:
    Transmitters: no data
    Receivers: 2,950,000—319/1,000 pop. (1983)
Television:
    Transmitters: no data
    Receivers: 570,000—62/1,000 pop. (1983)

GUYANA

THE SINGH FAMILY

Totaram Singh, age 37 (1)
Josada Singh, 32 (2)
Gaeta Singh, 11 (3)
Victor, 10 (4)
Devi, 5 (5)
Getrie, 2 (6)

1 dog

SISTERS VILLAGE
December 6

5:00. Full of zest, Josada heads down the wooden steps to the kitchen while the rest of the family continues to sleep. Friday is her favorite day. It's payday at the sugarcane refinery and the ideal day to get some money from the workers going to and from their shift. Just at the end of the market and at the entrance to the village, Josada's house lies along the road to the refinery. She has it all planned.

On Wednesdays she goes to the Georgetown market. Imports are restricted in Guyana, and milk, wheat flour, corn oil, and many other ingredients indispensable for traditional cooking are unavailable. But Josada has a whole network of clandestine suppliers. In Guyana the black market flourishes. Without it, Josada would be unable to prepare the recipes her ancestors brought from India at the end of the last century. She has nothing but scorn for local products. "Rice flour is too heavy! Peanut oil leaves an aftertaste!" she claims. "And powdered milk is too expensive."

On Thursdays, with the help of her husband and children she prepares her cakes made from pumpkin, coconut, and assorted spices. The cakes will be baked fresh throughout the next day, and sold to the workers passing by. The family works late into the night. Josada insists that her children stay home from school on Thursdays and Fridays. This chance for extra money is more important to her than her children's education.

6:00. Josada hands her husband his lunch, and Totaram joins the groups of men and women carrying machetes to the trucks parked outside the factory. They cram in. Jam-packed, the convoy bumps off in the direction of the fields where the peasants will cut sugarcane all day.

6:30. The first blast of the refinery siren warns the workers that there is another half hour until the shift change. On Fridays, a spontaneous market forms, and the merchants set up their stalls on both sides of the road. The first vendors to arrive get the permanent shelves; the others set up their trestles. In a few minutes a colorful market of fruits, vegetables, and clothes emerges. The cool morning air is pleasant, but soon the sunshades will be unable to contain the overwhelming heat.

The workers arriving for the day shift look just as tired as those leaving after a night's work. The swarming mass parts to let through the tractors of the independent farmers who have come to deliver their sugarcane. Sugar and rice are Guyana's main exports.

7:30. Josada's wares are starting to sell. She has roused her ten- and eleven-year-old children, Victor and Gaeta, to take care of the café. Gaeta places the freshly baked cakes on the counters, and Victor grinds the ginger for the beer that customers drink with their cakes. Gaeta really should be in school; to enter high school, she must pass an examination before she is twelve. If she fails, she will have two more years of elementary school and then no alternative but to look for a job. This deadline doesn't appear to bother her. She seems content to sell her mother's cakes. There are few customers. The oversized café is run-down, its shelves are covered with dust, paint is peeling off the walls, and cobwebs fill the corners.

Five-year-old Devi is stretched out with her little sister in the jute hammock. Josada's two youngest children are the only ones who are allowed some leisure, and today they know that the only way to avoid their mother's short temper is to keep out of sight.

11:30. The refinery siren lets loose its lunchtime blast. Totaram and his crew seek out some shade for their break. Totaram discreetly opens his lunch bucket; in it he finds the cheapest rice sold on the market. He misses the more sustaining corn-flour *rotis* (bread) that Josada used to make for him. He talks little and gets back to work with the crew quickly. There is no time to lose; they are paid according to the weight of the cane they bring to the factory. Working in the fields at breakneck speed, they cut and stack the cane whose branches were burned the day before. The fire trims the cane, chases away the rats, and kills the venomous snakes that live among the stalks. The men then pile the bundles of cane into barges stationed along the vast network of canals that run through the sugarcane fields. They strive to fill two barges a day, which will earn them a barely sufficient wage.

At home Josada sits outdoors with her sister Reena at the table. Their feet dangle as they eat rice and fish with their fingers. Four doors away, Reena has a bar, which also opens on Fridays. She sells nothing but rum. Her place does not look much better than Josada's, but paint is a luxury on the black market.

The oven is going full blast. Josada has been saving kerosene all week. Victor watches the shop while Gaeta squats in the courtyard washing the dishes. Totaram has installed an outside tap at ground level because the country's water pressure is so low that kitchen taps no longer work. The dishwater runs down through the yard and into the field behind the house. This is also where they dump their garbage. The smell is terrible and attracts thousands of gnats.

4:00. The day shift ends and the makeshift market comes to life. The returning field workers are unrecognizable, covered from head to foot with burned cane soot. A feeling of anticipation fills the air as the workers line up at the windows of an eight-sided wooden booth where three cashiers are passing out brown envelopes. Three policemen watch as the men and women get their envelopes and go off by themselves to furtively count their money.

There is nothing special to celebrate, but it is difficult to resist the modest pleasures offered by the market and by Josada's café and her sister's bar. The week's debts also have to be repaid. Unfortunately, many workers will have spent their pay before they even reach home.

7:00. The merchants pack up their stalls. There are fewer and fewer customers at Josada's café. She goes off to her sister's bar, and the children greedily snatch up the remaining cakes before it's time to close. Totaram helps his children sweep the floor and sees Devi and Getrie off to bed. Putting Gaeta in charge, he leaves with a friend. There are no distractions in the village; the movie theater closed long ago.

9:00. In Reena's bar some slightly tipsy customers empty the last bottles of rum. Josada makes her way home, looking forward to a good night's sleep and a day of rest. She expects her husband to be there. At dawn tomorrow the siren will remind Totaram that Saturday is not a day of rest for him.

It's the weekly opening of the café attached to the house. Like the house, it is run-down, the paint is peeling off the walls, and its empty shelves are covered with dust and cobwebs

Gaeta, Victor, and Devi are not going to school today. Their mother insists that they stay home and help her

GUYANA

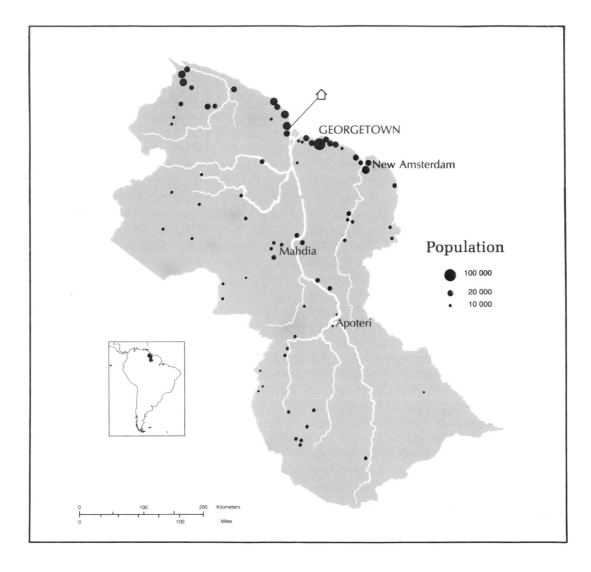

THE NAME: From Arawak, meaning "land of many
  waters"

THE PEOPLE: The Guyanese

GEOGRAPHY
  Low coastal plains
  South of the coast: hilly sand and clay area
  South and west: mountains and interior savannas
  Max. altitude: 3,031 m. (9,094 ft.) (Mt. Roraima)
Area: 214,969 sq. km. (83,000 sq. mi.)
Density: 3.9 pers./sq. km. (10 pers./sq. mi.) (1986)
Arable land: 2% (1987)
Forest: 76%

Climate: Tropical, but northeast trade winds mitigate
  the heat along the coast, where two wet seasons,
  from April to August and from November to
  January, alternate with two dry seasons.

CAPITAL: Georgetown, pop. 72,049 (1976 est.)

LANGUAGE: English (official)
  Creole is spoken by all except the Amerindians,
    who still speak their dialect.
  Hindu and Urdu are used for religious purposes.

RELIGION: (1980)
  Christian: 42%   Muslim: 9%
  Hindu: 37%   Other: 6%

POPULATION: Total—953,000 (1985)
  Annual growth: 1.9% (18,107) (1980–85)
  Doubling time: 35 yrs.
  Urban: 32% (1985) (est. for year 2000: 42%)
  Rural: 68%

AGE GROUPS: (1980)
  13% less than 5 yrs.
  41% less than 15
  54% less than 20
  28% from 20 to 39
  13% from 40 to 59
   6% 60 yrs. and over

ETHNIC GROUPS: (1980)
  East Indian: 51%
  Black: 31%
  East Indian and black: 11%
  Amerindian: 5% (9 tribes)

HISTORY
  Originally inhabited by American Indians
  1596: Dutch founding of Georgetown (Stabrock)
  1621: Dutch colonization
  1796: Occupied by the British
  1814: Becomes British Guiana
  1928: British Guiana made a Crown Colony
  1953: Constitution is granted
  May 26, 1966: Independence
  February 23, 1970: Becomes a republic within the
    Commonwealth

FAMILY
Marital status, for population 14 yrs. and
    older: (1980)
  Married: 48%
  Common-law: 9%
  Visiting union: 3%
  Separated from husband or partner: 12%
  Never had husband or partner: 23%
Female head of household: 24% (1980)
Fertility rate: 3.0 (1985)
Births out of wedlock: no data
Teenage births: no data
Contraception: 30.8% (1975)
Government's position on family planning: Considers
  present and prospective fertility rates satisfactory
  and permits the family-planning services provided
  by a private organization.

SOCIAL INDICATORS
Life expectancy: 69 yrs. (male: 66; female: 71) (1985)
Infant mortality: 36/1,000 births (1985)
Crude birth rate: 27/1,000 pop. (1985)
Crude death rate: 6/1,000

Health:
  Access to health services: 89% (1984)
  Births attended by trained health personnel:
    93% (1984)

HOUSING
Persons per household: 5.2 (1985)
Electricity: 31% without (1980)
Access to safe water: 80% (urban: 100%; rural: 60%)
  (1983)
Source of water: (1981)
  Piped inside: 36%
  Piped outside: 20%
  Public standpipe: 25%
  Other: 19%
Toilet facilities: (1981)
  Flush: 13%
  Latrine: 67%
  Other: 20%
Building materials: (1981)
  Wood: 24%
  Cement: 32%
  Other: 25%

EDUCATION
Literacy: 92% (male: 94%; female: 89%) (1970)
Gross enrollment ratio: (1983)
  First level: 90% (completing in 1980–84: 84%)
  Second: 55%
  Third: 2.0%
Educational attainment, for population 25 yrs. +:
  (1980)
  None: 8%
  First level: incomplete: 73%
  Second: entered: 17%
  Third: 1.8%

ECONOMIC ACTIVITY
Economically active population: no data
Agriculture: 36% act. pop.; 40% of GDP
Mines: 4% act. pop.; 18% of GDP
Industry: 20% act. pop.; 15% of GDP
Services: 40% act. pop.; 27% of GDP
Per capita GNP: 500 U.S.$ (1985)
Population in absolute poverty: no data
National currency/per U.S.$: 4.25 dollars (1985)
Principal resources: Sugar, rice, bauxite

COMMUNICATIONS
Radio:
  Transmitters: 8 (1979)
  Receivers: 350,000—381/1,000 pop. (1983)
Television: (1986)
  The information available suggests that no
    television service has yet been introduced in the
    country.

PARAGUAY

THE BURGES GUERRERO FAMILY

Simeón Burges Alonso, age 38 (1)
Catalina Guerrero de Burges, 28 (2)
Liz María Cristina Burges Guerrero, 8 (3)
Alfredo Ramón, 5 (4)
Edgar Alcides, 7 (5)
Aldo Damián, 7 months (6)

2 ducks
5 guinea hens
20 chickens
3 pigs
1 horse
1 cow
1 calf   1 dog
1 bull   2 cats

CABALLERO
July 22

The department of Paraguarí. It takes six hours by a wood-burning steam locomotive to travel the 100 kilometers between the capital and the village of Caballero. Then one hour on foot or half an hour on horseback through fields of cassava separated by small stands of trees, on a road washed out by frequent torrential rains, before one finally reaches the Burges home, where the days and nights are punctuated by the cries of a baby demanding his bottle.

6:00. Simeón walks out of the family bedroom and across the breezeway to the kitchen to light the wood stove. As if on cue, the ducks, guinea hens, chickens, pigs, cats, and dog leave the yard and clamor at the kitchen door. Once the fire is going, Simeón pushes past the animals with a load of sugarcane in his arms. They are in a frenzy until the cane is chopped and placed at their feet.

Simeón and his family live on ten acres of land owned by his father. He and two of his seven brothers work the land and share the produce. Each family has a small garden for their personal use. Simeón worries about what will happen to them when his aging father dies. Will the land be divided among all seven brothers? If so, he will no longer have enough land to feed his wife, Catalina, and his children. His sole source of money comes from chopping wood, which he has time to do only in winter. Simeón might be forced to work in the city, as he has done several times already. By working on construction sites, he managed to buy the materials to build his sixty-square-meter house.

Baby Aldo slung on her hip, Catalina enters the kitchen to make *mate*, an herbal tea. She shares the *mate*, steeping in a cup made from a dried gourd, with her husband. Their children are on holiday, and there is nothing to prevent them from staying in bed. But the aroma of their special *mate* with milk simmering on the stove brings forth three little faces from the corners of the bed. A

neighbor walking past the house with his team of oxen is the signal for Simeón to saddle his horse and join his brothers in the cassava fields.

7:30. Eight-year-old Liz sweeps the courtyard clean after the animals and levels the sand in front of the terrace. Liz already takes her role as a woman seriously. She can almost take care of the house and practices when her mother is out. She watches the baby while issuing orders and reprimands to her brothers. Her mother has gone to milk the cow at her in-laws' farm. The elderly couple moved to the village to be closer to the medical clinic, and two of their sons live on the farm alone. Catalina stops by to supervise their breakfast. "Two single men don't know how to look after a house," she says.

After the calf has drunk his fill, Catalina has just enough milk for the baby to drink that day. She takes her time coming home from the fields, gazing proudly at her home in the distance. "My house is beautiful," she says. Having an attractive home is highly valued in Paraguay, and families that can afford it paint or whitewash their houses every year.

9:00. In the bright midmorning sun Catalina scrubs the wash near the well while her daughter rinses the clothes and hangs them out to dry in the sun. Baby Aldo is asleep, and little Alfredo has been assigned the task of keeping the pigs out of the kitchen. The child is delighted by this responsibility and makes a game of it, using his stick to allow the chickens through so they can lay their eggs in the nest in the corner of the room. Edgar has gone to spend the day at his grandmother Guerrero's house. He makes many stops along the way. Each house belongs to an aunt, uncle, or cousin.

11:00. Aldo wakes up crying, and even capable Liz can't subdue his persistent whining. Catalina comes to the rescue with a song and a hug and the promise of lunch. At least it's easier for Catalina now that she has a new stove. Last year there was only a hole in the ground. Thanks to a loan from the Ministry of Agriculture, a number of families in the area were able to buy stoves. Catalina attended free cooking classes in the village. Now she takes more pleasure in preparing meals. She would be even happier if the kitchen was more comfortable. It still has a dirt floor and the half walls are unsquared lumber. The south-facing wall is made of cane, but Catalina loves the sunlight it lets in. A new wall would cost 7,000 pesos.

Simeón comes home from the fields. Alfredo runs to greet him and grabs the horse's reins to lead him to the shade. The horse is the boy's best friend. Alfredo then accompanies his father to a cousin's house. Catalina doesn't wait for them. She has her lunch with Liz: rice with cooked beef and herbs, served with manioc instead of bread.

1:15. Back at last, Simeón and Alfredo wait for Catalina to serve them at the table; she has kept their food warm. The animals are alert, waiting for a few scraps, and the unbearable squalling of the guinea hens drowns out the men's talk. Using a long pole, Liz knocks a grapefruit off the tree for dessert.

After lunch, Simeón saddles the horse for Catalina. She is taking Aldo to the village for his vaccination. The rhythm of the ride will send the future horseman off to sleep immediately. After seeing them off, Simeón tends the garden. The herbs, onions, and salad greens are ready for picking. In a few months, there will be carrots, cabbages, and tomatoes too. Traditionally these vegetables were not part of the Paraguay diet, but the government is attempting to stress their nutritional value, and Simeón has taken the time to learn how to grow them.

4:30. Catalina returns home and finds her children freshly washed and playing marbles in the yard. Alfredo is reunited with his pet. He unharnesses it and brings it some coconut leaves. Now Simeón can leave to drink *terrere* (*mate* with cold water) with the men. Before darkness falls Catalina goes into her kitchen. Even now the fire from the stove barely lights the dim room. "It will be much more pleasant next year when we have electricity,' she says. There is already electricity in the village of Caballero, but the homeowners on the rural roads have not yet organized themselves to pay for the connection.

6:00. When Simeón returns home, the children lower their voices and look for quieter games. Simeón does not like crying and arguments and demands that his house be well ordered and clean. Catalina accepts this machismo authority. "My husband is not like the others," she says. "He is gentle with me and the children." Simeón differs from other men in Paraguay who are used to having several women at the same time. (The 1870 War of the Triple Alliance, in which four-fifths of the male population were killed, and the 1932 Chaco War have resulted in a considerable disparity between the male and female population.)

Simeón lights the acetylene lamp and washes himself while the children eat an omelette and black-bean salad. Then the little ones give up their places to their parents, who linger at the table to chat.

9:00. Catalina puts a thermos of hot milk and some clean diapers next to the bed for the baby during the night. In the next bed, the children sleep huddled together like puppies. Simeón peers down into Aldo's crib. For the moment, the baby's still form and the quiet breathing of his other children satisfy Simeón's need for orderliness. The whole family rests for a few hours until a hungry Aldo awakens them all.

Having an attractive home is highly valued in Paraguay and families that can afford it paint or whitewash their houses every year. Simeón went to work in the city to earn the money to build his

Cooking is easier now that Catalina has a stove. Last year there was only a hole in the ground. She would be happier if the kitchen was more comfortable and if the chickens would lay their eggs somewhere else. What she likes the most is the sunlight that comes through the cane wall

PARAGUAY

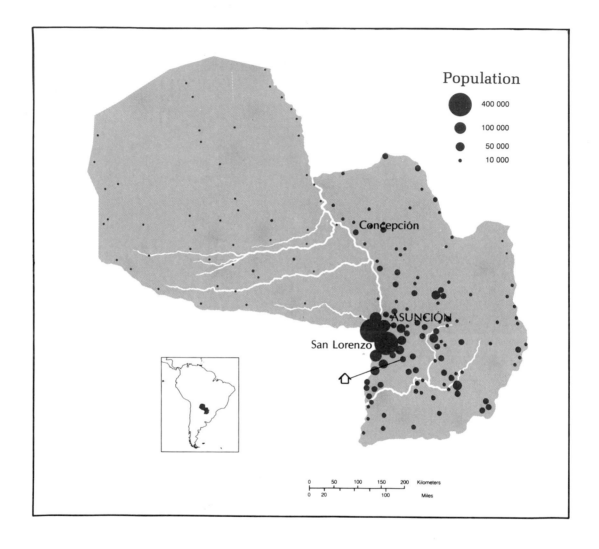

THE NAME: From Guarani, meaning "place with great rivers"

THE PEOPLE: The Paraguayans

GEOGRAPHY
The Paraguay River divides the country into two disparate regions:
    East: rolling terrain, with wooded hills, tropical forests, and fertile grasslands
    West: the Chaco, a semi-arid flat region
    Max. altitude: 850 m. (2,720 ft.) (Cerro San Rafael)
Area: 406,752 sq. km. (157,048 sq. mi.)
Density: 7.9 pers./sq. km. (21 pers./sq. mi.) (1986)
Arable land: 5% (1987)
Forest: 50%

Climate: Subtropical with abundant rainfall and only a short dry season from July to September, when temperatures are lowest.
Capital: Asunción, pop. 457,210 (1982)

LANGUAGE: Spanish and Guarani (official)

RELIGION
    Majority Catholic

POPULATION: Total—3,700,000 (1985)
    Annual growth: 3% (111,000) (1980–85)
    Doubling time: 24 yrs.
    Urban: 44% (1985) (est. for year 2000: 51%)
    Rural: 56%

AGE GROUPS: (1982)

15% less than 5 yrs.	28% from 20 to 39
41% less than 15	14% from 40 to 59
52% less than 20	6% 60 yrs. and over

ETHNIC GROUPS: Assimilation has been so complete that less than 5% is clearly identifiable as either white or Indian.

HISTORY

Originally inhabited by the Guarani Indians
1524: Arrival of Spanish explorer Alejo García
1528–31: Exploration by Sebastian Cabot
1537: First Spanish settlement in Asunción
1776: Establishment of Viceroyalty of the Río de la Plata
May 14, 1811: Independence and rejection of Buenos Aires' leadership
1865–70: Defeated in war against the Triple Alliance (Argentina, Brazil, and Uruguay); loses 55,000 square miles of territory and more than half its population
1932–35: Chaco War; Paraguay settles boundary dispute with Bolivia
1954–86: Military coup; General Alfredo Stroessner assumes power; has been reelected since.

FAMILY

Marital status, for population 12 yrs. and older: (1982)
Single: 44%
Married: 39%
Consensually married: 10%
Widowed: 4%
Separated: 1.5%
Divorce is illegal.
Female head of household: no data
Fertility rate: 4.7 (1985)
Births out of wedlock: no data
Teenage births: 11% (1982)
Contraception: 30% (1984)
Government's position on family planning: Has recently adopted the view that the rate of population growth is satisfactory.

SOCIAL INDICATORS

Life expectancy: 66 yrs. (male: 63; female: 68) (1985)
Infant mortality: 44/1,000 births (1985)
Crude birth rate: 35/1,000 pop. (1985)
Crude death rate: 7/1,000
Health:
Access to health services: 56% (urban: 89%; rural: 44%) (1980–83)
Births attended by trained health personnel: 22% (1984)

HOUSING

Persons per household: 5.2 (1982)
Electricity: 83% without (1982)
Access to safe water: 25% (urban: 46%; rural: 10%) (1983)
Source of water: (1982)
Public reservoir: 11%
Well: 81%
River and other: 8%
Toilet facilities: (1982)
Flush: 10%
Other: 70%
None: 10%
Building materials: (1982)
Brick: 47%
Wood boards: 30%
Esteques (bamboo): 15%
Adobe: 6%
Thatched roofs: 51%
Dirt floor: 59%

EDUCATION

Literacy: 87% (male: 90%; female: 85%) (1982)
Gross enrollment ratio: (1984)
First level: 101% (completing in 1980–84: 48%)
Second: 31%
Third: 9.7%
Educational attainment, for population 25 yrs. +: (1972)
None: 12%
First level: incomplete: 58% (complete: 10%)
Second: entered: 6%
Third: 2%

ECONOMIC ACTIVITY

Economically active population: 24% (male: 55%; female: 14%) (1982)
Agriculture: 50% act. pop.; 26% of GDP
Mines: 0% act. pop.; 0% of GDP
Industry: 15% act. pop.; 26% of GDP
Services: 35% act. pop.; 48% of GDP
Per capita GNP: 860 U.S.$ (1985)
Population in absolute poverty: (1978)
Urban: 19%
Rural: 50%
National currency/per U.S.$ (1985): 240 guarani
Principal resources: Soybeans, cotton

COMMUNICATIONS

Radio:
Transmitters: 56 (1979)
Receivers: 260,000—75/1,000 pop. (1983)
Television:
Transmitters: no data
Receivers: 82,000—24/1,000 pop. (1983)

PERU

THE TORRES FAMILY

Francisco Torres Ponce, age 44 (1)
Mercedes Calara, 30 (2)
Rosa Luz Torres, 10 (3)
Anna Luisa, 9 (4)
Adriana Felicita, 7 (5)
Marinela, 4 (6)
Marixa, 3 (7)

1 cat and her kittens

LLANAVILLE
September 27

It is midnight when Francisco stumbles noisily into the shack. He is drunk, as he is almost every night. His wife, Mercedes, and their five daughters are asleep in the only bed, and he passes out beside them. Mercedes is awakened by the noise and the lack of room in the bed. She is sad. If only she could change things! She wonders if she and her children will rise from their misery.

The Torres family lives in Llanaville, one of Peru's vast shantytowns, quaintly called *pueblos jovenes* (young cities). In reality this city outside Lima is a community of decrepit hovels that dot the pampa, a barren sandy Peruvian plain that stretches to the sea. Francisco and Mercedes are among the many poor Indians who have come down from the mountains and now make up one-third of Peru's urban population. Among the few slum dwellers who are not squatters, the Torres family built their shack two years ago in a shantytown where land ownership is recognized by the government. Francisco has twelve more months to build a cement house; if he fails to do so, he will have to return half of his hundred-square-meter plot to the community. Meanwhile they have been living in a one-room hut made of mats, scrap lumber, and bits of iron from the garbage dumps.

10:30. Under a heavy gray sky, Mercedes hangs her wash on the line, occasionally glancing up to see if her daughter Rosa Luz has returned from the public taps with water. Ten-year-old Rosa Luz is notoriously slow. Sometimes it takes her half a day to fetch two buckets. Mercedes complains about her sluggishness, but in all likelihood it is the result of malnutrition.

The Torres children have all had their battle with hunger. The peasants don't realize that lack of food causes many of their diseases and even death. Four of the Torres children have not survived their first birthday, yet Mercedes is pregnant

with her tenth. This baby will be born under questionable hygienic circumstances. As with all her other children, Mercedes will labor and deliver on the kitchen table.

Finally Mercedes sees Rosa Luz in the distance. Now she can wash the breakfast dishes and prepare lunch. Her four other daughters stop their game of jump rope and run to join their sister.

12:30. Mercedes lights the little kerosene stove and boils water in one of her two blackened tins. The girls stand around the table (the only place where there is room to congregate) waiting for her to serve the meal. Lunch consists of a bowl of rice and a small piece of fish that Francisco brought the night before. Francisco does not join his family for meals. He left the house at four in the morning to catch a bus to take him to the sea. He is a fisherman who works for anyone who has a boat. Although wages are low and easily spent on drink, his family can usually count on fish to eat.

After serving her daughters, Mercedes sits at one end of the bench and distractedly rubs her swelling stomach. Halfway through the day, she is already exhausted. She had her first child at fifteen and ever since has had one pregnancy after another. "All the boys have died," she says. "I hope the next one is a girl." Her husband insists on a sixth child. Francisco believes that the odd number five brings bad luck—as long as they have only five children one will die.

Mercedes defers to her husband's will even though it is rooted in ignorance and superstition. Life with Francisco is hard and brings no hope. He has not dug the hole needed for the outside toilet, and the family relieve themselves farther out in the pampa. "When I come home, it's to rest, not work," says Francisco. Nor has he built a cement water tank even though a truck would deliver water right to their door. Some of their neighbors have cement tanks and receive water weekly. But Francisco would much rather pay for his rum than for his water.

Fortunately, Mercedes has friends who help out. This morning she has done her laundry at the home of a friend who has water and electricity services. There are also some public services. Her daughters attend a school built by the community with the help of UNICEF. The Torres family could have more advantages if Francisco were only willing. In Llanaville people often pool their resources and work together on Sundays and holidays to help build each other's houses.

Lunch finished, the children wipe their noses and don their threadbare school uniforms. Because the school is new, ten-year-old Rosa Luz is in the same class as seven-year-old Adriana. Marixa, the youngest, remains behind clinging to her mother's skirts. She's not very big for her three years—again, probably the result of poor eating. The child settles down on the bed and plays with the four flea-ridden kittens. Meanwhile, her mother stacks the dishes for Rosa Luz to wash and passes the broom over the damp earth floor. There is a perpetual mist on Peru's desert coast at this time of year; it penetrates the straw roof and keeps the hovel's floor damp and unhealthy.

2:00. Marixa follows her mother down the sandy streets to the community center, which lies adjacent to the school. Mercedes comes here to take a course in dressmaking in the hope of earning a little money. There is a small fee for the course,

and it took Mercedes months to save for it. Unfortunately that meant cutting back on the family's food and kerosene. Mercedes dreams that one day she will get a job in the city and her efforts will be rewarded.

The center has become a focal point for the community and is alive with activities: parents' meetings, distribution of food donated by international organizations, vaccination clinics, and adult education and training. It is a source of hope and inspiration for many slum dwellers.

6:00. Home from school, the girls pile their uniforms in the three cardboard boxes that serve as a cupboard. They put their old clothes back on and disappear into the pampa. Rosa Luz stays behind to do her chores while her mother prepares the rice they will eat for dinner. Mercedes will not have to call her children. Night falls suddenly on the poorly lit pampa and sends the girls running home. They now must make do with the table as their playground before eating their meager meal.

8:00. Mercedes sets aside Francisco's portion of rice. The wick is burning in the pot, and Mercedes has to put it out to save oil. Shivering in the darkness, mother and daughters have no alternative but to go to bed. Like kittens in search of warmth, the children huddle against their mother. Surrounded by the five little bodies, Mercedes relaxes a little and falls asleep.

The Torres family are among the many poor Indians who have come down from the mountains to make up one-third of Peru's urban population. They have built their one-room hut with mats, scrap lumber, and bits of iron from the garbage dumps

The next baby will be born under questionable hygienic circumstances. As with all her other children, Mercedes will labor and deliver on the kitchen table

PERU

THE SALAZAR SAAVEDRA FAMILY

Manuel Salazar Balderrama, age 39 (1)
Luisa Saavedra de Salazar, 32 (2)
Isabel Salazar Saavedra, 15 (3)
Ester, 11 (4)
Eduardo, 13 (5)
Luis, 6 (6)

CÉSAR VALLEYO
September 23

5:30. For more than an hour, the Saavedra family have been trying to ignore the pandemonium outside their barricaded door. The racket of thousands of crowing roosters combines with a cacophony of buses, trucks, and cars as they rumble through the streets of the César Valleyo shantytown carrying workers to the city of Lima. Finally, Luisa and Manuel give in. Luisa unbolts the bedroom door, moves the chair that blocks the front door, and unbolts that as well. Meanwhile her husband pushes the dining table away from the courtyard door. Slum families like the Salazar Saavedras who own a few luxury items such as their black-and-white TV set, secondhand refrigerator, and radio are constant prey for robbers. Satisfied that her home is intact, Luisa switches on the radio. Salsa blares, livening up the dawn a little.

In her no-nonsense voice, she rouses her children. "It's quarter to six already! What are you waiting for?" Everyone jumps out of bed except six-year-old Luis. It is his privilege as the youngest to be overlooked until eight o'clock. Manuel sits with his son Eduardo breakfasting on coffee and a piece of bread, and helps him with a paper he is preparing for school on working conditions in Peru, something Manuel knows a lot about. Manuel is happy to help his son. He had to work hard himself to finish high school and has only one ambition: to send his children to the university.

6:30. Manuel runs to catch the bus for the hour-long trip through the endless belt of shantytowns surrounding the capital. There are 321 *pueblos jovenes* (young cities) housing the flood of peasants who have migrated from the mountains to Lima's medical and educational facilities and employment opportunities. Manuel is a mechanic in an electronic parts factory and is lucky to have a regular job in a time when unemployment is so high. This stability has greatly improved the family's standard of living. Ten years ago they were

living, like most other Peruvian peasants who flock to the city, in a shack with no water or electricity. The Salazar Saavedras are squatters and, like 86 percent of the shantytowns' inhabitants, do not own their land. They have no assurance that they will be allowed to remain where they are, but that prevents no one from building a permanent dwelling.

It took Manuel eight years to earn enough money to build his house. He spends his weekends laying the bricks he buys bit by bit. Half the walls in the kitchen are unfinished. Now they have electricity, which was finally made available to those who could afford it. The community fought long and hard for electricity and public water, and most houses in César Valleyo now have a tap in their yards.

Luisa fills a basin with water for washing the dishes; next to her, Isabel rushes to brush her teeth. The school bus is due in three minutes. Isabel is a quiet, studious girl who spends her free time lost in her school books. Next year she will graduate, and she plans to study law or journalism at the university. She has just seen a documentary on Greece and the Homeric myths, and talks wistfully about going there one day. It's hard for children to get out of slums, but Isabel might be one of the few to do so.

Eduardo and Ester go to school in the afternoon only, but Luisa insists that they get up at the same time as the others to help with the housework. Daylight begins to break through the thick layer of perpetual gray clouds that cloak this part of Peru. It enters the bedroom through the gap between the tin roof and the walls. Ester shoos Luis out of bed, and in the semi-darkness she makes the beds and straightens the single cupboard in which clothes and linens are stored. With a swish of his broom, Eduardo pushes his drowsy little brother out to the kitchen and continues sweeping the main room's gray cement floor.

He pushes the table against the wall and stacks the chairs in a corner as in a ballroom after a dance. When someone wants to sit down, he takes one from the stack.

10:00. After feeding her son and sending him out to play, Luisa stays in the kitchen. By the time one meal is finished, she is already at work on the next. Eduardo goes shopping while she cleans the rice. Across the street from their house, peasants and fishermen come every day to set up their stalls and sell their produce. Eduardo buys fish for to-night's dinner. When he returns he and Ester will do school work until lunchtime.

12:00. As soon as they have downed their lunch, Eduardo and Ester start to worry about leaving on time. Like their sister, they go to a private school in Lima. This is a deliberate choice on the part of their father, who, like many Peruvians, thinks that the education there is better than in the public school system. He is proud of paying fees for his children's education. Little Luis doesn't have to hurry; this is his first year of school and his parents have decided to try out the recently built public school in César Valleyo.

1:00. Luisa stacks the dishes and covers the vegetables with a piece of cloth to protect them from the neighborhood cats and chickens, who are always on the lookout for open kitchens. She changes and waits until Isabel arrives home from school before leaving for her adult education class, so that the house will not be left unattended. Luisa is finishing her fifth year of elementary school. She had no schooling and married very young, so she had to wait until her children were in school before she could complete her own education. Their parents' obvious commitment to learning makes a great impression on the children, who appreciate going to school.

2:00. Isabel fills a bowl with rice, takes a chair from the corner, and installs herself at the end of the table with her books. Her studies absorb her completely and she is oblivious to the noise from the street. She will do her homework there until dinnertime.

5:30. School's out. Eduardo sits down near Isabel and begins studying. Ester and her mother, an inseparable pair, are in the kitchen. They chatter away like two friends while they prepare the meal. Luis, a little clown, stands at the end of the table talking nonsense to Eduardo and Isabel, who sit with their schoolwork and try not to laugh. Having failed to distract them, he turns on the television. Nothing special, just another soap opera. He watches it anyway.

7:30. With his family gathered in the kitchen, Manuel helps with the final preparations of *ceviche*, a favorite Peruvian dish of raw fish marinated with lime. In the main room, the whole family take their places on one side of the table, one beside the other, facing the wall. This evening's conversation is dominated by more news of a general strike planned for tomorrow. These strikes by workers wanting better working conditions occur often in response to the country's economic and social instability. In theory, Manuel would like to participate; in reality, it would cost him a day's pay. If the transportation system is paralyzed it will be impossible to get into the city, and he decides to leave at five o'clock to avoid any demonstrations.

9:00. Father and son sit down for a game of checkers. Beside them, Isabel is watching a movie on television. Luis is outside with a friend, and now Luisa calls him in. Luis sits on Isabel's knees as they all watch a movie on TV. One hour later everyone slowly prepares for the night. After checking that no one else needs to use the outside toilet, Manuel pulls the table in front of the courtyard door. From now on, only the chamber pot is available. He bolts the door facing the street and puts the chair in place. The bedroom is divided into two sections by a low cement partition. On one side there are two bunk beds for the men and on the other a double bed for the three women. Before Luisa joins her daughters, she sets the alarm clock in the futile hope that maybe the next morning she'll wake up to its ring instead of the noise of the street. Even now, the dull roar of the traffic can be heard in the background. Silence will not fall until deep in the night when the last car has passed.

It began as a shack, and after eight years of buying the bricks bit by bit, there is still the kitchen to finish

By the time one meal is finished, Luisa is already at work on the next

PERU

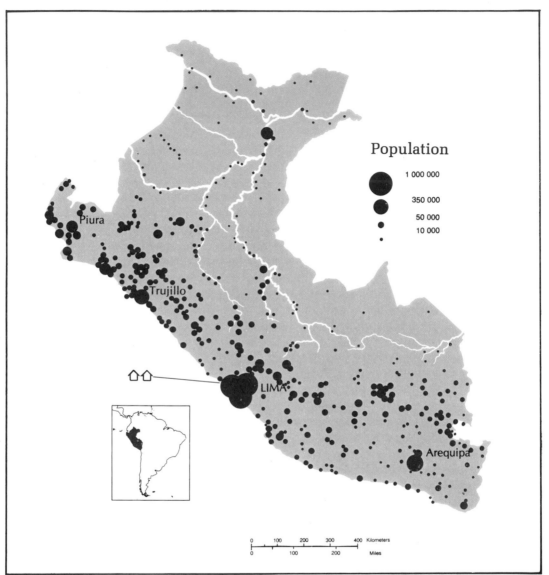

Population

- 1 000 000
- 350 000
- 50 000
- 10 000

Piura

Trujillo

LIMA

Arequipa

0   100   200   300   400 Kilometers

0   100   200   Miles

THE NAME: From the river Veru (Incan), which Spaniards understood as "Peru"

THE PEOPLE: The Peruvians

GEOGRAPHY
From west to east: the wide coastal desert, consisting of arid plains and foothills; the Andes Mountains (the Sierra); the eastern jungles (the Selva)
Max. altitude: 6,770 m. (22,211 ft.) (Huascarán)
Area: 1,285,216 sq. km. (496,224 sq. mi.)
Density: 15 pers./sq. km. (39 pers./sq. mi.) (1986)
Arable land: 3% (1987)
Forest: 54%

Climate: The coastal area is arid and mild; the Andes, temperate to frigid; and the eastern lowlands, tropically warm and humid.

CAPITAL: Lima, pop. 3,968,972 (1981)

LANGUAGE: Spanish and Quechua (official)

RELIGION
Majority Catholic

POPULATION: Total—19,700,000 (1985)
Annual growth: 2.6% (512,200) (1980–85)
Doubling time: 28 yrs.
Urban: 67% (est. for year 2000: 75%)
Rural: 33%

AGE GROUPS: (1981)
   17% less than 5 yrs.
   41% less than 15
   52% less than 20
   28% from 20 to 39
   14% from 40 to 59
   6% 60 yrs. and over

ETHNIC GROUPS
   Indian: 46%
   Mestizo: 38%
   White: 15%

HISTORY
   Human habitation dates back to 8000 B.C.; several
      advanced cultures developed until the 14th
      century
   1438: Expansion of the Inca Empire
   1524: Francisco Pizarro explores Peru
   1532: Spanish conquest of the Inca Empire
   1544: Creation of the Viceroyalty of Lima
   July 28, 1821: Independence
   1836–39: Peru-Bolivia confederation
   1879–84: War of the Pacific; Peru and Bolivia lose
      territory to Chile
   1895: Formation of Democratic Party
   1930: Military coup; followed by alternating periods
      of civilian administration and military dictatorship
   1980: Return to civilian and democratic
      administration

FAMILY
Marital status, for population 12 yrs. and older: (1981)
   Single: 39%
   Married: 38%
   Common-law: 12%
   Widowed: 7%
   Separated from husband or partner: 2%
   Divorced: 0.4%
Female head of household: 22% (1981)
Fertility rate: 4.7 (1985)
Births out of wedlock: no data
Teenage births: 13% (1977)
Contraception: 43% (1984)
Government's position on family planning: Considers
   the rate of population growth too high. It now
   provides direct support to family-planning services
   in order to reduce levels of fertility, both in relation
   to population growth and to family well-being.

SOCIAL INDICATORS
Life expectancy: 60 yrs. (male: 58; female: 62) (1985)
Infant mortality: 94/1,000 births (1985)
Crude birth rate: 36/1,000 pop. (1985)
Crude death rate: 10/1,000

Health:
   Access to health services: 17% (1980–83)
   Births attended by trained health personnel:
      44% (1984)

HOUSING
Persons per household: 4.9 (1981)
Electricity: 54% without (1981)
Access to safe water: 52% (urban: 73%; rural: 18%)
   (1983)
Source of water: (1981)
   Piped inside: 38%
   Piped outside: 4%
   Fountain, well: 27%
   River, streams: 30%
Toilet facilities: (1981)
   Without: 71% (rural: 98%)
Building materials: (1981)
   Adobe: 48%   Wood: 7%
   Concrete: 31%   Other: 14%

EDUCATION
Literacy: 82% (male: 90%; female: 74%) (1981)
Gross enrollment ratio: (1982–85)
   First level: 112% (completing in 1980–84: 70%)
   Second: 65%
   Third: 21.5%
Educational attainment, for population 25 yrs. +:
   (1980)
   None: 24%
   First level: incomplete: 27% (complete: 17%)
   Second: entered: 11%
   Third: 10%

ECONOMIC ACTIVITY
Economically active population: 31% (male: 47%;
   female: 16%) (1981)
Agriculture: 35% act. pop.; 8% of GDP
Mines: 8% act. pop.; 20% of GDP
Industry: 12% act. pop.; 20% of GDP
Services: 45% act. pop.; 52% of GDP
Per capita GNP: 1,100 U.S.$ (1985)
Population in absolute poverty: (1977)
   Urban: 49%
National currency/per U.S.$: 15.89 inti (1987)
Principal resources:
   Agriculture: coffee, cotton, rice, fishing
   Industries: copper, silver, zinc, petroleum

COMMUNICATIONS
Radio:
   Transmitters: 189 (1977)
   Receivers: 3,100,000—166/1,000 pop. (1983)
Television:
   Transmitters: no data
   Receivers: 950,000—51/1,000 pop. (1983)

SURINAME

THE SOETOWIDJOJO FAMILY

John Wagijo Soetowidjojo, age 28 (1)
Jakijm Soetowidjojo, 27 (2)
Sindy Soetowidjojo, 9 (3)
Leny, 5 (4)
David, 4 (5)
Jenelee, 2 (6)

10 chickens
6 ducks

POMORA
December 12

5:00. Along the estuary banks in the village of Pomora, men have been stacking baskets of dried and smoked fish on the two boats belonging to John Soetowidjojo and his cousin. The pink hues of dawn appear just as the dories, now full to overflowing, head up the Suriname River to the market at Paramaribo.

Two hours later John and his cousin will moor their little boats alongside larger ones which have already unloaded their cargoes of shark and tuna. The market will be in full swing, and thanks to John's salesmanship, he will have no trouble finding buyers for the village's fish.

John owns two other boats and hires Guyanese fishermen to set his lines and nets in the middle of the vast river estuary. As the sun rises, the fishermen in the village start their boat engines.

On the sandy beach, a woman is already at work, sorting the fish landed by her husband at dawn. Wrapped in her sarong, John wife's, Jakijm, walks quietly through the village and joins the young woman at the river's edge, Jakijm also sorted fish when she was first married; the Soetowidjojos' early years together were hard, like those of all the young couples in the village of Pomora.

At first, John rented a boat and made do with a single net, the traditional wedding present from his parents. He worked the nets and lines himself, and while he was fishing, Jakijm would clean, smoke, and dry the fish. Soon there were babies hanging on to her skirts, but fortunately Jakijm was able to leave them with their grandmothers. In time they were able to buy and equip their first boat, then save for a second boat and buy more nets and lines. Now they have three employees. In spite of their years of hard work, John and Jakijm are serene, peaceful people.

Jakijm's family was one of the first to settle on the beach at Pomora. When her father arrived, he found only three people here. Now there are a dozen houses lining the banks of the estuary.

At this hour of the morning, an enchanted stillness reigns; only the birds can be heard.

7:15. Suddenly the silence is shattered by the cries of a baby, which evoke a similar response from all the other babies in the village. Hearing her baby son Jenelee's distinctive cry, Jakijm runs the short distance to her house. It's time for his breakfast. Jakijm savors these moments of intimacy with her youngest, as another baby will soon arrive. "It will be the fifth and last," says Jakijm. His hunger satisfied, Jenelee frolics with his mother, who lavishes all her love on him. Jakijm's two older children, Sindy and Leny, are away at boarding school in Paramaribo, as there is no school in Pomora. They come home only on weekends. Jakijm also has a four-year-old son being raised by her sister, who is sterile. Only three doors away, David comes every day to play with his little brother.

8:30. The village of Pomora still has no running water, and Jakijm fills her tub in the drums that catch rainwater off the roof. She washes the dishes on a large windowsill that slants down to the ground outside. Greasy water and bits of food spill down into the yard and the ducks and chickens splash about in the mud fighting for the scraps.

Jakijm goes out onto the veranda overlooking the river to clean the vegetables for their midday meal. It will be a traditional Javanese lunch. Vegetables fried lightly in oil, and meat and fish rolled in batter, then simmered in a highly spiced sauce. From the veranda, Jakijm can watch the village women and the hired help (most of whom come from Guyana) place the drying trays on wooden frames in front of each house. Before they spread the fish out to dry, they examine the sky carefully. The white puffy clouds above are not the kind that bring sudden torrential downpours. People here know the telltale signs of nature's moods by heart.

10:00. The morning fishermen tie up their boats. Each man tips the contents of his baskets onto the table in front of his house. Their families immediately set to work, sorting, cutting, and cleaning the fish. Whatever catfish they have they take to the smoke pits. Jakijm squats in the midst of their catch, a knife in her hand. She doesn't need to do it—the hired help could do the work—but she likes cleaning the fish, and chatting with the fishermen is a pleasant way to pass the time.

10:30. John returns. He has succeeded in selling the village's entire catch. He distributes the proceeds of the sale equally among the fishermen. From the market he has brought beans, carrots, cabbage, and a chicken. He doesn't like fish himself. Before entering the house he removes his shoes and picks up Jenelee. The child yawns and rests his head on John's shoulder; it's siesta time for father and son.

12:00. The whole village bustles around the tables and the smoke pits. A dark cloud appears on the horizon, and suddenly, as if in response to a silent alarm, everyone runs to the drying trays. Just as the last basket has been brought to safety under wooden pavilions, the heavens open and huge raindrops begin to fall. When the skies clear, the fish are put back out to dry. The people of Pomora have an infallible instinct.

The thunder of the rain on the corrugated-iron roof has awakened John and his son. Covered with a white cloth, their meal is waiting on the table. Husband and wife each help themselves and find a place to sit on the spotless linoleum floor. Jakijm shares the contents of her plate with her son: one mouthful for Mommy, one for Jenelee.

1:00. As she relaxes on the veranda, Jakijm watches her husband at work. With the help of his employees, John unloads his three boats, which have returned laden with the last catch of the day, while his brother sets out his last net for the night.

5:30. The generator that supplies the village's electricity has been turned on, so Jenelee can watch cartoons on television. Activity in the village has not yet ceased. The morning fishermen prepare their nets, bait the lines, and stack the sacks of dried and smoked fish for tomorrow's trip to the market. Out of sight, in the improvised bathroom beside the house, Jakijm and Jenelee bathe each other with buckets of rainwater. This game is a daily ritual that mother and son enjoy equally. Jenelee, all clean and scrubbed in his pajamas, comes running in happily and jumps on his father's stomach. Stretched out on the living-room floor, John has been listening to a record by his favorite Javanese singer. Suriname is one of the most ethnically diverse countries in Latin America, and each ethnic group has kept its own cultural traditions.

8:00. Leaving father and son to their rowdy game, Jakijm goes to her sister's house to give David a good-night kiss and take a final walk around the village and along the beach. She always enjoys a few moments of solitude for herself. Everyone has gone home. On her way back, she passes a few fishermen on the beach making final preparations for tomorrow's fishing.

9:00. The hum of the generator will lull the Soetowidjojos to sleep. Their lights are left on, but it doesn't matter. At eleven o'clock, the electricity is shut off and Pomora is plunged into darkness.

The spring floods forced the Soetowidjojos to move the house back thirty feet, but from the veranda Jakijm can still see her husband unloading his three fishing boats

Jakijm scrubs the linoleum floor with special care. Her family prefers to eat sitting comfortably on the floor. One mouthful for Mommy, one for Jenelee

SURINAME

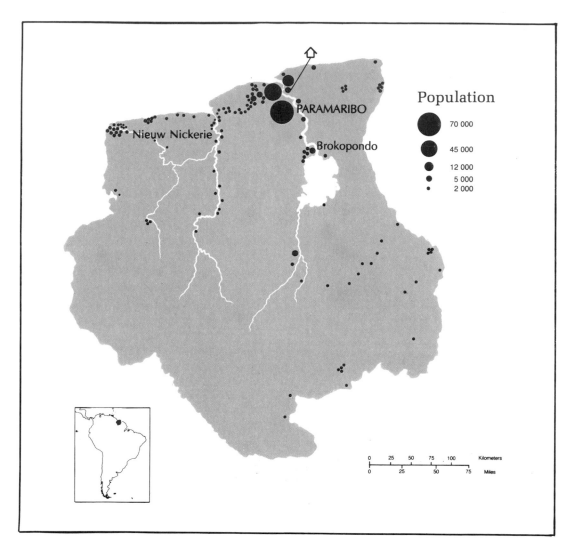

Population

● 70 000

● 45 000

• 12 000

· 5 000

· 2 000

PARAMARIBO

Brokopondo

Nieuw Nickerie

| | 0 | 25 | 50 | 75 | 100 | Kilometers |
| 0 | | 25 | | 50 | | 75 | Miles |

THE NAME: From the Amerindian tribe the Surinas

THE PEOPLE: The Surinamese

GEOGRAPHY
Narrow coastal plain, central zone forested and broken by scattered savannas
The southern low mountain ranges
Max. altitude: 1,230 m. (4,635 ft.) (Juliana Top)
Area: 163,265 sq. km. (63,037 sq. mi.)
Density: 2.3 pers./sq. km. (5.9 pers./sq. mi.) (1986)
Arable land: 0% (1987)
Forest: 96%
Climate: Tropical, with uniformly high temperatures and rainfall. No recognized dry season.

CAPITAL: Paramaribo, pop. 67,718 (1980).

LANGUAGE: Dutch (official)
English widely spoken. The lingua franca is a pidgin English, Taki-Taki.
Most children go to private schools to learn their ethnic language—Hindi, Javanese, and Chinese.

RELIGION
Hindu: 26%
Catholic: 22%
Muslim: 6%

POPULATION: Total—375,000 (1985)
Annual growth: 1.1% (4,125) (1980–85)
Doubling time: 33 yrs.
Urban: 43% (1985) (est. for year 2000: 49%)
Rural: 57%

AGE GROUPS: (1980)
17% less than 5 yrs.
51% less than 15
66% less than 20
17% from 20 to 39
12% from 40 to 59
6% 60 yrs. and over

ETHNIC GROUPS
East Indian: 37%
Creole: 31%
Indonesian: 15%
Bush Negro: 10% (ancestors of the slaves who fled to the jungle, living according to African traditions)
Amerindian: 2.7%
Chinese: 1.7%
European: 1%

HISTORY
Originally inhabited by the Surinen
1593: Becomes a Spanish possession
1602: First Dutch settlements
1651: English settlers
1667: The Netherlands acquires Suriname from Britain in exchange for its rights in New Amsterdam (New York)
1799–1802 and 1804–26: British rule
1863: Abolition of slavery
1954: Internal autonomy
November 25, 1975: Independence
1980: Military coup brings Colonel Daysi Bouterse to power

FAMILY
Marital status, for head of household only: (1980)
Married: 60%
Widowed: 4%
Divorced: 4%
Unmarried: 30%
Female head of household: no data
Fertility rate: 3.6 (1980–85)
Births out of wedlock: no data
Teenage births: no data
Contraception: no data
Government's position on family planning: Considers rates of natural increase and fertility satisfactory.

SOCIAL INDICATORS
Life expectancy: 69 yrs. (male: 66; female: 71) (1985)
Infant mortality: 33/1,000 births (1985)

Crude birth rate: 27/1,000 pop. (1985)
Crude death rate: 6/1,000
Health:
Access to health services: no data
Births attended by trained health personnel: 80% (1984)

HOUSING
Persons per household: 4.1 (1980)
Electricity: 18% without (1980)
Access to safe water: no data
Source of water: (1980)
Piped inside: 41%
Piped outside: 22%
None and other: 38%
Toilet facilities: (1980)
Flush: 41%
Other: 57%
Building materials: (1980)
Mostly wood
Huts: 11% (bush Negroes live in huts)
Houses of questionable quality: 22%

EDUCATION
Literacy: 65% (male: 68%; female: 63%) (1978)
Gross enrollment ratio: (1984)
First level: 113%
Second: 66%
Third: 6.9%
Educational attainment: no data

ECONOMIC ACTIVITY
Economically active population: no data
Agriculture: 20% act. pop.; 13% of GDP
Mines: 5% act. pop.; 7% of GDP
Industry: 5% act. pop.; 50% of GDP
Services: 40% act. pop.; 30% of GDP
Per capita GNP: 2,580 U.S.$ (1985)
Population in absolute poverty: no data
National currency/per U.S.$: 1.79 guilders (1985)
Principal resources: Bauxite (and its derivatives: alumina and aluminum)

COMMUNICATIONS
Radio:
Transmitters: 16 (1979)
Receivers: 220,000—627 per 1,000 (1983)
Television:
Transmitters: no data
Receivers: 43,000—121/1,000 pop. (1983)

URUGUAY

THE SACCO FAMILY

Alvaro Sacco Irigoin, age 35 (1)
Graciela Sacco Villacieva, 35 (2)
Alvaro Sacco, 14 (3)
Juan Manuel, 12 (4)
Martín, 10 (5)

MONTEVIDEO
July 15

Juan Cabaal Street is gray. The whole of Montevideo is gray. It's an austere old city in dire need of a fresh coat of paint. The rainy July weather and the current economic crisis do nothing to dispel this impression of drab silence.

8:00. Graciela Sacco enters her cozy living room, still half asleep and bundled up in a long rose dressing gown. She heads straight for the fireplace. The dry eucalyptus wood catches fire immediately, filling the room with its strong aroma. The fire lowers the ever-present humidity a bit, but nothing can completely dry up the moisture that peels the paint off the walls.

This morning, Graciela isn't in her usual hurry. Her boys have winter vacation, and she and her husband have taken Thursday and Friday off to be with them. And Monday the eighteenth is Uruguay's national holiday, so they have almost a week's vacation. Graciela puts the breakfast jams, caramel spread, and hot coffee on the table. The family will help themselves to toast. She prepares for a morning in the kitchen. Tomorrow she will go to see her mother in the country, and she is making food for the men to eat in her absence.

Alvaro joins his wife, happy that for once he can savor his coffee and read his newspaper while sitting in front of the fire. He and Graciela normally leave at seven o'clock for the Pension Fund office, where they both work. She spends eight hours at the main office, and he spends six in the accounting department. At one o'clock Alvaro returns and makes lunch for the three boys, then leaves for his afternoon job as a taxi driver. Alvaro's car represents a double resource, since he rents it every morning to a friend who uses it in the same way. For the last three years, with the recession, Alvaro has had to work fourteen hours, instead of the eight he once did, in order to maintain his standard of living and give his children what they need.

11:00. Ten-year-old Martín enters the living room and climbs onto his father's lap. He loves to start his day with a cuddle. Alvaro couldn't ask for more. He is a loving man who gives each of his children the attention and affection they need. Three heirs, however, are sufficient; he has no intention of having more.

Juan and Alvaro Jr. finally emerge from their bedroom. They were up late last night and are all set to loaf around in their pajamas, but their mother insists that they get dressed. Graciela is an organized woman, but she has neither the money for a cleaning lady nor a great deal of time to spend on the housework. Each member of the family therefore has to pitch in according to the schedule posted on the kitchen wall. Today it's Martín's turn to do the shopping, Juan sets the table, and Alvaro Jr. makes the beds. The house is transformed into a clean, pleasant living space to the accompaniment of a Brazilian samba.

The boys have time for a game of basketball in the garden before lunch. Alvaro bought this particular house eight years ago because of the spacious garden. The lawn, trees, and barbecue pit make it an ideal place for the family's ritual weekend *asados* (grilled meat). And the boys can invite their friends to play.

2:00. Chicken, salad, and crème caramel are eaten with gusto, and then it's time to drive the boys to the community athletic center. Alvaro gets the taxi out of the garage. Even today he will cruise for several hours.

At the center, the boys and girls have been competing all week, and today there are the finals for the handball, basketball, and water polo players. As a basketball captain, Alvaro Jr. picks his team, including his brother and the prettiest girls in the club. He has good taste, but is a bad loser. He will have to get over this if he ever realizes his ambition of becoming a physical education teacher. Juan, however, is much more relaxed. Every point scored brings an enthusiastic outburst and a chance to give his brother a hearty bear hug.

At home, Graciela is happy. It's so rare that she has a day's freedom that she can't decide what to do. First she reads a bit, then picks up her knitting. Then she decides to surprise her men with one of her special cakes.

6:00. Graciela doesn't know where the day went, and it's already teatime. Alvaro never misses that, despite his busy schedule. On his way home, he picks up little Martín at the athletic center. Martín isn't much of a sports fan. A gentle spirit, he is the family poet and artist.

7:00. Alvaro is back on the streets. Graciela prepares the evening meal, and Martín watches the never-ending adventures of Popeye and Olive Oyl on the television while puttering with his collection of treasures. Martín is a real pack rat. In a wooden box, he squirrels away bits of wool and pieces of cardboard that had been destined for the garbage, which he uses for his artwork. He is never idle. Everyone makes fun of him a little, but tonight it's in the famous box that Graciela finds what she needs to make Juan an Indian cos-tume for the athletic center's end-of-the-season dance.

9:00. The house has grown chilly, and Graciela joins Martín by the fire. The meal is ready, but no one is there to eat it. It's nine-twenty when Alvaro comes in, and he is worried because the boys are still not home. Just then, the telephone rings. It's Juan. They have played a game of Ping Pong with some friends and are taking the bus. They'll be home in half an hour.

10:00. Juan and Alvaro Jr. arrive all excited and worn out, kiss their parents, collapse on the car-pet, and describe the day's victories and defeats. The end of their narrative is accompanied by the wolfing down of a ham-and-cheese pancake, Gra-ciela's famous cake, and several pieces of fruit.

The boys sprawl on the cushions in front of the TV. No matter how tired they are, they won't miss the South American basketball finals, especially since Uruguay has a good chance. Alvaro, less fanatical than his sons, helps his wife clean up the kitchen, and ends his day with a shower.

11:30. Alvaro and Graciela's bedroom is next to the boys', so Graciela closes the door to cut down the unrelenting noise of their card playing and roughhousing. Vacations are like candies: to be savored to the very end.

Alavaro bought the house because of the spacious garden. It is an ideal place for the ritual weekend asados (grilled meat)

The city might be austere and in need of a fresh coat of paint, but inside the gray walls the Saccos have made a warm, welcoming, and pleasant home

URUGUAY

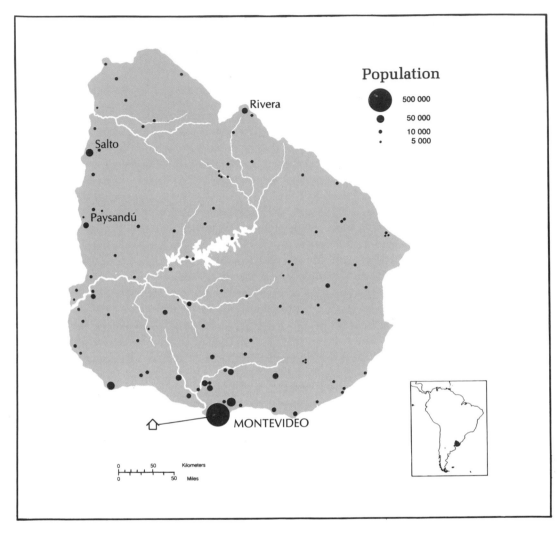

THE NAME: From Guarani, meaning "river of the birds"

THE PEOPLE: The Uruguayans

GEOGRAPHY
   Vast lowlands; coastline features attractive beaches; abundant pastureland on the plains.
   Max. altitude: 501 m. (1,644 ft.) (Cerro Mirador)
Area: 176,215 sq. km. (68,037 sq. mi.)
Density: 17 pers./sq. km. (43 pers./sq. mi.) (1986)
Arable land: 8% (1987)
Forest: 4%
Climate: Warm, temperate, with mild winters and warm summers. Wettest months are from March to June, but there is no dry season.

CAPITAL: Montevideo, pop. 1,298,546 (1980)

LANGUAGE: Spanish

RELIGION:
   Catholic: 66%
   Other: 30%

POPULATION: Total—3,000,000 (1985)
   Annual growth: 0.7% (21,000) (1980–85)
   Doubling time: 90 yrs.
   Urban: 85% (1985) (est. for year 2000: 88%)
   Rural: 15%

AGE GROUPS: (1980)
   9% less than 5 yrs.
   27% less than 15
   36% less than 20
   27% from 20 to 39
   23% from 40 to 59
   15% 60 yrs. and over

ETHNIC GROUPS
White: 76%
Mestizo: 5%
Other: 19%

HISTORY
Originally inhabited by the Charruas
1516: Spanish discovery by Juan Díaz de Solis
1726: Establishment of Montevideo
1776: Creation of the Viceroyalty of the Río de la Plata
1811–20: Struggle for independence
1816: Portuguese invasion
August 25, 1825: Independence
1839–51: Civil war
1865–70: War with Paraguay followed by military rule
1903: Election of President José Batlle y Ordóñez, a social and political reformer
1951: Adoption of a new constitution
1973: Military dictatorship
1981: Return to democracy

FAMILY
Marital status: no data
Female head of household: 20.8%
Fertility rate: 2.7 (1985)
Births out of wedlock: no data
Teenage births: 14.6% (1981)
Contraception: no data
Government's position on family planning: Has no policy designed to modify levels of fertility. The government currently provides direct support to family-planning programs.

SOCIAL INDICATORS
Life expectancy: 71 yrs. (male: 67; female: 74) (1985)
Infant mortality: 39/1,000 births (1985)
Crude birth rate: 19/1,000 pop. (1985)
Crude death rate: 10/1,000
Health:
Access to health services: 80% (1980–83)
Births attended by trained health personnel: no data

HOUSING
Persons per household: 3.4 (1975)
Electricity: 20% without (1975)
Access to safe water: 79% (urban: 95%; rural: 3%) (1984)
Source of water: no data
Toilet facilities: None: 8% (1975)
Building materials: (1975)
Concrete: 89.8%
Wood or zinc: 3.8%
Other: 3.5%

EDUCATION
Literacy: 94% (male: 93%; female: 94%) (1975)
Gross enrollment ratio: (1983)
First level: 109% (completing in 1980–84: 88%)
Second: 67%
Third: 20.8%
Educational attainment, for population 25 yrs. +: (1975)
None: 10%
First level: incomplete: 10% (complete: 37%)
Second: entered: 17%
Third: 6%

ECONOMIC ACTIVITY
Economically active population: 42% (male: 54%; female: 32%) (1984)
Agriculture: 11% act. pop.; 8% of GDP
Mines: 0% act. pop.; 0% of GDP
Industry: 32% act. pop.; 33% of GDP
Services: 57% act. pop.; 59% of GDP
Per capita GNP: 1,650 U.S.$ (1985)
Population in absolute poverty: (1980)
Urban: 25%
National currency/per U.S.$: 101.43 pesos (1985)
Principal resource: Cattle

COMMUNICATIONS
Radio:
Transmitters: 94 (1981)
Receivers: 1,700,000—573 per 1,000 pop. (1983)
Television:
Transmitters: 33 (1983)
Receivers: 370,000—125/1,000 pop. (1983)

VENEZUELA

THE VISSLAMIL FAMILY

Adonay Benito Visslamil, age 39 (1)
Deicy Beatrice de Visslamil, 33 (2)
Adonay José Visslamil, 8 (3)
Carlos Eduardo Visslamil, 4 (4)
Melisa Raquel Visslamil, 8 months (5)

ZULIA
January 10

5:00. The rattle of a pebble thrown at the window wakes Deicy. Her neighbor has come to fetch her for their morning workout. Deicy is determined to lose the pounds she gained during her last pregnancy. She pulls on her jogging outfit and slips outside.

Taking small steps, the two women jog around the perimeter of Campo Rojo, one of the many oil camps in the area. All the streets are the same, laid out in symmetrical blocks, and the houses are built according to the same plan. Only their dimensions vary, depending upon the rank of the people who rent them, all employees of the Lagoven oil company. It is still dark, and Deicy relishes the silence of the empty streets.

6:00. Still out of breath, Deicy wakes her children before heading off to the kitchen. Because her boys do not like to eat breakfast in the morning, she makes a snack for them to eat during recess. She also prepares her salad for lunch.

Leaving his little brother buried under the sheets, José showers and sits down on the living-room sofa to recite his lessons to María, their *muchacha* (live-in maid). A precocious child, José learns easily and sometimes is too far ahead of his class.

Deicy, her hair neatly brushed and her face made up, is wearing a pretty dress. She heats a bottle of milk, grabs a bag of diapers, and pushes open the door of the bedroom where Melisa is sleeping. The daylight awakens the child, and she sits up in bed smiling at her mother. Melisa spends the mornings at her grandmother's house with her five cousins and a good-natured *muchacha* whose job it is to cater to their every need. Melisa loves it there and usually lets her mother leave for work without any fuss.

6:30. Adonay Benito comes home from work with the daily newspaper and a bottle of milk tucked under his arm. He is a supervisor of the repair department for 150 boats that make the run from one oil platform to another in Lake Maracaibo. This week he is working the night shift. Today he will drop off the baby and drive Deicy to school, where she teaches physical education in the morning, as her adored 1956 Ford is in the shop. Adonay doesn't mind; he loves to drive his new air-conditioned American car. He went to Miami especially to buy it. In spite of Venezuela's temperate climate, the area around Maracaibo is noted for its constant, scorchingly hot temperatures. Walking anywhere at all is out of the question.

7:15. José and Carlos are impeccably dressed in their school uniforms: blue jeans and beige shirts. María helps Carlos up the steps of the bus, and the two children run to the back to join their friends, who are making an enormous racket. They go to a private school run by nuns. Deicy and her husband are convinced that this kind of education is best for the boys and are contemplating sending José to a military academy.

María tidies up the kitchen and two bedrooms and runs the vacuum cleaner over the floor, drowning out the perpetual drone of the air conditioner. María is a good worker, but she is only sixteen and dreams of more; the Visslamils don't expect her to stay long. In the shuttered living room, Adonay sits in front of the Christmas tree, which is due to come down. He reads the newspaper without a shred of guilt and expects Deicy to deal with it next weekend. Later, after a quiet morning at home, Adonay drives the three blocks to his parents' house. The family members are extremely close and visit each other every day. Twenty-four hours without news of each other and the Visslamil clan panics.

11:30. Adonay has run a few errands and goes to fetch Deicy. On their way home they stop to pick up Melisa. Her mother-in-law surprises Deicy with a covered plate containing one of her secret family dishes. No dinner to prepare! Back home, Adonay plays in the living room with Melisa, while Deicy serves lunch in the kitchen. Carlos is home and breathlessly tells his mother all about his morning as he tosses back his soup. Deicy contents herself with the salad and piece of chicken that she is allowed on her diet.

José takes his place at the table and fills his plate two or three times. His favorite foods are *arepas* (corn-meal griddle cakes) and hamburgers. "He is too fat," groans Deicy, but José grimaces and turns a deaf ear. His family is always talking about diets, but the country's traditional cooking is rich and delicious, and they always give in to its temptations.

2:00. It is siesta time, a sacrosanct institution, and bedtime for Adonay. The lowered shutters have kept the house cool. Deicy locks the door. Every day the children resist, but Deicy's authority overrules the arguments and within five minutes the boys are asleep.

5:00. After the siesta, Deicy helps Carlos write his letters. She keeps a close watch on her children's progress in school. Today, José received a black mark. Impatient to show he knew the answer, he whispered it to his friend, and now he must listen to his mother's sharp reprimand.

When their homework is finished, the children are allowed to play video games on the television in their bedroom. With the same enthusiasm with which children exchange baseball cards, José exchanges video games with his cousins. But the special treat is when they get to join their parents in their bedroom and watch a movie on a videocassette recorder and on a giant television screen. The VCR is an important part of family life, and the rented films make the round of all the relatives.

Deicy fills the washing machine in the laundry/maid's room behind the house. Next to her, María sits in front of her own television set, lost in her daily soap opera. Melisa sits in her playpen in the living room, squealing as she watches everyone else move around. She would like to pull herself from one piece of furniture to the next, but the vast array of crystal and china knickknacks scattered around the house make this impossible. She will have to wait until one of the boys takes pity on her and picks her up.

6:00. The sun is low in the sky by the time Deicy leaves for her second jog. The streets are swarming with people, and the gardens are overflowing with children. At last there is an opportunity to breathe in cool air and chat with the neighbors. Cars and the next trip to Miami are the favorite topics.

On her return Deicy showers, leaves the children to play outside, and goes to church to say a rosary for a neighbor who died a week ago. Then she returns home to prepare supper.

9:00. Deicy wakes her husband when she goes into the bedroom carrying his supper on a tray. He eats in bed, takes a shower, and heads back to the boats. Adonay has to be at the shipyard by ten o'clock. This week he can't go to his company's club, where he watches baseball games on TV and drinks beer with his friends. He misses this when he works nights.

9:30. After letting her sons take advantage of the cool night, Deicy calls them inside. A few minutes later, everyone is in bed watching TV. "Not more than half an hour," Deicy calls to her sons.

Adonay went to Miami to buy his huge air-conditioned American car. In spite of Venezuela's temperate climate, the area around Maracaibo is noted for its constant, scorchingly hot temperatures

Adonay's sister drops in and distracts the baby so the rest of the family can enjoy their meal

VENEZUELA

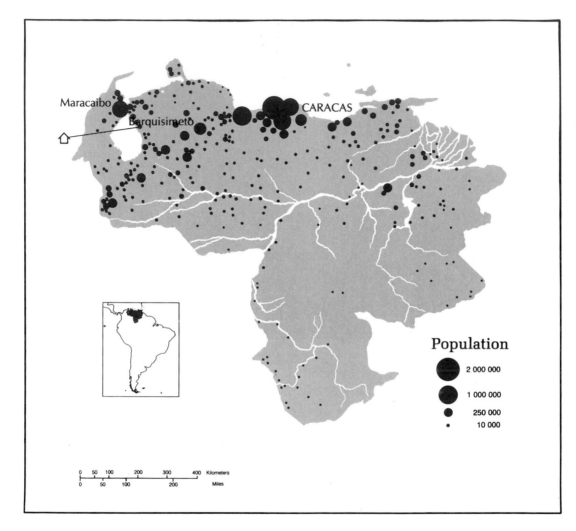

Maracaibo

Barquisimeto

CARACAS

Population

2 000 000

1 000 000

250 000

10 000

0 50 100 200 300 400 Kilometers

0 50 100 200 Miles

THE NAME: From Italian meaning "little Venice"; given by Amerigo Vespucci

THE PEOPLE: The Venezuelans

GEOGRAPHY
Northwest: Andes Mountains and adjacent hill country
North of the mountains: coastal zone
Center: low-lying grass plains (*llanos*)
Southeast: vast area of high plateaus and rolling plains
    Max. altitude: 5,007 m. (16,423 ft.) (Pico Bolívar)
Area: 912,050 sq. km. (352,144 sq. mi.)
Density: 18 pers./sq. km. (46 pers./sq. mi.) (1986)
Arable land: 4% (1987)
Forest: 35%
Climate: Varies with altitude from tropical to temperate: coastal areas are humid.

CAPITAL: Caracas, pop. 1,816,901 (1981)

LANGUAGE: Spanish

RELIGION
    Majority Catholic

POPULATION: Total—17,300,000 (1985)
    Annual growth: 2.8% (484,400) (1980–85)
    Doubling time: 26 yrs.
    Urban: 87% (1985) (est. for year 2000: 99%)
    Rural: 17%

AGE GROUPS: (1981)
    15% less than 5 yrs.
    41% less than 15
    52% less than 20
    30% from 20 to 39
    13% from 40 to 59
    5% 60 yrs. and over

ETHNIC GROUPS
Mestizo: 67%
White: 21%
Black: 10%
Indian: 2%

HISTORY
Inhabited by Carib and Arawak Indians
1498: Discovery by Christopher Columbus
1547: Spanish colonization
1811: Independence: royalist forces maintain control
1812–21: War of independence, led by Simón Bolívar, who creates Greater Colombia (with Colombia, Panama, and Ecuador) and is named president
July 5, 1821: Independence from Spain
1821–30: Part of the Republic of Gran Colombia
1830: Becomes an independent republic
Succession of dictatorships
1958: First democratic election

FAMILY
Marital status, for population 12 yrs. and older: (1981)
Married: 32%
Common-law: 16%
Separated: 3%
Divorced: 1%
Widowed: 2%
Single: 44%
Female head of household: 21% (1982)
Fertility rate: 3.9 (1985)
Births out of wedlock: no data
Teenage births: 17% (1981)
Contraception: 49% (1984)
Government's position on family planning: Considers the rates of fertility and natural increase to be satisfactory, but has acknowledged the need for a continued expansion of family-planning programs.

SOCIAL INDICATORS
Life expectancy: 69 yrs. (male: 66; female: 72) (1985)
Infant mortality: 38/1,000 births (1985)
Crude birth rate: 32/1,000 pop. (1985)
Crude death rate: 5/1,000
Health:
Access to health services: no data
Births attended by trained health personnel: 82% (1984)

HOUSING
Persons per household: 5.3 (1985)
Electricity: 11% without (1981)
Access to safe water: 81%
Source of water: (1981)
Piped inside: 61%
Piped outside: 24%
Not piped: 15%
Toilet facilities: (1981)
Full bathroom with shower: 29%
Building materials: (1981)
Brick, block, concrete: 79%
Adobe, mud: 12%
Palm, cane, and other: 7%
Wood: 3%

EDUCATION
Literacy: 85% (male: 86%; female: 83%) (1981)
Gross enrollment ratio: (1984)
First level: 109% (completing in 1980–84: 68%)
Second: 45%
Third: 23%
Educational attainment, for population 25 yrs. +: (1981)
None: 24%
First level: incomplete: 47%
Second: entered: 22%
Third: 7%

ECONOMIC ACTIVITY
Economically active population: 32% (male: 47%; female: 18%) (1981)
Agriculture: 15% act. pop.; 6% of GDP
Mines: 5% act. pop.; 27% of GDP
Industry: 25% act. pop.; 15% of GDP
Services: 55% act. pop.; 52% of GDP
Per capita GNP: U.S.$ 3,410 (1985)
Average monthly family income: 3,134.89 bolivares (1982)
National currency/per U.S.$: 7.02 bolivares (1984)
Principal resource: Petroleum

COMMUNICATIONS
Radio:
Transmitters: 210 (1977)
Receivers: 6,800,000—415/1,000 pop. (1983)
Television:
Transmitters: 42 (1977)
Receivers: 2,100,000—128/1,000 pop. (1983)

Central America

BELIZE

THE WADE FAMILY

Wilson Dery Wade (Parks), age 36 (1)
Leone Margaret Flowers (Maggy), 30 (2)
Curtis Antony Wade, 14 (3)
Erwin Ernesto (Winy), 12 (4)
Wilson Leroy (Didi), 11 (5)
Oscar Alexander, 10 (6)
Allan James, 4 (7)

11 chickens and turkeys
2 ducks
3 pigs
3 dogs
2 horses

CROOKED TREE
December 6

5:00 At cockcrow, Wilson Dery Wade, otherwise known as Parks, leaves his tiny house's only room. The whole family sleeps there together; four-year-old Allan with his mother and father and the four other boys head to foot in two curtained-off bunk beds.

Maggy follows her husband into the kitchen, another little thatched-roof cottage. On his way to work, Parks will nibble on Maggy's homemade rolls. He jumps into his boat to cross the swampy lake that separates the village of Crooked Tree from the main road, taking his rifle with him in case he sees some game on the way. When he gets to the road, a fellow worker will pick him up and drive him to his employer's land.

The Wades have lived on their little piece of property for thirteen years. They tore down the dilapidated old shack that was there before and used the materials to build the two huts. Their great dream is a real house made out of cinder blocks that will never need any repair, but that will have to wait until the fruit trees show a profit.

For a few dollars, Parks rents twenty acres of land from the government, with stands of pine, oak, and cashew. Among the plants he has added are citrus trees, areca palms, and coconut palms. At present, only the sale of wood and cashew nuts brings in money, so Parks works as a farm laborer.

6:00. Back in bed, snuggling with her last youngster, Maggy calls to the other boys. They all shuffle sleepily outside and collapse on a bench under the shade of an oak. Their mother allows them these few minutes to rest before setting about their chores. The boys are well disciplined, and their mother has a carefully worked-out schedule for them. Maggy only has to say "Eh, man" in her firm, lilting voice and all her children spring to attention. She gets to stay in bed while her sons perform their jobs. Curtis, the oldest, cuts the wood and lights the fire; Didi and Winy make three trips to the public fountain, returning each time with a twenty-liter bucket on their heads. Oscar meanwhile sweeps the sandy soil around the house clean of animal droppings and sprinkles ashes down the pit toilet at the bottom of the garden.

6:45. "You can get up now, Mum." The house is clean, and powdered chocolate and water is boiling on the wood fire. Maggy doesn't use the gas stove because butane is too expensive. She serves the breakfast of bread and chocolate on the table, while Winy washes yesterday's dishes in a bucket and puts them out on a board to dry. The bamboo walls of the cottage are papered with newspaper and pages from American fan magazines—a constant reminder of the American dream to which most Belizians aspire.

Maggy scolds her boys as they dawdle while getting dressed for school. The boys have grown up half naked, and wearing a shirt is torture. For school, however, it's compulsory. Fortunately, going barefoot is allowed. The Wade boys are a bit like their father, preferring sports and games to studying. They hurry down the sandy lane that snakes between the scattered houses of Crooked Tree. Maggy owns neither a watch nor a radio and relies on the sun's position for time. This morning she was a little off. School is a large wooden room in which the classes are separated by screens. There are fewer and fewer children in the classes: the effects of slow population growth and a wave of emigration to the city and abroad are beginning to make themselves felt.

Alone, Maggy enjoys the peace and quiet. She often goes fishing in the morning, but today she is doing the laundry under the shade of a tree. She scrubs the ground-in dirt from her sons' pants on a washboard and puts the linens to soak in a basin. Then she goes off to cook some fish for the dogs. That and oranges are their favorite food.

Some young men from the village pass by, pick a piece of fruit, chat for a while, and go down to the water's edge. There is no work in Crooked Tree and not much more in Belize City. They would like to obtain visas to rejoin their families, who are already in the United States, but America's doors are getting harder and harder to open. Maggy's sons never miss an opportunity to remind her that they don't intend to stay here when they grow up, but rather will seek their fortune in the big world. Little by little Maggy is growing used to the idea of their departure.

9:00. Little Allan has sneaked back home from kindergarten, where he has been registered since the beginning of the year. He hates being parted from his mother and knows what to say and do to get his way. "If I were the mummy and you were the baby," he says, "I'd let you stay home." Maggy inevitably capitulates. She adores children and would have liked to have eleven, like her mother. But the times are too hard for that. "There's no question of a sixth child," she says. "The house is so small, there's not even room for a doll."

12:00. The schoolboys eat a frugal lunch—a big bowl of watered-down coffee enriched with evaporated milk, a portion of fish, and two rolls. Before they return to school, they fetch lake water for their mother so she can rinse the laundry.

2:00. Maggy's day continues serenely. She likes to go back to bed in the afternoon, not to sleep, but to read. She has a large collection of used Harlequin romances, and when her neighbors go into town, she asks them to bring back more of them. The lovers in today's book take her to Egypt. "It's my way of escaping and traveling a little," she says. Allan snuggles up to his mother, and before he falls asleep, whispers, "Let me bite your lips first."

4:00. Maggy doesn't put her book down until she hears the children's voices in the lane. It's time

to bake her daily batch of bread. Curtis puts big logs on the fire so that there will be a heaping bed of embers. Meanwhile his brothers bring down two coconuts. Maggy grates and presses the coconut meat to extract the milk. She mixes the flour, fat, and coconut milk in a large plastic bowl. She has a skillful touch: in less time than it takes to tell it, the dough is mixed and rolled into a ball. Now it just has to rise.

Didi feeds the rest of the grated coconut to the chickens, while Allan, armed with a stick, repels the pigs and dogs who try to steal it. Curtis, Winy, and their friends play soccer in front of the house. Parks arrives and sits down in the doorway, his rifle between his knees. He referees the soccer match, during which he is able to shoot two wild pigeons flying by.

5:00. The embers are as red as Maggy wants them, and she goes to work under the shade of a palm tree. She flattens the dough and shapes it into rolls which she places on the bottom of a large iron pot. She covers the pot with an earthenware dish filled with a layer of coals. In her own way, Maggy has invented an efficient oven. The rolls are crusty and golden.

5:30. At dusk, thousands of fireflies swarm around the house. In the kitchen, father and sons wait impatiently for Maggy to serve them the wild pigeons and the delicious new bread.

7:00. Maggy and Parks put the children to bed. Then they saunter off in the moonlight to watch television at a neighbor's. Crooked Tree has no electricity, but this television runs off a battery. It comes, of course, from the United States, a present from friends who were able to emigrate, and is such a rarity that this evening there are thirty people gathered in front of it. With fresh eyes they watch a very old soap opera which has seen better days.

Two small thatched huts, twelve square meters for the bedroom and the same for the kitchen. The Wades want a real cinder-block house

The promise of the American dream papers the kitchen walls, but the gas stove sits abandoned in a corner because butane is too expensive

BELIZE

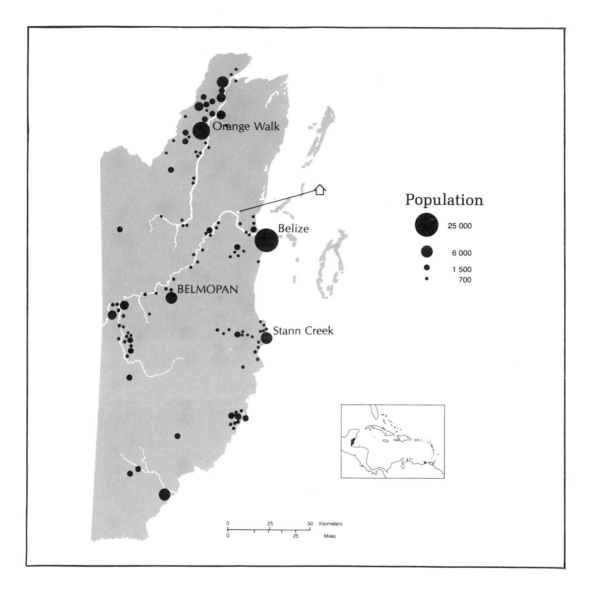

THE NAME: From a Mayan word meaning "muddy water"

THE PEOPLE: The Belizians

GEOGRAPHY
North: part of the Yucatán plateau
Flat and swampy coastal area, fringed by 450 cays and the world's second-largest barrier reef
South—Maya Mountains
Max. altitude: 1,104 m. (3,580 ft.) (Victoria Peak)
Area: 22,963 sq. km. (8,866 sq. mi.)
Density: 7 pers./sq. km. (18 sq. mi.) (1986); 75% of the territory is inhabited

Arable land: 2% (1987)
Forest: 44%
Climate: Tropical, with high rainfall and small annual range of temperature. The rainy season extends from May to February.

CAPITAL: Belmopan, pop. 8,000 (1980 est.)

LANGUAGE: English (official), Spanish Creole
62% bilingual; 16% trilingual
50.6% have English as mother tongue
31.6% have Spanish
6% have Mayan
3.3% have Ketchi

RELIGION
Catholic: 62%
Anglican: 12%
Other Protestant: 18%

POPULATION: Total—160,000 (1985)
Annual growth: 1.7% (2,720) (1980–84)
Doubling time: 25 yrs.
Urban: 50%
Rural: 50%

AGE GROUPS: (1980)
17% less than 5 yrs.
46% less than 15
58% less than 20
24% from 20 to 39
12% from 40 to 59
 6% 60 yrs. and over

ETHNIC GROUPS
Creole: 40%
Mestizo: 33%
Garifuna: 8% (African-Carib from St. Vincent)
Mayan: 7% (natives)
White: 4%
Ketchi: 3%
East Indian: 2%

HISTORY
300 B.C.–A.D. 900: Mayan civilization
1638: English settlement in St. George's Cay
1798: After many attempts to take the settlement Spain is defeated
1862: British Honduras (former name) becomes a Crown Colony
1964: Internal autonomy
September 21, 1981: Independence within the Commonwealth

FAMILY
Marital status, for females 14–44 yrs.: (1980)
Married: 38%
Common-law: 17%
Visiting union: 5%
No longer with husband or partner: 8%
Never had husband or partner: 20%
Female head of household: 27% (1983)
Fertility rate: 4.5 (1980)
Births out of wedlock: 54% (1983)
Teenage births: 21% (1982–83)
Contraception: no data
Government's position on family planning: Believes that the maintenance of moderately high rates of fertility and natural increase is appropriate for the country. Family planning is supported in order to decrease the morbidity and mortality levels of women of reproductive age.

SOCIAL INDICATORS
Life expectancy: 68 yrs. (male; female: no data) (1980)
Infant mortality: 23/1,000 births (1985)
Crude birth rate: 38/1,000 pop. (1980)
Crude death rate: 4/1,000

Health:
Access to health services: 89%
Direct access: 56% (9% for rural pop.)
Mobile clinics: 33%
Deliveries in medical centers: 63% (1982)

HOUSING
Persons per household: 5.3 (1980)
Electricity: 40% without (1980)
Access to safe water: (1985)
Urban: 86%
Rural: 49%
Source of water: (1980)
Piped inside: 19%
Piped outside: 27%
Public standpipe: 15%
Other: 39%
Toilet facilities: (1980)
Flush: 22%
Pit: 49%
Other: 29%
Building materials: (1980)
Primarily wood
Housing quality: 20% questionable
                 60% poor
                 10% very poor

EDUCATION
Literacy: 91% (male: 91%; female: 91%) (1970)
Gross enrollment ratio: (1982)
First level: 82%
Second: no data
Educational attainment, for population 25 yrs. +: (1980)
None: 11%
First level: incomplete: 75%
Second: entered: 12%
Third: 2.6%

ECONOMIC ACTIVITY
Economically active population: 33% (male: 50%; female: 15%) (1980)
Agriculture: 50% act. pop.; 30% of GDP
Mines: 0% act. pop.; 0% of GDP
Industry: 15% act. pop.; 25% of GDP
Services: 35% act. pop.; 45% of GDP
Per capita GNP: 1,190 U.S.$ (1985)
Population in absolute poverty: no data
National currency/per U.S.$: 2.00 dollars (1985)
Principal resources:
Sugar
Money from emigrants abroad is important to GNP

COMMUNICATIONS
Radio:
Transmitters: 11 (1983)
Receivers: 79,000—506 per 1,000 pop. (1983)
Television:
Transmitters: no data
Receivers: no data

COSTA RICA

THE SALAS VARGAS FAMILY

Luis Enrique Salas Villalovos, age 41 (1)
María Tulia Vargas Rodríguez de Salas, 41 (2)
Anabelle Salas Vargas, 21 (absent)
Grace María, 19 (3)
Mario Enrique, 18 (4)
María del Rocio, 16 (5)
Maricela, 13 (6)
Roy Alberto, 3 (7)
Jacqueline Salas Villalovos (cousin), 10 (8)
Shirley Salas Villalovos (cousin), 7 (9)

7 cows
6 calves
1 dog
25 chickens
2 rabbits
1 cat and 1 kitten

BARRANCA DE NARANJO
December 22

4:00. During the dry season, from December to March, the wind buffets the wooden house of the Salas Vargas family. Awakened by a particularly violent gust, Luis Enrique shakes awake his elder son, Mario, to accompany him down the hill to milk the cows. Their animals are good milk producers, and today there is enough to fill two large white metal cans. Mario and his father hoist the heavy loads onto their shoulders for the winding climb up the mountain's dirt road to the main highway, where the truck from the cooperative passes by to collect the milk. The evening milking is for the family.

5:30. In the lean-to attached to the side of the house, María Tulia picks up a few logs from the pile arranged carefully along the wall and throws them into the open-fire cement stove that dominates the shed. Electricity is so expensive that she is reluctant to use the electric stove in the kitchen every day. This morning the wood fire will be in constant use. It's three days before Christmas and the Salas Vargas women will prepare hundreds of holiday tamales for family and friends. María looks forward especially to seeing her grandchildren, who will arrive on Christmas Day.

Mario and his father return, and María Tulia serves them breakfast. Luis Enrique snatches up his sleepy three-year-old son and carries him to the table. His morning meal finished, Mario goes across the family compound to fetch his uncle Carlos. Carlos' house is attached to his parents' house, where his widowed sister also lives with her two little girls. After building his house, Carlos helped his brother Luis Enrique build his own sixty-square-meter home, which is connected to their father's by a breezeway.

7:30. Nineteen-year-old Grace is the first of the three sisters to awake. During the school year the entire family is up at five o'clock, and the girls help with the farm chores before the school bus comes. This morning, however, they have slept in. In this part of the world Christmas takes place during summer vacation. The coffee beans are also harvested at this time, with a short break to observe the holiday. The young people who join the harvest are paid according to the weight of the beans picked. For many of them, like Grace's younger sisters, it's a chance to have fun and flirt with the boys. María, in particular, always manages to choose a row of trees that will bring her closest to her current favorite. But Grace has more serious ambitions. She wants to become a teacher, and her university career depends on her holiday earnings. In contrast to her sisters, she hardly talks at all in the fields.

Maricela and María join their mother and Grace, and over an ample breakfast of tortillas and fresh cream, they discuss investing their future earnings (a fortune to them) in fabric for new dresses.

8:30. It's time for the three sisters to do their chores. As they go down to the cow shed with Roy following at their heels, they are joined by their two little cousins, Jacqueline and Shirley. The two young girls will keep an eye on their cousins while the older girls untie the cows and clean out their stalls. This is not normally the girls' job, but today they are helping out because Mario and Uncle Carlos have gone to sell cabbages in the market and their father has taken the bus to Naraja to fetch help for a cow that has just calved. The placenta has not emerged and the cow lies on its side, breathing with difficulty. Roy and his cousins crouch near the sick animal while Maricela forks the grass into a big manual chaffcutter, mixes it with oats and molasses, and fills the mangers.

10:30. Luis returns with the barber. "He knows as much as a vet and charges much less," explains Luis. The man actually does seem to know what he is doing. With swift action, he removes the placenta, gives the cow an injection to prevent infection, and gets the animal back on its feet. While he is there, Enrique asks him to look at the other cows, since there is an epidemic raging that has already killed several animals in the district. The younger children haven't moved an inch from his side.

12:30. María Tulia serves her family lunch. Back from the market, Mario sits with his plate on his knees and watches the report of the bicycle tour of Costa Rica. All the international stars are participating and, at the moment, a Guatemalan is in the lead. "Not surprising," says Mario. "They train in their mountains, and they're higher than ours!"

Indifferent to their brother's enthusiasm, the girls quickly wash the dishes. They have work to do this afternoon. Making two hundred tamales is no small order. Jacqueline and Shirley settle down with Roy to watch Donald Duck on television. They practically live at María Tulia's, where the atmosphere is much livelier.

In the shed, María Tulia surveys her simmering pots of chicken, pork, beef, vegetables, and spices. A delicious aroma fills the house with the spirit of Christmas, accompanied by holiday songs on the radio. Even serious Grace sings the choruses along with her sisters as she presses the boiled corn through a sieve to make mush. María and Maricela lay out the plantain leaves on the table. When everything is cooked, they will spread successive layers of corn paste, meat, rice, and vegetables on each leaf, then tie each packet before placing it in the refrigerator. This season brings many visitors to the house, and no one is allowed to leave without having tasted a tamale. "The longer you keep them, the better they get," claim the girls.

3:00. After a short siesta, Mario helps his father bring in the cows and milk them. Enrique is very organized and demands as much from Mario as from himself. He is grateful to have a son who never shirks a task. Enrique was a policeman in his youth, but it was a poorly paid profession no matter how hard he worked at it, and he did not like the violence. He took over the family farm when his father retired and is much happier. "Now I'm independent," he says, "and the harder I work, the more I can give to my family."

8:00. After supper, the sons and daughters kneel around their parents' bed to say a rosary. In a corner, Roy's crib is full of ironing. He doesn't sleep in it anymore; Enrique dotes on his younger son and lets him sleep between himself and his wife. When the prayer is over, father and son both lie down and soon are sleeping deeply.

As he does every evening, Mario goes off to join his friends. Thanks to the district farmers' association, of which Enrique is chairman, the young people have a place to meet. The building is half café, half party room. The association has also proved the farmers with running water, electricity, and a paved road into town.

The girls go to their grandfather's to watch *Esperanza*, a soap opera that no one wants to miss. María Tulia takes advantage of the quiet evening to compile the list of New Year's presents that she will buy tomorrow for her grandchildren.

9:00. When Mario returns, his three sisters tease him as usual, demanding news of his girlfriend. Mario merely smiles. He joins them in a board game called Gran Banco: with a few good throws of the dice and a little luck the winner is declared a millionaire. "Mother, would you make us some delicious chocolate?" asks Maricela in her nicest voice. María Tulia lovingly serves her children before going to bed.

10:30. The game would go on forever if they didn't have to get up at dawn tomorrow. Mario is the privileged one with a room all to himself. In the next room, the three girls sleep in the same bed. Even when the lights are out, the darkness is not total. The harsh light of the rural road's streetlamp shines through the transparent curtains.

Enrique's house is attached to his father's by a breezeway. His brother Carlos, who lives across the way, supervised the building of the three houses

Maricela and María join their mother and Grace, and over an ample breakfast of tortillas and fresh cream, they discuss investing their future earnings (a fortune to them) in fabric for new dresses

COSTA RICA

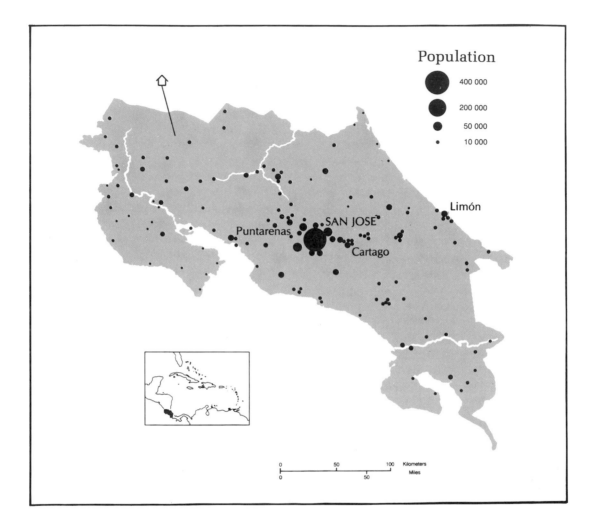

Population
- 400 000
- 200 000
- 50 000
- 10 000

Limón
SAN JOSE
Puntarenas
Cartago

0   50   100   Kilometers
0   50   Miles

THE NAME: From Spanish, meaning "rich coast"; given by Christopher Columbus

THE PEOPLE: The Costa Ricans

GEOGRAPHY
Narrow Pacific coastal region
Four cordilleras in the center of the country, bordered by plains that extend east to the Caribbean Sea and west to the Pacific Ocean.
Max. altitude: 3,820 m. (12,529 ft.) (Chirripó Grande)
Area: 51,100 sq. km. (19,730 sq. mi.)
Density: 53 pers./sq. km. (138 pers./sq. mi.) (1986)
Arable land: 13% (1987)
Forest: 31%
Climate: Warm and damp in the coastal lowlands, but cooler on the central plateau.

CAPITAL: San José, pop. 274,832 (1983)

LANGUAGE: Spanish

RELIGION
Majority Catholic

POPULATION: Total—2,600,000 (1985)
Annual growth: 2.6% (67,600) (1980–85)
Doubling time: 25 yrs.
Urban: 50% (1985) (est. for year 2000: 56%)
Rural: 50%

AGE GROUPS: (1984)
13% less than 5 yrs.	13% from 40 to 59
37% less than 15	7% 60 yrs. and over
48% less than 20	
32% from 20 to 39	

ETHNIC GROUPS
White and Mestizo: 97%
Black: 2%
Indian: 1%

HISTORY
Originally inhabited by independent Indian tribes (Boruca, Carib, Chorotega, Corobici, and Nahua)
1502: Discovery by Christopher Columbus
1563: After 60 years of fighting the Indians, the Spanish establish a permanent settlement. Founding of Cartago, which was administered as part of the Captaincy of Guatemala
September 15, 1821: Independence from Spain Joins Mexican Empire
1823–38: Member of the United Provinces of Central America
1890: First free election begins a tradition of democracy
1917–19: Dictatorship of Federico Granados
1948: Revolution; army is proscribed and replaced by a civil guard.

FAMILY
Marital status, for population 15 yrs. and older: (1984)
Single: 38%
Married: 45%
Consensually married: 10%
Widowed: 3%
Separated from husband or partner: 2%
Divorced: 1%
Female head of household: no data
Fertility rate: 3.4 (1985)
Births out of wedlock: no data
Teenage births: 19%
Contraception: 66% (1984)
Government's position on family planning: In 1983 the rate of population growth was regarded as satisfactory. Services are provided throughout the country to enhance the welfare of the family.

SOCIAL INDICATORS
Life expectancy: 73 yrs. (male: 70; female: 76) (1985)
Infant mortality: 19/1,000 births (1985)
Crude birth rate: 30/1,000 pop. (1985)
Crude death rate: 4/1,000
Health
Access to health services: 79% (urban: 100%; rural: 63%) (1980–83)
Births attended by trained health personnel: 93% (1984)

HOUSING
Persons per household: 4.8 (1984)
Electricity: 97%
Access to safe water: 93% (urban: 100%; rural: 82%) (1984)
Source of water: (1984)
Piped inside: 87%
Piped outside: 13%
Toilet facilities: (1984)
Flush: 66%
Latrine: 29%
Other: 4%
Building materials: (1984)
Wood: 60%
Mixture of wood and concrete: 35%
Adobe: 1%
Other: 4%

EDUCATION
Literacy: 88% (male: 89%; female: 88%) (1973)
Gross enrollment ratio: (1984)
First level: 101% (completing in 1980–84: 75%)
Second: 42%
Third: 22%
Educational attainment, for population 25 yrs. +: (1973)
None: 16%
First level: incomplete: 49% (complete: 18%)
Second: entered: 6%
Third: 6%

ECONOMIC ACTIVITY
Economically active population: 36% (male: 53%; female: 19%) (1985)
Agriculture: 28% act. pop.; 25% of GDP
Mines: 0% act. pop.; 0% of GDP
Industry: 22% act. pop.; 27% of GDP
Services: 50% act. pop.; 48% of GDP
Per capita GNP: 1,300 U.S.$ (1985)
Population in absolute poverty: no data
National currency/per U.S.$: 50.62 colones (1985)
Principal resource: Coffee

COMMUNICATIONS
Radio:
Transmitters: 123 (1981)
Receivers: 205,000—86/1,000 pop. (1983)
Television:
Transmitters: no data
Receivers: 181,000—76/1,000 pop. (1983)

EL SALVADOR

THE FRAILE PAZ FAMILY

Juan Antonio Fraile Castro, age 53 (1)
Jesús Paz, 46 (2)
Ana Hidalia Paz, 26 (absent)
Lidia de Carmen Paz, 22 (absent)
Juan Elizabeth Paz, 18 (3)
Ana Francisca Paz, 13 (4)
María Catalina Fraile, 7 (5)
Juan Antonio Fraile Paz, 5 (6)
Evelyne Galimet, 3 (7)
Carlos Alberto Fraile, 4 (8)

3 chickens
1 rooster

CANTON LA MAJADA
November 19

5:45. A small earthquake rumbles through the hills of El Salvador's coffee-growing region. The Fraile Paz family's wooden hut creaks at every joint, their beds shake, and it seems as though the wind will sweep away the insecurely attached corrugated-iron roof. In one of the two rooms Jesús Paz coughs and hacks incessantly. She has had bronchitis for months and her perpetual cigarette smoking aggravates it terribly. Beside her, her three-year-old granddaughter, Evelyne, starts to cry. The quake has awakened everyone. Juan Antonio switches on the radio to find out the time, and he and his wife get up. They put on the same clothes from yesterday and the day before. They have no choice.

Juan Antonio and Jesús leave their house, set in the midst of the coffee plantation where they work, and make their way down the hill. It takes Juan twenty minutes to reach the owner's house, where he meets David, his young helper. The two men go to the cow shed to clean out the stalls and mix the feed, while Jesús continues walking for another half hour to the main road. She is on her way to a farmer's to buy a rooster for her three hens: "A house is not a house without a rooster," she says.

Jesús and Juan Antonio have already lived in many parts of the country—moving from one place to another, fleeing the war zones of their country's civil war, constantly seeking a quieter life, a job, a house. But all in vain. A year ago, when they lived in Apancayo, the coffee plantation owner sought Juan out to tend his cows and sheep. Livestock are rare in the mountains and not one of his fifty employees knew how to look after animals. Juan had no reason to refuse the owner's offer. Now he has some security. The wages are low, but regular, and his wife and eighteen-year-old daughter can work on the estate. The owner thinks that women make better pickers than men.

The coffee is late this year and the rainy season is approaching. There is a danger that the strong winds will blow the beans off the trees. The pickers are impatient for the owner's signal to begin the harvest. The other twelve plantations in the cooperative have already started picking. But the owner insists on his coffee beans being heavy and ripe. More weight means more money. Jesús and Elizabeth look forward to bringing home a little money. "But only God and the master know when," says Jesús, sighing.

7:00. The roasting plant siren of the coffee cooperative reminds the peasants that a new day has begun. Elizabeth, up since her parents' departure, prepares breakfast. She lights the wood fire, boils the water, and cooks the *frijoles*. The beans are of poor quality and take two hours to cook, an hour more than usual. To make tortillas, Elizabeth washes corn boiled the night before and grinds it. It takes all her strength to turn the mill, and the movement hurts her back. Then she pounds the paste on a flat stone with a rolling pin and shapes it into little cakes with a quick, skillful movement of the hands. The meal will be ready just in time for her father's return at nine o'clock.

Elizabeth is pregnant with her second child. The first, Carlos, was conceived in a moment of passion, as often happens at harvesttime. Her lover disappeared after the harvest. The father of the second child, who is already married and has other children, visits her from time to time. Elizabeth never knows when he will arrive or when he will leave. He says that he will take her away, that he will find her a house and take care of her. A passive, withdrawn girl, Elizabeth has chosen to believe him.

Evelyne can't get warm and is curled up on the ground, her dirty dress wrapped around her legs. She watches the two little boys amuse themselves by seeing who can pee the farthest. With little result, thirteen-year-old Francisca sweeps the porch that serves as a kitchen with a broom made of coffee leaves. The wind eddies and blows, further scattering the ashes and garbage. When Elizabeth and Jesús go off to the harvest, Francisca will look after the house and the children on her own. This morning she does the family laundry.

9:30. Juan Antonio and his helper take off again on horseback as soon as they have eaten their breakfast. They will spend the rest of the morning up on the mountain taking the cows and sheep to pasture and water.

12:00. Jesús returns with a rooster and some corn under her arm. The hens' cackle grows louder and louder, and they start to squabble. "Finally some happiness in this house!" exclaims Jesús. She places the sack of corn she has just bought under one of the beds. Since the war the employees on the estate have stopped growing corn on land provided by the owner because their harvest was often stolen as soon as it was ripe.

Jesús has hardly sat down when Evelyne climbs up on her knees. She loves her little granddaughter and has enormous patience with children. She has had nine herself. Three daughters by one man who then left her for another woman. One of them died, the second lives on the coast with her three children, and Lidia, Evelyne's mother, lives wherever she can find work. She comes to visit her daughter when she has money and can get time off.

2:00. Juan and David are back, and the menu is the same as for the previous meal. The tortillas are dipped in bean soup. If there is soup left over, they make more tortillas. If there are tortillas left over, they make more soup. The men leave for the estate, loaded with spinach for the owner and grass for the young calves. The heat is intolerable, and the women stretch out under the orange tree to cool off. Jesús is tired, but, with the children running around and shouting, there is no possibility of a siesta for her.

3:00. As always when the rainy season is approaching, the sky darkens suddenly at this time of day. A thick fog settles on the mountain and the wind rises. It grows cold, and the family take shelter inside and listen to the radio. The music lulls the little ones to sleep. The women welcome the sight of a pickup truck making its way up the estate's dirt road to fill the now empty oil drum with water. This supply must last for a week.

4:00. The wind has scattered the washing that was drying on the line and on the branches, and Francisca runs about picking up the clothes. The co-op siren blows. It is time to prepare the evening meal: the beans will take just as long to cook and more corn will have to be ground for the tortillas.

7:00. Gathered under the kitchen roof and sheltered from the wind, the family eats the last meal of the day. A single lamp lights their faces and the plates on their knees. Juan is tired and doesn't talk much. He prefers to listen, as Jesús shares the gossip she has gleaned during her journey. The children know they must be quiet during the adults' conversation. The lamp is extinguished early to save oil. There is nothing to do now but go to bed, hoping that the earth will not tremble, the roof will stay on, and Mother's cough will get better. They all need a good night's sleep.

*Jesús and Juan
Antonio have
already lived in
many parts of the
country—fleeing
the war zones,
seeking a quieter
life, a job, a house.
But all in vain*

*After the harvest,
the owner allows
his employees to
take the prunings
of the coffee trees
for firewood*

EL SALVADOR

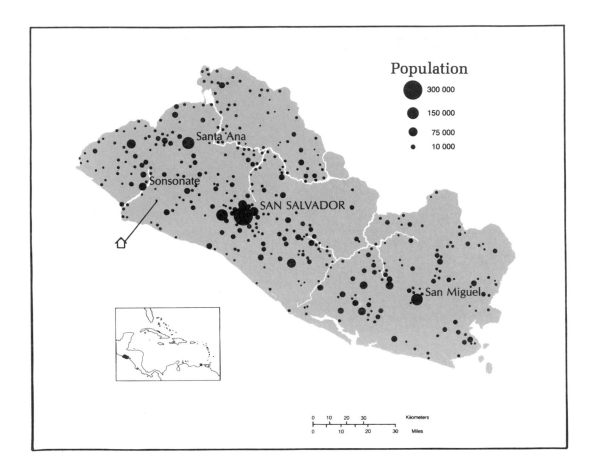

Population
- 300 000
- 150 000
- 75 000
- 10 000

Santa Ana

Sonsonate

SAN SALVADOR

San Miguel

Kilometers 0 10 20 30
Miles 0 10 20 30

THE NAME: In honor of the Catholic Saviour

THE PEOPLE: The Salvadoreans

GEOGRAPHY
Mountain ranges running east to west divide the country
into three distinct regions:
South: narrow Pacific coastal belt
Center: subtropical region of valleys and plateaus
with rich volcanic soils
North: mountainous region; several volcanoes still
active
Max. altitude: 2,381 m. (7,812 ft.) (Santa Ana
volcano)

Area: 21,041 sq. km. (8,124 sq. mi.)
Density: 233 pers./sq. km. (604 pers./sq. mi.) (1986)
Arable land: 34% (1987)
Forest: 6%
Climate: Tropical in the coastal lowlands, but temperate
in the uplands. Distinct wet and dry seasons.

CAPITAL: San Salvador, pop. 445,054 (1983 est.)

LANGUAGE: Spanish (official), Pipil (native Indian
language)

RELIGION
Majority Catholic

POPULATION: Total—5,600,000 (1985)
Annual growth: 2.9% (162,400) (1980–85)
Doubling time: 27 yrs.
Urban: 39% (1985) (est. for year 2000: 53%)
Rural: 61%

AGE GROUPS: (1980)
18% less than 5 yrs.
45% less than 15
56% less than 20
27% from 20 to 39
12% from 40 to 59
5% 60 yrs. and over

ETHNIC GROUPS
Mestizo: 92%
Indian: 6%
White: 2%

HISTORY
Originally inhabited by Pipil Indians
1524: Conquest by Spaniard Pedro de Alvarado
Administered until its independence as part of the
Captaincy of Guatemala
September 15, 1821: Independence
1821–40: Member of the United Provinces of
Central America
Political turmoil until 1931, the beginning of a
succession of military dictatorships
1969: Brief war with Honduras due to immigration
of Salvadoreans to Honduras
1984: Election of President José Napoleón Duarte

FAMILY
Marital status: (1978)
Common-law: 43%
No other data available
Female head of household: 22%
Fertility rate: 5.3 (1985)
Births out of wedlock: 69% (1979)
Teenage births: 21% (1982)
Contraception: 48% (1984)
Government's position on family planning: Has
incorporated a national population policy into its
general strategy of development, including family
planning within its health objectives.

SOCIAL INDICATORS
Life expectancy: 66 yrs. (male: 63; female: 68) (1985)
Infant mortality: 65/1,000 births (1985)
Crude birth rate: 39/1,000 pop. (1985)
Crude death rate: 8/1,000
Health:
Access to health services: no data
Births attended by trained health personnel:
35% (1984)

HOUSING
Persons per household: 5 (1981)
Electricity: 51% without (1981)
Access to safe water: 51% (urban: 67%; rural: 40%)
(1983)
Source of water: (1978)
Piped inside: 28%
River: 35%
Well: 22%
Other: 15%
Toilet facilities: (1978)
Flush: 62%
None: 37%
Building materials: (1978)
Adobe: 30%
Cane and earth: 28%
Concrete and concrete-adobe mixture: 23%
Wood: 6%
Straw and other: 13%

EDUCATION
Literacy: 69% (male: 68%; female: 69%) (1980)
Gross enrollment ratio: (1983–84)
First level: 70% (completing in 1980–84: 68%)
Second: 24%
Third: 11.9%
Educational attainment, for population 10 yrs. +:
(1980)
None: 30%
First level: incomplete: 61%
Second: entered: 7%
Third: 2%

ECONOMIC ACTIVITY
Economically active population: no data
Agriculture: 50% act. pop.; 24% of GDP
Mines: 0% act. pop.; 0% of GDP
Industry: 18% act. pop.; 18% of GDP
Services: 32% act. pop.; 58% of GDP
Per capita GNP: 820 U.S.$ (1985)
Population in absolute poverty: (1977–84)
Urban: 20%
Rural: 32%
In 1983, 69.75% of the population lived with less
than the minimum salary (300 colones a month);
each economically active person supports 4.3
persons.
National currency/per U.S.$: 2.50 colones (1985)
Principal resources: Coffee, cotton, sugar

COMMUNICATIONS
Radio:
Transmitters: 75 (1979)
Receivers: 1,900,000—363/1,000 pop. (1983)
Television:
Transmitters: no data
Receivers: 340,000—65/1,000 pop. (1983)

GUATEMALA

THE VELÁSQUEZ PÉREZ FAMILY

Benjamin Velásquez Pérez, age 36 (1)
Johana María Velásquez, 31 (2)
Dalila Guadalupe Velásquez, 10 (3)
Nemias Nicolás, 8 (4)
Jonathan Crispin, 5 (5)
María Guadalupe Pérez, 64 (6)

7 chickens
5 ducks

TOTONICAPÁN
October 22

6:00 Benjamin turns on the radio a little too loud but nobody reacts. He shuffles toward the door, climbing into the trousers that he left on the back of the chair the night before. This year it is Benjamin's turn to pick up the mail from Totonicapán as part of his volunteer work for the community. His plastic cowboy hat on his head, his stomach empty, he marches quickly off.

When he opens the door, the cold, thin mountain air takes his breath away. It will take him twenty minutes to climb down to the valley where the bus passes. The path on the edge of the cliff is so narrow and steep that it takes all his concentration to navigate it. Above Benjamin is a majestic green and yellow sweep of mountains embroidered with an iridescent mosaic of terraced fields. And as always, the silhouette of the Santa María volcano looms in the distance.

Inside their cool adobe house the children are happy to remain snuggled under their warm blankets while their mother, Johana, lights the wood fire. They are on summer vacation. Johana thinks that her children are wasting their time in school. The classes are overcrowded, often sixty to seventy children in each room, and Johana does not like the teachers. "They come from the city to teach but don't bother to learn Cakchiquel [the native language]," she complains. "Our children have to learn Spanish to be educated."

7:00 Johana drinks a cup of coffee and goes out on the patio in the back of her house to begin her day's work. Like most of the residents in the Juchanep township, she is an artist. Using brightly colored cotton twine, Johana weaves beautiful belts of intricate patterns. She hangs one end of her weaving on a post and attaches the other end to a leather harness around her waist. It takes her four days to finish one belt, which she sells for 4 quetzals ($4.00) to a wholesaler. It probably cost

her three-quarters of this amount to make each belt, but Johana and the other artisans do not conduct their business in a modern fashion, which computes profits in terms of time spent and materials purchased.

The children are up and scampering about their mother. When they were small, Johana carried them on her back as she wove. By the time they could walk, their mother's work had already become a part of their lives and so the children accept her lack of attention to them. They are independent, and the older ones naturally look after the younger. Now they leave for their grandparents' house across the patio. It's a lively home and their gentle grandmother is always willing to spend time with them. Their aunt Rachel and uncle Nefteli also live there. Rachel is a widow who has returned home to run the household after her husband was shot to death. When asked who killed him, she replies, "Who knows." In view of the country's current social instability, it could be dangerous for Rachel to try to find out. Now she makes tortillas for breakfast. Afterward she will change her old running shoes for a pair of dress shoes and go into Totonicapán to do the shopping.

Their arms crossed in front of them, the children bow slightly and greet each of the adults present, as is their tradition. *"Buenos días, Mama. Buenos días, Papa. Buenos días, Tía Rachel. Buenos días, Tío Nefteli."* The adults return the greeting and Grandfather blesses them.

This tradition has been lost in many Guatemalan homes, but Grandmother makes sure it is observed by her family.

Breakfast begins like every other meal, with Grandfather sitting near the fire saying grace. Grandfather was baptized and married as a Catholic. But his faith weakened over the years, and one day some particularly persuasive Jehovah's Witnesses got his ear. Grandfather made up his mind then, and the family left one church for the other. Now Grandfather spends several hours every day reading the Bible and spreading God's word.

8:00. After eating tortillas, eggs, and chili sauce and drinking a good cup of coffee, Tío Nefteli bows, thanks his parents and sister, and leaves for work. He is a weaver and will spend the next eight hours at a large loom in a small, dimly lit adobe shack. Mayan myth has it that weaving was invented by Ixehel, goddess of the moon. In ancient days weaving was the sacred duty of women and farming the sacred duty of men. But land has become less plentiful in modern times and men have taken over many of the big looms. It takes Nefteli three and a half days to weave a *corte*, a piece of cloth seven yards long which will become a colorful skirt when wrapped around a woman's waist. The skirts are tied with long belts like those Johana makes. A traditional Quiche woman will have two skirts, one for everyday wear and one for special occasions. The woven colors are dazzling, and the designs reflect each region and ethnic group. They are old Mayan patterns influenced by the art of the Spanish conquistadors. Nefteli dreams of having a wife who still dresses in a *corte*, but the younger Indian women are becoming more and more Westernized.

Like his sister Rebecca, who is a nurse in the city, they refuse to wear the traditional clothing, preferring shirts and trousers.

8:30. The children go out to the corn fields to play on the dirt paths between the rows. The corn will be ripe in twenty days. Tired of the long vacation, the children look forward to the harvest. At last they will be able to share in the family's work. The corn for the year's tortillas will have to be picked, dried, and stored. Later the oats and wheat will be cut. This family is fortunate. Grandfather owns twenty-six *cuerdas* (almost three acres) of land, the fruit of his lifetime's labor.

10:30. Benjamin returns from Totonicapán and climbs up to the top of the mountain to cut wood for cooking. Sometimes he brings back enough for Grandfather to sell for lumber. In three weeks he will no longer have time to do this, for he will go to work for the large landowners. Benjamin hopes one day to buy a field of his own—a daunting prospect in a country where farmland sells for around $4,000 an acre.

1:00. Johana joins her children in Grandmother's kitchen. They eat tortillas, little tamales, and broth for lunch. There is time for only a moment's rest, a brief conversation; then it's back to work. Grandfather loses himself in his Bible, and Nemias and Jonathan look for new games to play. Johana takes only one day a week to go to the city to shop and bathe in the warm water of the large public baths. Nevertheless, Johana is peaceful and content—perhaps because much of her work involves creating things of beauty and her family keeps alive traditional values and rituals.

5:00. Dalila is happy to finally have work of her own and goes off proudly to the mill to get their corn ground, carrying a plastic bowl on her head. Her return tells Johana that her workday is over. As she puts her weaving aside, Benjamin appears with a load of wood on his back. He dumps the wood in a corner of the patio and enters the house to light the cooking fire for his wife.

7:00. It's time for the children to give their grandmother and Tía Rachel some peace and quiet, to receive their grandfather's blessing, and to welcome home the artisan who has once again resumed her role as homemaker. The warmth of the fire replaces the warmth of the day's sunshine, and Johana's hands busy themselves with corn dough so her family can eat tortillas. The weary woodcutter showers with a pail of cold water, and all the people in the countryside light their kerosene lamps and send their children to bed.

It is a lively home where the gentle grandmother makes sure that Quiche traditions are respected by her family

Breakfast, like every other meal, begins with Grandfather sitting near the fire saying grace

GUATEMALA

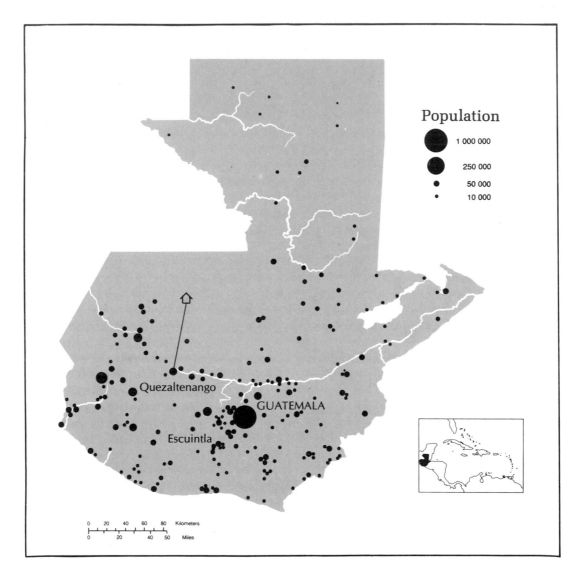

Population

- 1 000 000
- 250 000
- 50 000
- 10 000

Quezaltenango

GUATEMALA

Escuintla

0 20 40 60 80 Kilometers
0 20 40 50 Miles

THE NAME: From Aztec *guauhtemallan*, meaning "land of the trees" or "land surrounded by trees"

THE PEOPLE: The Guatemalans

GEOGRAPHY
Center: mountainous region
Pacific plain: narrow belt between mountains and ocean
The lowlands have fertile river valleys
Max. altitude: 4,220 m. (13,845 ft.) (Tajumulco volcano)
Area: 108,889 sq. km. (42,042 sq. mi.)
Density: 74 pers./sq. km. (192 pers./sq. mi.) (1986)

Arable land: 17% (1987)
Forest: 39%
Climate: Tropical in the coastal lowlands, but more temperate in the central highlands area. Well-marked wet season from May to October.

CAPITAL: Guatemala City, pop. 754,243 (1981)

LANGUAGE: Spanish (official)
35% of the people speak Quiche.
There are 23 autochthonous languages.

RELIGION
Majority Catholic

POPULATION: Total—8,000,000 (1985)
  Annual growth: 2.8% (224,000) (1980)
  Doubling time: 22 yrs.
  Urban: 40% (1985) (est. for year 2000: 54%)
  Rural: 60%

AGE GROUPS: (1981)
  18% less than 5 yrs.
  45% less than 15
  56% less than 20
  27% from 20 to 39
  13% from 40 to 59
   5% 60 yrs. and over

ETHNIC GROUPS
  Mestizo and Ladinized Indian: 47%
  Indian: 43%
  White: 9%

HISTORY
  From 2000 B.C. until A.D. 800 Guatemala was the
    center of the Mayan civilization
  1524: Conquest by Spanish Pedro de Alvarado
  1542: Foundation of the Captaincy of Guatemala
  September 15, 1821: Independence
  Until 1823: Associated with Mexico
  1824–39: Member of the United Provinces of
    Central America
  1839–71: Succession of military dictatorships under
    the leadership of Rafael Carrera
  1871: Liberal revolution
  1951–57: Social and agrarian reforms expropriate
    the holdings of foreign plantation owners
    (including the United Fruit Co.)
  1954: With U.S. support, the government is
    overthrown and expropriated land returned
  1955: Dictatorial presidencies lead to rule by
    revolutionary junta followed by continuous
    political instability

FAMILY
  Marital status, for population 15 yrs. and older: (1981)
    Single: 25%
    Married: 35%
    Common-law: 28%
    Widowed: 8%
    Divorced or separated: 4%
  Female head of household: 14% (1981)
  Fertility rate: 5.9 (1985)
  Births out of wedlock: 51% (1980–81)
  Teenage births: 18% (1979)
  Contraception: 25% (1984)
  Government's position on family planning: Does not
    express a point of view on the rate of population
    growth or the level of fertility, but there is a
    national family-planning program.

SOCIAL INDICATORS
  Life expectancy: 61 yrs. (male: 59; female: 62) (1985)
  Infant mortality: 65/1,000 births (1985)
  Crude birth rate: 42/1,000 pop. (1985)
  Crude death rate: 10/1,000

Health
  Access to health services: 34% (urban: 99%; rural:
    55%) (1980–83)
  Births attended by trained health personnel: no
    data

HOUSING
Persons per household: 5.2 (1985)
Electricity: 61% without (1980)
Access to safe water: 51% (urban: 99%; rural: 55%)
  (1983)
Source of water: (1980)
  River and other: 68%
  Private well: 15%
  Public standpipe: 11%
  Public well: 11%
Toilet facilities: (1980)
  Pit: 28%
  None: 48%
  Other: 24%
Building materials: (1980)
  Adobe: 36%
  Wood: 31%
  Concrete: 13%
  Cane: 10%
  Cane and earth: 7%
  Other: 4%

EDUCATION
Literacy: 46% (male: 54%; female: 38%) (1973)
Gross enrollment ratio: (1982–84)
  First level: 76% (completing in 1980–84: 38%)
  Second: 17%
  Third: 7%
Educational attainment, for population 25 yrs. +:
  (1973)
  None: 94%
  First level: 38%
  Second: entered: 5%
  Third: 1%

ECONOMIC ACTIVITY
Economically active population: 28% (male: 48%;
  female: 8% (1981)
Agriculture: 55% act. pop.; 25% of GDP
Mines: 1% act. pop.; 1% of GDP
Industry: 17% act. pop.; 19% of GDP
Services: 27% act. pop.; 55% of GDP
Per capita GNP: 1,250 U.S.$ (1985)
Population in absolute poverty: (1977–84)
  Urban: 21%
  Rural: 25%
National currency/per U.S.$: 1.00 quetzal (1985)
Principal resources: Corn, coffee

COMMUNICATIONS
Radio:
  Transmitters: 115 (1979)
  Receivers: 340,000—43/1,000 pop. (1983)
Television:
  Transmitters: no data
  Receivers: 203,000—26/1,000 pop. (1983)

HONDURAS

THE GIRÓN RAMÍREZ FAMILY

Majim Ramírez, age 45 (1)
Emilia Girón, 24 (2)
Juan Gilberto Girón, 10 (3)
José Santos, 8 (4)
Pablo, 6 (5)
Martha Esperanza Bartita, 4 (6)
José Wilfredo Ramírez Girón (Willy), 8 months (7)

1 dog and her 5 puppies
1 cat
10 chickens
3 ducks

GRUPO PAJONAL, COMAYAGUA
November 4

Emilia gets up in the dark, patters across the dirt floor of her one-room house, and lights the fire for the morning coffee. The fact that her family is still sleeping just a few feet away does not stop her from speaking aloud. She converses with herself, running through the chores for the day, while her ten-year-old son, Juan, lying closest to her on an old car seat with broken springs, murmurs as if in response. Morning comes early with Mother's conversations. Just as she places the pot on the fire, eight-month-old Willy wakes up crying. Emilia puts him to her breast, and nudging Juan aside, sits down on the old car seat. Her husband, Majim, will serve the coffee.

Majim turns on the radio, but the batteries are so low that the announcement of a plot against the President of the Republic is barely audible. Nobody pays attention anyway. The life and daily concerns of the poor farmers in Honduras are so far removed geographically and politically from the seat of the government that it's almost like listening to news from another country. Just as the reporter begins to speak of Indira Gandhi's assassination in India, Majim turns off the radio.

Before it gets too hot, Juan and his younger brother José set off for their first trip to the river, pulling a homemade cart loaded with a dozen plastic jerry cans. It is a half-hour walk to the river, and it will take three trips to fetch enough water to last the day. Majim goes out into his field to pick corn for the children to strip so that he can sell it in the Comayagua market on Sunday.

Four years ago, Majim left the arid country of the Tibuca region for Comayagua. He was able to take advantage of a short-lived agrarian reform and, along with forty other families, was granted four *manzanas* (seven acres) of barely arable land. He is still waiting, without making too much fuss, for the papers that confirm his title. "It takes a long time," he was told in the town.

8:00. Once the men have left for work, Emilia can relax in her tiny kitchen. She prepares a break-

fast of tortillas and beans, watched avidly by the emaciated dog, who lies passively feeding her puppies.

Emilia's first husband was killed in a settling of accounts. Left on her own, with four children, she went from the countryside to the city to work as a maid. Juan, who was then seven years old, left school to look after his brothers and sister while his mother was away. One day Emilia came to the Comayagua area to harvest tomatoes. There she met Majim, a widower, who was immediately smitten and asked her to move in with him. Little Willy came along soon after, and Juan was finally able to start elementary school.

9:30. Majim returns from the fields. By now the boys have been to the river and back twice. Everyone takes refuge from the heat in the coolness of the house. When he met Emilia, Majim lived at his mother's house with his young daughter. Leaving his daughter with her grandmother, he moved his new family into a cardboard shack until he could save enough money to build a real house with a tiled roof. The roof is now finished, but the house walls are still just interwoven branches tightly knotted together and the gaps need to be filled in with mud. Soon they will have to have proper shelter. At night the wind blows through the walls, and the children often have colds. Emilia pesters Majim to finish the house. He promises to do so as soon as he has sold the corn, harvested the *frijoles*, and picked the watermelons. But in all likelihood he will not be able to make the hundreds of trips to the river that would be needed to mix the mud.

The whole family has breakfast. Emilia eats hers with Willy at her breast. With practiced hands the children hungrily scoop up the beans with their tortillas. Between harvests Emilia often runs out of beans and has only tortillas for her children.

10:30. Majim picks up his wheelbarrow and goes off to pick more corn. Juan and José make their last trip to the river. In an hour it will be too hot to do anything until the afternoon. Willy does not want to leave his mother's breast, and Emilia is always cheerfully compliant. Pablo and Martha have nothing much to play with. They amuse themselves by watching the chickens. When a hen lays an egg on the bed, they grab it and shove it into a cardboard box. The chickens and the ducks are very thin. From time to time, Emilia picks them up, weighs them in her hand, and decides against making a meal out of them for her family. Today's lunch will be the same as every other meal: beans and tortillas.

2:30. Siesta is over. At last the sun has moved behind the house, and the family can tend to their afternoon chores. Emilia gathers some dead twigs to fashion into a broom and sweeps the yard.

Majim sits in the shade and watches his step-sons shell the corn. First the children wrap the dried ears in netting and place them on large plastic sheets. Then they beat the bundles with heavy sticks to loosen the kernels. Majim wonders how many sacks they will be able to fill. He could produce more if he worked all his land instead of only half. He would like to go ahead, but he cannot afford a plow animal and he does not have enough energy to do the extra plowing himself. He will wait until the children get big enough to help him in the fields. Pablo takes advantage of his step-father's inactivity to hunt for lice in his hair.

3:00. Today at Emilia's neighbor's house the women of the community are meeting with the representative of the Honduran Federation of Peasant Women. The Federation has donated six pigs for the mothers to raise and sell. One is already sick and the others are not getting enough food. The representative tells the women that the pigs have to be well fed in order to be sold and recommends using leftovers. "But what leftovers?" Emilia asks. "Our kitchens are bare." The representative, whose parents are peasants too, looks flustered. "Perhaps you could grow some food," she says. "Perhaps,"

replies Emilia kindly. "But who will look after our children and give us tools and seeds? Can the Federation help us?" The representative leaves, promising to discuss these unforeseen problems with her organization's leaders.

Emilia returns in the late afternoon. The heat is even more unbearable. With Willy at her breast, and Pablo and Martha clutching her skirts, Emilia goes to the river to wash some clothes and cool off in the cold water under the bridge.

6:00. The sun has set behind the mountains and the full moon is on the rise. After their beans, the men go to play football in the moonlit field while the women visit from shack to shack with their babies on their arms. All over the world, in places where there is no electricity, families take advantage of this extension of natural light.

7:30. Full moon or not, it's bedtime for the smallest children. Emilia lights the house by placing a burning wooden stick from the fire in the middle of the dirt floor. She lifts Pablo into the hammock which hangs over the two beds and covers Martha, who always protests at this point. As for Willy, he is already asleep in his parents' bed, his fists tightly clenched.

9:00. Juan returns to the uncomfortable car seat and quickly falls asleep, oblivious for now to his mother's voice, which can be heard as she lies in bed telling her husband about the afternoon's meeting. As they drift off to sleep, Martha begins to cry. Her life has been tough since Willy was born. She had to give up her place in her parents' bed and go and sleep with José. She can't snuggle up to her brother they way she could to her mother. "I have to go," wails Martha. "Get up, go, and get back into bed," says her mother from the next bed. Sniffling, Martha gets up, squats on the dirt floor at the end of her bed, and lies down again. Her crying has awakened Willy, who needs only to nuzzle at his mother's breast to fall back to sleep.

The boys wrap the dried ears of corn in netting and place them on large plastic sheets. Then they beat them with sticks. They put the shelled corn in bags to sell in the city

It takes all of José's strength to mash the cooked corn. Then Emilia will roll the dough on the flat stone to make tortillas

HONDURAS

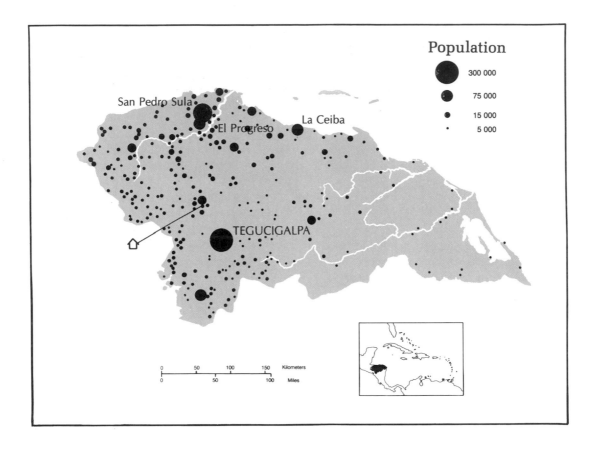

THE NAME: From Spanish *hondo*, meaning "deep"; Christopher Columbus noticed the area's deep waters

THE PEOPLE: The Hondurans

GEOGRAPHY

Two major mountain ranges bisect the country from northwest to southwest; lowlands along both coasts

Max. altitude: 2,866 m. (9,403 ft.) (Las Minas)

Area: 112,088 sq. km. (43,277 sq. mi.)

Density: 40 pers./sq. km (104 pers./sq. mi.) (1986)

Arable land: 16% (1987)

Forest: 33%

Climate: Tropical in the coastal lowlands, but temperate in the mountainous regions. Rainy season from May to November.

CAPITAL: Tegucigalpa, pop. 539,042 (1985 est.)

LANGUAGE: Spanish

RELIGION

Majority Catholic

In 1982, it was estimated that there are 50 different religious sects, the most influential being the Unificacionista Church.

POPULATION: Total—4,400,000 (1985)

Annual growth: 3.4% (149,600) (1980–85)

Doubling time: 22 yrs.

Urban: 40% (1985) (est. for year 2000: 52%)

Rural: 60%

AGE GROUPS: (1981)

19% less than 5 yrs.	25% from 20 to 39
48% less than 15	12% from 40 to 59
58% less than 20	4% 60 yrs. and over

ETHNIC GROUPS:

Ladino: 90% (mixed Spanish and Indian)

Indian: 7%

Black: 2%

White: 1%

HISTORY

Mayan civilization until 1st millennium A.D.
1502: Discovery by Christopher Columbus
1523: Beginning of permanent Spanish settlement
1570: Part of the Captaincy of Guatemala
September 15, 1821: Independence from Spain
1821–38: Member of the United Provinces of Central America
November 5, 1838: Becomes an independent state
1932–49: Dictatorship under President Carías Andino
1957: Adoption of constitution
1969: Brief war with El Salvador, due to immigration of Salvadoreans in Honduras Peace treaty drawn up in 1980
1982: Civilian government elected; the military remains powerful and retains control of security decisions

FAMILY

Marital status, for population 15 yrs. and older: (1974)
  Married: 27%
  Common-law: 27%
  Separated from husband or partner: 10%
  Other: 35%
Female head of household: 22% (1974)
Fertility rate: 6.0 (1985)
Births out of wedlock: no data
Teenage births: 19% (1979)
Contraception: 35% (1984)
Government's position on family planning: Believes that the population growth rate is too high and that it impedes development. The government provides direct support to family-planning services, as a means of both reducing population growth and improving family well-being.

SOCIAL INDICATORS

Life expectancy: 61 yrs. (male: 59; female: 63) (1984)
Infant mortality: 76/1,000 births (1985)
Crude birth rate: 42/1,000 pop. (1985)
Crude death rate: 9/1,000
Health:
  Access to health services: 60% (1980–83)
  Births attended by trained health personnel: 50% (1984)

HOUSING

Persons per household: 5.7 (1985)

Electricity: 59% without (rural 89%) (1974)
Access to safe water: 69% (urban: 91%; rural: 55%) (1983)
Source of water: (1974)
  Piped inside: 20%
  Piped outside: 38%
  Other: 41%
Toilet facilities: (1974)
  None: 42% (rural: 66%)
Building materials: (1974)
  Cane and earth: 36%
  Wood: 26%
  Adobe: 16%
  Concrete: 12%
  Other: 10%

EDUCATION

Literacy: 57% (male: 59%; female: 55%) (1974)
Gross enrollment ratio: (1984–85)
  First level: 102% (completing in 1980–84: 27%)
  Second: 33%
  Third: 10%
Educational attainment, for population 25 yrs. +: (1983)
  None: 34%
  First level: 51%
  Second: 4%
  Third: 3%

ECONOMIC ACTIVITY

Economically active population: 44% (male: 75%; female: 13%) (1984)
Agriculture: 62% act. pop.; 28% of GDP
Mines: 3% act. pop.; 3% of GDP
Industry: 12% act. pop.; 23% of GDP
Services: 23% act. pop.; 46% of GDP
Per capita GNP: 720 U.S.$ (1985)
Population in absolute poverty: (1977–84)
  Urban: 14%
  Rural: 55%
National currency/per U.S.$: 2.00 lempiras (1985)
Principal resources: Coffee, bananas, wood

COMMUNICATIONS

Radio:
  Transmitters: 153 (1979)
  Receivers: 200,000—49/1,000 pop. (1983)
Television:
  Transmitters: no data
  Receivers: 52,000—13/1,000 pop. (1983)

MEXICO

THE GARCÍAS HERNÁNDEZ FAMILY

Sixto Hernández, age 44 (1)
María Catanina Garcías Hernández, 34 (2)
Reyes Garcías Hernández, 16 (3)
Alfredo, 14 (4)
Gerardo, 10 (5)
Francisco, 8 (6)
Angélica, 8 (7)
Pascuala, 2½ (8)

2 chickens
2 turkeys
1 pig
3 cows
4 ducks
1 dog

TANCUILIN
September 25

5:00. The call of nature awakens Pascuala. In the darkness, her mother, Catanina, hunts on her hands and knees for the flashlight on the floor. She switches it on and accompanies her toddler outside to squat on the ground near the door. This wakes the boys, lined up in a row like onions on the kitchen floor. Sixteen-year-old Reyes gets up to pile twigs inside the three stones that form the hearth. He lights the fire, places the pot of water on top, and goes back to bed.

The cane-and-thatch house of the Garcías Hernández family perches on the green slope of a mountain in the Huasteca region of central Mexico. A dirt path leads down from the house to the main road winding through groves of orange trees and along a river. The family's two teenagers descend every morning, Alfredo on foot for high school in Chipolco and Reyes on a wobbly bicycle for the technical college in Halpila.

6:30. After sharing morning coffee with their father, the boys leave for school. Sixto is determined that all his family will be well educated. An uneducated farmer, Sixto grows enough corn, coffee, avocados, and bananas for the family's consumption and enough oranges to sell. Yet two days a week, to make ends meet, he hires himself out as a laborer to large landowners. "Picking oranges is a lot of work for only a little profit," says Sixto. "We must carry them on our backs all the way to the main road to sell them to wholesalers. I don't understand why everything I buy gets more and more expensive, but I never get more for my oranges."

Picking up his machete, Sixto leaves the yard for the elementary school. One day a week, he volunteers to work for the community. This morning he and another local man will prepare adobe and patch the holes in the classrooms' walls.

Ten-year-old Gerardo and eight-year-old Francisco will soon follow their father up the mountain. But before they leave for school, they bring water to the three cows that are grazing in a small pasture surrounded by orange trees.

8:00. Pascuala follows her mother around the house and pretends to share in the housework. The little girl's greatest delight is imitating her mother. Today she has refused to go the *kinder* (nursery school), which is adjacent to the elementary school. "It's so boring," she exclaims. Her gentle and patient mother lets her do as she pleases.

Catanina's friend stops by. She has walked for two hours to bring her nieces to school. Catanina ties up Angélica's hair. She surveys her critically and nods, knowing her daughter will pass the teacher's inspection for clean hands, hair, and clothes. The three girls leave for school on the dirt road that winds its way up among the houses. It has started to drizzle, and the path is becoming slick and treacherous. Catanina, her friend, and Pascuala sit down to clean and sort beans as the final schoolbell rings.

10:00. Catanina rolls out the corn dough on the flat stone to make it smooth so that the tortillas will be soft. She could use the press to flatten them, but Sixto prefers tortillas made the old-fashioned way, by hand. Those are the best! Catanina proves him right.

With its walls of blackened cane, the kitchen smells of charred wood and smoke and the *frijoles* simmering on the fire. Today Catanina will make an omelette with mushrooms which her friend picked in the woods on the way down to school. Mother and daughter chat as they prepare the meal. Each day Pascuala learns new words in Spanish or Nahuatl, her native language. Her colorful conversation never fails to amuse Catanina, who bursts out laughing as she clasps her belly, where the next child is already stirring.

10:30. The bell rings for school recess and a

midmorning meal. The children run down the mountains in the pouring rain. In each house rice and beans are waiting for them. They eat heartily and leave as quickly as they arrived.

Sixto returns and sits next to the only table in the house; it is so low that he cannot slide his knees underneath. In front of him, Pascuala drinks black-bean juice and continues her monologue. A torrential rain falls on the house. The ducks huddle on the doorstep and the chickens take shelter inside. Slowly and calmly, as is her nature, Catanina lets down her hair and combs the long tresses. Unable to resist his little girl's charm, Sixto breaks into hearty laughter.

1:00. School is over and the children tumble down the muddy track shouting at the top of their lungs. Gerardo and Francisco race up the meadow to milk the cows and bring back a pail of milk that Catanina will sell to the neighbors. Angélica goes down to the river to fetch water, returning with one heavy bucket on her head and another in her hand. Catanina reheats the beans for her hungry teenagers and has the oldest one chop wood for the kitchen fire.

Sixto goes back to the elementary school. The new doctor from the regional clinic is coming to meet the men and to discuss the importance of obtaining medical assistance for their families. The school principal will also be present to remind the fathers that school is compulsory for their children and that the early school years are the most important for their development. Too often the peasants keep their children home to work.

3:00. Catanina leaves for the river with her children. She washes their clothes, imitated by Pascuala. Angélica washes the corn for tomorrow's tortillas, while the boys fool around. They soap themselves and rinse off by diving into the water. At this hour of the day, the riverbank is a lively place. Most of the families on the mountain slope are here. The river runs swift and wide. Indians from the opposite side have difficulty crossing it in their small boats. They come to the settlement to buy rice and beans and then make the equally laborious return journey back to the mountains, where they live in extreme isolation.

Everyone is sparkling clean. They climb back up to the house, the girls carrying the washing and corn and the boys a pail of water. No one ever comes home from the river empty-handed.

5:30. Alfredo and Gerardo take turns grinding the cooked corn and making dough for the evening tortillas. Once in a while, they toss a handful to the chickens and to Mariposa, the dog, who watches their every movement. Catanina hangs out the washing, hoping that it will not rain again. Angélica hands her the clothes, singing over and over the chorus of a hymn learned at school: "Gracias a Dios" ("Thanks Be to God").

6:30. No sooner are the tortillas and eggs ready than a plate is held out. It is dark by the time Catanina can sit to eat her portion. The family does not want to waste a candle. Their eyes gradually grow accustomed to the darkness, where dim shadows perched on Lilliputian chairs can only just be made out. The conversation continues in the darkness.

8:00. On her hands and knees, Catanina lays out the mats and blankets on the concrete bedroom floor. She sleeps there with Sixto and their two daughters. The boys prefer the coolness of the kitchen's dirt floor. For another half hour, they listen to the tinny radio, argue, and burst into noisy laughter. Pascuala is lying near her mother, tossing and turning in her sleep. In her calm voice, Catanina tells everyone to be quiet. Without a complaint, they all obey.

In the yard, the ducks waddle on the small pile of sand that will one day be used to build Sixto's dream, a concrete house with a tin roof

During their school recess, the children come home for a meal. They eat at the only table in the house

MEXICO

THE GÓMEZ SALINAS FAMILY

Miguel Hinogoza Salinas, age 35 (1)
María de Jesús Gómez de Salinas, 28 (2)
Francisca Hinogoza Gómez de Salinas, 8 (3)
Humberto, 7 (4)
Carlos, 5 (5)
Primo, 4 (6)
Adriana, 3 (7)
María de Jesús, 1 (8)

3 horses
1 pig
3 dogs
1 cat
30 chickens
1 turkey   1 pigeon   15 cows

LA PRAESITA
September 20

The *ranchitos* of the tiny hamlet of La Praesita lie scattered on the scrubby desert plain. The stone walls have absorbed the coolness of the desert night, and the houses enclosed within enjoy temporary relief from the day's blazing sun.

In the yard of one *ranchito* some thirty hens and chicks leave their tree and begin scratching around for some grains of corn. Finding nothing, they make their way to the house and discover the door mistakenly left open. The chickens pour in. Irritated cooing noises indicate that the invaders have awakened the house's pigeon which flies down from its perch and joins the hungry legion. Hens, chicks, turkeys, cat, and kittens surround the beds, noisily demanding their breakfast.

María de Salinas pays no attention to the cacophony that has become her morning alarm clock. Nonchalantly she prepares her baby's bottle. Furious at this lack of attention, the animals redouble their squawks and cries. Suddenly María's patience is exhausted. She shoos them outside with energetic kicks and latches the door.

7:00. It is still cool in the stone house, and the children stay snug under the covers. School has been canceled because of a teachers' meeting. This doesn't particularly please the two older children who just started school last week. Francisca and Humberto amuse their younger brothers and sister by showing them pictures in their new school books. Their baby sister nurses on her bottle and immediately goes back to sleep.

María takes advantage of the children's quiet to go to the mill. Every night María boils dry corn. In the morning she rinses the kernels and takes them to the mill to be ground. In the course of the day María will make at least a hundred tortillas for her family.

On her way back from the mill, she stops at one of the four *tiendas* (small family stores), which is owned by her in-laws. Her husband, Miguel, is sure to be there. Up at dawn, he heads for the pasture and brings his cows back to the *ranchito* and milks them. Then he visits with his brothers until María has prepared breakfast. María buys a piece of sausage, picks up her pail of cornmeal, and returns home.

8:30. Surrounded by hungry children, María prepares breakfast at the table. Her sister Ana arrives and distracts the children for her. María is diligent but moves quite slowly and is consequently sometimes overwhelmed by work. Her family often come to her rescue. Now she plugs her mixer into the hanging light-bulb socket and grinds a batch of fresh chilis for salsa. To save time, she cooks the first batch of tortillas on the gas stove. The rest will be cooked in a traditional stone oven built in the kitchen wall.

The children take their places at the table without being asked. Three-year-old Adriana is the greediest. A bit more sauce to finish off the tortillas and then one more tortilla to finish off the sauce. In her infant walker, little María de Jesús wheels around the table begging a mouthful from everyone. Mexican babies are familiar with the taste of peppers long before they can walk.

10:00. Miguel has returned and eaten his breakfast and now he leads the three horses to graze under the trees on one of his five scattered pieces of land. The coarse, dry grass that grows among the huge cacti is sparse and hard to find. Miguel cuts it and takes it to his horses, who stand tethered in the shade of small desert trees.

Meanwhile María lights the wood fire in the stone oven. Seated in front of the hearth, she cooks the rest of the tortillas for the day, to the accompaniment of Julio Iglesias' melodious voice over the radio. The dogs and the cat are asleep at her side. But her moment of tranquillity is soon shattered. The heat of the day has driven the children inside and they are arguing loudly. As always, it's seven-year-old Humberto who is the culprit. "You're going to get it," threatens his mother. A familiar refrain.

1:30. The whole family gathers for the main meal of the day: a stew of beans, tomatoes, and wild summer squash. The family garden does not yield much. "The seeds are expensive," complains Miguel. "The rainy season drowns the vegetables; the dry season dries them up. Too much effort for too little result."

After lunch, eight-year-old Francisca helps her mother straighten up while the other children play. She is an accomplished housekeeper and sweeps up the garbage that her mother dumps outside the door. When her pile is big enough, she buries it in a corner of the yard.

3:30. María has made cheese from the morning milk and now, escaping the shrieking noise of her children, sets off to do the laundry. In this dry climate, the dust permeates everything, and the clothes must be washed every day. María sets up her tin tub and washboard by the tap in the yard. In another tub under the flow of tepid water the baby splashes beside her. Primo and Carlos want to cool off, and when their mother leaves to hang the wash they jump into the vacant tub. Their "bath" for the day is more entertaining than cleansing.

5:30. María, followed by her brood, returns to her in-laws' store for a bucket of prickly pears and to see the next installment of *Guadalupe*. This popular soap opera's heroine has so many fans there is no more room in the store. On her way home María stops at her mother's house. These family visits are daily occurrences. The heat and the harsh conditions of the land deplete people's energy quickly, and much time is spent simply sitting around and exchanging small talk. The children are restless, and Humberto is once again on the warpath. María's threats are ignored, but Miguel, just returned from taking the cows back to the fields, gives the boy his inevitable spanking.

6:00. Leaving his son sobbing in the yard, Miguel heads for Mariano Vásquez Square, where the men of the village congregate, holding their horses by their bridles. The oldest of them remembers the square's hero, who was assassinated for having fought against the landowners. It was due to his efforts that the peasants came to own their own land, and every year there is a celebration in his memory.

7:00. The air has finally cooled down. The mosquitoes have reappeared, and the hens have settled down in their favorite tree. Around the table, the children drink hot chocolate before going to bed. Humberto and Francisca chase two recalcitrant chickens out from under the beds. The little ones are excited and continue to play, but once in their room they collapse. María finds them asleep in a heap. She tucks the boys into one bed and the girls in another. The pigeon perches on the frame of his favorite picture: the Lord's Last Supper.

8:00. María washes the dishes, boils the corn for tomorrow's tortillas, makes up the night bottle for the baby, and puts a great cauldron of water on the stove to sterilize it for drinking. Miguel sits near her and makes book covers out of newspaper to protect his children's school books. The mariachi band sing their hearts out on the radio while the two adults finish their labors under the harsh light of a single bulb.

The gate of the ranchito faces Mariano Vásquez Square. The small hamlet's elders remember the hero, whose fight against the landowners has enabled peasants like Miguel to own their own land today

In her infant walker, little María de Jesús goes around the table begging a mouthful of chili tortilla from everyone. Mexican babies are familiar with the taste of peppers long before they can walk

MEXICO

THE HERNÁNDEZ FAMILY

Jesús Hernández Ortiz, age 28 (1)
María del Pilar Ríos de Hernández, 27 (2)
José de Jesús Hernández (Chui), 5 (3)
Oliver, 3 (4)

GUADALAJARA
October 10

6:00. The Hernández family's duplex apartment is on one of Guadalajara's busiest streets. The infernal noise of cars, motorcycles, and trucks blends with the shouts of children passing by on their way to the church and school next door. The early-morning commotion does not disturb the Hernández family, who have no problems sleeping late.

8:15. The heels of Pilar's slippers clatter as she runs down on the tiled staircase. Still more than half asleep, she lights the water heater and prepares two bottles of chocolate milk for her young sons. She delivers the first to Oliver, whose bed is squeezed into a narrow alcove at the top of the stairs, and the second to Chui, who has his mattress on the floor next to his parents' bed. Then Pilar falls back into bed for fifteen minutes more of luxurious sleep.

But she sleeps too long and now the children are late. Showered and dressed, they run to the door followed by their young parents. At the last minute, Pilar pulls a sweater over each of their heads to protect them from the brisk morning air. She lets go of them only after receiving a kiss from each one and making the sign of the cross over their heads. The boys climb joyfully into their father's truck and head off for half a day at the *kinder* (nursery school). Once the door has closed, Pilar breathes a sigh of satisfaction: "Ouf!" Three whole hours of peace and quiet.

9:15. Jesús returns to eat his breakfast: coffee, scrambled eggs, sausage, and tortillas, prepared by his wife. They gossip about their friend Pablo, who had dinner with them yesterday. "He's still single at the age of twenty-nine, a sign that he is not taking life seriously," remarks Pilar. "We must convince him to get married." She would love to continue—other people's lives fascinate her—but Jesús has to leave for work.

Jesús owns a small ceramic-tile workshop that he inherited from his father. During the day, he looks for new customers and purchases materials to replenish his stock. His five employees produce the tiles; Pilar does the paperwork and looks after the store, which is just off the kitchen. Pilar and Jesús are saving to renovate the apartment, which they own, and they are ambitious enough to eventually achieve their dream despite the runaway inflation that makes it particularly hard for the middle class.

Still in her dressing gown, Pilar washes last night's dishes as she glances with interest at a television program on the private lives of Mexican artists. The laundry must be hung out to dry, the furniture dusted, the floors washed. Pilar tries to do her work around the small apartment without completely losing sight of the television.

11:00. Pilar takes a break to shower. She strives to look impeccably elegant, and dressed now in a silky blouse and trousers, she sits at the counter that separates her kitchen from the dining room and begins the delicate operation of painting her eyelids. A skillful blend of gray and white, a line of black pencil, crowned by long false eyelashes, and Pilar looks as rich as any of her favorite soap opera heroines. She has no plans to leave her house, but wants to look her best for the customers who come throughout the day to order tiles. Pilar knows that the success of the tile business will enable them to move into a bigger home and a nicer neighborhood. She is more than ready to move up the social ladder as well.

12:00. School is out. Students from the school next door climb into their parents' waiting cars as Jesús drops his two boys off in front of the apartment. The tranquil, clean house is instantly turned into a circus arena. Each time Chui picks up a toy, Oliver tries to grab it. He screams, jumps up and down, and hurls himself at the furniture, knowing his mother will then make sure he gets his way. If Chui complains, his mother threatens him with a spanking. It is tough to be the older son.

Pilar sends her sons outside to play so that she can finish making lunch in peace. Less than five minutes later, Chui runs in shouting, "Oliver broke Mrs. González's living-room window with the ball!" Pilar orders her sons inside, but the telephone rings before she has time to run and apologize to Mrs. González or to reprimand her son. It's a girlfriend on the line. For fifteen minutes Pilar chats and complains about the mischief caused by her offspring. She hangs up to call a glazier who might come to repair the damage before nightfall. "She should have put bars on the windows like everybody else," sighs Pilar. "That would prevent these problems." Another two thousand pesos down the drain. In the last week, Oliver has smashed the glass of the coffee table and broken the color television set. "That child would have to be tied up to ensure that anything worked properly in this house," Pilar says, exasperated. Still, she leaves the disciplining of the boys to her husband.

2:00. After inspecting their hands for dirt, Pilar sits her children on high stools at the counter. They eat their rice, bananas, french fries, and meat without taking their eyes off the Flintstones cartoons on television. When Jesús returns, the couple take their children's place and over lunch discuss the day's business. Jesús asks his wife to allow more time to fill the orders that are flooding in. Right now their employees have more work than they can handle, even by working overtime.

Jesús eats lightly, changes into his soccer clothes, and leaves for the stadium for his weekly match. After that, he will have a sauna at his club. He's making an extra effort these days to lose a few kilos. This weekend Pilar and Jesús will attend a family baptism, where they will be the godparents. When Jesús tried on his formal suit, he was shocked that he could hardly get into it. Pilar goes to their club only on Sundays and then mostly to visit with friends and let her children work off their energy.

4:00. Jesús has punished Chui and Oliver for their morning's carelessness. No going outside to play or bothering their mother. The only thing left to do is to take refuge upstairs on their parents' comfortable bed to watch cartoons on television. Pilar has reserved the television set in the dining room to watch her four daily soap operas, especially her favorite one, *Guadalupe*. Since she has to press the clothes they will wear to the christening, Pilar sets up the ironing board in front of the television.

7:00. Dinner is casual and light. Pilar takes the tortillas that she buys weekly out of the freezer. She reheats them, fills them with ham and tomatoes, and serves them with cups of milky coffee. The family eat their fill. Jesús takes a big helping before leaving to watch a basketball game. He won't lose a single kilo tonight.

8:30. Her husband gone, Pilar piles up the dishes in the sink. There will always be time tomorrow to wash them. Tonight, she cannot summon up the energy and goes upstairs to wash off her makeup, change into her dressing gown, and lie down between her two sons, who are once again hypnotized by the TV set. Pilar deposits them in their bed and settles down to watch an American film and wait for Jesús.

11:00. Jesús climbs into bed with Pilar to watch one last film. Tonight the couple again fall asleep with the light from the set flickering on their faces.

For the last two years Jesús and Pilar have owned their duplex apartment. Ambitious, they will certainly succeed, despite the runaway inflation, in renovating their home

Their hands are clean. The children will have their meal without taking their eyes off the Flintstones cartoons on television

MEXICO

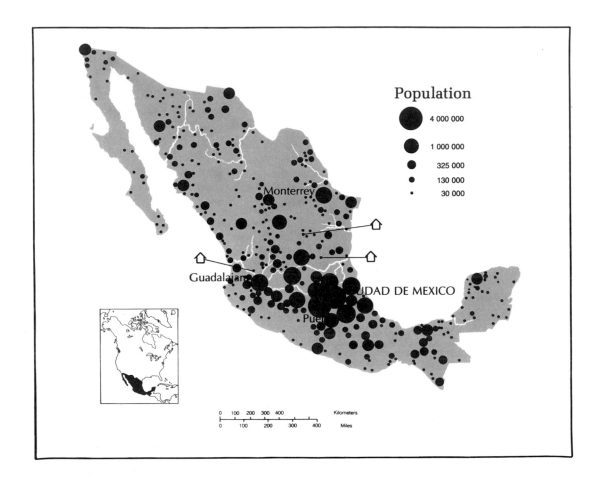

Population

- 4 000 000
- 1 000 000
- 325 000
- 130 000
- 30 000

Monterrey

Guadalajara

CIUDAD DE MEXICO

Pue

Kilometers
0 100 200 300 400

Miles
0 100 200 300 400

THE NAME: From the Indian tribe Mexica, meaning "nomadic" and "primitive people of the north"

THE PEOPLE: The Mexicans

GEOGRAPHY

Country of extraordinary physical variety
> Large central volcanic plateau rimmed by coastal lowlands enclosed by the eastern and western ranges of the Sierra Madre
> From a low desert plain in the north, the plateau rises to 2,600 m. (8,000 ft.) in the center
> Max. altitude: 5,569 m. (18,700 ft.) (Orizaba Peak)

Area: 1,972,547 sq. km. (761,604 sq. mi.)
Density: 40 pers./sq. km. (103 pers./sq. mi.) (1986)
Arable land: 13% (1987)
Forest: 23%
Climate: Varies with altitude: arid and semi-arid in the north, with extreme temperatures; humid tropical climate in the south; temperate in the central highlands.

CAPITAL: Mexico City, pop. 9,191,295 (1979 est.)

LANGUAGE: Spanish (official), Indian dialects

RELIGION
Majority Catholic

POPULATION: Total—79,000,000 (1985)
  Annual growth: 2.6% (2,054,000) (1980–85)
  Doubling time: 28 yrs.
  Urban: 70% (1985) (est. for year 2000: 77%)
  Rural: 30%

AGE GROUPS: (1980)
  19% less than 5 yrs.
  46% less than 15
  57% less than 20
  27% from 20 to 39
  12% from 40 to 59
  5% 60 yrs. and over

ETHNIC GROUPS
Mestizo: 60%
Indian: 30% (56 different groups)
White: 9%
Black: 1%

HISTORY
From 1500 B.C.: Olmec, Zapotec, Toltec civilizations
950–1300: Mayan civilization
1400–1500: Prominence of the Aztec civilization
1519: Aztecs conquered by Hernando Cortes
1810–21: Wars of independence
September 16, 1810: Independence
1845–48: War with the United States; Upper California and New Mexico ceded to the United States
1876–1910: Dictatorship of Porfirio Díaz
Foreign interests purchase almost three-quarters of Mexico's mineral resources
1910–17: Revolution, which cost over a million lives
1929: The National Revolutionary Party, the PRI, takes power

FAMILY
Marital status, for population 10 yrs. and older: (1978)
Single: 29%
Married: 52%
Consensually married: 10%
Widowed: 7%
Separated: 2.3%
Divorced: 0.7%
Female head of household: no data
Fertility rate: 4.3 (1985)
Births out of wedlock: no data
Teenage births: 16% (1980)
Contraception: 48% (1984)
Government's position on family planning: Views population as a fundamental aspect of development. Its official policy is to decrease population growth, chiefly by modifying fertility.

SOCIAL INDICATORS
Life expectancy: 66 yrs. (male: 64; female: 68) (1985)
Infant mortality: 50/1,000 births (1985)
Crude birth rate: 33/1,000 pop. (1985)
Crude death rate: 7/1,000
Health:
Access to health services: 45% (1980–83)
Births attended by trained health personnel: no data

HOUSING
Persons per household: 5.5 (1980)
Electricity: 25% without (1980)
Access to safe water: 74% (urban: 91%; rural: 40%) (1983)
Source of water: (1980)
Piped inside: 50%
Piped outside: 16%
Other: 34%
Toilet facilities: (1980)
Flush: 45%
Other: 48%
None: 7%
Building materials: (1980)
Concrete: 74%
Adobe: 19%
Other: 7%

EDUCATION
Literacy: 83% (male: 92%; female: 80%) (1980)
Gross enrollment ratio: (1984)
First level: 116% (completing in 1980–84: 66%)
Second: 55%
Third: 15%
Educational attainment, for population 25 yrs. +: (1980)
None: 38%
First level: incomplete: 32% (complete: 17%)
Second: entered: 6%
Third: 5%

ECONOMIC ACTIVITY
Economically active population: 33% (male: 48%; female: 18%) (1980)
Agriculture: 36% act. pop.; 7% of GDP
Mines: 8% act. pop.; 23% of GDP
Industry: 18% act. pop.; 15% of GDP
Services: 38% act. pop.; 55% of GDP
Per capita GNP: 2,080 U.S.$ (1985)
Population in absolute poverty: no data
National currency/per U.S.$: 256.87 pesos (1985)
Principal resources: Coffee, cotton, silver, petroleum

COMMUNICATIONS
Radio:
Transmitters: 872 (1983)
Receivers: 13,020,000—173/1,000 pop. (1983)
Television:
Transmitters: 405 (1983)
Receivers: 8,100,000—108/1,000 pop. (1983)

NICARAGUA

THE BRIONES FAMILY

Lucía Briones Pérez, age 32 (1)
Ligia María Briones Rodríguez, 14 (2)
Naraya Patricia Briones Rodríguez, 11 (3)
Arturo Alberto Briones Rodríguez, 7 (4)
Alba Nubia Vargas Briones (cousin), 17 (5)
Francisco Javier Vargas Briones (cousin), 16 (6)
Denis Vargas Briones (cousin), 15 (7)
Nelson Antonio Vargas Briones (cousin), 13 (absent from photo)
Edrulfo Iván Rodríguez (cousin), 14 months (8)

1 dog
3 ducks

ESTELÍ
November 12

The sun's first rays peek above the roof of the Briones family's little wooden house and awaken the colors of the flowers and fruit trees in the small interior garden. Lucía Briones turns on the radio, and eight children come from the house's two bedrooms to congregate in the kitchen and listen to the first news broadcast of the day. Estelí is a small rural town that lies at the base of the mountains where the country's civil war is being fought. The daily broadcasts have become a vital part of the family's existence. Lucía serves coffee and cake. The older children will prepare a real breakfast of tortillas and sour cream after she leaves for work.

6:45. Lucia reminds everyone of their chores. Dressed in jeans and a shirt to protect her from the chilly November morning, she leaves the house. Her daugher Patricia accompanies her as far as the end of the road, on her way to buy meat. She must get in line early, as the meat will all be sold by midday. Lucía's nephew Javier leaves as well. He is an electrical mechanic for the government transportation company. Like most of Nicaragua's young adults, he works during the day and attends school in the evening.

Lucía Briones has an unusually large household to manage by herself. She has adopted her four nieces and nephews whose parents were casualties of the war. She also cares for her sister's baby while the mother finishes her studies in biology in Cuba. The baby's father, an agricultural engineer and tobacco expert, is working in the North in the war zone.

For the past fifteen years, Lucía has worked for the national tobacco company. Until last year she rolled tobacco in the town factory, a tiring and monotonous job. Now she has been transferred to the company's day-care center and is in charge of the infants. The promotion brought her a much-needed wage increase. Left alone by her husband six years ago, Lucía has struggled to provide enough food for the children. Fortunately, another sister, who is a teacher in the northern part of the country, sends her money for clothes.

8:00. The younger children stay home until their afternoon classes. They have an impressive sense of responsibility and carry out their assigned daily tasks quietly. Patricia makes the beds, cleans the rooms, and wipes a cloth over the red earth tiles on the living-room floor. Then she sweeps the patio. In one corner of the garden, Nubia washes the diapers and baby clothes in a cement tub. In another corner, Ligia lights the fire to cook the black beans. Gas is scarce and to economize, long cooking jobs are done over a wood fire. Nelson and Denis then leave with a gas bottle; they will have to stand in line for at least three hours to exchange their ration card for this month's allotment.

Patricia grumbles a little this morning. It's her turn to look after her little cousin, Edrulfo Iván, when she could be preparing for her examination this afternoon. She'll get a chance when the baby naps later on in the morning.

10:30. Breakfast has been eaten, the baby is sleeping, and the house is silent. The children are concentrating on their studies. It is examination time and school ends in ten days. During a study break the children excitedly discuss their vacation, which in fact is three months of work harvesting coffee beans. All over Nicaragua students and teachers volunteer for the coffee harvest, the country's primary resource. Even Javier will go. His employer is required to give him leave. "The young people for the harvest, the adults for the defense of the nation," reads a popular political slogan. The Briones children feel strongly about helping their country.

Seventeen-year-old Nubia has been arguing with her aunt Lucía. Lucía relies on Nubia to look after the house and the baby while she is at work and doesn't want Nubia to go to the harvest. But Nubia looks forward to this summer's harvest, even though it is in an area where there is fighting between government forces and the Contra rebels. For her the harvest is also fun, a chance to be with and act like other children her age. It's an incongruous image. In a country torn by war, amid coffee fields protected by Sandinista soldiers, students and teachers harvest as people have harvested through all time, with enthusiasm and festivity.

Lucía worries about all of them despite the protection of the Sandinista army. She has the painful memory of the death of her fifteen-year-old son barely a year ago. "He said it was his duty to go and fight for his country," Lucía explains. She did not oppose his going, and he did not return. She also thinks of her children's father, who left the country during the revolution and has not been heard from since. Lucía wants to protect those who are left.

11:30. The girls close their books to prepare lunch. Nelson and Denis return with the gas. The boys are volunteers for the militia and contribute one day or night a week for civil defense—guarding bridges, schools, and other strategic points. Since the death of their brother and cousin, their adolescent zeal has been tempered, and they will wait until they're seventeen, when they will be drafted for their compulsory military service.

Ligia serves the meal: rice, beans, and a few pieces of boiled beef. After eating, the students shower, change, and head off to class, leaving Nubia behind for the afternoon. She and the baby will take a short nap, after which she will quickly iron all the family's clothes. Electricity is so expensive that even though they have a refrigerator, it stays unplugged.

4:00. Home from work, Lucía relaxes for a few minutes in the rocking chair watching her little nephew playing at her feet. She loves children but doesn't want any more. "My family has doubled in a short time," she says. "And I don't want any more men in my house. Things are fine as they are." Her mother arrives from the countryside, where she lives alone. Her plot of land is in the war zone; every other day she comes to Estelí to sell eggs, chickens, or vegetables and buy her ration of rice and sugar. Today she brings three ducks for the family to fatten for the New Year's celebration. She leaves to catch the bus home, and Lucía rises to prepare the evening meal of eggs, beans, and tortillas.

5:45. The streets of the town are swarming with students coming from and going to their classes. Finished with their dinner, Javier and Nubia search for their friends and join the crowd. The rest of the family sit at the table and converse. As night falls, the wooden house trembles and their voices are drowned out by army helicopters coming in to land at the military base, a mere two blocks away. Lucía gets up from the table to go to the yard. As she leaves the kitchen, she unscrews the light bulb and takes it with her to the outdoor socket. The bulb accompanies Lucía from room to room, leaving the rest of the house in darkness.

7:30. With dinner over, a few clothes washed, and the baby in his pajamas, Lucía resumes rocking in the chair with little Edrulfo Iván on her lap. Only half paying attention, she watches the television set, which is so old it leaves the viewer guessing at pictures. She rocks the child for a long, long time.

At the end of the
afternoon, the
streets of the small
rural town swarm
with students
coming from and
going to their
classes. Night
students are as
numerous as those
attending high
school during
the day

Lucía
has adopted
her sister's
orphans.
Conscious of the
work and financial
responsibility this
entails, each one
participates in his
own way to make
things easier
for her

NICARAGUA

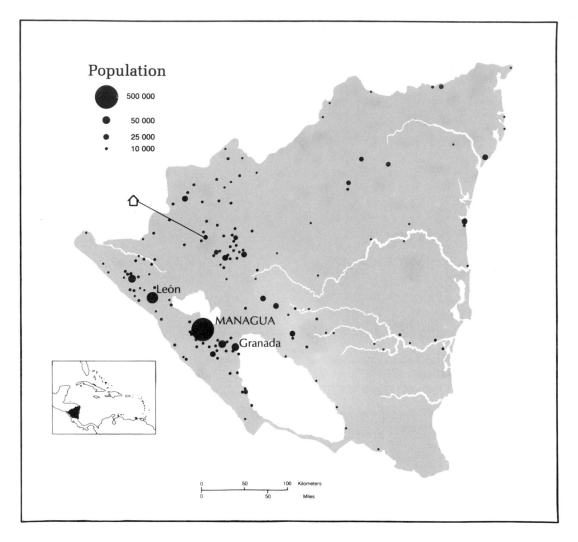

THE NAME: From Nahuatl, named after the cacique Indian chief Nicarao Cali

THE PEOPLE: The Nicaraguans

GEOGRAPHY
Pacific zone: coastal basins and valley near the coast with volcanic range of Las Maribias running parallel
Atlantic zone: swampy coastal lowlands (Mosquito Coast)
Central and northern zone: a sparsely populated wilderness of timbered plains and rolling hills
Max. altitude 2,107 m. (6,913 ft.) (Mogotón)
Area: 130,000 sq. km. (50,193 sq. mi.)
Density: 23 pers./sq. km. (59 pers./sq. mi.) (1986)
Arable land: 10% (1987)
Forest: 31%

Climate: Tropical, with a wet season from May to October; temperatures vary with altitude.

CAPITAL: Managua, pop. 608,020 (1979 est.)

LANGUAGE: Spanish (official)
On the Atlantic coast literacy programs are conducted in Miskito, Sumu, and English.

RELIGION
Majority Catholic

POPULATION:
Total: 3,200,000 (1985)
Annual growth: 3.3% (105,600) (1975–80)
Doubling time: 20 yrs.
Urban: 57% (1985) (est. for year 2000: 69%)
Rural: 43%

AGE GROUPS: (1980)

17% less than 5 yrs.	25% from 20 to 39
48% less than 15	11% from 40 to 59
59% less than 20	5% 60 yrs. and over

ETHNIC GROUPS
Ladino: 86% (17% white; 70% mixed)
Negro: 9%
Indian: 5%

HISTORY
Originally inhabited by Indians who migrated from
  South America
1502: Discovery by Christopher Columbus
1520s: Settlement established by Hernández de
  Córdoba
Administered as part of the Captaincy of Guatemala
1740–86: Britain claims Mosquito Coast as a
  protectorate
September 15, 1821: Independence
1821–39: Member of the United Provinces of
  Central America
1856–57: U.S. soldier William Walker seizes
  presidency but is ousted by alliance of Central
  American states
1912–33: Occupation by U.S. Marines
1934: Assassination of General Augusto César
  Sandino, whose guerrilla group had been defying
  the U.S. intervention since 1927
1936: Dictatorial Somoza regime
1962: Creation of FSLN, the Sandinista National
  Liberation Front
1979: Somoza flees the country; the Sandinistas
  take power

FAMILY
Marital status, for population 10 yrs. and older: (1971)

Single: 49%	Common-law: 17%
Married: 28%	Widowed: 2%

Female head of household: 26% (Managua: 60%) (1980
  est.)
Fertility rate: 5.7 (1983)
Births out of wedlock: no data
Teenage births: no data
Contraception: 9% (1984)
Government's position on family planning: Considers
  the current rates of fertility and natural increase to
  be satisfactory. Family-planning services are
  provided within public health services, and the
  government supports the activities of private
  organizations.

SOCIAL INDICATORS
Life expectancy: 62 yrs. (male: 60; female: 62) (1985)
Infant mortality: 69/1,000 births (1985)
Crude birth rate: 43/1,000 pop. (1985)
Crude death rate: 9/1,000
Health
  Access to health services: 80% (urban: 100%; rural:
    60%)
  Births attended by trained health personnel: 43%
    (1982)

HOUSING
Persons per household: 5.7 (1984)
Electricity: 59% without (1971)
Access to safe water: 53% (1983) (urban: 91%; rural:
  10%)
Source of water: (1971)
  Well: 31%
  River and other: 30%
  Piped inside: 28%
  Piped outside: 6%
  Public standpipe: 5%
Toilet facilities: (1971)
  Flush: 20%
  Other: 80% (latrine: urban: 64%; rural: 18%)
Building materials: (1980)
  The majority of houses are made of wood and
  adobe. In 1972 an earthquake destroyed a large
  part of Managua, including 90% of the shops, small
  industries, markets, and hospitals and the majority
  of schools and churches. In 1979 an important
  program of reconstruction was begun.

EDUCATION
Literacy: male: 87%; female: 87% (1982)
Gross enrollment ratio: (1984)
  First level: 99% (completing in 1980–1984:
    27%)
  Second: 43%
  Third: 11%
Educational attainment, for population 25 yrs. +:
  (1971)
  None: 54%
  First level: incomplete: 42%
  Since 1979, great efforts have been made in literacy
  and education. In 1982 there were more adults
  registered in educational programs than students at
  the secondary level.

ECONOMIC ACTIVITY
Economically active population: no data
Agriculture: 43% act. pop.; 21% of GDP
Mines: 2% act. pop.; 1% of GDP
Industry: 37% act. pop.; 48% of GDP
Services: 37% act. pop.; 48% of GDP
Per capita GNP: 770 U.S.$ (1985)
Population in absolute poverty: (1977–84)
  Urban: 21%
  Rural: 19%
National currency/per U.S.$: 26.50 cordobas (1985)
Principal resources: Coffee, cotton

COMMUNICATIONS
Radio:
  Transmitters: 87 (1979)
  Receivers: 850,000—278/1,000 pop. (1983)
Television:
  Transmitters: no data
  Receivers: 205,000—67/1,000 pop. (1983)

PANAMA

THE RÉREZ FAMILY

Gustavo Sáez Rérez, age 36 (1)
Reina Ildaura Rérez, 30 (2)
Diana Isela Sáez Rérez, 12 (3)
René, 10 (4)
Maciel Milagros, 4 (5)

15 chickens
1 dog
1 cat

LLANO LARGO
January 15

The sound of a truck engine starting up has awakened all the roosters in the village of Llano Largo. Their chorus erupts in every garden and echoes across the green shrubby coastal plain. Shifting the gears of his old truck, Gustavo Rérez sets off on the hundred-kilometer trip to the market at Aguadulce, where every Wednesday he sells his tomatoes and watermelons. The profits are the Rérez family's main source of income, and must cover the rent for the two hectares of land Gustavo farms, the wages for the young laborer he employs, and the cost of gasoline.

5:50. "What time is it?" Every day at this time twelve-year-old Diana's question comes bouncing over the half wall of cement blocks that separates the children's bedroom from their parents'. Her mother, Reina, stretches out her arm and pulls the string hanging from the corrugated-iron roof. The harsh light from the bulb drives Diana out of bed. After bathing with a pan of water and brushing her teeth at the tap in the dark courtyard, Diana takes her carefully hung school uniform out of the house's only cupboard.

A neighbor has seen the light at the Rérez place and immediately comes over to their stuccoed cement house to buy bread. Still in her nightdress, Reina gets up and serves her first customer. Over the past month her *tienda* (store) has become a new source of income for the family. The inventory has already doubled, and the living room has been completely taken over by shelves, a counter, and dozens of sacks and boxes. Reina would like to have her living room back, but adding a room now will cost them the same as it did to build the whole house thirteen years ago.

Diana finishes the oatmeal that her mother has made and, clutching her sandwich in her hand, joins her friend in the street. High school students and town workers alike head in the same direction to catch the bus to Los Santos. The women, balancing on their stiletto heels, walk carefully over the rocky ground. The farm laborers squeeze into trucks provided by the owners of the huge banana and sugar plantations nearby.

7:00. Ten-year-old René folds up his camp bed and leans it against the wall of the room he shares with Diana. Without uttering a word, he goes through the same motions as his sister. He won't really wake up until he gets to the village school and joins his friends. His silence goes unnoticed by his mother, who is rather shy and untalkative herself. Reina sweeps the house inside and outside, collecting a pile of papers and orange peels. The garbage will be burned at one end of the half acre of land she shares with her in-laws.

8:00. Little Maciel appears, yawning. She needs long nights of sleep to recover from her strenuous days. In a few minutes she will disappear and not return until sunset. Her mother never worries about Maciel's comings and goings. She has two grandfathers, two grandmothers, and dozens of uncles and aunts whom she visits each in turn. Bright and good-natured, Maciel is also tough and independent, and anyone bold enough to oppose her is rewarded with a monumental outburst of temper.

11:00. Reina spends the morning serving her neighbors, who come to buy a pound of rice, a stick of butter, or a can of tomato sauce. From time to time, wholesalers drive up in trucks to sell Reina more stock. "This product is imported directly from the United States, señora. It's excellent!" Reina allows herself to be persuaded.

At lunchtime, Reina searches the shelves, trying to vary the usual menu of rice and black beans. Finally she decides on one of the chickens scratching behind the house. The chase begins. Tommy, the dog, refuses to participate, as it's already much too hot to get excited about a chicken. From his prone position, the dog watches as Reina runs after the chicken with a stone in her hand and deftly knocks the bird unconscious.

1:00. School is out, and the store fills up with children who have come to spend their pocket money on candy or sherbet. Diana saves her pocket money by walking back from Los Santos, which takes a good hour. She arrives at the same time that Gustavo returns from the market. Behind the house in a thatched-roof shelter that serves as a kitchen, the chicken soup simmers on the open-fire adobe stove. Reina still uses the wood fire instead of her gas stove. It's more economical, and she thinks the food tastes better. Outside, the family takes advantage of the winter breeze; a scorching one by other people's standards. In a couple of months, it will be even more intolerable. Old people, like Reina and Gustavo's parents, prefer to live in their traditional adobe houses with tile roofs, which stay cool inside. Like most younger poeple, however, Gustavo prefers a corrugated-iron roof and cement blocks. "It's hotter," he admits, "but I'll never have to repair it." It's this decison that forces the family outside two to three hours a day when their house becomes like an oven. No need to hurry. There won't be any customers; everyone's staying in the shade.

4:00. Diana installs herself on the front porch, and puts her books and notebooks on top of the sewing-machine cabinet to do her homework. She is a good student, and her hard work earned her a scholarship to cover the first three years of high school. She is very proud of saving her parents the high cost of education, including registration, uniform, books, and fees. René is less studious and postpones the learning of the Ten Commandments in his catechism. Today he will go with his father to buy this week's cow. Every Thursday night, Gustavo and his laborer slaughter and bleed an animal in the yard, and then Reina cuts it up in the kitchen. The meat will be ready for sale by dawn. This is the third source of income

for the family. Gustavo and Reina are hard workers, and a well-matched couple. Although not outwardly affectionate and demonstrative, they have organized their life together well. They have used birth control to plan their family so that they will never want for anything. "My children eat their fill, are well dressed, and can go to school," states Reina proudly. "When I was little, it was rare to see people with shoes; today it's rare to see them going barefoot. There will be still more progress by the time my children have grown up."

5:00. The family relaxes on the porch as teenagers stop by to buy a Coca-Cola and chat. All the chairs and most of the steps are occupied and a lively discussion is underway. One of the high school students is worried about going to the university— afraid of going to the capital, to such a big city. The girls vie with one another as they discuss the men in their lives, Saturday night's dance, and Carnival, which is just around the corner. Gustavo is preoccupied with the details of the next *junta* (community cooperation to build an adobe house) and Sunday's cockfight. He has a vested interest, as two of his birds will be fighting. Reina passes her family plates of food. Balancing their dinner on their knees, they all praise the chicken with rice.

7:55. "The crickets are singing this evening," Gustavo observes with satisfaction. "That means that the night will be cool." Someone notes the time, and the patio suddenly empties. Television sets are switched on in every house. The last hour of the day is devoted to Lionella, a soap opera heroine. The Rérez family take their seats in their living room/store, where the TV set stands on a shelf. The children balance on sacks of rice and black beans and the parents take to their chairs for an hour of romantic drama that makes Reina cry and makes the rest of the family hungry. They eat oranges, passing the paring knife to each other in silence. The peels pile up for Reina to sweep away tomorrow.

The old people prefer to live in their traditional tile-roofed adobe houses, which stay cool in hot weather. Gustavo prefers corrugated iron and cement blocks: "It's hotter, but I'll never have to repair it," he says

Every Thursday night, Gustavo slaughters a cow in the yard. Reina is up all night butchering it on the kitchen table. The meat will be ready for sale at dawn

PANAMA

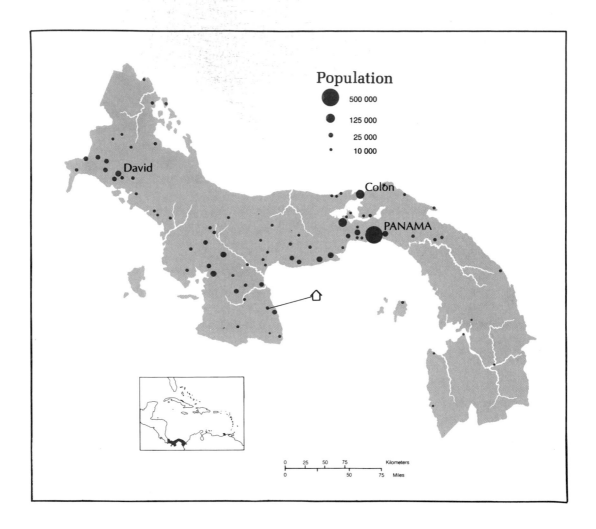

THE NAME: From Indian, meaning "abundance of fish"

THE PEOPLE: The Panamanians

GEOGRAPHY
Central mountain ranges bordered by coastal lowlands
Eastern regions covered by dense tropical forests
Max. altitude: 3,475 m. (11,401 ft.) (Barú volcano)
Area: 77,082 sq. km. (29,762 sq. mi.)
Density: 28 pers./sq. km. (72 pers./sq. mi.) (1986)
Arable land: 7% (1987)
Forest: 53%
Climate: Tropical, but tempered by sea breezes; little seasonal variation in temperatures; rainy season from April until December.

CAPITAL: Panama City, pop. 424,204 (1984 est.)

LANGUAGE: Spanish

RELIGION
Majority Catholic

POPULATION: Total—2,200,000 (1985)
Annual growth: 2.2% (48,400) (1980–85)
Doubling time: 32 yrs.
Urban: 52% (est. for year 2000: 67%)
Rural: 48%

AGE GROUPS: (1980)

12.9% less than 5 yrs.	28.8% from 20 to 39
39.1% less than 15	14.0% from 40 to 59
50.3% less than 20	6.7% 60 yrs. and over

ETHNIC GROUPS
Mestizo: 70% (mixed)
Antillean: 14% (blacks)
White: 9%
Indian: 7%

HISTORY
There may have been as many as 750,000 Indians when the Spanish arrived, but exploitation, disease, and murder decimated them
1501: Discovery by the Spanish
1821: Independence from Spain and union with Gran Colombia (a confederation consisting of Ecuador, Panama, Colombia, and Venezuela)
November 3, 1903: Breaks away from Colombia to grant the United States the right to control the Panama Canal in perpetuity
1914: Opening of the canal
1968: Coup under Colonel Omar Torrijos Herrera
1977: Panama Canal Treaty, giving jurisdiction to Panama and the responsibility of operation to the United States until 1999

FAMILY
Marital status, for population 15 yrs. and older: (1980)
Single: 28%
Married: 28%
Common-law: 28%
Widowed: 6%
Separated from husband or partner: 9%
Divorced: 1.2%
Female head of household: 21% (1980)
Fertility rate: 3.3 (1985)
Births out of wedlock: 71% (1980)
Teenage births: 21% (1981)
Contraception: 61% (1984)
Government's position on family planning: Considers the rate of population growth to be satisfactory and feels that there is no need for intervention.

SOCIAL INDICATORS
Life expectancy: 72 yrs. (male: 69; female: 73) (1985)
Infant mortality: 25/1,000 births (1985)
Crude birth rate: 27/1,000 pop. (1985)
Crude death rate: 5/1,000
Health:
Access to health services: 81% (1980–83)
Births attended by trained health personnel: 83% (rural: 65%) (1984)

HOUSING
Persons per household: 4.9 (1984)
Electricity: 35% without (1980)
Access to safe water: 62% (urban: 97%; rural: 26%) (1983)
Source of water: (1980)
Piped inside: 45%
Piped outside: 31%
Not piped: 25%
Toilet facilities: (1980)
Flush: 44%
Other: 44%
None: 12%
Building materials: (1980)

Concrete: 51%	Straw, cane, and other: 13%
Wood: 26%	Dirt floor: 21%
Adobe: 10%	

EDUCATION
Literacy: 86% (male: 86%; female: 85%) (1980)
Gross enrollment ratio: (1983–84)
First level: 105% (completing in 1980–84: 73%)
Second: 59%
Third: 25%
Educational attainment, for population 25 yrs. +: (1980)
None: 17%
First level: incomplete: 27% (complete: 23%)
Second: entered: 12%
Third: 8%

ECONOMIC ACTIVITY
Economically active population: 32% (male: 46%; female: 18%) (1980)
Agriculture: 26% act. pop.; 10% of GDP
Mines: 0% act. pop.; 0% of GDP
Industry: 18% act. pop.; 21% of GDP
Services: 56% act. pop.; 69% of GDP
Per capita GNP: 2,100 U.S.$ (1985)
Population in absolute poverty: (1977–84)
Urban: 21%
Rural: 30%
National currency/per U.S.$: 1.00 balboa (1985)
Principal resources: Bananas, sugar

COMMUNICATIONS
Radio:
Transmitters: 93 (1977)
Receivers: 335,000—160/1,000 pop. (1983)
Television:
Transmitters: 10 (1977)
Receivers: 255,000—122/1,000 pop. (1983)

The Caribbean

ANTIGUA and BARBUDA

THE ANTHONY FAMILY

Willmot Anthony, age 31 (1)
Charmaine Anthony, 24 (2)
Oniecia Anthony (Nixie), 9 (3)
Janiecia, 7 (4)

1 dog
2 sheep
6 chickens

JENNING VILLAGE
June 3

5:00. Willmot has been watching television for the past half hour. He is never able to sleep more than three or four hours a night. Now he would like some company and turns up the radio so loud that Charmaine has no choice but to get up. She goes straight into the kitchen, cleans her teeth in the sink, and makes coffee. Then while listening to the daily religious broadcasting, she begins preparing noodles, chicken wings, and dumplings for tomorrow's Sabbath meal. The Anthonys are part of a small group of Seventh-Day Adventists and on Saturdays are forbidden to work or even to cook. Janiecia wakes Nixie and they climb into their parents' bed. The cartoons are about to start.

6:30. In the small crowded family room, Charmaine pushes the chairs and table against the wall to clear a spot for her morning exercises; already a strong, large-framed woman, she doesn't want to gain more weight. After a fifteen-minute workout she goes into the shower. The plumbing was installed in 1982, but in spite of endless election promises of piped domestic water, their supply still comes from the communal tap, and they bathe using a saucepan. "Promises, promises," complains Willmot.

7:00. Willmot sweeps the ground around his four-room wooden house while chatting with Charmaine, who sits on the cement stoop braiding the girls' hair. She wraps their heads in scarves so that their hair will be flawless until the afternoon when it's time for school. Because of the shortage of schools on the island of Antigua, their classrooms are occupied by the secondary school in the morning. Leaving her girls munching pieces of bread, Charmaine goes to catch the bus. For the past two years she has worked as a domestic and has had to trust Janiecia and Nixie to fend for themselves in the morning. She is comforted by the knowledge that her husband's family live scattered around the small village.

After their mother has left, Nixie sets about doing the laundry while her sister washes the dishes, standing on a stool. These two young girls are just as competent at keeping house as any grown woman. They finish quickly so they will have time to play with their cousin.

8:00. Willmot sets off for St. John's, Antigua's capital, in search of a jack to lift up the floor of the house. The rains have damaged one of the beams, and it urgently needs replacing. Even if it rots wood, rain is always welcome. This year Antigua is again suffering from drought. When the rainy season arrives, however, it often brings nothing but devastation. The water streams over the hard rutted earth, hardly penetrating, and floods the flatlands. The houses have to be built on raised cinder blocks. Willmot's task will be easy for him, as he is a carpenter. His job, working for the government, gives him a regular salary and flexible working hours, so he can occasionally take time off to fill private contracts or, like today, do his own work.

11:15. Janiecia and Nixie hastily do their homework and walk to the store to buy bread for their lunch. Even though the sun keeps going behind the clouds, it is hot, and the girls make their way slowly through the dirt yards and small scrubby clearings, chatting and laughing together.

Always the little mother, Nixie prepares lunch for herself and for her sister. The knife is blunt and she impatiently struggles to cut the hard sausage for the sandwiches they wash down with a large glass of ginger beer. Then they have to put on clean dresses for school. Nixie is upset to find that the sole of her shoe is yet again hanging by a thread. She tries to repair it, borrowing her father's tools and attempting vainly to drive a nail into the plastic sole. Nixie dreams of having new shoes, but she won't ask for them; she knows that her parents will buy her a pair when they can.

12:30. Willmot arrives just in time to say goodbye to the girls. He had thought that the errand would take him an hour at most, but now he has lost the whole morning. He has a hasty lunch and starts on the repairs.

Willmot and Charmaine lived with Willmot's mother until Nixie was born, at which point they felt the need to get married and be independent. They built a wooden bungalow with their own hands and soon wanted to expand. Willmot went to work in the Virgin Islands, where wages are higher. In a couple of years, they were able to add a concrete kitchen, a bathroom, and another bedroom. Now they just have to save for a bed, and the girls can each have their own room.

When Willmot was a child, Antigua was still a British colony and the land on which the house now stands was a sugarcane field. Since independence, the great plantations have gradually disappeared. Antigua's main source of income now is the tourists who come for its white-sand beaches and turquoise sea. Once the plantations were abandoned, the fields were occupied by squatters. When the government finally agreed to sell the land, Willmot became the owner of the hundred square meters surrounding his house.

2:00. The countryside is silent except for the sound of Willmot's hammer—and his voice. He has put on a country-and-western record, and since he knows the words by heart, he sings along as he works. When Charmaine returns in the late afternoon, she changes from her dress into shorts and

seems more at ease. Now she will not leave her kitchen for several hours. This is where she loves to be. She likes to cook, and it is the most spacious room in the house. In addition, she can survey her neighbors from the window over the sink.

4:30. Home from school, Nixie and Janiecia obey their mother's order to change their clothes and fetch two or three buckets of water. In exchange, they're allowed to watch television until dinnertime.

6:30. Tonight Willmot will be responsible for putting his daughters to bed. Charmaine is going to a rehearsal at church. She has the leading role in a play which will be performed at the next church gathering. The social lives of the island's families often revolve around the congregation that they belong to, and Charmaine looks forward to spending two weeks this summer on a holiday retreat with other women in her church group. "Off you go." Willmot shoos his daughters off the bed and settles down to watch a football game on television.

10:30. When Charmaine returns, Willmot hasn't moved. He has just switched from the football game to a movie. The cable carries seven American channels, so Willmot can, if he wants, watch television twenty-four hours a day. Charmaine lies down beside him. Not much of a viewer herself, she snuggles against her husband and falls asleep.

When Willmot was a child, Antigua was still a British colony and the land on which the house now stands was a sugarcane field. The main source of income now is the tourists who come for the white-sand beaches and the turquoise sea

The girls go to school only in the afternoon. Because of the shortage of schools on the island, their classrooms are occupied by the secondary school in the morning

ANTIGUA and BARBUDA

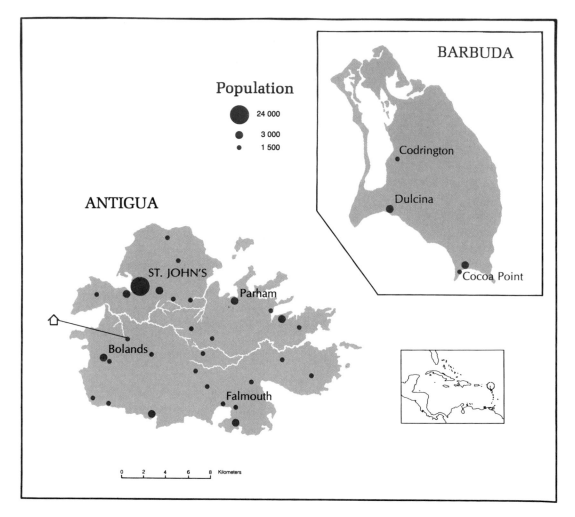

THE NAME
Antigua: From Santa María la Antigua, a church in Seville, Spain

Barbuda: From the Spanish tree called "the bearded fig"

THE PEOPLE: Antiguans and Barbudans

GEOGRAPHY
Antigua: composed of volcanic rock, coral, and limestone; renowned for its 365 sandy beaches
  Max. altitude: 405 m. (1,330 ft.) (Boggy Peak)

Barbuda: flat coral island with a large lagoon on one side
  Max. altitude: 304 m. (1,000 ft.) (Rodunda)

Area:
  Antigua: 280 sq. km. (108 sq. mi.)
  Barbuda: 160 sq. km. (62 sq. mi.)

Density: 176 pers./sq. km. (456 pers./sq. mi.) (1986)

Arable land: 18% (1987)

Forest: 16%

Climate: Tropical, but drier than most West Indies islands; the hot season is from May to November, when rainfall is greater.

CAPITAL: St. John's, pop. 36,000 (1980)

LANGUAGE: English; English patois is widely used.

RELIGION: (1970)
  Anglican: 44%
  Other Protestant: 30%
  Moravian: 16%
  Catholic: 10%

POPULATION: Total—80,000 (1985)
  Annual growth: 1.3% (1,040) (1980–85)
  Doubling time: 71 yrs.
  Urban: 45% (1980 est.)
  Rural: 55%

AGE GROUPS: (1970)

16% less than 5 yrs.	20% from 20 to 39
47% less than 15	15% from 40 to 59
58% less than 20	7% 60 yrs. and over

ETHNIC GROUPS
Black: 95%
Mixed: 3.5%
White: 1.5%

HISTORY
Antigua
1493: Discovery by Christopher Columbus
1628: British colonization
November 1, 1981: Independence within the
   Commonwealth
Barbuda:
1628: British colonization
1680: Granted to the Codrington family; originally
   intended as a slave-breeding farm, but never
   became one
1860: Annexed to Antigua

FAMILY
Marital status, for population 15 yrs. and older: (1982)
   Married: 28%
   Common-law: 13%
   Visiting union: 45%
   Not in union: 27%
Female head of household: no data
Fertility rate: 2.5 (1984)
Births out of wedlock: 81% (1983)
Teenage births: 28% (1982)
Contraception: no data
Government's position on family planning: Has created
   a pilot family-planning program operated on the
   concept of community-based distribution of
   contraceptives.

SOCIAL INDICATORS
Life expectancy: 73 yrs. (male, female: no data) (1985)
Infant mortality: 30/1,000 births (1985)
Crude birth rate: 15/1,000 pop. (1980–85)
Crude death rate: 5/1,000
Health:
   Access to health services: no data
   Births attended by trained health personnel: 83%
   (1982)

HOUSING
Persons per household: 3 (1980)
Electricity: Majority has access.
Source of water: (1970)
   Piped: 17%
   Public standpipe: 64%
   Other: 19%
Toilet facilities: (1970)
   Flush: 17%
   Other: 61%
Building materials: (1970)
   Wood: 76%
   Concrete: 17%
   Other: 7%

EDUCATION
Literacy: 89% (male: 90%; female: 88%) (1982)
Gross enrollment ratio: (1982)
   Primary school: 100%
   Most students stay in school until age 16, after
      which there is a large dropout rate.
Educational attainment, for all ages: (1970)
   None: 15%
   First level: incomplete: 79%
   Second: entered: 5%
   Third: 1%

ECONOMIC ACTIVITY
Economically active population: 50% (male: 26%;
   female: 35%) (1975)
Agriculture: 9% act. pop.; GDP: no data
Industry: 20% act. pop.
Services: 71% act. pop.
Per capita GNP: 2,020 U.S.$ (1985)
Population in absolute poverty: no data
National currency/per U.S.$: 2.70 East Caribbean
   dollars (1985)
Principal resource: Tourism

COMMUNICATIONS
Radio:
   Transmitters: 5 (1979)
   Receivers: 20,000—256/1,000 pop. (1983)
Television:
   Transmitters: no data
   Receivers: 19,000—244/1,000 pop. (1983)

THE BAHAMAS

THE MAJOR FAMILY

Peter Major, age 32 (1)
Arlene Major, 32 (2)
Tracey Major, 8 (3)
Peter Jr. (P.J.), 5 (4)
Ryan, 2 (5)

1 dog

NASSAU
August 2

7:00. It's a hot, muggy August morning in Nassau, and in the Majors' small residential neighborhood most people are still asleep inside their cool cement bungalows. The streets are empty and peaceful. The children are on summer vacation, and as it is the island's slow season for tourism, many Bahamians take this time to travel.

8:30. Like a sleepwalker, Peter Major emerges from his bedroom and walks to the kitchen, barely noticing his three children, who have been sprawled in front of the TV since seven o'clock. As if on automatic pilot, Peter fixes his coffee and heads for the shower in his own bathroom. He didn't get home until dawn and hopes the stream of water will rejuvenate him enough to face the day's work. Peter has been working his way up in hotel management, and this year he has been promoted to director of personnel. Last night was Peter's night out. An articulate and sociable man, Peter gets along extremely well with people, including hotel guests, who often become family friends.

Arlene wakes Ryan, who grumbles a little. He likes to take life easy. This morning, however, he has to learn to bow to the dictates of bureaucracy; he needs a passport for his first trip abroad, a week at Disney World with his mother, Aunt Hazella, Aunt Maggy, his brother, his sister, and his cousins. Arlene likes to travel, and Florida is on the doorstep for Bahamians, who go there on vacation, to go to school. or simply to go shopping.

After dropping her husband off at work and Tracey and P.J. with her mother-in-law, Arlene drives to the passport office. It's already jammed. Part of the crowd is standing in line; there are children running all over the place. The service is slow, but fortunately Arlene has lots of time. Like her children, she is on vacation. She works as a high school counselor and teaches courses in English literature at a college in Nassau. She is a friendly, compassionate woman, and students often

show up at the house just to visit her, even during the summer.

2:00. Arlene picks up the two older children from her mother-in-law, who served them lunch in her absence. No sooner are they home than Tracey puts a Disney movie on the VCR. It must be the tenth time they've seen it, but the children love all the twists in the story and laugh in anticipation of the best parts.

Arlene has to call her sister Maggy in Freeport to arrange the final details of the trip. This could take her all afternoon. They have no phone, and she has to drive to her sister-in-law's and hope that she can get a fast connection. Telephone service on the island is awful. The Majors have been waiting for a telephone ever since they moved into their house four years ago. The answer is invariably that there are no lines available yet. And when one has a phone, the service is not much better. It can take hours to call from Nassau to Freeport, and often it is easier to call overseas than to get through to another island in the chain.

3:30. The call did take a while, long enough for Hazella to set Arlene's hair, and now Arlene wonders whether she should stop back at the house before going shopping. She tells herself not to worry. Ryan always has a long siesta, Tracey is a responsible girl, and P.J. is doubtless in front of the television.

Tracey gets up to help her mother carry six large grocery bags in from the car. Once again the car's trunk won't close, and Arlene sighs impatiently. The old Mustang is falling to pieces, and Arlene hopes that this year they will be able to trade it in for a Volvo. She is the one who uses the car the most. All year long she acts as chauffeur for her own children and some others in the neighborhood who go to the same private school. Public transportation is poor in the area, and a car is an absolute necessity for shopping. Mother and daughter put the groceries away in the cupboards, the refrigerator, and the freezer. Arlene then starts straightening up with a decided lack of enthusiasm. She would rather be packing than cleaning. She and Peter have been saving for years to have their own house built, and this is the year! They have bought the lot, and the house will soon be finished. While tidying up Ryan's drawer, Arlene sorts through his baby clothes. He was an accident, and the couple won't have any more children. Arlene will take the baby clothes to a young student who has just had a baby. Arlene gets upset every time she hears of another girl who must leave school. Despite all the government's efforts to encourage young people to go to school and prepare for their future, there are still too many teenage pregnancies.

Ryan pulls up a chair so he can look out the window, his favorite spot to stand with his pet poodle and daydream. But this afternoon it's raining, as it has every day for the past two weeks. The washing is still damp after two days on the line. Arlene will have to take the clothes to the laundromat to get them dry, as she does all through the rainy season.

6:00. The rain has stopped. Arlene attempts to convince her children that some fresh air would do them good, but they insist on staying glued to the television while she goes to pick Peter up from work. The drive takes longer than usual. Arlene has to take several detours to avoid construction on the highway. The old British colonial capital is being given a facelift before playing host to the Commonwealth heads of government. Arlene enters the lobby of the hotel and finds her husband in animated conversation with one of the guests. Peter introduces Arlene and tells her they have just been invited to the States for a visit. This happens often to the Majors. They recently spent two weeks in Canada.

7:00. Tonight the children will sleep over at Aunt Hazella's. With their large families, the Majors have no difficulty finding babysitters. Arlene takes the curlers out of her hair. Once a week, Peter takes his wife out. Often they go out with friends, but this evening there's just the two of them. Peter has decided to eat dinner at the hotel where he works. The food is excellent, and once again they succumb to the temptation of two Bahamian specialties—conch salad and lobster tail. Afterward, Arlene and Peter leave for one of Paradise Island's discotheques. After a few dances, Peter goes to greet a friend but never takes his eyes off his wife. Woe betide anyone so bold as to ask her to dance. Arlene smiles indulgently at her husband's possessiveness.

2:30. The couple arrive home exhausted but relaxed. The heat in the house is unbearable, and they immediately open the windows, which they had shut as a security precaution. Their poodle wouldn't be much use in keeping burglars away.

Peter has promised that their new house will have ceiling fans everywhere and air conditioning in the bedrooms

It must be the tenth time P.J. has seen this children's movie, but he laughs delightedly in anticipation of the best parts

THE BAHAMAS

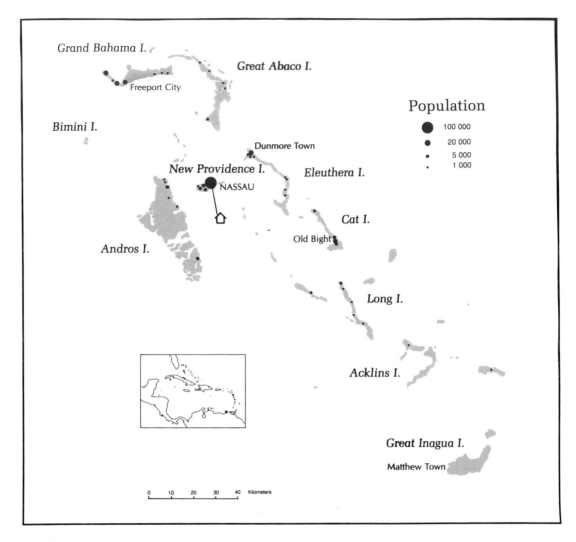

THE NAME: From Spanish *bajamar*, meaning "shallow water"

THE PEOPLE: The Bahamians

GEOGRAPHY
   Archipelago of 700 islands and more than 2,000 cays and barren rock formations
Area: 13,939 sq. km. (5,382 sq. mi.) (700 islands)
Density: 17 pers./sq. km. (43 pers./sq. mi.) (1986)
Arable land: 1% (1987)
Forest: 23%
Climate: Subtropical: winters are mild and summers warm. Rainfall varies across the islands.

CAPITAL: Nassau (on New Providence Island), pop. 135,437 (metropolitan area) (1980)

LANGUAGE: English

RELIGION
   Baptist: 29%
   Anglican: 23%
   Catholic: 23%
   Other: 25%

POPULATION: Total—200,000 (1985)
   Annual growth: 2% (4,000) (1980–84)
   Doubling time: 39 yrs.
   Urban: 58%
   Rural: 42%

AGE GROUPS: (1980)
   14% less than 5 yrs.   29% from 20 to 39
   38% less than 15   15% from 40 to 59
   50% less than 20   6% 60 yrs. and over

ETHNIC GROUPS
Black: 80%
Whites and persons of mixed descent: 20%

HISTORY
Originally inhabited by Arawak Indians (the Lucayans)
1492: First landing of Christopher Columbus on the island of San Salvador
1629: British possession of islands; no settlements
1659: Settlement on New Providence
1717: Becomes Crown Colony
1782–83: Spanish rule
1834: Abolition of slavery
July 10, 1973: Independence

FAMILY
Marital status: (1980)
Single: 68%
Married: 22%
Common-law: 5%
Widowed: 3%
Separated: 3%
Divorced: 0.5%
Female head of household: 35% (1980)
Fertility rate: 2.5 (1980–85)
Births out of wedlock: 61% (1982)
Teenage births: 22% (1978)
Contraception: no data
Government's position on family planning: Considers the rates of fertility and natural increase to be too high. The current policy seeks to reduce the population growth rate.

SOCIAL INDICATORS
Life expectancy: 70 yrs. (male, female: no data) (1980)
Infant mortality: 23/1,000 births (1985)
Crude birth rate: 25.1/1,000 pop. (1981)
Crude death rate: 5.4/1,000
Health:
Access to health services: no data
Births attended by trained health personnel: 99% (1984)

HOUSING
Persons per household: no data
Electricity: 22% without (1980)
Access to safe water: no data
Source of water: (1980)
Piped inside: 60%
Piped outside: 4%
Not piped: 13%
Toilet facilities: (1980)

Flush: 63%	Other: 7%
Pit: 28%	None: 2%

Building materials: (1980)
Concrete: 55%
Wood: 32%
Other: 13%

EDUCATION
Literacy: 90% (male: 91%; female: 90%)
Gross enrollment ratio: (1984)
First level: 62%
Second: 37%
Third: no data
Educational attainment: no data

ECONOMIC ACTIVITY
Economically active population: 42% (male: 47%; female: 36%) (1980)
Agriculture: 9% act. pop.; 8% of GDP
Mines: 0% act. pop.; 0% of GDP
Industry: 14% act. pop.; 12% of GDP
Services: 77% act. pop.; 80% of GDP
Per capita GNP: 7,070 U.S.$ (1985)
Population in absolute poverty: no data
National currency/per U.S.$: 1.00 dollar (1985)
Principal resource: Tourism

COMMUNICATIONS
Radio:
Transmitters: 5 (1979)
Receivers: 117,000—527/1,000 pop. (1983)
Television:
Transmitters: no data
Receivers: 36,000—162/1,000 pop. (1983)

BARBADOS

THE WILLIAMS FAMILY

Vincent Braithwaite, 52 (1)
Dorie Williams, 27 (2)
Richard Braithwaite, 9 (3)
Debbie Williams, 7 (4)
Dwayne Williams, 5 (5)
Shawn Williams, 3 (6)

ST. MICHAEL
April 20

5:30. Somewhere in St. Michael a cock crows, a reminder that this neighborhood of bungalows and tiny yards was once a peaceful village. Now houses have sprung up between the villages and the capital of Bridgetown, making it seem like a single town.

In the yellow wooden house at the end of Palm Tree Place, Shawn and Dwayne climb into their mother's bed, impatient to start the day. Dorie is less enthusiastic; for her it's another day of work as a salesclerk in the photography section of a department store downtown. The first thing Dorie does is to take the two boys to their great-aunt's house. As she has done every day during this Easter vacation, Auntie takes the boys with her to the beach, where she meets her friends. In a few hours the beach will be overrun by the thousands of tourists who flock to the island and its marvelous stretches of white sand. The locals, "Bajans," as they're called, use the early-morning hours when their beaches are deserted to exercise or go for a peaceful walk alone. Auntie goes in the water up to her waist and joins the circle of old people chatting as they enjoy the cool sea water on their bodies. Shawn and Dwayne bury themselves in the sand, start to build a sand castle, then play in the waves.

6:30. Dorie takes a cold shower, puts on her makeup and a pretty dress, and pours herself a cup of coffee. Her father, Vincent, is already busy with one of his Saturday do-it-yourself projects, repairing a burner on the stove. Her little brother, Richard, wakes and joins them for a minute. Dorie never sees much of him. This morning he will disappear to play with cousins his own age.

Dorie spent her childhood in this house, with her parents and five brothers. At that time it was very small and typically "Bajan," like the neighbors' houses. Thanks to his regular salary as a civil servant, Vincent has little by little been able to make improvements. First he added a cinder-block

kitchen at the rear of the house; this contains a sink, cupboards, and a table large enough for the whole family to gather round. Then he installed a bathroom to replace the outhouse in the yard. Several years later, he had saved enough to transform the interior of the little house. Four rooms were created and concrete walls replaced the wooden ones. Finally, fifteen years after the project began, Vincent installed new wood siding. Since the house is less than three meters from the street, wood is the only material allowed by law. The little house with the gabled roof has become an attractive bungalow with a formal dining room and a living room, where Granddaddy keeps his piano.

7:30. Now it's time for Dorie to catch the bus. Today she works only half a day. Before she leaves, she politely asks her father to return the bottles piling up on the back stoop. Vincent, an affable but proud man with a great sense of dignity, deigns to comply with his daughter's request.

Dorie has been the mistress of the house since their mother's departure. Vincent's wife left with three of their sons to help subsidize their studies in the United States. She works there as a nurse. At the time, Dorie's husband, David, was also working abroad. After several years, he returned, but Dorie still could not rely on his financial and emotional support and decided to stay with her father and little brother Richard. David went back to live with his mother. Their daughter, Debbie, is visiting there right now. She enjoys being with her father. Dorie was brought up to value marriage and the family, and she regrets that she cannot provide the same environment for her own children.

8:30. Auntie brings the children home and heads off to town in high spirits to do her shopping, leaving Granddaddy to take over the babysitting. The children play outside with the neighbors' two daughters, while Vincent cleans up the yard, picking up windblown papers and coconuts that have fallen from the trees. Then he collects the bottles.

The children are not allowed to play in the house when Vincent is around. He likes a tidy, quiet house. But they do have the porch and the street, where there is little traffic. The four children have difficulty agreeing on a game, but they know better than to shout. Otherwise the sleeping mother of the two little girls is likely to get angry, and that would certainly lead to a spanking for the girls. She works nights and doesn't like to be disturbed.

10:30. Granddaddy leaves for the government printing office. He does not normally work on weekends, but he has to finish a document before Monday. Vincent says goodbye to his grandsons and reminds them to be good and stay out of the house. The neighbors' girls are seven and eight and will be responsible for them. They will wake their mother if need be. Shawn and Dwayne are perfectly content with this. They love having older playmates as babysitters.

1:30. Dorie arrives home with a net bag full of groceries. She sets about preparing the traditional weekend midday meal of *coucou*, a gumbo of fine cornmeal and okra, served with salt fish. Finally alone inside, Shawn tries to give his mother a hard time. But Dorie is in too good a mood and is all patience now that she can look forward to a day and a half off from work.

The whole family sits down to Dorie's delicious dinner, to which Vincent pays appropriate compliments. His daughter is as good a cook as his wife. After lunch the boys go into their bedroom to watch TV.

4:30. Granddaddy is dressed in his Sunday best. For the past half hour he has been waiting for a friend to drive him to church, where the choir he sings in has been invited to perform at a Methodist wedding. "How can someone make a man wait when he's all dressed up!" he grumbles, loosening his tie in the fierce heat. Singing is Vincent's pas-

sion; every day he has either rehearsal or a mass to sing.

Saturday afternoon is Dorie's only time for leisure during the entire week. Tomorrow, she must do the laundry and the housework. Now she stretches out on the bed with the boys to watch TV. Auntie drops in for her daily visit, and they all move even closer together to give her some room. The program is an American thriller, but not thrilling enough to keep Shawn awake. He falls asleep in the crook of his mother's arm.

7:00. Vincent, back from church, gratefully sheds his shirt and tie. He showers, puts on some cologne, and dresses, island style, in a light pair of slacks and a cotton shirt. He declares, to nobody in particular, "I'm going out." Vincent is a great socializer, and Dorie never questions her father's comings and goings. Tonight, she turns down the invitation of a friend to go disco dancing. Dorie prefers to relax at home.

7:30. Debbie returns, driven home by her father. Dorie offers her husband some leftovers from lunch; she knows how much he enjoys her cooking. And what could be a better ending to the evening than a family game of dominoes. Shawn is too young to play with them; he gets bored and tries every trick he knows to distract the players. His mother reminds him at least a dozen times of the existence of the leather belt hanging behind the door, but Shawn's charm saves him from a spanking.

9:30. David has gone. Dorie is propped up like a pasha on a pile of pillows watching a movie on television. One after the other, the children fall asleep around her. Suddenly a wave of music emanates from the living room, drowning out the television actors' voices. Granddaddy and three comrades from the choir have gathered around the piano, as they often do in the evening. Dorie covers the children with a light sheet and goes off to her room. She falls asleep, lulled, as she has been throughout her childhood, by the deep voices singing gospel songs in perfect harmony.

The house was very small and typically "Bajan," like the neighbors' houses. Its transformation into an attractive middle-class bungalow took fifteen years' savings

A neighbor, whose little house is rather cramped, often visits Dorie. She comes over to do the laundry. Her two daughters regularly share the family meal

BARBADOS

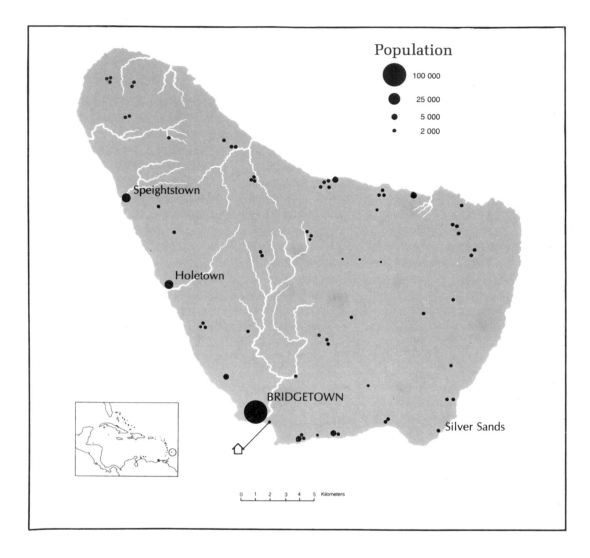

Population

● 100 000

● 25 000

• 5 000

· 2 000

Speightstown

Holetown

BRIDGETOWN

Silver Sands

0 1 2 3 4 5 Kilometers

THE NAME: From the Spanish tree called "the bearded fig"

THE PEOPLE: The Barbadians (or Badjans)

GEOGRAPHY
Flat lowlands rising from the west coast in a series of terraces to a ridge in the center, encircled by coral reefs
Max. altitude: 337 m. (1,115 ft.) (Mt. Hillaby)
Area: 430 sq. km. (166 sq. mi.)
Density: 581 pers./sq. km. (1,506 pers./sq. mi.) (1986)
Arable land: 77% (1987)
Forest: 0%

Climate: Subtropical, with a rainy season from June to November.

CAPITAL: Bridgetown, pop. 7,466 (1980)

LANGUAGE: English

RELIGION: (1980)
Anglican: 40%
Pentecostal: 8%
Methodist: 7%
Catholic: 4%
Other Protestant: 22%
None or not stated: 20%

POPULATION: Total—253,000 (1985)
  Annual growth: 0.3% (759) (1980–85)
  Doubling time: 78 yrs.
  Urban: 42% (est. for year 2000: 55%)
  Rural: 58%

AGE GROUPS: (1980)
  9% less than 5 yrs.
  28% less than 15
  41% less than 20
  30% from 20 to 39
  15% from 40 to 59
  14% 60 yrs. and over

ETHNIC GROUPS: (1980)
  Black: 92%
  White: 3%
  Mixed: 3%

HISTORY
  Originally inhabited by Arawak Indians
  1518: Spanish landed; no settlement
  1627: British colonization
  1834: Abolition of slavery
  1958–65: Part of the West Indies Federation
  November 30, 1966: Independence within the
    Commonwealth

FAMILY
Marital status, for population 14 yrs. and older: (1980)
  Never married: 56%
  Married: 33%
  Widowed: 8%
  Divorced or legally separated: 2%
Female head of household: 45% (1980)
Fertility rate: 1.9 (1980–85)
Births out of wedlock: 74% (1974)
Teenage births: 25% (1978)
Contraception: 47% (1980)
Government's position on family planning: Continues
  to give its steady support to population control
  activities, in an effort to lower the rate of
  population growth and thereby enhance
  socioeconomic development.

SOCIAL INDICATORS
Life expectancy: 73 yrs. (male: 70; female: 76) (1985)
Infant mortality: 11/1,000 births (1985)
Crude birth rate: 18/1,000 pop. (1985)
Crude death rate: 9/1,000
Health:
  Access to health services: no data
  Births attended by trained health personnel:
    98% (1984)

HOUSING
Persons per household: 3.63 (1980)
Electricity: 17% without (1980)
Access to safe water: 100% (1984)
Source of water: (1980)
  Piped inside: 61%
  Piped outside: 21%
  Public standpipe: 10%
  Other and none: 8%
Toilet facilities: (1980)
  Flush: 44%
  Pit: 52%
  Other: 4%
Building materials: (1980)
  Wood: 57%
  Concrete: 26%
  Mixture of wood and concrete: 12%

EDUCATION
Literacy: 99% (male: 99%; female: 99%) (1970)
Gross enrollment ratio: (1984)
  First level: 110%
  Second: 93%
  Third: 19%
Educational attainment, for population 25 yrs. +:
  (1980)
  None: 1%
  First level: incomplete: 64%
  Second: entered: 33%
  Third: 3%

ECONOMIC ACTIVITY
Economically active population: 46% (male: 52%;
  female: 40%) (1983)
Agriculture: 16% act. pop.; 18% of GDP
Mines: 3% act. pop.; 2% of GDP
Industry: 19% act. pop.; 20% of GDP
Service: 62% act. pop.; 60% of GDP
Per capita GNP: 4,630 U.S.$ (1985)
National currency/per U.S.$: 2.01 Barbados dollars
  (1985)
Population in absolute poverty: (1977)
  Urban: 23%
  Rural: 23%
Principal resource: Tourism

COMMUNICATIONS
Radio:
  Transmitters: 1 (1977)
  Receivers: 191,000—758/1,000 pop. (1983)
Television:
  Transmitters: 2 (1977)
  Receivers: 55,000—218/1,000 pop. (1983)

CUBA

THE FONSECA FAMILY

Juan Fonseca Molina, age 71 (1)
Dolores Romero Hernández (Lolita), 56 (2)
Héctor Péres González, 42 (3)
Elizabeth Fonseca Romero (Betty), 31 (4)
Yamila Rodríguez Fonseca, 14 (5)

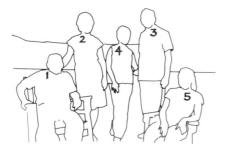

HOLGUIN
January 22

8:00. On Saturdays, Yamila gets to stay in bed until eight o'clock, a real treat considering that she's usually up at six. Outside her room she hears her grandparents' muted conversation. Juan is ready for his daily outing to the peasants' free market.° He says the walk keeps the circulation going in his old legs, but he especially likes meeting other grandfathers who, like him, are still able to make themselves useful. Today, Lolita is counting on him to unearth some country onions that she can't find in the government supermarket.

Now Yamila hears her stepfather, Héctor, telling Lolita to keep a close eye on his wife. He leaves the tiny apartment and won't return until tomorrow morning. Héctor has worked at the Holguin Polytechnic Institute for the past seventeen years; he is now deputy director. This evening the Institute has organized a concert for live-in students who come from Cuba's other provinces and from abroad to study. It is Héctor's turn to monitor the activities.

Betty is supposed to stay in bed if she wants to be sure of not losing the baby she is carrying. Her two previous abortions have increased her chances of a miscarriage. This morning, despite her husband's concern, nothing is going to stop her from taking her examination on the history of the workers' movement. Like most Cubans, Betty is an eternal student and is determined to get her diploma in educational psychology before the baby arrives in July. Since her divorce, immediately after Yamila's birth, she has channeled all her energies into her teaching career and her studies. After eleven years of living alone and five years of adult education, she met Héctor, a middle-aged bachelor, and remarried. At first she was reluctant to keep their baby, but Héctor's desire and her love for him prevailed.

Betty doesn't like being so helpless and having her mother serve her coffee and rolls in bed. But Lolita is the most willing of nurses and now fills the bucket of warm water for her daughter's bath.

° Since the time of this writing, the government has closed down the peasants' market because of fraudulent practices.

For the past week the pressure has been too low for the residents on the top floor to use the shower. Bathed and dressed, Betty walks down three flights of cement stairs while Lolita watches her every step from the landing above. To be on the safe side, she takes a taxi. On the way, she passes the modern, well-kept day-care center where she has already registered her unborn child. From six weeks to six years, the baby will be cared for by day-care workers and teachers at the government's expense. "I'll be able to work without worrying," Betty says. "My father will pick the baby up after school, as he did for Yamila. That way they will become good friends too."

9:00. After breakfast, still in her nightgown, Yamila goes out on the balcony and sneaks a glance at an apartment window across the way. Today she's determined to talk to the boy who lives there. She's completely infatuated. The young man is already in the complex's courtyard, where college students hang out on weekends and listen to salsa music. The music is playing full blast as the boys practice for the next dance. Lolita joins her granddaughter on the balcony. "Young people nowadays think of nothing but having a good time," Lolita says, remembering that there was not much time for leisure when she was young. Her eyes follow the little children as they chase each other laughing through the trenches that will become the foundation of a fallout shelter being built by the community on "Defense Sunday" (every fourth Sunday). Each week, everyone participates in projects organized by the CDR, the Committee for the Defense of the Revolution. Every building has its own CDR, headed by a chairman and a vice-chairman who are responsible for planning and for members' participation in its activities. This morning there is a blood-donor clinic, and the truck is already waiting for the donors.

Back in her room, Yamila arranges her dolls on her brightly colored bedspread and opens her wooden chiffonier to choose today's clothes. She prefers the foreign look. "I'm constantly making her pretty little dresses, and she always wears this old T-shirt and shorts that come from I don't know where," Lolita complains.

Before graduating from primary school, Yamila, like all students, will have to put in the statutory thirty days' work in the countryside this summer. Next year, when she attends high school, she has a choice. Either she can board in the countryside, where the high schools are located, dividing her time between studying and working in the fields, or she can take an entrance exam to a city "vocational" school, where there are programs for gifted students. Yamila is sure to get in, with her 98 average over the last three years. Since primary school, she has been participating in a compulsory career orientation program organized by the Ministry of Education. Each year students register for a career that interests them, and for the entire year professionals from that field come to explain their work. After this year's program, Yamila dreams of becoming an engineer. Yamila's ambition will be no burden on her parents. If she works hard and is bright enough, she will reap the benefits her country offers—free education and no sex discrimination in the workplace. And where does Yamila's interest in boys fit in? With a smile she answers, "For the moment, the only thing that interests me is to graduate and possibly work or study abroad."

10:00. Lolita tries hard to keep the eighty-five-square-meter apartment immaculate. "Everyone does the same as I do," Lolita maintains. The Board of Health checks people's homes regularly for cleanliness, to prevent the spread of disease, especially among small children. The Fonsecas gave up their family home three years ago. It needed a lot of repair and was too far from the community services which the older couple felt they needed. The medical clinic, the supermarket, and schools are all close by.

There is a housing shortage in Cuba, but Juan was lucky. He found the apartment through the classified ads. The former tenants of this three-bedroom apartment wanted a house and they agreed to swap after the government judged the two dwellings to be of comparable value. Since then Juan has become the owner of the apartment, while the new inhabitants of the house have continued to pay rent to the government. Soon, however, they will benefit from a July 1985 law

which gives all those who have paid rent to the government for twenty years ownership of their homes.

11:30. Lolita moves into the kitchen. When she married Juan he was a widower with four sons. Even though the sons are all married now, they often visit unexpectedly, and Lolita always provides an ample feast. If the family ration book is insufficient, little delicacies can be had from the parallel market, which is official but more expensive. That is where Lolita got the chicken she is preparing now. The family can afford it, with Héctor's and Betty's salaries and Juan's pension.

2:00. Lolita takes a small tray to Betty, who has gone to bed. She passed her exam, but the effort has exhausted her and she falls asleep immediately after lunch. The afternoon is quiet. While Juan has his siesta, Lolita goes out on the back balcony to do her laundry in the built-in outdoor sink. Yamila has gone off to buy Héctor a bottle of cologne for his birthday.

5:00. Before joining her friends in the courtyard, Yamila runs downstairs with bags of empty bottles, boxes, paper toothpaste tubes, and drug bottles that Lolita has been saving for a month. The recycling of raw materials is a national policy and the proceeds from the sale will be used to pay the salaries of the CDR's regional and provincial organizers.

7:30. Lolita cleans up the kitchen after a light dinner. She is always the first and the last to be busy in the house. She likes to sew in the evening but today goes down into the courtyard with Yamila to participate in a *cyclo de estudio*, a community meeting in which a neighborhood comrade is delegated by the committee to read and explain President Fidel's most recent speech.

9:00. Lolita bolts the door and joins Juan in bed. Betty stretches out on the sofa beside her daughter. There is always a musical special and two foreign films on television on Saturdays. The first film is one of those old American war films, and the subject of the second will remain a mystery. Betty and Yamila have fallen asleep.

A July 1985 law gives all those who have paid rent to the government for twenty years ownership of their homes

If the ration book is insufficient, supplies can be bought in the parallel market, which is more expensive. The family can afford it, though, with Héctor's and Betty's salaries and Juan's pension

CUBA

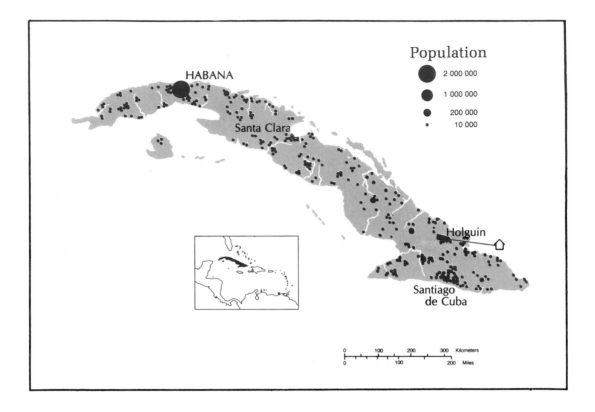

THE NAME: From Arawak, meaning "fields, land used for cultivation, garden"

THE PEOPLE: The Cubans

GEOGRAPHY
Central calcareous lowlands and hills bordered by mountains to the north and the Sierra Maestra to the southwest
Max. altitude: 1974 m. (6,476 ft.) (Pico Turquino)
Area: 114,524 sq. km. (44,218 sq. mi.)
Density: 85 pers./sq. km. (221 pers./sq. mi.) (1986)
Arable land: 29% (1987)
Forest: 17%
Climate: Semi-tropical; rainy season from May to October.

CAPITAL: Havana, pop. 1,992,620 (1984)

LANGUAGE: Spanish

RELIGION:
Catholic: 85% (10% practicing)
Protestant, Jewish, Afro-Cuban cults: 15%

POPULATION: Total—10,038,000 (1985)
Annual growth: 0.6% (60,228) (1980–85)
Doubling time: 58 yrs.
Urban: 72% (1985) (est. for year 2000: 80%)
Rural: 28%

AGE GROUPS: (1981)
7% less than 5 yrs.
30% less than 15
42% less than 20
29% from 20 to 39
18% from 40 to 59
11% 60 yrs. and over

ETHNIC GROUPS: (1981)
White: 66%
Black: 12%
Mulatto and mestizo: 22%

HISTORY
Originally inhabited by the Ciboney, the Guanahatabey, and finally the Arawak (or Taino)
1492: Discovery by Christopher Columbus

1511: Diego de Velázquez establishes first Spanish settlement; serves as a base for the conquest of the American continent

1762–63: British occupation

1886: Abolition of slavery

January 1, 1899: Independence

1901: The United States obtains right to oversee Cuban foreign and internal affairs

May 20, 1902: Becomes an independent republic; followed by U.S. military rule

1959: Fidel Castro overthrows dictator Fulgencio Batista

1960: Deterioration of relations with the United States, as Castro begins to transform Cuba into a socialist state and most U.S.-owned property is nationalized without compensation

1961: Attempt by the United States to overthrow Castro fails (Bay of Pigs)

1971: Cuba signs economic pact with the Soviet Union

FAMILY

Marital status, for population 14 yrs. and older: (1981)
Single: 22%
Married: 38%
Common-law: 21%
Widowed: 7%
Separated from husband or partner: 5%
Divorced: 7%
Female head of household: 28% (1981)
Fertility rate: 2.0 (1985)
Births out of wedlock: no data
Teenage births: 28% (1981)
Contraception: 60% (1984)
Abortions: 76.1/100 live births (1980)
Government's position on family planning: Considers levels and trends of fertility acceptable and provides direct support to family-planning and sex-education programs.

SOCIAL INDICATORS

Life expectancy: 74 yrs. (male: 72; female: 75) (1985)
Infant mortality: 15/1,000 births (1985)
Crude birth rate: 17/1,000 pop. (1985)
Crude death rate: 7/1,000
Health:
Access to health services: no data
Births attended by trained health personnel: 99% (1984)

HOUSING

Persons per household: 4.1 (1981)
Electricity: 17% without (rural: 54%) (1981)
Access to safe water: no data
Source of water: (1981)
Piped inside: 53%
Piped outside: 21%
Other: 9%
Toilet facilities: (1981)
Flush: 50%
Other: 41%
None: 9%
Building materials: (1981)
Concrete: 54%
Wood: 35%
Cane: 9%
Adobe: 2%

EDUCATION

Literacy: 98% (1981)
Gross enrollment ratio: (1984)
First level: 106%
Second: 75%
Third: 20%
Educational attainment, for population 25 yrs. +: (1981)
None: 4%
First level: incomplete: 23% (complete: 28%)
Second: entered: 40%
Third: 6%

ECONOMIC ACTIVITY

Economically active population: 36% (male: 50%; female: 23%) (1980)
Agriculture: 23% act. pop.; 15% of GDP
Mines: 2% act. pop.; 3% of GDP
Industry: 25% act. pop.; 47% of GDP
Services: 50% act. pop.; 35% of GDP
Per capita GNP: 1,410 U.S.$ (1979)
Population in absolute poverty: no data
National currency/per U.S.$: 0.90 peso (1984)
Principal resources:
World's largest exporters of sugar
Nickel

COMMUNICATIONS

Radio:
Transmitters: 150 (1983)
Receivers: 3,121,000—316/1,000 pop. (1983)
Television:
Transmitters: 58 (1983)
Receivers: 1,658,000—168/1,000 pop. (1983)

DOMINICA

THE BERTRAND FAMILY

Myrtle Bertrand, age 30 (1)
Glen Larocque, 13 (2)
Nick Larocque, 12 (3)
Carson Larocque, 9 (4)

DUBLANC
May 27

5:15. The farmers of the village of Dublanc squeeze into a few pickup trucks for the drive over the mountain. Overlooking the sea, Dublanc's side of the mountain does not get enough rain for crops, so the farmers each have one or two acres in the interior. Dublanc is famous throughout the country for its large crops of bananas and citrus fruits.

Myrtle steps adroitly between the bodies of her three sons sleeping on the floor, grabs her basket, and runs to take her position on Dublanc's single street. Myrtle hasn't a minute to lose. She must get rid of yesterday's unsold bread before the other women take their freshly baked loaves out of the village oven. Only a few women can bake and sell bread at the bakery cooperative. Myrtle got this chance to earn some money when a friend temporarily lent Myrtle her spot. She is worried, wondering how she is going to repay the money she borrowed for flour and yeast. Her only hope is to sell off the fifteen small loaves she has left and try to collect from the people who owe her. "I never make any profit," she says. "And no one here can afford to pay more than the twenty-five cents [ten cents U.S.] a loaf I charge now. Some people owe me as much as three dollars, and I will have to make a terrible fuss to get it back."

A few minutes later, Carson walks by his mother with a chamber pot on his head. He will empty it in the river that flows into the nearby sea. His brothers dump the old clothes they use as a mattress into a flour sack and slide it under Myrtle's bed. When Carson returns, the three boys climb the path up the lush green mountainside to have coffee at their grandmother's house.

6:30. Even though school doesn't start until eight o'clock, Glen and Nick set off, taking with them bread, cheese, and grapefruit juice. This morning they have to catch the bus at the main road. The bus is expensive, but fortunately the boys' father, who is a truck driver and lives in the next village, drives them to the school in St. Joseph three times

a week. Myrtle receives no other assistance from the father of her three children. Her only income is the 20 East Caribbean dollars ($8 U.S.) she has been receiving each month since being elected to the job of municipal counselor, collecting taxes, overseeing public work, and the like. This meager salary must pay for her food, her rent to her uncle, and the electricity bills.

Myrtle never lived with her sons' father and doesn't know how many other women have children by him. Myrtle herself does not know how many half brothers or sisters she has. This is not unusual with many Caribbean people. Many of their African forebears practiced polygamy, and when they became slaves, the traditional family unit was deliberately destroyed by their masters. Male slaves were allowed only to impregnate the women, leaving the responsibility of raising the children to the mothers. Many Caribbean men still have children by several women and do not feel bound to any of the mothers.

The bakers take the loaves out of the village oven. Now nobody will want to buy her bread, so Myrtle abandons her post. She unlocks the door of the little shack behind her house which she uses as a kitchen. Ever since she lost a saucepan and some light bulbs, she never forgets to padlock the door when she leaves. Picking up the bowl with the dirty dishes, she sets off for the river. Myrtle doesn't waste any time. It is better to do as many chores as possible before the sun comes up over the mountain. Afterward, it's too hot.

The riverbank is bustling. Myrtle sees her mother there, despite the fact that she has water in her yard. One of her sons sent the money for the tap from Canada, where he lives. But she still prefers the company of the village women. "I'm not alone so much and the clothes get whiter here," she maintains. Myrtle could have running water too, but the cost of the pipes and the installation work is too much for her. In any case, the village tap is close by, and there is no shortage of arms in the house for carrying water.

9:00. Myrtle returns from the river on the path that winds between the closely built little wooden houses. Although most of its inhabitants have left, the village is far from silent. Children's voices from the day-care center, radios, and the cocks create a constant hum.

12:00. Carson and his friends return from the primary school. They have an hour to eat but won't spend long at home, where there is not much more than a piece of bread to chew on. They rush down to the river for a swim, since the village is suffocating in the noonday heat. The houses are too close together for the sea breezes to circulate. The children float down the river on old inner tubes. They don't swim in the sea. The rocky seashore serves as the village dump and an open-air toilet for those too lazy to go to the public toilets at the other end of the village. The stench makes the prospect of swimming there nauseating.

1:30. Once Carson goes back to school, Myrtle remains in her kitchen for a while. First, an old childhood friend comes by for a chat. He has taken another day off to recover from the wild nights of the long Easter weekend. He wasn't the only one living it up. Most of the younger of Dublanc's 450 residents gathered in Shake a Leg, the village disco. It is in a little house, hardly any bigger than Myrtle's, run by her best friend, Nalda, who opens the disco every Friday and Saturday night.

Now Nalda arrives. The three friends exchange gossip. Myrtle talks about her boyfriend in the capital, who will probably come next Saturday, but mostly she talks of her financial problems. Myrtle looks to the men in her life for love only. She knows she will have to fulfill by herself her dream of buying chairs for her sons to sit in while they do their homework. The boys are serious and

are doing well at school, and Myrtle sees their success as her chance for a better future. The students arrive home, change into their old clothes, and are off. They spend little time around the tiny house, but they are never far if Myrtle needs them for a chore.

3:30. The women of Dublanc, Myrtle among them, gather in the shadow of an open wooden shed where the farmers crate bananas. They prepare sandwiches and fruit juice and sit down with their crocheting while they wait for the arrival of the country's Minister of Education. Today the Minister, representing the Adult Education Service, will donate a stove and a sewing machine to the village women's club.

When the Minister arrives, the women stand, nervous and slightly awed. In the fields beside the shed, the men, back from work, play soccer as if nothing is happening. The women must unload the donations on the truck by themselves. In her first public speech, the village municipal secretary invites the Minister to return, provided he doesn't come empty-handed. He laughs at her bold naïveté.

7:00. Myrtle fries pieces of chicken in coconut oil. She hopes to find the money to buy a bottle of gas for her little two-ring stove, but the deposit required is much too high. In the meantime, she uses the brazier fueled with the charcoal that her mother makes every two months. The boys eat their chicken and bread wherever they please.

8:30. The village is quiet this evening. The Shake a Leg is closed, and the inhabitants are recuperating. Myrtle and Nalda are chatting on the doorstep and listening to the music of radios playing throughout the village. Inside the little house, Glen, Nick, and Carson have pulled the rags out of the flour sack. It's time to make up their bed.

The village is suffocating in the noonday heat. The houses are too close together for the sea breezes to circulate

Every time she goes out, Myrtle locks the door of the tiny kitchen shack. Too many of her possessions have disappeared

DOMINICA

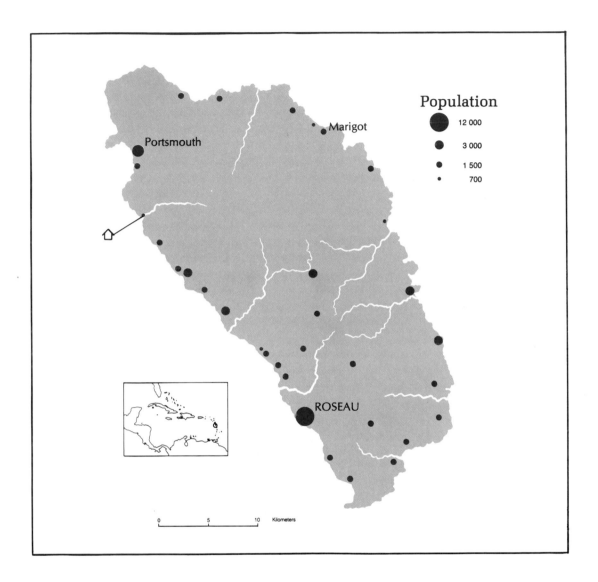

THE NAME: From Latin *Dominica*, meaning Sunday (the day on which Columbus first sighted the island)

THE PEOPLE: The Dominicans

GEOGRAPHY

High volcanic peaks carpeted by deep forests, cut by more than 350 rivers and punctuated with lakes and waterfalls; some volcanoes are still active and 37% of area has a high risk of erosion.

Max. altitude: 1,447 m. (4,747 ft.) (Morne Diablotin)

Area: 752 sq. km. (290 sq. mi.)

Density: 98 pers./sq. km. (290 pers./sq. mi.) (1986)
Arable land: 23% (1987)
Forest: 41%
Climate: Tropical, tempered by sea winds, which can reach hurricane force. Rainfall is heavy in the mountainous area.

CAPITAL: Roseau, pop. 8,346 (1981)

LANGUAGE: English (official), French patois

RELIGION

Catholic: 78%
Protestant and other: 22%

POPULATION: Total—76,000 (1985)
    Annual growth: 0.7% (532) (1980–85)
    Doubling time: 41 yrs.
    Urban: 29% (1980)
    Rural: 71%

AGE GROUPS: (1980)
    11% less than 5 yrs.
    40% less than 15
    53% less than 20
    25% from 20 to 39
    13% from 40 to 59
    11% 60 yrs. and over

ETHNIC GROUPS: (1981)
    Black: 91%
    Mixed: 6%
    Carib (Amerindian): 2%
    White and other: 1%

HISTORY
    Originally inhabited by Arawak and Carib Indians
    1493: Discovery by Christopher Columbus
    1700s: French colonization
    1759: Captured by the British
    1778: Retaken by the French
    1783: Restored to Britain by the Treaty of Paris
    1834: Abolition of slavery
    1871: Part of Federation of the Leeward Islands
    1940: Transferred to the jurisdiction of the
       Windward Islands group with Grenada, St.
       Vincent, and St. Lucia
    1967: Self-governing member of the West Indies
       Associated States within the British
       Commonwealth
    November 3, 1978: Independence within the
       Commonwealth

FAMILY
Marital status, for population 14 yrs. and older: (1980)
    Married: 31%
    Common-law: 12%
    Visiting union: 7%
    Not in union: 50%
Female head of household: 39% (1980)
Fertility rate: 3.4 (1975–80)
Births out of wedlock: no data
Teenage births: 24% (1980)
Contraception: no data
Government's position on family planning: Supports
    family planning and has issued a policy statement
    indicating the acceptance of family planning as an
    integral part of maternal and child health services.

SOCIAL INDICATORS
Life expectancy: 75 yrs. (1987)
Infant mortality: 13/1,000 births (1987)

Crude birth rate: 21.4/1,000 pop. (1978)
Crude death rate: 5.3/1,000
Health:
    Access to health services: no data
    Births attended by trained health personnel: 96%
       (1983)

HOUSING
Persons per household: 4.3 (1981)
Electricity: 70% without (1980)
Access to safe water: no data
Source of water: (1980)
    Piped inside: 22%
    Piped outside: 10%
    Public standpipe: 47%
    Other: 21%
Toilet facilities: (1980)
    Flush: 23%
    Pit: 50%
    Other: 27%
Building materials: (1980)
    Wood: 62%
    Concrete: 19%
    Mixture of concrete and wood: 19%

EDUCATION
Literacy: 94% (male: 89%; female: 94%) (1970)
Gross enrollment ratio: no data
Educational attainment, for population 25 yrs. +:
    (1981)
    None: 6.6%
    First level: incomplete: 81%
    Second: entered: 114%
    Third: 2%

ECONOMIC ACTIVITY
Economically active population: 34% (male: 45%;
    female: 23%) (1981)
Agriculture: 65.3% act. pop.; GDP: no data
Mines: 0% act. pop.
Industry: 23% act. pop.
Services: 33% act. pop.
Per capita GNP: 1,150 U.S.$ (1985)
Population in absolute poverty: no data
National currency/per U.S.$: 2.70 East Caribbean
    dollars (1985)
Principal resources: Bananas (42% of export revenue in
    1983), coconuts, limes and other citrus fruits

COMMUNICATIONS
Radio:
    Transmitters: 3 (1979)
    Receivers: 44,000—550/1,000 pop. (1983)
Television: no data

DOMINICAN REPUBLIC

THE FERNÁNDEZ FAMILY

Conrado Fernández, age 48 (1)
Melania de Jesús García de Fernández, 38 (2)
Grizelda Antonia Fernández, 13 (3)
Julia Antonia, 9 (4)
Ana Augustina, 8 (5)
Pedro Pablo, 6 (6)
Héctor del Carmen, 8 (7)
Carmen Toribio, 13 (8)
Anna Luisa Gómez, 65 (9)

SANTIAGO
June 30

5:30. Inside the Fernández house in Mirador, one of Santiago's shantytowns, Conrado hurries to fill out 160 receipts. He must hand these out to his fellow members of the Sociedad Unidad do Rosario (a neighborhood solidarity association) in return for their donation of one peso each. Yesterday Conrado took up a collection for the family of a friend who died recently. Conrado's is a combative and generous spirit. For him it is a question of survival. As he writes, he hums the songs coming from a little radio that reverberates in the house like an old saucepan.

Lack of work forced Conrado to leave the countryside. He exchanged his house in the village for this four-room, fifty-square-meter wooden shack in Mirador. When he arrived with Melania, there were only five houses. Today, ten years later, the exodus from the countryside seems endless, and the shantytown is bursting at the seams. The houses are piled one on top of the other, and new arrivals are condemned to live in the dumps on the slum's outskirts without water or electricity.

Conrado's mother and Melania sip cups of thick coffee. Melania smokes one of her ever-present cigarettes and Anna Luisa one of her cigars, despite the bad cold that makes her cough. Grandmother is an inveterate smoker, dividing her passion between the pipe and the cigar.

6:00. Melania sweeps the house and the courtyard, an act that will be repeated many times in the course of the day. The windblown dust is one of the plagues of the neighborhood. It infiltrates the house through the cracks in the poorly joined planks, through the termite holes in the wood, through the gap between the tin roof and the top of the walls, and through the always open doors.

6:30. Conrado heads out into the streets of Mirador and hails a taxi already crammed with workers going downtown. Each passenger pays 35 centavos, a small sum but nevertheless one that many cannot afford. For the past five years, Conrado has worked

as a clerk in the records section of the Ministry of Finance. He was lucky enough to keep his job at the last change of government, despite a large turnover of positions.

Conrado spends twice as much as he earns to feed his family. For the last five years he hasn't even been able to buy himself a shirt. His house is falling apart, and he can't consider having any repairs done. Conrado owes one year's wages to the Almiradora Cooperative Credit Union. In spite of everything, Conrado is in a privileged position. He has a job, whereas most of the other people in the slum are unemployed and overwhelmed with debt.

7:00. The children are on vacation, so they drink their coffee and lounge around the house. Melania demands that Grizelda, Carmen, and Julia help her. They wash the gray cement floor without ever succeeding in making it look clean. At least they can wash it twice a day with water from the tap in the yard, which wasn't possible in February, when they had to fill buckets at the public fountain. Conrado and his neighbors fought for ten years to get running water. They still need a school building. The church and several houses are turned into schools during the day, but it is not enough. Most of the children remain illiterate.

10:00. In their room, Julia and Ana, inseparable playmates, play house with an old doll. Beside them, Pedro is confined to his bed with a high fever. Melania doesn't know the cause. She lets the child sleep in the hope that the fever will break by itself. It is useless to panic yet. There are no medical services in Mirador, and no money to consult a doctor in town. Too many of Melania's friends are losing their children to illness. They can rely only on their prayers.

12:00. Melania cooks rice and beans and serves it in plastic bowls to the family around the table. The wind sweeps in through the door, carrying blasts of unbearable heat along with the dust. Paving the streets is one of a long list of demands.

1:00. Grizelda and Carmen wash the dishes and tidy the kitchen. Grizelda sings as she works. She dreams of being a star. Anna Luisa sips another cup of coffee and smokes her cigar as she listens appreciatively to Grizelda's sweet voice. Melania keeps her sick son company. Conrado's wife, who often seems overwhelmed by raising her family, is not an activist like her husband and doesn't even try to participate. Unfortunately, she doesn't take advantage of the information sessions organized by women in the community. These sessions are intended to help women gain a better understanding of hygiene and contraception, to learn how to cook more economically and sew and care for their children. But Melania is generous and has opened her house to Héctor, a little nephew stricken with polio, and Carmen, whose father has died. Both children had been abandoned by their mothers, and now live as members of the Fernández family.

3:00. Melania and Anna Luisa sit and smoke in silence at the table. The grandmother never has much to say. The children have gone off to play with friends. Home from work, Conrado sets about his social work. Once again he has to collect money to aid a family whose mother died this morning of lung cancer, which claims many victims here. "I wonder whether it's caused by the dust that we constantly breathe," says Conrado.

5:30. The heat has abated, and from the cramped, uncomfortable houses people begin to fill the alleys. While she cooks dinner, Melania makes coffee for visitors who have come with Conrado. People in search of help, advice, and encouragement always seek out his company. This year, in addition to his work for the Sociedad Unidad do Rosario, Conrado is chairman of the Almiradora Cooperative Credit Union. He never has a minute to himself.

6:30. The evening's menu is the same as at noon: black beans and rice. As soon as he has wolfed down his dinner, Conrado disappears to kneel beside the coffin of his friend, and then to a meeting of the Cooperative. Grizelda and Carmen plan to stroll through the neighborhood for a while. Melania and the younger ones watch the passersby from the doorstep, as Grandmother puffs furiously on her pipe.

9:00. Julia and Ana are dead tired and fall asleep very quickly in one of the children's room's three beds. Grandmother has her own room, which Conrado built for her. She sleeps with Héctor, her protégé. She tucks him in, places the chamber pot under the bed, and slips under the mosquito net. Grizelda and Carmen want to hang around the busy streets a little longer, but Melania lays down the law, and they come in. There are no streetlights, and too often violence erupts at night. Pedro's condition hasn't changed, and Melania's anxiety grows. Maybe Conrado will know what to do. While the rest of the family sleeps, Melania stays on the doorstep smoking cigarettes and waiting for her husband to return.

*The dust
penetrates the
cracks in the
poorly joined
planks, the termite
holes in the wood,
and the gaps
between the tin
roof and the top
of the walls*

*Melania is
generous and has
opened her house
to Héctor and
Carmen. Both
children have been
abandoned by
their mothers*

DOMINICAN REPUBLIC

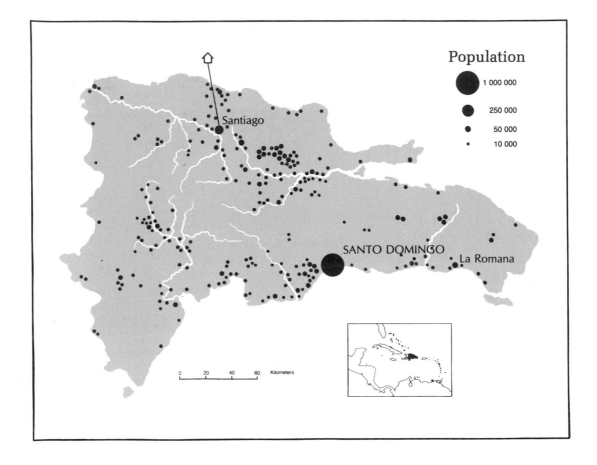

THE NAME: From Latin *Dominica*, meaning Sunday (the day on which Columbus first sighted the island)

THE PEOPLE: The Dominicans

GEOGRAPHY
Cordillera Central, the principal mountain range, crosses the middle of the country.
In the upper central part lies the Cibao, a fertile valley known as the food basket of the country.
Max. altitude: 3,175 m. (10,417 ft.) (Pico Duarte)
Area: 48,442 sq. km. (18,704 sq. mi.)
Density: 128 pers./sq. km. (332 pers./sq. mi.) (1986)
Arable land: 30% (1987)
Forest: no data
Climate: Maritime tropical; ocean currents and trade winds moderate the heat. Rainy season from May to November.

CAPITAL: Santo Domingo, pop. 817,645 (1970)

LANGUAGE: Spanish

RELIGION
Majority Catholic

POPULATION: Total—6,243,000 (1985)
Annual growth: 2.3% (143,589) (1980–85)
Doubling time: 28 yrs.
Urban: 56% (1985) (est. for year 2000: 68%)
Rural: 44% (1985)

AGE GROUPS: (1980)
17% less than 5 yrs.
48% less than 15
59% less than 20
25% from 20 to 39
12% from 40 to 59
 5% 60 yrs. and over

ETHNIC GROUPS
Mulatto: 73%
White: 16%
Black: 11%

HISTORY
Originally inhabited by Carib Indians
1492: Discovery by Christopher Columbus
1697: France and Spain divide Hispaniola
1795: French conquest
1809: Two-thirds of island returned to Spain
1821: Independence as the Dominican Republic;
    overrun by Haitian troops within weeks and
    occupied until 1844
February 27, 1844: Independence
1882–99: Democratic government under Ulises
    Heureaux
1916–24: U.S. occupation
1930–61: Dictatorship of General Trujillo
1963: Election of Juan Bosch, leader of the
    democratic left
1965: U.S. intervention against pro-Bosch forces
1966–78: Authoritarian government under Joaquín
    Balaguer
1978: Election of Antonio Guzmán of the
    Dominican Revolutionary Party
1982: Election of President Salvador Jorge Blanco,
    DRP

FAMILY
Marital status, for population 15 yrs. and
    older: (1980–83)
    Married: 24%
    Common-law: 28%
    Divorced: 1%
    Separated: 5%
    Other: 42%
    41% of couples married for the first time will
        separate.
    20% of unions are made before the age of fifteen.
Female head of household: no data
Fertility rate: 3.9 (1985)
Births out of wedlock: no data
Teenage births: 11% (1976)
Contraception: 50% (1984)
Government's position on family planning: Considers
    fertility to be too high. The government has an
    active program to bring about its reduction, which
    includes direct support for family planning.

SOCIAL INDICATORS
Life expectancy: 64 yrs. (male: 61; female: 73) (1985)
Infant mortality: 70/1,000 births (1985)
Crude birth rate: 32/1,000 pop. (1985)
Crude death rate: 8/1,000

Health:
Access to health services: 80% (1980)
Births attended by trained health personnel: 51%
    (1984)

HOUSING
Persons per household: 5.3 (1980)
Electricity: 41% without (1981)
Access to safe water: 60% (urban: 85%; rural: 32%)
    (1983)
Source of water: (1981)
    Piped inside: 2%   Not piped: 46%
    Piped outside: 26%   Other: 5%
Toilet facilities: (1981)
    Flush: 14%
    Other: 63%
    None: 23%
Building materials:
    Wood: 36%
    Concrete: 30%
    Straw: 27%

EDUCATION
Literacy: 69% (male: 68%; female: 69%) (1981)
Gross enrollment ratio: (1983)
    First level: 112% (completing in 1980–84): 72%
    Second: 45%
    Third: no data
Educational attainment, for population 25 yrs. +:
    (1970)
    None: 40%
    First level: incomplete: 42% (complete: 4%)
    Second: entered: 10%
    Third: 2%

ECONOMIC ACTIVITY
Economically active population: 34% (male: 48%;
    female: 20%) (1981)
Agriculture: 49% of act. pop.; 18% of GDP
Mines: 4% act. pop.; 25% of GDP
Industry: 49% act. pop.; 18% of GDP
Services: 3% act. pop.; 54% of GDP
Per capita GNP: 790 U.S.$ (1985)
Population in absolute poverty: (1978)
    Urban: 45%
    Rural: 43%
National currency/per U.S.$: 3.11 pesos (1985)
Principal resource: Sugar

COMMUNICATIONS
Radio:
    Transmitters: 188 (1979)
    Receivers: 1,200,000—201/1,000 pop. (1983)
Television:
    Transmitters: no data
    Receivers: 550,000—92/1,000 pop. (1983)

GRENADA

THE ABRAHAM FAMILY

Adna Abraham, age 39 (1)
Aron Abraham, 16 (2)
Cloyde, 8 (3)
Delon, 3 (4)

1 pig
6 chickens
2 cats and their kittens
1 dog

PEARLS
April 29

An early-morning downpour has saturated the half-acre yard surrounding the Abrahams' new little house, and the spices and fruits that grow in Adna's garden have released their fragrant perfume into the dawn air. Nature's bounty has rightly earned Granada the name Spice Island.

6:00. Adna has slept very little. She was up late last night at a neighbor's, honoring the tradition that a person's friends gather forty days after his death to sing psalms with the family.

Adna wakes her three boys, who sleep on the floor, and leaves the house carefully. There is no doorstep, and the muddy ground is slippery. She lights the charcoal fire, and the kitchen is soon filled with the aroma of hot chocolate spiced with cinnamon. The chocolate is fresh from the cocoa trees behind the house. Adna dreams of one day having a kitchen in the house. However, the charcoal fire blackens the walls too much, so she has to put up with this makeshift cabin until she can afford gas. At least, for the past four months Adna has had a brand-new house, which she built with her cousin Jim's help. In exchange for his labor, she allowed Jim to build a room with a private entrance at the back for his own use. To protect the wood, the exterior walls of the house have been coated with used oil collected from gas stations. Building the house took Adna longer than she had planned. The first load of wood was stolen soon after it was delivered, and she had to save for several more years.

6:30. On their way to the banana and coconut plantations, the farm workers file past the wooden houses lining the country road. It is not easy to tell the difference between the men and the women, and indeed, in the fields there is none. The women are just as strong as the men. As single heads of households, most Grenadian women have learned to fend for themselves. Leaving the two older boys in charge of their own breakfast and of little De-

lon, Adna ties her apron over her old dress, pulls on her rubber boots, and sets her cap on her head. In one hand she takes her heavy machete, in the other a thermos of fresh grapefruit juice. Then she falls in behind Cousin Teresa at the end of the line. Both women greet Cousin Mariette, who is leading her goats to pasture in the opposite direction. Adna can call half of her neighbors Cousin. Her extended family has been growing in this part of the country since the end of slavery.

Adna's other dream is to have a job that doesn't require as much physical effort. Self-delusion is, however, pointless, and Adna doesn't believe that she will achieve her goal on this side of the grave. Three days a week she works on the plantations. The rest of the time she devotes all her energy to maintaining her garden. Citrus, mangos, bananas, avocados, tamarinds, breadfruit, and guava all do their part to balance her budget. The spices give Grenadian dishes an unforgettable taste, and the many Grenadians who have emigrated to Trinidad to work impatiently await the weekly boats which bring products from their homeland.

7:00. Hidden by a few sheets of metal, Cloyde bathes in the garden behind the house. Dressed in his school uniform, he joins the children streaming down the dirt road to the bus that will take them to the primary school.

Delon plays underneath the house with his dog. He is a happy child. Adna adopted him when his mother could no longer be bothered with him, and he is the family's pet. His snack and his school bag are waiting. In an hour, Cousin Yolande will take him and the other younger children in the neighborhood to the day-care center in Paradise, a little community twenty minutes away. Yolande has to be constantly on the alert; the island's motorists drive fast, with little concern for pedestrians.

8:30. Left to himself, Aron decides, not for the

first time, to play hooky. In June he will graduate—just barely—from his seventh year of school, and the only thing he's interested in is becoming a mechanic. Adna has tried to discourage him, without much success. "There aren't enough cars here. He'll become unemployed and, like so many others, will have to leave the island to find work," she says. Unless Aron changes his mind, she is afraid that she cannot count on much help from him in the future. She has so much difficulty making ends meet. Aron's father has left the island. Cloyde's father visits his son only on rare occasions, and his generosity is as infrequent. Beyond that there are only the few pennies that Cousin Jim pays her, but they depend on whatever work he can get.

10:00. Until the afternoon, the only signs of life along the Abrahams' rural road are a few very young children who remain at home with their grandparents and Adna's neighbor and cousin Mariette. It is as if time has stood still. But life has changed nevertheless. Even the children can remember when the road was no more than a track and there were no taps or public showers for those without running water. "We built our road with our own hands, with financial help from international organizations," says Mariette proudly. She is always the first to become involved in community activities, and her standards for living set an example for all her neighbors.

3:30. Back from the plantation, Adna asks Aron to go to Cousin Mariette's to pick up a sack of dried coconut, from which she extracts oil for cooking. "Yes, Cousin," he replies agreeably, relieved that his errant behavior has gone unnoticed. After hearing his mother addressed as Cousin by all the neighbors since childhood, he has acquired the habit.

The late-afternoon heat doesn't bother the children. Home from school, they begin a cricket match on the road, using a branch from a coconut tree as a bat. Girls play too. As long as Cousin Mariette is around, there is no discrimination; she is a great believer in the equality of the sexes.

7:30. Adna gives Delon a bath and dresses him in clean clothes for the next day, in which he will sleep. She takes this time for a bit of affection with the boy. She is a quiet, introverted woman, and these moments don't come often to her. After half an hour of semi-darkness, Adna lights the oil lamp. As soon as all the neighbors can agree, she will have electricity. Some of them don't want to pay the extra cost of installing the poles and prefer to wait until others provide it; then all they will have to do is hook up.

Aron and Delon eat their dinner of *callalou* (a green vegetable similar to spinach) and fried bananas with fresh lemon juice at the little table in the main room. Even though he can't see anything at all, Cloyde prefers to eat in the kitchen with Adna, perched on top of a sack of chick-peas.

8:00. Adna takes some old clothes from the boxes at the foot of the bed that serve as a cupboard. She spreads the clothes on the ground and covers them with a sheet to make her sons' bed. Delon clings to Cloyde and embarks on a series of questions—why this? . . . why that?—before he falls asleep.

Adna fills the iron with embers from the hearth. Kneeling in front of a cloth spread on the ground, she irons the boys' school uniforms with a sure hand. Adna likes to go to bed early. Finally she stretches out on her mattress in her room. Near the bed, the cats and their kittens are purring. The air is hot and heavy. Even though it is still too early for the rainy season, Adna falls asleep to the sound of the rain falling on the tin roof.

To protect the wood, the exterior walls of the house are coated with used oil collected from gas stations

Adna dreams of one day having a kitchen in the house. However, the charcoal fire blackens the walls too much, so she has to put up with this makeshift cabin until she can afford gas

GRENADA

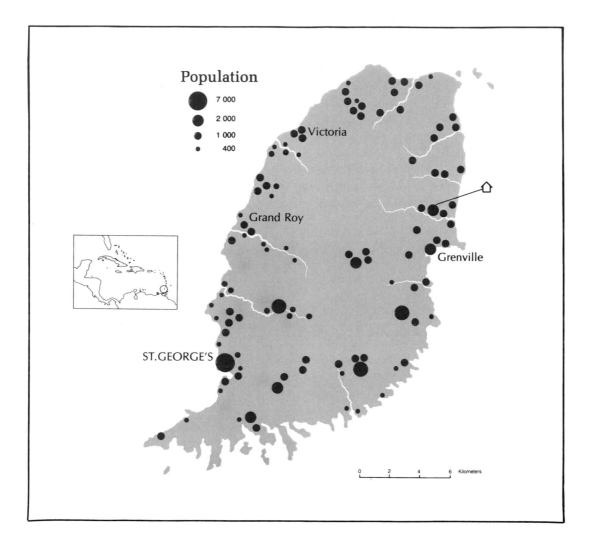

Population

- 7 000
- 2 000
- 1 000
- 400

Victoria

Grand Roy

Grenville

ST. GEORGE'S

0 2 4 6 Kilometers

THE NAME: From Granada, Spain; given by Spanish sailors

THE PEOPLE: The Grenadians

GEOGRAPHY
  Mountainous island of volcanic origin
  Rain forest in the center bordered by coastal plains
  Southern coast with sandy beach
  Max. altitude: 1,840 m. (2,757 ft.) (Mt. St. Catherine)
Area: 344 sq. km. (133 sq. mi.)
Density: 331 pers./sq. km. (857 pers./sq. mi.) (1986)
Arable land: 41% (1987)
Forest: 9%

Climate: Semi-tropical. Mild season from January to May. Average annual rainfall: 1,500 mm. on coast to 3,800 mm. in mountains. Average temperature: 28°C. (82°F.).

CAPITAL: St. George's, pop. 7,500 (1982 est.)

LANGUAGE: English

RELIGION
  Catholic: 58%
  Anglican: 18%
  Seventh-Day Adventist: 6%
  Pentecostal: 4%
  Methodist: 3%
  Other Protestant: 24%

POPULATION: Total—112,000 (1985)
 Annual growth: 1% (1,120) (1980–85)
 Doubling time: 37 yrs.
 Urban: 39% (1985)
 Rural: 61%

AGE GROUPS: (1980)
 12% less than 5 yrs.
 39% less than 15
 52% less than 20
 25% from 20 to 39
 13% from 40 to 59
 10% 60 yrs. and over

ETHNIC GROUPS
 Black: 82%
 Mixed: 13%
 East Indian: 3%
 White: 1%

HISTORY
 Originally inhabited by Carib Indians
 1498: Discovered by Christopher Columbus
 1650: French colonization
 1674–1762: British and French battle for possession
 1762: British rule, with the exception of five years of French rule (1779–83)
 1967: Associated with the United Kingdom
 February 7, 1974: Independence
 1979: Creation of People's Revolutionary Government by Maurice Bishop
 1983: Execution of Bishop by PRG; government replaced by Revolutionary Military Council, followed by U.S. invasion

FAMILY
Marital status, for population 14 yrs. and older: (1981)
 Married: 29%
 Common-law: 13%
 Visiting union: 7%
 Separated from husband or partner: 14%
 Never had husband or partner: 33%
Female head of household: 45% (extended family: 46%)
Fertility rate: 3.18 (1983)
Births out of wedlock: 83% (1983)
Teenage births: 27% (1978)
Contraception: no data
Government's position on family planning: Concerned with the implications of increased population on employment, housing, nutrition, etc., the government asserts the right of the individual to have access to knowledge about contraception and the means to regulate family size.

SOCIAL INDICATORS
Life expectancy: 72 yrs. (male, female: no data) (1987)
Infant mortality: 14/1,000 births (1985)
Crude birth rate: 25/1,000 pop. (1984)
Crude death rate: 7/1,000
Health:
 Access to health services: no data
 Births attended by trained health personnel: 50% (1983)

HOUSING
Persons per household: 2.9 (1985)
Electricity: 61% without (1981)
Access to safe water: no data
Source of water: (1981)
 Piped inside: 34%
 Piped outside: 24%
 Not piped: 51%
Toilet facilities: (1981)
 WC linked to sewer: 4%
 WC not linked: 23%
 Pit: 62%
 None or other: 20%
Building materials: (1981)
 Concrete, wood, adobe, straw, cane, and other

EDUCATION
Literacy: 98% (male: 98%; female: 98%) (1970)
Gross enrollment ratio: (1982)
 First level: 88% (completing in 1980–84: no data)
Educational attainment, for population 25 yrs. +:
 (1981)
 None: 2%
 First level: incomplete: 88%
 Second: entered: 9%
 Third: 2%

ECONOMIC ACTIVITY
Economically active population: no data
Agriculture: 30% act. pop.; 25% of GDP
Mines: 0% act. pop.; 0% of GDP
Industry: 15% act. pop.; 20% of GDP
Services: 55% act. pop.; 20% of GDP
Per capita GNP: 970 U.S.$ (1985)
Population in absolute poverty: no data
National currency/per U.S.$: 2.70 East Caribbean dollars (1985)
Principal resources: Cocoa, bananas, nutmeg

COMMUNICATIONS
Radio:
 Transmitters: 3 (1979)
 Receivers: 38,000—345/1,000 pop. (1983)
Television: no data

HAITI

THE BARTHÉLEMY FAMILY

Albert Barthélemy, age 50 (1)
Mercegrace Barthélemy, 49 (2)
Detanie Beauchamps, 22 (absent)
Mercenise Barthélemy, 20 (3)
Amors, 17 (4)
Indianise, 14 (5)
Alfese, 8 (6)

1 horse
1 donkey
1 bull
1 calf
5 chickens

LA BROUSSE
July 8

6:00. Mercenise sits up on her straw mat and nudges her sister. Indianise, who is a deaf-mute, knows that her sister's gesture is an order. She rises obediently, puts the wicker basket filled with empty jerry cans on the donkey, and leaves for the spring.

Mercenise shoos her brother off their mat, dampens the dirt floor, and sweeps it with a broom made of dry branches. The house's only room is divided into the sections by a curtain. On this side the furniture consists of a table and two chairs. The parents sleep on the smaller side, where a number of boxes of clothing, two jerry cans, and seven plates—the household's entire supply—are stacked beside the bed.

7:30. A neighbor comes to fetch Albert. Every Thursday and Friday the men of La Brousse and Foison contribute their labor to the construction of a road connecting their two villages. Albert opens the door carefully to prevent pieces of the dry mud wall from crumbling. The Barthélemys have lived in their house for twenty years, and only the thatched roof is intact. This is the sole benefit of the drought which has plagued the country for years. Rain would surely destroy the old roof and, as there is no more straw in the country, Albert could never afford to replace it.

In a house as poor as hers, Mercegrace has no housework and no breakfast to serve her children. She washes herself and places Alfese in the shade in front of the house. From the age of four, *ti-moune* (little one, as all Haitian children are called) has not been able to walk and must drag himself painfully along on his hands. He spends hours in the same spot, sometimes playing with two bits of wood, but most often staring at the horizon and singing incomprehensible songs he makes up himself. Alfese will never go to school.

Mercegrace often sits down beside Alfese and lets her gentle, sad eyes wander. Two of her children are severely handicapped, and a daughter "got sick in the chest" last year and died. Mercegrace doesn't know why, just as she doesn't know that Alfese's sickness is called polio.

In the garden, Amors cuts the cornstalks and cane leaves to feed the animals. They are so dried out that they are of no use for humans. He examines the stalks carefully, though, to see if any edible ears are among them. This would be the only food the family could hope to have today.

8:30. Some cousins drop by for a few minutes on their way to the mountain to make charcoal, the peasants' main financial resource. As one of them says: "When there are no more trees, we will cease to exist." Everyone in the country cooks with charcoal. Gas and electricity are simply unaffordable.

When Albert was young, this part of the Northwest was green and covered with tropical forests. Deforestation has dried out the soil, and the lack of moisture prevents the formation of clouds large enough to produce rain. The land is now so desolate that the inhabitants are forced to abandon it and choose between two equally tragic alternatives: to move to the dismal shantytowns clustered around the capital or to escape by sea as boat people with neither papers nor money. The odds against landing on a welcoming shore are heavy. Albert is one of those who don't want to move. He puts his fate in "God's hands."

10:00. Mercenise walks around looking for something—anything—to do. The house and the kitchen are as bare as the garden is dry, and the peasants that have not left are dispersed around the countryside. Mercenise is lonely. She is waiting to marry her fiancé, but she will need a miracle to fill the little box in which she hopes to collect her trousseau. Without it, there can be no ceremony. Tradition requires that the bride bring some linen and dishes, while the groom builds the house. Her father keeps postponing Mercenise's plans. Albert is vigorously opposed to *vivavek* (common-law marriage), which is practiced by the majority of the population. As a devout Catholic, he insists on a nuptial blessing and refuses to allow his daughter to "live in sin."

More to the point, though, Albert is in debt. Last year he had to pay for the church burial of one daughter and the wedding of his oldest. "Really bad luck," he says. "Everything happened at once." The 50 percent interest rates are usurious. Albert will never repay the loan even if he lives to a ripe old age. Here again he puts his trust in God.

Resigned to her fate, Mercenise sits down in the shade. Indianise, back from the spring, has reoccupied her usual corner of the garden. Ignored by everyone, possibly because she is a living reminder of the family's misfortune, Indianise withdraws into her dream world. From time to time, Mercegrace takes a pinch of snuff or throws a pebble at the head of a chicken to keep it away from the house. The scrawny birds might get fat enough to sell someday.

11:00. Amors has found an edible ear of corn and a piece of sugarcane in the garden. In the little shack that serves as a kitchen, Mercenise piles up a few bits of wood from the ground and lights the fire. She grills the corn and divides it into six portions. Albert returns and joins the family; he chews his few grains slowly. Afterward, each person sucks on a little piece of cane. The day's single meager meal must be made to last as long as possible.

2:30. The heat drives everyone into the cool shade of the house. Mercegrace spreads a mat on the ground for Alfese's nap and strokes him, murmuring, "Go to sleep, *ti-moune*." She sits down next to him to braid Indianise's hair, while Albert embarks upon his daily ritual of Bible reading. For a couple of hours, he recites the gospels. Sometimes he hesitates, stumbling over a word or a phrase, occasionally even beginning an entire paragraph over again and interrupting the recital

to check that his family has properly understood the meaning of the story. Everyone enjoys this time, when they forget their daily misery.

Afterward, Amors sets off to receive his year-end report card, which is handed out at the school, an hour's walk over the mountain. Mercenise throws a small pebble in the direction of Indianise, who is dozing. The only time the family communicates with her is when they need water. Indianise immediately unhitches the donkey by the door and sets off. Many children meet at the spring; a boy her own age helps Indianise fill the jerry cans. Her face relaxes, and she smiles.

6:00. Albert empties the water from the jerry cans onto the young tobacco plants behind the house and covers them again with banana leaves to slow the evaporation. For all his care, he is not sure that he can save the harvest from the drought.

8:00. As darkness falls, the women watch the silhouettes of Albert and Amors feeding the animals and tying them up for the night. Mercegrace spreads her children's two mats on the ground. She lays Alfese on one of them, covers him with a sheet, and climbs into her own bed.

9:30. His family asleep, Albert sits on the edge of his bed and examines his son's report card by the light of kerosene burning in an old powdered-milk bottle. Amors will move up into the next class, but at seventeen he can hardly read and still needs another two years to graduate from primary school. It is unlikely, however, that his father will be able to pay the school fees for the coming year. Even those who are less poor take an average of eleven years to finish primary school. "And what use is a graduation certificate to Amors if I can't send him to college in Port-au-Prince?" asks Albert. But he will continue to try to finance his son's education. He dreams of seeing Amors leave for the city to earn money and help his family out of their poverty.

Only the thatched roof is intact—a benefit of the drought which has plagued the country for years

One ear of corn divided among six people and a bit of cane to suck on as dessert constitute the only meal of the day

HAITI

THE LAMBERT FAMILY

Vilbre Lambert, age 40 (1)
Gladys Clervil, 40 (2)
Pierre Michelet Clervil, 17 (3)
Joël Lambert, 10 (4)
Rosis Lambert, 8 (5)
Rosa Lambert, 4 (6)
Meprisa Lambert (father's daughter), 8 (7)
Jesusla Lambert, 1 (8)

"CITY OF BROOKLYN"
July 13

The fading moonlight shines on the sheet-metal shacks of the "City of Brooklyn," casting an ethereal glow that transforms the squalor of one of Haiti's poorest slums—a squalor that becomes harshly visible with the rising sun. The early-morning silence is broken by delirious chants coming from a makeshift chapel belonging to Haitian Baptists who practice Christianity laced liberally with voodoo and African idolatry. The starving slum dogs accompany the rising voices, filling the dawn air with an eerie otherworldly lament.

Gladys Lambert lies with her eyes closed, listening to the sounds of people in the alley hurrying to the morning market with their sorry baskets of goods perched on their heads. Her husband lies asleep beside her, and one-year-old Jesusla is curled against her right breast. Gladys waits for all the others to wake, holding on, it seems, to the only peaceful time in her unfortunate life.

6:00. When Gladys and her family open their doors, they join the rest of their neighbors, squatting naked with their washbasins in front of their houses. People spit and urinate on the garbage-strewn ground. Children run to and fro carrying chamber pots on their heads; they empty them in the vacant field that leads to the slum. The shantytown has no running water or sewers, and as the children dump their pots, they must dodge people squatting on the ground relieving themselves in full view of their neighbors.

Gladys' oldest son goes to stand in line at the water tank in the neighboring shantytown. Water there costs only five centimes (one penny) a bucket instead of the ten centimes in the "City of Brooklyn." A man collects the money at each tap for its private owner.

Forty-five minutes later, Pierre Michelet comes struggling through the doorway, one bucket of water balanced on his head, the other dripping in his hands. He looks exhausted. Gladys is gambling everything on her oldest son. Every month she borrows 10 gourdes ($2 U.S.) at 50 percent interest to send Pierre to a private school. "He'll study," Gladys says hopefully, "and get a good job

that will make enough money to repay my debt and give me money to help us live." Most Haitian students take an average of eleven years to complete the country's six-year primary school program. And seventeen-year-old Pierre is no exception. He still has two more years to go. Like many mothers, Gladys is blind to her son's lack of ability. In addition to the difficulties inherent in slum life, Pierre is sickly and does not have enough energy to realize his mother's ambition.

7:30. Gladys' husband, Vilbre, has already disappeared in the slum's labyrinth. Vilbre is a professional beggar. Every day, dressed neatly, his little purse tucked under his arm, he begs, centime by centime, for the 20 gourdes he needs to pay for his monthly medical attention. Vilbre has tuberculosis, probably contracted when he worked as a *faltra* (feces) collector, shoveling the slum's excrement from the vacant field. Vilbre always gets the money he needs. He has nine children by four different women, and one of his sons always helps him out. "Vilbre runs away," Gladys says. "He hates it when the children follow him around asking for a few centimes for something to eat." Gladys resents bearing all the responsibility for providing for her children. Vilbre's daughter Meprisa has come to live with them, and it's just one more mouth that Gladys must feed. She is a strong, compassionate woman and treats Meprisa as one of her own, but she cannot excuse her husband despite his illness. Both Lamberts, however, prefer their life in the shantytown to the one they led in the country.

8:00. Gladys spreads peanut butter on manioc biscuits, hands them to the four younger children, and shoos them out the door. They are on vacation. Gladys sweeps and washes the crude cement floor.

Their fifteen-square-meter shack has two rooms which she rents for 10 gourdes a month. The walls consist of a jumble of tin sheets nailed onto a frame made from small branches. Gladys has covered them with pieces of cardboard and pages from magazines. This is where her "customers" come. From the outside, no one would suspect that Gladys has a store, but word gets around quickly in shantytowns. Between the bed and the table, beside the door, she places a plank on a pile of cardboard. There she displays tiny packets of groceries—two centimes' worth of sugar, three centimes of salt, five centimes of detergent; that is all the poor can afford. Gladys serves everyone with Jesusla hanging at her breast.

9:00. Calling Rosis in to mind the store, Gladys goes to see her neighbors. She visits an old woman who lies naked and motionless on her bed, her body devoured by cancer. Gladys takes the emaciated woman in her arms and sets her on a chair. She will return several times in the course of the day to change the dying woman's position. As Gladys leaves, a friend calls to her from the door of another shack. She is clutching her younger daughter who is delirious with fever. Malaria is a constant danger here, but before the mother can go to a doctor, she must find money to pay for the visit and the drugs. The friend turns to Gladys for sympathy and support. Gladys' attentiveness and her ability to listen quietly are invaluable to people who experience the indignity of death and starvation daily. Her final visit is to a shack where triplets were born a week earlier. One of them has diarrhea, and dehydration has set in. Again, no money, no doctor. Nothing to do but ask for God's mercy. Turning to God is often the only alternative for the majority of Haitians.

10:30. Children wait impatiently around Pierre Michelet, who squats in front of an outdoor brazier grilling peanuts. He sells *royales*, peanut butter spread on manioc biscuits. Those children who have scrounged up two centimes eagerly await their one treat of the day. Then they skip away in single file through the narrow passages around the houses. Some of the children are permanently on vacation, while others attend school every year. It's all a question of money. Watching their children go by, the women smile, forgetting their problems for a moment.

By early afternoon the sheet-metal houses have become uninhabitable ovens. Gladys pours a little water into a plastic bowl and sits Jesusla in it. Somewhat refreshed, the baby dozes, and Gladys sits with her neighbors, their backs against the walls, in the filigree of shade. While they talk, they plait each other's hair. Other women weave baskets of straw to sell in the market. Two young women carrying buckets of water on their heads walk by, hoping that some of the mothers will pay twelve centimes for a bucket. No one moves in the intense heat.

5:00. Gladys prepares a puree of bananas and carrots for her baby. The other children will have rice and kidney beans. The meals are not always as filling; sometimes there is nothing but bread and peanut butter.

A storm breaks over the mountain of Pétionville, home of the city's more fortunate citizens, whose gardens will benefit from the precipitation. The excess water rushes down the streets of Port-au-Prince to the slum. Children along the way bathe and play in the flood of muddy, but free, water. The slums of Port-au-Prince are built on a former swamp that lies a meter below sea level. When the rains are severe, the "City of Brooklyn" becomes a muddy pool and whole families must spend the night on tables and chairs.

6:45. It is cooler now. The merchants and beggars return, and the shantytown comes to life again. The air fills with the aromas of spices and grilled fish. A noisy brawl breaks out between two women weaving baskets, and a crowd forms around them. Jesusla sits on the filthy ground and is attacked by clouds of mosquitoes. Her skin is already completely covered with sores. Gladys rinses her off in a tub, and breast-feeds her before bed.

7:30. Meprisa lights the homemade kerosene lamp fashioned from a jam jar. The slum is connected to the electricity grid, but the residents couldn't pay their bills, so the power was cut off.

8:30. The afternoon storm didn't cause too much damage, so the three girls spread their beds made out of cardboard boxes on the ground near their parents' bed. Gladys lays rags on top, and the girls pile onto them and fall asleep immediately. The boys sleep head to toe on a cot. Vilbre comes home just in time to go to bed. Husband and wife have little to say to each other, so Gladys puts out the lamp. "Until tomorrow," she mutters quietly. Another Haitian might add, "If God in his mercy so wills."

Gladys prefers the life in the shantytown to the one she had in the country. "Here at least I am not alone," she says

By early afternoon, the sheet-metal houses have become uninhabitable ovens. Gladys pours a little water into a bowl and cools her baby

THE LAMBERT FAMILY • 203

HAITI

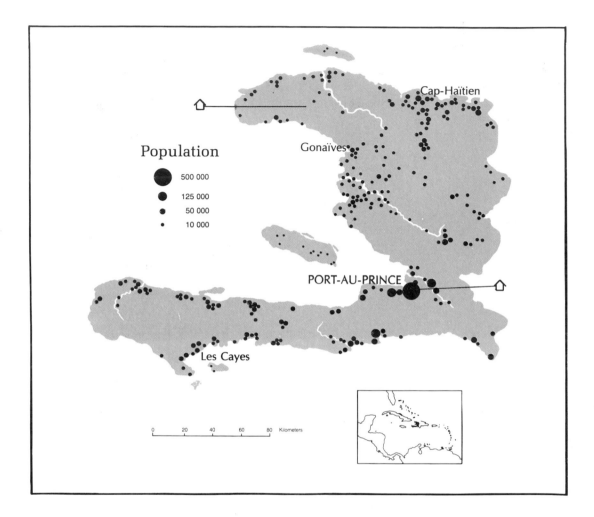

THE NAME: From aboriginal Amerindian *ayti*, meaning "mountainous country"

THE PEOPLE: The Haitians

GEOGRAPHY
> Mountainous country; from west to east, mountain ranges alternate with fertile lowlands.
> Max. altitude: 2,680 m. (8,793 ft.) (Pic La Selle)

Area: 27,750 sq. km. (10,714 sq. mi.)

Density: 191 pers./sq. km. (495 pers./sq. mi.) (1986); 42% of the population occupies 12% of the residential area, with densities of more than 800 persons per hectare.

Arable land: 33% (1987)

Forest: 2%

Climate: Tropical, but cooler in the mountains and on the coast. Rainy season from May to November.

CAPITAL: Port-au-Prince, pop. 738,342 (1984 est.)

LANGUAGE: French (official)
> Creole spoken by all; only 10% speak real French.

RELIGION
> Catholic: 80%
> Baptist: 10%
> Pentecostal: 4%
> Seventh-Day Adventist: 1%
> Voodooism (folk religion)

POPULATION: Total—6,585,000 (1985)
> Annual growth: 2.5% (164,625) (1980–85)
> Doubling time: 30 yrs.
> Urban: 27% (1985) (est. for year 2000: 39%)
> Rural: 73%

AGE GROUPS: (1981)

15% less than 5 yrs.	28% from 20 to 39
41% less than 15	15% from 40 to 59
51% less than 20	6% 60 yrs. and over

ETHNIC GROUPS
Black: 90%
Mixed: 10%

HISTORY
Originally inhabited by the Cibomey, the Arawak, and finally the Caribs

1492: Discovered by Christopher Columbus

1644: Founding of Port-de-Paix by the French

1801–3: Occupation of the entire island of Hispaniola by Toussaint L'Ouverture, a former slave, and his guerrilla bands, who abolish slavery and introduce a constitution

January 1, 1804: Jean Jacques Dessalines declares independence and proclaims himself emperor

1844: Separation from the Dominican Republic and creation of Haiti

1915–34: Occupation by U.S. Marines

1957–71: Dictatorship of François Duvalier (Papa Doc)

1971–86: Jean Claude Duvalier (Baby Doc) succeeds his father and declares himself president for life

1986: Dictator Baby Doc flees Haiti for exile in France

FAMILY
Marital status, for population 10 yrs. and older: (1982)
Single: 33%
Married: 18%
Common-law: 33%
Widowed: 6%
Separated from husband or partner: 9%
Divorced: 0.2%
Female head of household: 33% (1983)
Fertility rate: 5.0 (1985)
Births out of wedlock: no data
Teenage births: no data
Contraception: 7% (1984)
Government's position on family planning: Believes that the population growth rate is too high. The Five-Year Plan (1981–86) sets forth measures to reduce fertility through family planning and increasing the participation of women in development activities.

SOCIAL INDICATORS
Life expectancy: 54 yrs. (male: 52; female: 55) (1985)
Infant mortality: 123/1,000 births (1985)
Crude birth rate: 41/1,000 pop. (1985)
Crude death rate: 14/1,000
Health:
Access to health services: no data
Births attended by trained health personnel: 20% (1983)

HOUSING
Persons per household: 4.4 (1977)

Electricity: 84% without (urban) (1976)
Access to safe water: 33% (urban: 58%; rural: 25%) (1983)
Source of water: (1976)
Piped inside: 11% urban (no piped water in rural areas)
Toilet facilities: (1980)
Urban canalization of rainwater and the sewer system: 5%
Building materials: No data. The available information suggests that the majority of buildings are made of adobe.

EDUCATION
Literacy: 35% (male: 38%; female: 32%) (1982)
Gross enrollment ratio: (1983)
First level: 76% (completing in 1980–84: 45%)
Second: 16%
Third: 1%
An average of 12.5 years is needed to graduate from primary school. Only 11% of the students will complete 6 years of primary school without repeating. (1984)
Educational attainment, for population 25 yrs. +: (1982)
None: 77%
First level: incomplete: 15%
Second: entered: 7%
Third: 1%
Population that knows how to read and write: 23% (1980)
Pop. 6–24 yrs. who do not attend school: 62% (1982)
Pop. 6–26 yrs. who attend primary school: less than 50% (1983)

ECONOMIC ACTIVITY
Economically active population: 44% (male: 71%; female: 37%) (1983)
Agriculture: 74% act. pop.; 32% of GDP
Mines: 1% act. pop.; 1% of GDP
Industry: 6% act. pop.; 22% of GDP
Services: 19% act. pop.; 45% of GDP
Per capita GNP: 310 U.S.$ (1985)
Population in absolute poverty: (1977–84)
Urban: 55%
Rural: 78%
National currency/per U.S.$: 5.00 gourdes (1985)
Principal resource: Coffee

COMMUNICATIONS
Radio:
Transmitters: 48 (1979)
Receivers: 120,000—23/1,000 pop. (1983)
Television:
Transmitters: no data
Receivers: 19,000—3.6/1,000 pop. (1983)

JAMAICA

THE CLARK FAMILY

Bernice Clark, age 38 (1)
Lester Richardson (Richie), 39 (2)
George Brown, 18 (3)
Sharon Brown, 17 (4)
Jenifer Thompson, 11 (5)
Christopher Thompson, 10 (6)
Shernette Richardson, 6 (7)
Patrick Richardson, 4 (8)

LINSTEAD
February 11

5:30. The Alcan bauxite company's train enters the little town of Linstead and comes to a noisy halt right in front of Bernice Clark's tiny house. In their bedroom Bernice and Richie start to talk over the sleeping bodies of their two children, Shernette and Patrick.

Half an hour later, the train's departing whistle rouses the whole town. Bernice, followed by the two youngest, goes into the kitchen, which she calls the cupboard because it's so small. On the couch in the main room, her son George, barely awake, lies with his ear glued to his homemade radio. In the camp bed across from him, Sharon leaves her sleeping younger sister. She slips into a skirt and T-shirt and goes outside to wash up under the coconut palms. Then she opens the window, as she does every morning, giving George, Jenifer, and Christopher the final signal to get up. They watch their dutiful sister as she folds the blankets, stuffs them into the cardboard box at the foot of the bed, and scrubs the wooden floor of the room and the veranda with a brush made from dried coconut.

7:30. Bernice serves Richard his café au lait and bread in bed. Richie is the father of Shernette and Patrick and has minimal contact with Bernice's four other children. He takes no responsibility for their keep. Despite her minimum wage, Bernice contributes three-quarters of the rent and pays for her own children's food and tuition. Richie is not working today. He has a job with the bauxite company only one or two weeks a month. Alcan is now the only employer in the area. If it shuts down like the other bauxite company did recently, there would be another few thousand unemployed.

First served, first to leave. Where to? "I'm going to walk the street, man!" Richie will chat with his friend the stationmaster, and then hang out in the shoe shop. Bernice accepts this. "Men never stay home and you really don't know how long they'll be around," she says.

8:00. As she does every morning, Sharon braids Jenifer's hair, sweeps the yard, and irons the school uniforms. Jenifer and Christopher then join the other students for the half-hour walk out of town to school. Bernice has put a sandwich and a cookie into their satchels for lunch. Christopher and Jenifer were born while Bernice was working as a maid. She was not well informed about birth-control methods at the time. Although she never lived with their father, he comes to see the children from time to time and sometimes gives Bernice a little money.

The eldest children, George and Sharon, have never known their father. He left Jamaica for the United States when Sharon was barely a month old and has never been heard from since. George and Sharon have been pressuring Bernice to make inquiries at the American Embassy, and she has reluctantly done so. "They want a photo of their father so badly. If they don't get any news, I'm afraid they'll go off to find him." Sharon and George are learning a trade and intend to emigrate as soon as possible. Sharon is attending secretarial school, and George has just finished carpentry courses at a technical school. The three pairs of brothers and sisters do not interact much. Their only family bond is to their mother, and this won't be enough to keep George and Sharon in Jamaica.

8:30. George leaves for the furniture shop. This is his first year of work. He loves his craft but is frustrated at having nothing more to do than turn bed legs. He works privately on the side so as not to lose his skills. His customers are pleased with his work, but they forget to pay their bills. "People here are willing to pay crazy prices for imported goods," says Bernice, "but they don't want to pay George for the time it takes him to make a piece of furniture and for the price of the materials he has to buy." George always tries to give some of his salary to his mother, but she encourages him to save it for his own needs.

9:00. Sharon takes the two youngest with her. She will drop them off at the kindergarten on her way to secretarial school. Alone at last, Bernice listens to a phone-in show on the radio while she does the laundry and washes the dishes. The debate surges around the lack of a secondary school.

Then she takes a short break to chat with her neighbor. The two woman lean on the front fence as they watch a car drive up the street. "Mrs. Barry's going to have her electricity cut off again," says the neighbor, recognizing the utility company car as it parks in front of the woman's house. "I don't understand the government," Bernice says angrily. "They know how much unemployment there is and how little money we have." As the car drives away, they wonder who its next victim will be.

Bernice doesn't like her house; she finds it too small. She would like to move, but apart from the difficulty of finding another, she could not consider paying more rent. The owner of this house has emigrated to the United States and has locked up two rooms, one of which is the bathroom, where he stores his belongings. The family is squeezed into the remaining forty-six square meters and has to put up with a toilet in the yard. The owner also left an unpaid water bill and the water was cut off. It would cost three months' salary to have it reconnected, which is out of the question, so Bernice fetches water from the neighbors' houses.

Bernice goes to the market. The children would be pleased if she could find some rice as a change from plantains and potatoes. She investigates all the shelves, eventually finds what she wants, and begins to negotiate. The merchant will give her a good price for the rice only if she will buy some other items that he can't sell and that Bernice has no need for. "Everything works by blackmail," she complains as she returns without rice.

3:30. Everyone is home from school. Jenifer and Christopher lounge around on the veranda while Bernice washes their uniforms. This is a daily task. Sharon will iron them tomorrow morning. At the moment, she is doing her shorthand exercises before helping her mother with dinner. Always near their mother, Patrick and Shernette sit on the kitchen doorstep sucking their thumbs.

5:30. There are yams and—not terribly fresh—fish for dinner this evening. When the dishes are done, Bernice leaves with Christopher for the health clinic, where she does the cleaning. Without her ten-year-old's help, she would not be finished until eleven o'clock. She prefers working there to being a domestic at an employer's constant beck and call. Also, the government now regulates wages and working hours, which makes exploitation more difficult.

9:00. George makes a final trip to the neighbors' for water. Then he walks around the town for a while. He spends the rest of the evening listening to the radio, singing along with the reggae tunes he knows by heart. The evening is calm, and the children are eventually lulled to sleep by his music.

Bernice and Christopher return. She sticks her head in the living-room door and checks that her family is there. Knowing that Richie will be home late, she slides into bed beside the two youngest. George sings quietly in the darkness.

The owner of the house has emigrated to the United States but retains the use of two rooms, one of which is the bathroom, to store his things

In Bernice's room, the table is squeezed in between the bed and the door

JAMAICA

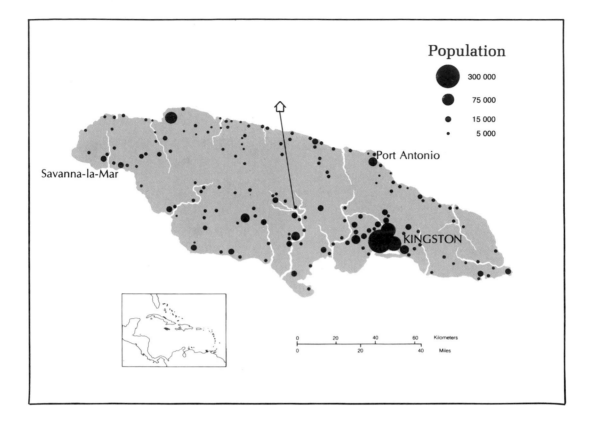

THE NAME: From Arawak *xaimaca*, meaning "land of wood and water"

THE PEOPLE: The Jamaicans

GEOGRAPHY
> Mountains covering about 80% of the island
> Coastal lowlands and valleys
> Hills and limestone plateaus in central and western areas of interior
> Max. altitude: 2,344 m. (17,402 ft.) (Blue Mountain Peak)
> **Area:** 10,991 sq. km. (4,244 sq. mi.)
> **Density:** 197 pers./sq. km. (511 pers./sq. mi.) (1986)
> **Arable land:** 24% (1987)
> **Forest:** 17%
> **Climate:** Varies with altitude. Tropical at sea level and temperate in the mountain areas. Rainfall is seasonal, with striking regional variations.

CAPITAL: Kingston, pop. 696,300 (metropolitan area) (1982 est.)

LANGUAGE: English

RELIGION
> Baptist: 18%
> Anglican: 15%
> Seventh-Day Adventist: 7%
> Methodist: 6%
> Catholic: 8%

POPULATION: Total—2,336,000
> Annual growth: 1.4% (32,704) (1980–85)
> Doubling time: 34 yrs.
> Urban: 54% (est. for year 2000: 64%)
> Rural: 46%

AGE GROUPS: (1980)
> 12% less than 5 yrs.
> 38% less than 15
> 50% less than 20
> 27% from 20 to 39
> 13% from 40 to 59
> 10% 60 yrs. and over

ETHNIC GROUPS
Black: 76%
Mixed: 15% (black and white)
East Indian and Afro East Indian: 3%
White: 3%

HISTORY
Originally inhabited by the Arawak Indians
1494: Discovered by Christopher Columbus
1509–1655: Spanish colonization
1655: British colonization
1838: Abolition of slavery
1865: Establishment of Crown Colony
August 3, 1962: Independence within the Commonwealth

FAMILY
Marital status, for population 14 yrs. and older: (1982)
Married: 25%
Common-law: 16%
Visiting union: 3%
Separated from husband or partner: 11%
Never had a husband or partner: 3%
Female head of household: 38% (1982)
Fertility rate: 3.1 (1985)
Births out of wedlock: no data
Teenage births: 27% (1981)
Contraception: 52% (1984)
Government's position on family planning: Has indicated that its anticipated population size is excessive and that levels of population growth are too high. A policy-formation body, vested with full statutory responsibility for family planning, has been established.

SOCIAL INDICATORS
Life expectancy: 74 yrs. (male: 70; female: 76) (1985)
Infant mortality: 20/1,000 births (1985)
Crude birth rate: 27/1,000 pop. (1985)
Crude death rate: 5/1,000
Health:
Access to health services: no data
Births attended by trained health personnel: 89% (1984)

HOUSING
Persons per household: 3.4 (1984)
Electricity: 51% without (1982)
Access to safe water: 86% (1983)

Source of water: (1982)
Piped inside: 31%
Piped outside: 21%
Public standpipe: 17%
Private catchment: 8%
Other: 2.4%
Toilet facilities: (1980)
Pit: 48%
WC linked to sewer: 17%
WC not linked: 18%
None and other: 17%
Building materials: (1982)
Concrete: 57%
Wood: 27%
Mixture of wood and concrete: 8%
Other: 9%

EDUCATION
Literacy: 96% (male: 96%; female: 96%) (1970)
Gross enrollment ratio: (1982–83)
First level: 106% (completing in 1980–84: 80%)
Second: 58%
Third: 6%
Educational attainment, for population 14 yrs. +: (1981)
None: 2%
First level: incomplete: 70%
Second: entered: 28%
Third: no data

ECONOMIC ACTIVITY
Economically active population: 47% (male: 50%; female: 43%) (1982)
Agriculture: 21% act. pop.; 7% of GDP
Mines: 5% act. pop.; 9% of GDP
Industry: 21% act. pop.; 25% of GDP
Services: 53% act. pop.; 60% of GDP
Per capita GNP: 940 U.S.$ (1985)
Population in absolute poverty: (1977–84)
Rural: 80%
National currency/per U.S.$ (1984): 5.56 Jamaican dollars
Principal resources: Sugar, bauxite

COMMUNICATIONS
Radio:
Transmitters: 19 (1979)
Receivers: 890,000—394/1,000 pop. (1983)
Television:
Transmitters: no data
Receivers: 200,000—89/1,000 pop. (1983)

ST. KITTS (St. Christopher) and NEVIS

THE ARCHIBALD FAMILY

Loraine Archibald, age 39 (1)
Sharon Archibald, 22 (absent from photo)
Blondell Archibald, 20 (2)
Roslyn, 18 (3) *Geraldine, 16* (4)
Hazel, 14 (5) *Fastina, 10* (6)
Jeanette, 3 (7) *Jason, 4* (8)

1 dog	*3 cows*
1 cat	*7 goats*
1 pig	*16 chickens*

LOWER CAYON
June 10

5:25. Loraine stretches out her arms and pulls the cord hanging from the ceiling. Her tiny room is flooded with light. Outside, dawn is having difficulty asserting itself. The sky is heavy with gray clouds, harbingers of the rainy season. Even the birds hesitate to sing. In any case, their song would be drowned by the gospel music blaring from the radio. Loraine usually has it turned up to such a level that no member of the family can sleep. She empties the chamber pots and finishes getting ready for her day by pouring a bucket of water over her head. She slips into the same work clothes she wore yesterday, sticks a cap on her head, picks up the bag containing her lunch, grabs her machete, and announces her departure loudly. At the last moment, Loraine unhooks the heavy belt hanging behind the door and wraps it around her ample waist. This is the belt that makes little Jeanette run—and also cry when it is used to administer a spanking.

Loraine walks quickly down the lane to the village's main road. Every hour she wastes costs her $2.40 E.C. (90 cents, U.S.), money she cannot afford to lose. The sugarcane harvest is coming to an end at the Brighton Estate, the plantation where she works. Starting next week, she will work no more than three days a week, weeding and spraying the fields.

6:00. Like all the inhabitants of the village, Roslyn goes to fill two buckets at the public tap. The water pressure is so low that the taps in each family's yard do not work; neither does the shower at the bottom of the Archibalds' garden. This is the dry season, and the sugar plantation has first priority in the use of the water from the almost empty reservoir.

Hazel and Fastina, as the youngest schoolgirls, have the daily task of sweeping the chicken droppings from the yard, feeding the pigs, and picking up the garbage blown in by the wind. Every year the twelve villages on the island compete for the title of "Most Beautiful Village," and as a result, every house is carefully maintained and surrounded with flowers.

6:20. Blondell arrives to drop off her son, Jason, with her sisters before she leaves for work at a factory that manufactures components for television sets. Jason has been crying all night. Blondell just moved into a new house last week, and Jason misses his grandmother and his "aunt" Jeanette terribly. Jason and Jeanette suck their thumbs while watching Blondell make herself a mayonnaise sandwich in preparation for her day. She hasn't quite adjusted to her new independence either.

Roslyn meanwhile spreads a sheet on the table in order to iron her skirt. She never leaves the house without looking flawless. She is heading for the square at Cayon, which last night was alive with children, lovers, and basketball players. This morning, it is full of workers who will ride the minibus to the capital, the country's only town. Roslyn works in an American factory that makes underwear and swimsuits for export. She gives 40 percent of her salary to her mother and deposits the rest in the bank. Her first goal is to buy herself a bed and turn the little alcove that serves as a clothes closet into a bedroom. She is tired of sleeping in the same room as her three sisters, but she won't leave home to alive alone like Blondell. "I need my family," she says.

8:20. Geraldine sweeps and washes the floors. Hazel and Fastina braid each other's hair, finish their mangos, and set off for school, taking Jason to the day-care center on the way. Blondell will pick him up after work. Jeanette has a cold and will stay home and be looked after by Geraldine, who is delighted to miss school. She would love to quit school and work in a factory so she could buy all the things that her three older sisters have.

9:00. Sharon, the oldest, emerges from her room at the back of the house, which she has built out of cement blocks. The only one of the seven sisters with a private space of her own, she padlocks it whenever she leaves. Woe betide anyone bold enough to play with her many jars of cream. Sharon's aloofness annoys her sisters, but they accept her oddity. At twenty-two, she has no children and no boyfriend either. An individualist, she practices a different religion than the rest of the family. She is a Seventh-Day Adventist and is forbidden to speak or work on Saturdays. This morning she is preparing to be away for a week. Sharon is a nurse in town and sleeps in the hospital when she is on night duty. Like her other working sisters, she pays her mother for room and board.

10:00. Geraldine's repeated warnings have no effect on Jeanette, who is running around shouting, not acting very sick at all. The only way to restore calm is a good spanking. After the tears have subsided, Jeanette goes to sleep. The old wooden house falls silent and even seems large. Its sixty square meters of living space feels very cramped, though, when all the girls are together. Fortunately, the rent is minimal. The house belongs to Loraine's brother, who, like the rest of the Archibald family, has left to work in England. He will never reoccupy his little wooden house because he has bought himself a concrete house higher up in the village. He plans to move there in a few months after twenty-six years outside the country.

1:00. Loraine returns from the fields. She opens the refrigerator, pours herself a large glass of cold water, and sits down at the end of the table to watch Jeanette eat her soup. She rests for only a few moments, however, before taking a bath and heading straight for the kitchen, a sagging old hut in the backyard.

Loraine is an independent woman. She has always refused to marry. "Men are very nice, but once they get married, they change and become demanding. I prefer my freedom!" There have nevertheless been a number of men in her life, five in particular: the fathers of her seven daughters.

3:30. Back home from school, Hazel and Fastina put on their normal clothes—skirts and T-shirts with holes in them. Then, with Geraldine, they each carry a bucket of water on their heads to take to the cows and goats which the family raises and sells. The girls go down a deep ravine, cross a dried-up riverbed, and climb back up to the fields. They sit and look at the village and the sea while the cows drink their fill. Regardless of where you are on St. Kitts, it is always possible, by craning your neck slightly, to see the Caribbean's blue waters.

5:20. In the tiny living room, Jeanette is comfortably nestled against her mother's ample chest, sucking her thumb happily as the two watch *Sesame Street* on television, a privilege which the older children didn't have four years ago when there was no electricity. From now on, Loraine doesn't have to get up; she issues orders, and her daughters do the work. There are still buckets of water to be fetched, mending to be done, and washing to be spread out.

7:30. They all eat their chicken and potatoes when and where they wish, as there is no room for all of them at the table. Roslyn is getting ready to go out with a friend, and hopes she will run into her boyfriend. In any case, there is always a strong possibility that she will meet a half brother or half sister in the village. All the children in these intricate networks of relationships know each other and usually become close friends.

9:00. Loraine boils a pot of water on the kerosene stove. Every evening she fills a thermos with hot water in case someone should be ill during the night. After waking Jeanette and making her go to the bathroom, Loraine scoops up her little daughter and brings her to the bed they both share.

Geraldine is watching the end of a television program while her younger sisters get ready for bed. Roslyn comes in and checks that the doors are securely bolted before sliding onto the bed she shares with Geraldine. The uncomfortable box spring covered with old rags and the lack of space remind her of the importance of her savings.

Each house is carefully maintained and surrounded with flowers, and every year the island's twelve villages compete for the title of "Most Beautiful Village"

The girls play dominoes in the tiny room that serves as a dining room as their mother prepares dinner in the kitchen, a sagging old hut in the backyard

ST. KITTS (St. Christopher) and NEVIS

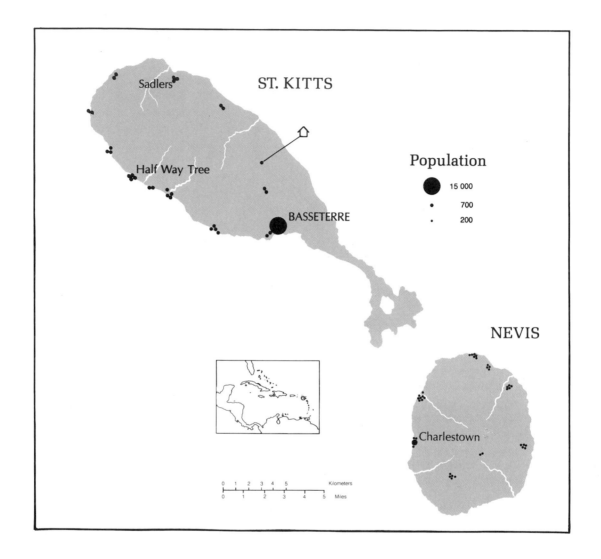

THE NAME
St. Kitts: short form of St. Christopher; given by
   Christopher Columbus
Nevis: from the Nevis Mountain in Scotland

THE PEOPLE: The Kittitians and Nevisians

GEOGRAPHY
   Volcanic mountain chain dominates central core of
     both islands.
   Max. altitude: 1,156 m. (3,792 ft.) (Mt. Liamuiga)
   Nevis: consists of a single mountain—Nevis Peak,
     985 m. (3,232 ft.)
Area: 269 sq. km. (104 sq. mi.); St. Kitts: 168.4 sq. km.
   (68 sq. mi.)

Density: 167 pers./sq. km. (433 pers./sq. mi.) (1986)
Arable land: 39% (1987)
Forest: 17%
Climate: Tropical, tempered by sea winds; low humidity
   and no recognized rainy season.

CAPITAL: Basseterre, pop. 15,000 (1980)

LANGUAGE: English

RELIGION
   Anglican: 37%
   Methodist: 29%
   Catholic: 7%
   Other Protestant: 31%

POPULATION: Total—46,000
  Annual growth: 0.7% (322) (1980–85)
  Doubling time: 45 yrs.
  Urban: 45% (1985)
  Rural: 55%

AGE GROUPS: (1980)
  12% less than 5 yrs.
  37% less than 15
  50% less than 20
  24% from 20 to 39
  12% from 40 to 59
  13% 60 yrs. and over

ETHNIC GROUPS
  Black: 94.3%
  Mixed: 3.3%
  White: 0.9%

HISTORY
  Originally inhabited by the Arawak and Carib
    Indians
  1493: Discovery by Christopher Columbus
  1623: English settlers arrive on St. Kitts
  1628: English settle on Nevis
  1627–1727: Anglo-French rivalry
  1783: Both islands become British
  1871–1956: Member of the Federation of the
    Leeward Islands
  1958: Joins West Indies Federation
  February 27, 1967: Autonomous within the
    Commonwealth
  September 19, 1983: Independence

FAMILY
Marital status, for population 14 yrs. and older: (1980)
  Married: 29%
  Common-law: 10%
  Visiting union: 6%
  Separated from husband or partner: 12%
  Never had husband or partner: 40%
Female head of household: 46% (1980)
Fertility rate: 3.6 (1980)
Births out of wedlock: no data
Teenage births: 28% (1981)
Contraception: no data
Government's position on family planning: no data

SOCIAL INDICATORS
Life expectancy: 64 yrs. (male, female: no data) (1985)
Infant mortality: 41/1,000 births (1985)
Crude birth rate: 25.4/1,000 pop. (1981)
Crude death rate: 10.1/1,000

Health:
  Access to health services: Given the island's small
    size, everyone has easy access to a medical
    center.
  Births attended by trained health personnel: 97%
    (1981)

HOUSING
Persons per household: 3.7 (1980 est.)
Electricity: 43% without (1980)
Access to safe water: No data, but it can be assumed
  that piped water is safe.
Source of water: (1980)
  Piped inside: 35%
  Piped outside: 11%
  Public standpipe: 41%
  Other: 13%
Toilet facilities: (1980)
  Flush: 30%
  Latrine: 60%
  Other: 10%
Building materials: (1980)
  Wood: 51%
  Concrete: 21%
  Mixture of wood and concrete: 25%

EDUCATION
Literacy: 98% (male: 98%; female: 98%) (1970)
Gross enrollment ratio: no data
Educational attainment, for population 25 yrs. +:
  (1980)
  None: 1%
  First level: incomplete: 30%
  Second: entered: 67%
  Third: 2%

ECONOMIC ACTIVITY
Economically active population: 40% (male: 49%;
  female: 31%) (1980)
Agriculture: 25% act. pop.; GDP: no data
Mines: 0% act. pop.
Industry: 29% act. pop.
Services: 46% act. pop.
Per capita GNP: 1,550 U.S.$ (1985)
Population in absolute poverty: no data
National currency/per U.S.$: 2.70 East Caribbean
  dollars (1985)
Principal resources: Sugar, tourism

COMMUNICATIONS
Radio:
  Transmitters: 2 (1979)
  Receivers: 21,000—313/1,000 pop. (1983)
Television:
  Transmitters: 4 (1983)
  Receivers: 4,500—67/1,000 pop. (1983)

St. Lucia

THE POPO FAMILY

Raphael Popo, age 30 (1)
Francisca Popo, 30 (2)
Alvin Popo, 12 (3)
Davis, 11 (4)
Ron, 8 (5)
Delia, 5 (6)

4 sheep
3 goats
2 cows
1 dog

BABONNEAU
May 6

5:30. Francisca bangs on the wall that separates her room from her children's. Her oldest son, Alvin, gets up and walks outside to the kitchen shack to light the fire. The morning mist clings to the lush, verdant slopes of the rain-forest mountains. After Dominica, St. Lucia is the greenest island in the Caribbean.

Half an hour later, Francisca rouses herself from slumber. Every day the child she is carrying feels heavier. Raphael has made coffee. This morning he fills an extra cup; his mother-in-law came yesterday to spend Mother's Day with her daughter and after breakfast will return by bus to her home in the capital. Seeing that his wife is in no mood to speak to him, Raphael leaves to take the livestock to pasture.

Alvin gathers up yesterday's dirty dishes and puts them outside on the ground. Then he goes to fill a dishpan with water at the only tap in the courtyard. In her room, Francisca gathers the children's school uniforms from the cardboard boxes that serve as cupboards. She irons the uniforms every day. Ron takes a basket and climbs to the top of the hill to wait for the truck that delivers bread every morning. Davis, the most studious, is excused from chores, as is Delia, who is still too small.

7:15. A sudden downpour causes everyone to run for shelter. It rains very hard, but only for a short time. In five minutes everyone is back at work. In silence, they listen to radio announcements of the local obituaries. Francisca always listens in case she knows any of the people who have died. The slightest piece of news travels fast on this small island, and commenting on neighbors' actions is the only excitement in the peaceful life of the country people.

Francisca has pulled out a bucket and sits down beside Alvin. The family's activities take place here, between the house and the shack that serves as a kitchen. As she does her daily laundry, she gives instructions to Davis, who is making breakfast: "Don't forget to put a little nutmeg and cinnamon in the hot chocolate. Not too much corned beef on the bread."

9:00. The children will barely be able to make it to school before the second downpour. They run up the hill, pursued by heavy gray clouds.

Francisca bathes under the outside tap and slowly climbs up the now slippery dirt road to the community health clinic. She is careful. Two years ago she lost a baby when she was eight months pregnant and almost died. This will be the last child—a girl, she hopes. Then she will have a tubal ligation. "I have to think of myself and of the children I have already." Francisca enters the clinic two hours late. With the experience of previous pregnancies, she knew that it was pointless to come earlier. A dozen pregnant women, seated uncomfortably on hard, narrow benches, still wait their turn.

Raphael has offered to rinse the laundry during her absence and hang it out to dry. A good excuse not to work in his banana grove this morning! He drank too much last night and the mere thought of all the things he has to do exhausts him. But Raphael is not apologetic. "I've got the right to rest a little bit. I've never been afraid of work." He spent three years working the harvest in the southern United States, under an agreement between the United States and the Caribbean governments. "But I'm finished with that slave work," Raphael says. "I've got what I wanted, and now I want to stay close to my family."

Thirteen years ago, Raphael built his wooden house with his own hands. It has four small rooms and is solidly built. The neighbors sought shelter at the Popos' when Hurricane Allen destroyed part of the island. "All we need now is one extra room," says Francisca. They have to wait until they accumulate some savings. "When I think of all the people living around us in mud houses with no running water or electricity, I think how lucky we are." The new room will be for the boys. They are growing fast and will soon outgrow their tiny room. And it will be built of cement, now that it is no more expensive than wood.

After the first year working abroad, Raphael bought a sofa and the piece of land surrounding the house. After the second, he brought back a television and hi-fi system. Then he installed a tap for running water. Finally he widened the path leading to the house and had electricity installed, sharing the cost with his neighbor.

12:00. Francisca leaves the clinic at the same time as the children get out of school. With Raphael's help, the meal is ready when they arrive home. Raphael's willingness to participate in the household chores is a rare quality among the men of this country. It helps Francisca forget all his other faults, the most outstanding being his numerous amorous escapades and the two children he has by other women on the island. Francisca has been angry at him since yesterday, though, when he left her at home and spent Mother's Day with his buddies. Eventually she will forgive him. They have lived together since they were sixteen. Francisca, however, doesn't have many illusions about love, even though Raphael decided three years ago to propose marriage to her. "He knows I'm a hard worker," she says, "and he was afraid someone else might notice it and snatch me up." For his part of the marriage contract, Raphael has promised to be faithful to his wife.

1:00. The children have returned to school, and Francisca and Raphael go out to work. The banana trees must be looked after every day and every stage of their development watched. The Federation that is responsible for the export of bananas has issued very strict regulations, which have to be obeyed, and that takes hours of work. Now they both wrap bunches of green bananas in blue plastic bags to prevent the windblown palms from blemishing the fruit. "They tell us foreigners don't buy marked bananas," says Raphael. Tomorrow Raphael will plant sweet potatoes. He follows the instructions of the farmer's almanac, whose growing seasons are governed by the phases of the moon.

4:00. Francisca is sitting in the shade, giving her swollen legs a rest. Delia has trotted off down the road. She spends a lot of time at the home of Raphael's mother, their closest neighbor.

School is out, but the boys cannot go out to play immediately. Ron carries charcoal into the kitchen, and Alvin goes to feed the cows. Alvin is the hardest worker at home, but Francisca complains about his performance at school. Davis is the most promising student. He lazily waters the garden. Physical work doesn't interest him. His ambition is one day to wear a suit and tie and work in the city.

5:30. Francisca prepares dinner in the cabin. She has given up the idea of having a kitchen in the house. Her husband would never be willing to give up the good taste of food cooked over a wood fire. In the garden, Raphael is planting two rows of lettuce, singing with the radio as he works. They grow a variety of vegetables and herbs, which Francisca sells at the market three times a week, their only regular source of income. The last rays of the sun illuminate the different green hues of the various fruit trees in the valley. Waves of rhythmic music float out of the house. "When there's music, it doesn't feel like you're working," says Raphael, pouring himself a small glass of rum, which he places on the side of the balcony. He seems a happy man. "To have my own land, my own house, no debts, and no boss, that was my dream. To be free."

6:00. It is raining very hard now. "Good," says Francisca. "The garden needs it." The door of the house shuts out the wind and the mosquitoes. Francisca has planned carefully so that she can have her meal while watching a soap opera on television. The boys eat their dinner at the table. Raphael prefers to eat alone when everyone else has finished. Meanwhile he can have a second glass of rum.

8:00. Alvin is entitled to a bed, while his two brothers make a mattress out of old clothes. Delia falls asleep on the couch. Beside her, Francisca watches one last program.

Before joining Raphael, who is already asleep, Francisca puts the chamber pot where everyone can get at it easily. She climbs in beside her husband and uses his shoulder as a pillow. Whatever she was pouting about is suddenly forgotten.

In contrast to the shack that serves as kitchen, the little wooden house is solid. The neighbors sought shelter at the Popos' when Hurricane Allen hit in 1980

Francisca has given up the idea of having a kitchen in the house. Her husband would never be willing to give up the good taste of food cooked over a wood fire

ST. LUCIA

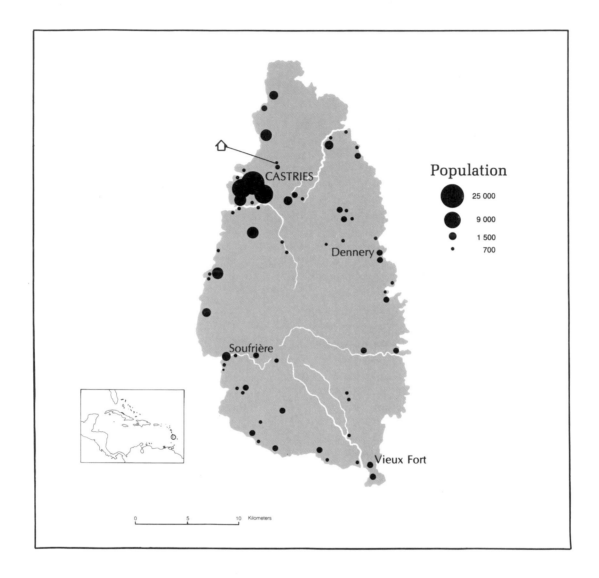

THE NAME: In honor of St. Lucy; island first sighted
   by the Spanish on St. Lucy's day

THE PEOPLE: St. Lucians

GEOGRAPHY
   Mountainous island of volcanic origin with fertile
      valleys
   Max. altitude: 950 m. (3,145 ft.) (Mt. Gimie)
Area: 616 sq. km. (238 sq. mi.)
Density: 195 pers./sq. km. (504 pers./sq. mi.) (1986)
Arable land: 27% (1987)
Forest: 13%
Climate: Tropical maritime; rainy season from May to
   August. Temperatures are uniform.

CAPITAL: Castries, pop. 47,600 (1979)

LANGUAGE: English (official)
   French-based patois is widely spoken.

RELIGION:
   Majority Catholic

POPULATION: Total—130,000 (1985)
   Annual growth: 1.6% (2,080) (1980–84)
   Doubling time: 28 yrs.
   Urban: 34% (1980)
   Rural: 66%

AGE GROUPS: (1980)

14% less than 5 yrs.	24% from 20 to 39
44% less than 15	12% from 40 to 59
56% less than 20	8% 60 yrs. and over

ETHNIC GROUPS:
Black: 87%
Mixed: 9%
East Indian: 3%
White: 0.6%

HISTORY
Originally inhabited by the Arawak and Carib Indians
1502: Discovery by Christopher Columbus
1605–38: Attempts by English to establish settlements
1650: French colonization
1814: France cedes island to Britain after a succession of wars
1838: Abolition of slavery
1871: Part of the Windward Islands
1958–62: Member of the Federation of the West Indies
January 3, 1967: Associate state of the Commonwealth
February 22, 1979: Independence within the Commonwealth

FAMILY
Marital status, for population 14 yrs. and older: (1980)
Married: 29%
Common-law: 16%
Visiting union: 7%
Separated from husband or partner: 13%
Never had husband or partner: 30%
Female head of household: 39% (1980)
Fertility rate: 4.5 (1984)
Births out of wedlock: 86% (1984)
Teenage births: 27% (1981)
Contraception: no data
Government's position on family planning: Considers the present rate of population growth to be excessive and plans to intensify family-planning activities to reduce it to a more satisfactory level.

SOCIAL INDICATORS
Life expectancy: 69 yrs. (male: 70; female: 75) (1980–85)
Infant mortality: 18/1,000 births (1985)
Crude birth rate: 30/1,000 pop. (1984)
Crude death rate: 6/1,000
Health:
Access to health services: no data
Births attended by trained health personnel: 99% (1979–81)

HOUSING
Persons per household: 4.6 (1980)
Electricity: 55% without (1980)
Access to safe water: No data, but it can be assumed that piped water is safe.
Source of water: (1980)
Piped inside: 23%
Piped outside: 16%
Public standpipe: 41%
Other: 20%
Toilet facilities: (1980)
WC linked to sewer: 7%
WC not linked: 12%
Pit: 51%
None: 22%
Other: 8%
Building materials: (1980)
Wood: 74%
Concrete: 12%
Mixture of wood and concrete: 9%
Other: 5%

EDUCATION
Literacy: 82% (male: 81%; female: 82%) (1970)
Gross enrollment ratio: (1981)
First level: 95%
Second: no data
Third: no data
Educational attainment, for population 25 yrs. +: (1980)
None: 18%
First level: incomplete: 75%
Second: entered: 7%
Third: 1%

ECONOMIC ACTIVITY
Economically active population: no data
Agriculture: 30% act. pop.; 30% of GDP
Mines: 0% act. pop.; 0% of GDP
Industry: 20% act. pop.; 15% of GDP
Services: 50% act. pop.; 55% of GDP
Per capita GNP: 1,240 U.S.$ (1985)
Population in absolute poverty: no data
National currency/per U.S.$: 2.70 East Caribbean dollars (1985)
Principal resources: Bananas, coconuts

COMMUNICATIONS
Radio:
Transmitters: 4 (1979)
Receivers: 96,000—758/1,000 pop. (1983)
Television:
Transmitters: no data
Receivers: 2,000—16/1,000 pop. (1983)

ST. VINCENT and THE GRENADINES

THE CHARLES FAMILY

Peggy Louis, age 85 (1)
Victor Charles, 62 (2)
Iris C. Charles, 35 (3)
Miranda Wood (Pet), 16 (4)
Martin Wood, 14 (5)

4 chickens
1 sheep
1 dog

LAYOU
May 1

5:30. It's Monday morning and May Day, the international workers' holiday. But Uncle Victor is all ready to leave for work in the fields; he owns and farms three acres. One hour later reggae music pours out of the neighbors' house and forces Iris Charles out of her bed.

Her daughter Miranda, nicknamed Pet, turns on her radio too. The newscaster is commenting on the Prime Minister's speech the day before. Iris attended the political rally organized in honor of the nationalization of one of the large coconut plantations in the northern part of the island. Every time the tiny country recovers land from foreign hands and becomes more independent, it's reason to celebrate.

Iris took advantage of the event to have a quiet word with her Prime Minister, who walked among the crowd. Iris has lost her job as municipal counselor. She had been in charge of her community for several years, collecting the taxes and looking after public works. Thanks to Iris, a pedestrian crossing was installed this year. "The young people drive like madmen down the narrow main road, and the shops play their music so loudly that it's impossible to hear a car coming. We had to protect ourselves." Iris is enraged at her removal. A village resident who had influential relatives managed to place his girlfriend in Iris' job. In such a small country, it is difficult to be in politics without having to do favors for your relatives. The Prime Minister listened and told Iris to come to his office next week. Iris hopes he will settle the problem.

To take her mind off her troubles, Iris decides to work on her bathroom. "The hardest part is cutting the tiles and making proper corners, but I do the best I can," she says as she wields the trowel. The work on the house never seems to end.

The history of Iris' house is typical for the island. Her grandmother owned what was then a little wooden house with a gabled roof. She had come down from the North, driven out, like all the inhabitants, by the eruption of the Soufrière volcano in 1902. When Iris was born, she was left in her grandmother's care by her mother, who went off to England to work. In the first years that Iris worked, before Miranda's birth, she decided to remodel the house. She saved up to buy two cement blocks per week and bought five hundred in all. She added two bedrooms, a kitchen and dining room, and finally, last Christmas, a bathroom. The children's father has helped financially with the most recent tile-buying project. Even though he has never lived with Iris, he has always been solicitous of his children's welfare; this is why he and Iris have always maintained a good relationship. Now that she is old, Mammy Peggy has put the ownership of the house in Iris' name. She is a proud, independent woman who instilled the same traits in her granddaughter, and although she would still have herself considered head of the household, the family matriarch relaxes under Iris' loving care.

Iris stops to check the alignment of the tiles and grunts with satisfaction. The roads of the country are lined with houses in the process of renovation. Everyone wants to give his old wooden shack a more modern appearance.

8:00. Martin is watering the garden. As usual, Iris had to raise her voice to get him to do it. "With the neighborhood sheep and goats roaming free, it's a wonder that our garden is as pretty as it is," Mammy Peggy complains. After gathering her hair in her eternal turban, she goes out to prune the shrubs. Mammy Peggy seems to be everywhere at once. She constantly finds thousands of little jobs to do. Iris keeps telling her to sit and let herself be spoiled. But the old woman needs to keep busy.

9:00. Miranda is in the kitchen preparing the midday meal of chicken, rice, and boiled plantains. She is seven months pregnant and can no longer attend school. When she told her mother the news, she was ashamed and afraid of the storm it would provoke. And at first Iris was furious. "Girls are so gullible; love, fine promises, they always allow themselves to be taken in," Iris says. She hopes that her daughter will resume her schooling in evening classes after the baby is born. Now that her anger has subsided, Iris impatiently awaits the baby's arrival. Miranda wants a girl. Her drawer is already full of baby clothes, and her boyfriend is building a crib.

12:00. They all help themselves to Miranda's meal when they get hungry. The tempo has slowed down today, and they are happy to talk to other relatives who stop by to visit. The family is large. Iris' mother alone has twelve children and twenty grandchildren. First the visitors go into the kitchen and greet Mammy Peggy, who prefers sitting cross-legged on the floor. Then they sit for a few moments in the living room, over which Iris maintains a proprietary watch. The backs and arms of the sofa and two red leatherette chairs are covered with lace antimacassars. On the little wooden table Iris has placed a basket that she crocheted, starched, and filled with plastic flowers. In one corner a cupboard holds the record player, the radio–cassette recorder, and the television, while in another there is a bookcase in which books and china knickknacks vie for space. On the pink and turquoise walls hangs a collection of little plates inscribed with pious thoughts and popular sayings.

3:00. Martin and Miranda have disappeared with their friends, and Iris returns to her tiles. Even though the village lies beside the sea, the young people prefer to climb the mountain and take the path to a secluded bay. There, Martin plays soccer until sunset and Miranda swims and flirts a bit with her boyfriend. Despite her swollen stomach, Miranda is still a teenager who likes to have a good time.

Uncle Victor comes in from the fields, bringing coconuts and a sackful of vegetables: peas, cucumbers, tomatoes, corn, sweet potatoes, yams, and manioc. His arrival spurs Mammy Peggy into action. She grates the coconut and the sweet potatoes to make a local pudding for the evening meal, while her son Victor lights the fire in the clay oven behind the house. This is also where they bake bread and cakes. "The gas stove in the kitchen is very practical, but certain things have to cook over a wood fire to be really fine," maintains Mammy Peggy. Victor feeds the sheep and chickens he keeps in the backyard.

6:00. Iris abandons the bathroom. The sun has set, and the sea breeze moves the curtains that divide the rooms. Miranda braids her mother's crinkly hair to prevent it from getting tangled during the night. Then it's Iris' turn to do the same for Miranda. This daily ritual is an intimate time for both mother and daughter.

Martin gets his trousers and his white shirt and shoes ready for tomorrow. At school he has been nicknamed Shineshoe because his shoes are always so highly polished. Martin doesn't care. He is serious, proud, and ambitious, which this year earned him a scholarship for the rest of his high school education.

8:00. The dessert pudding was a huge success. Miranda washes the dishes before spending an hour watching television. Mammy Peggy and Victor have fallen asleep head to toe on the bed in their room. Martin retires to his little room next to his mother's. Lying down on his camp bed, he listens to the radio, and as always, he falls asleep in his clothes.

9:00. Iris settles down beside Miranda, but not before remembering to light the insect coil, which burns all night to keep the mosquitoes away. The future grandmother looks at her little crammed room, wondering where she will put the crib for the child she will have to raise.

"With the neighborhood sheep and goats roaming free, it's a wonder that our garden is as pretty as it is," Mammy Peggy complains

Iris succeeded in remodeling the little wooden house by buying two cement blocks a week. The bathroom was installed last Christmas, and this morning Iris is laying the tiles

ST. VINCENT and THE GRENADINES

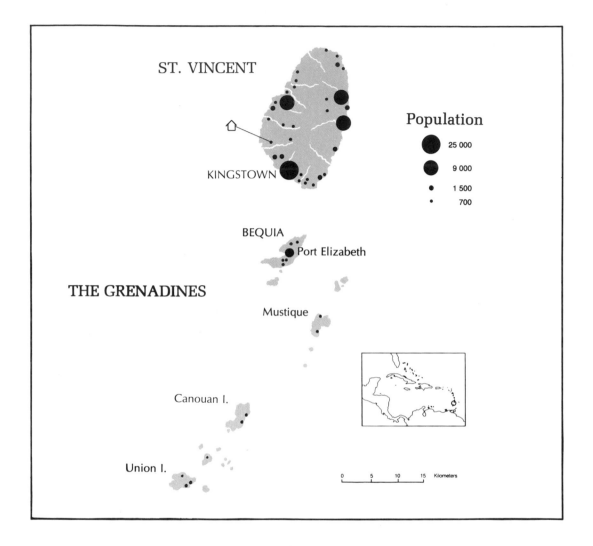

THE NAME
St. Vincent: In honor of St. Vincent; given by the
   Spanish
The Grenadines: from Spanish city, Granada

THE PEOPLE: The St. Vincentians

GEOGRAPHY
St. Vincent: volcanic island with volcano, La Soufrière,
   as the highest peak, 1,245 m. (4,048 ft.), still active.
The Grenadines: island chain stretching between St.
   Vincent and Grenada with white beaches and a
   coral reef
Area: 389 sq. km. (150 sq. mi.); St. Vincent: 344 sq. km.
   (133 sq. mi.)

Density: 360 pers./sq. km. (933 pers./sq. mi.) (1986)
Arable land: 50% (1987)
Forest: 41%
Climate: Tropical; rainy season from June to December.
   Rainfall varies from mountainous interior to the
   south.

CAPITAL: Kingston, pop. 24,764 (1982)

LANGUAGE: English

RELIGION: (1980)
   Anglican: 42%
   Methodist: 20%
   Catholic: 12%
   Other: 26%

POPULATION: Total—104,000 (1985)
  Annual growth: 0.9% (936) (1980–84)
  Doubling time: 35 yrs.
  Urban: 25% (1980)
  Rural: 75%

AGE GROUPS: (1980)
  15% less than 5 yrs.
  44% less than 15
  57% less than 20
  24% from 20 to 39
  11% from 40 to 59
  6% 60 yrs. and over

ETHNIC GROUPS
  Black: 66%
  Mulatto: 19%
  East Indian: 6%
  White: 4%
  Amerindian: 2%

HISTORY
  Originally inhabited by Carib Indians
  1498: Discovery by Christopher Columbus
  1627–1783: Alternating French and British
    occupations
  1783: British colonization
  1833: Part of the Windward Islands
  1958–62: Member of the West Indies Federation
  1969: Associate state of the Commonwealth
  October 27, 1979: Independence within the
    Commonwealth

FAMILY
Marital status, for population 14 yrs. and older: (1980)
  Married: 28%
  Common-law: 15%
  Visiting union: 6%
  Separated from husband or partner: 12%
  Never had husband or partner: 35%
Female head of household: 42% (1980)
Fertility rate: no data
Births out of wedlock: no data
Teenage births: 29% (1981)
Contraception: no data
Government's position on family planning: Concerned
  with the problems facing individuals in planning
  and spacing births, the government recently
  introduced a free national family-planning program.
  Fertility levels, which were very high, have
  declined since 1956, when the Family Planning
  Association was founded.

SOCIAL INDICATORS
Life expectancy: 69 yrs. (male: 67; female: 71) (1985)

Infant mortality: 33/1,000 births (1985)
Crude birth rate: 29/1,000 pop. (1984)
Crude death rate: 7/1,000
Health:
  Access to health services: no data
  Births attended by trained health personnel:
    73% (1981)

HOUSING
Persons per household: 4.8 (1980)
Electricity: 48% without (1980)
Access to safe water: No data, but it can be assumed
  that piped water is safe.
Source of water: (1980)
  Piped inside: 29%
  Piped outside: 13%
  Public standpipe: 45%
  Other: 12%
Toilet facilities: (1980)
  Pit: 69%
  None: 4%
  Other: 27%
Building materials: (1980)
  Concrete: 36%
  Wood: 45%
  Mixture of wood and concrete: 10%
  Wattle or adobe: 4%

EDUCATION
Literacy: 96% (male: 96%; female: 95%) (1970)
Gross enrollment ratio: (1982)
First level: 95%
Educational attainment, for population 25 yrs. +:
  (1980)
  None: 2%
  First level: incomplete: 88%
  Second: entered: 8%
  Third: 1%

ECONOMIC ACTIVITY
Economically active population: no data
Agriculture: 42% act. pop.; 40% of GDP
Mines: 0% act. pop.; 0% of GDP
Industry: 10% act. pop.; 10% of GDP
Services: 48% act. pop.; 50% of GDP
Per capita GNP: 850 U.S.$ (1985)
Population in absolute poverty: no data
National currency/per U.S.$: 2.70 East Caribbean
  dollars (1985)
Principal resources: Bananas, coconuts

COMMUNICATIONS
Radio:
  Transmitters: 1 (1979)
  Receivers: no data
Television: no data

TRINIDAD and TOBAGO

THE AJIM FAMILY

Tyrone Ajim, age 42 (1)
Leecil Ajim, 31 (2)
Muriel Ajim, 14 (absent from photo)
Meril, 13 (3)
André, 11 (4)
Ian, 10 (5)
Peter, 8 (6)

SANGRE GRANDE
November 28

Only seven kilometers of sea separate the island of Trinidad from the mainland of South America, but the calypso music on the radio reminds you that this is the Caribbean. The national highway that circumnavigates the island and links all the towns is paved, and all the asphalt is mined locally. Despite the paving, you need a great deal of patience to drive the forty kilometers between Port of Spain and the east coast; traffic tieups are one of the banes of the country.

The Ajim family has lived in the little town of Sangre Grande for twelve years. On Tyrone's meager teacher's salary they were able to build a house on land that he had bought before they were married. The house is built on concrete posts in the local style. It's one way of providing for future expansion. Eight years later, all Tyrone had to do was build walls between the posts in order to add a small apartment on the ground floor. This month he will complete a studio apartment using the same principle. He will then be able to pay off his bank loan with the money from the two rents and finally buy a fine air-conditioned car like everyone else. Judging by the traffic jams it's hard to believe that there is anyone in Trinidad who still does not have a car!

5:00. A cock, whose ownership is a mystery, walks down Baker Trace Street crowing. The sun appears behind the transparent curtains. The Rasta° plumber is hammering the walls on the ground floor. Sleep is impossible. Tyrone accepts the inevitable and gets up. This morning he dons shorts and T-shirt instead of his teacher's clothes; he's going to the market. The rest of the family remain in bed, recovering a little longer from Saturday night's parties, dancing, music, and movies.

° Rasta: from Rastafarian, a religious sect that began in Jamaica in the 1930s. Its adherents are notable for their systematic rejection of the rules of society, their appearance (knotted hair), and their use of *ganja* (marijuana). They eat neither meat nor salt and regard Africa (especially Ethiopia) as their homeland.

7:00. Meril turns on the hi-fi system and vanishes into the shower, enveloped in calypso melodies. Behind him, Muriel, André, Ian, and Peter argue about who's next. Their father returns, his arms loaded with fruits and vegetables, just as Leecil has had enough of the noise and decides to referee the shower squabble. One by one, the children reappear in the kitchen for breakfast. They find the downstairs neighbor there washing dishes. She is still waiting for the Rasta to finish his work.

8:00. With robotlike movements, the boys get their soccer equipment ready. They practice their break dancing with every move they make. This morning there is a soccer match at Biche, a little town twenty kilometers from Sangre Grande where Tyrone is the school principal. Leecil and Muriel will spend the morning in the kitchen preparing a creole Sunday dinner: Spanish rice, boiled plantains, sweet potatoes, chicken fricassee, and *callalou* (a green vegetable similar to spinach). It takes a long time to prepare, and it will be the only meal of the day.

11:00. Mary, another downstairs neighbor, comes in. She has washed her hair and applied straightener and has come to ask Leecil to put in rollers to wave it in the latest fashion. The two women sit outside in the shade. Leecil is a calm, gentle, energetic woman. Everyone appreciates having her around. She loves children, but her own are older, so she has decided to open a day-care center. When Tyrone has the money, he will add a room onto the ground floor. In the meantime, she looks after three babies in the house five days a week.

12:30. The boys return from their soccer game in high spirits. A little more break dancing before lunch. The movements are influenced by calypso rhythms, but their dancing is patterned after the style that originated in black neighborhoods in the

United States. The neighbors, still without water, join the happy family meal, which is enlivened by Meril, the comedian, whose antics comment hilariously on everyday life.

2:00. It would be unthinkable to spend a free afternoon shut up in the house, and equally unthinkable to play in the street in this tropical heat. But getting to the sea is difficult for a seven-person family without a car. The public minibuses are infrequent and always full. When the Ajims can't find a friend to drive them to the sea, they make the shorter trip to Tyrone's mother's house in the country instead. Today, it's Muriel who will sacrifice herself and stay home so they can all fit in a taxi. She will spend her afternoon doing the whole family's laundry, and her expression reveals that she is less than enthusiastic at the prospect.

Although most of the island is rural, there are very few farmers in Trinidad. The drilling of oil and tourism have tempted the inhabitants away from agriculture. Tyrone's parents, whose ancestors came from India over a century ago, are an exception. They have kept their dairy farm and share the house and farm work with the families of three of their children, eighteen people in all. When Tyrone's family arrives, the men gather for a game of cards and the women talk about Saturday night's dance. The children go off to play down by the river that meanders through the lush green valley. They are not the only ones looking for a cool spot: whole families are already there. Reggae, calypso, and pop music spill from the open doors of the cars in a joyful cacophony.

5:00. After a light Indian-style supper prepared by Grandmother, Tyrone and his family manage to hail a taxi near the road. At home, Muriel has finished the laundry and has shut herself in her room, still pouting at having had to miss the trip to the country and a swim in the river.

Peter goes to the video club on the corner to return two cassettes that every member of the family has seen twice. He chooses a new movie for the adults and a cartoon for himself. Sitting on the floor in the corridor, André is dismantling old toy cars. Out of the various parts he succeeds in making a new battery-driven car. He is very clever with his hands.

Ian is in the street playing cricket, a game inherited from the English colonists, with the neighborhood children. They will have to stop soon, as it is getting dark.

6:30. Muriel, Meril, and Ian finish their homework under their father's expert supervision. Tyrone answers their questions and encourages them to study, although he is aware that his children, unfortunately, are not as interested in school as he was at their age. In those days it was difficult to graduate. "Today there is no shortage of money or schools and less effort is required, yet the children are less studious," he complains.

8:00. The leftovers from the creole dinner are placed on the table, but Grandmother's snack was too filling and no one has much appetite. The Ajims settle down on the sofa to watch the new videocassette. Meril would rather go and listen to the neighborhood steel band practice for the island Carnival, which the Trinidadians proudly maintain is better than the one in Rio. The bands play their music on steel drums whose tops have been hammered to produce different notes. Originally the drums were made from oil barrels.

9:00. Tyrone opts for bed and a good night's rest before the next week begins. Leecil is also quietly preparing to go to bed. She will have three babies on her doorstep tomorrow morning.

The film is over and the boys retire to their room. Muriel bolts the door, switches off the light, and closes her door. Tomorrow there will be no pouting. She will be a schoolgirl again.

The house is built on concrete posts. The family lives on the upper floor; the ground floor is kept for future additions

Saturday is the evening of parties, enlivened by steel bands and calypso music. On Sunday the family gets together for a creole dinner

TRINIDAD and TOBAGO

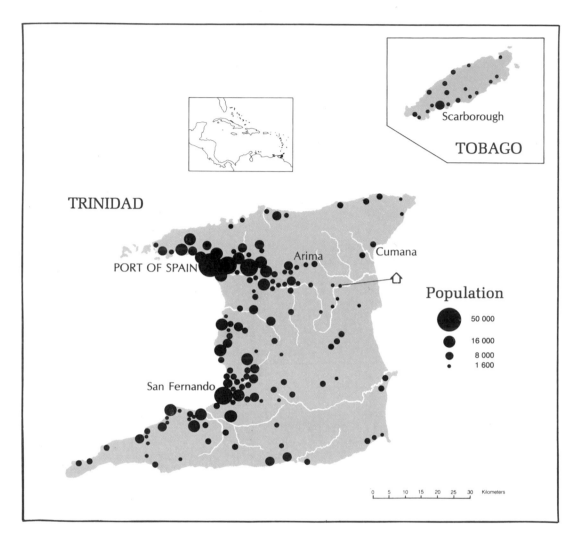

TRINIDAD

TOBAGO

Scarborough

PORT OF SPAIN

Arima

Cumana

San Fernando

Population

50 000

16 000

8 000

1 600

0 5 10 15 20 25 30   Kilometers

THE NAME:
Trinidad: when Columbus discovered the area, he
   approached from the south and saw three peaks
   which reminded him of the Catholic Trinity
Tobago: from "tobacco," because of the large
   plantations

THE PEOPLE: The Trinidadians and Tobagonians

GEOGRAPHY
Trinidad: geologically an extension of South America;
   separated from Venezuela by the 7-mile strait of
   the Gulf of Paria. Low mountain ranges cross from
   east to west, lowlands south and center.
Tobago: geographically part of the Caribbean; separated
   from Trinidad by a 19-mile channel. A ridge of
   volcanic origin lies along the center of the island.
   Max. altitude: 900 m. (3,085 ft.) (Mt. El Tucuche)

Area: 5,128 sq. km. (1,980 sq. mi.)
Density: 242 pers./sq. km. (626 sq. mi.) (1986)
Arable land: 31% (1987)
Forest: 44%
Climate: Tropical. Dry season from January to May.
   Temperatures are uniformly high year round.

CAPITAL: Port of Spain, pop. 59,649 (1982 est.)

LANGUAGE: English

RELIGION
   Catholic: 33%
   Hindu: 25%
   Anglican: 15%
   Muslim: 6%
   Other: 22%

POPULATION: Total—1,185,000 (1985)
Annual growth: 1.6% (18,960) (1980–85)
Doubling time: 34 yrs.
Urban: 21% (1985) (est. for year 2000: 28%)
Rural: 79%

AGE GROUPS: (1982)
11% less than 5 yrs.
34% less than 15
47% less than 20
31% from 20 to 39
14% from 40 to 59
8% 60 yrs. and over

ETHNIC GROUPS
Black: 41%
East Indian: 41%
Mixed: 16%
White: 1%

HISTORY
Originally inhabited by Carib Indians on Tobago and Arawak Indians on Trinidad.
Trinidad
1498: Discovery by Christopher Columbus
1532: Spanish government is appointed
1592: Spanish conquest and extermination of Amerindians
1797: British conquest
Tobago
1632: Dutch colonization as Niewe Walcheren
1737: British occupation
1781: French occupation
1802: British acquisition
1834: Abolition of slavery
1888: Amalgamation with Trinidad

1958–62: Member of the West Indies Federation
August 31, 1962: Independence within the Commonwealth
January 8, 1976: Proclamation of the republic

FAMILY
Marital status, for women 14 to 64 yrs.: (1980)
Married: 46%
Common-law: 13%
Visiting union: 2%
Separated from husband or partner: 9%
Never had husband or partner: 29%
Female head of household: 25% (1980)
Fertility rate: 2.9 (1980–85)
Births out of wedlock: 42% (1979)
Teenage births: 3% (1980)
Contraception: 55% (1984)
Government's position on family planning: Has indicated that the country's population growth rate is too high. It has formulated a number of policies in relation to fertility and family well-being and family-planning programs.

SOCIAL INDICATORS
Life expectancy: 69 yrs. (male: 67; female: 72) (1985)

Infant mortality: 22/1,000 births (1985)
Crude birth rate: 25/1,000 pop. (1985)
Crude death rate: 7/1,000
Health:
Access to health services: no data
Births attended by trained health personnel: 90%

HOUSING
Persons per household: 4.5 (1980)
Electricity: 16% without (1980)
Access to safe water: 99% (rural: 96%) (1983)
Source of water: (1980)
Piped inside: 49%
Piped outside: 16%
Public standpipe: 25%
Water truck, river, and other: 10%
Toilet facilities: (1980)
WC linked to sewer: 20%
WC not linked: 21%
Pit: 58%
Building materials: (1980)
Brick: 41%
Wood: 33%
Concrete: 13%
Wood and concrete: 7%
Other: 7%

EDUCATION
Literacy: 95% (male: 96%; female: 93%) (1980)
Gross enrollment ratio: (1982–84)
First level: 96% (completing in 1980–84: 52%)
Second: 76%
Third: 4%
Educational attainment, for population 25 yrs. +: (1980)
None: 1.3
First level: incomplete: 29% (complete: 43%)
Second: entered: 20%
Third: 3%

ECONOMIC ACTIVITY
Economically active population: 60% (male: 81%; female: 40%) (1985)
Agriculture: 10% act. pop.; 2% of GDP
Mines: 5% act. pop.; 35% of GDP
Industry: 34% act. pop.; 17% of GDP
Services: 51% act. pop.; 46% of GDP
Per capita GNP: 6,020 U.S.$ (1985)
Population in absolute poverty: (1977–84)
Urban: 35%
Rural: 45%
National currency/per U.S.$: 2.45 Trinidad dollars (1985)
Principal resource: Petroleum

COMMUNICATIONS
Radio:
Transmitters: 5 (1979)
Receivers: 360,000—313/1,000 pop. (1983)
Television:
Transmitters: 6 (1981)
Receivers: 310,000—270/1,000 pop. (1983)

North America

CANADA

THE JAMIESON FAMILY

Duncan Jamieson, age 43 (1)
Lise Jamieson, 44 (2)
Mark, 15 (3)
Ian, 13 (4)

1 dog

GOULAIS RIVER
September 20

Thirty minutes out of Sault Ste. Marie on the northwest road in the exact center of Canada's vast northern expanse lies the community of Goulais River and the brick ranch house of the Jamiesons. The Jamiesons live surrounded by hundreds of miles of spectacular forest wilderness and only minutes away from the magnificent beauty of Lake Superior, the largest freshwater lake in the world.

6:00. Duncan Jamieson turns off his alarm and goes to the kitchen to make himself coffee and two slices of toast. Today he has an almost two-hour drive to the bush (forest) to reach his tractor. Taking a sandwich from the refrigerator and the thermos of hot soup that his wife made the night before, Duncan climbs into his truck. Duncan is self-employed and cuts logging roads for the lumber industry. In winter when the snow makes driving his pickup truck slippery and dangerous, Duncan lives on site in a trailer, coming home only on Wednesdays and weekends. In July, his wife and two sons join him. Lise, a schoolteacher in Sault Ste. Marie, would like to take another kind of vacation someday, but April is the only possible month for Duncan, since the thaw makes his work impossible, and Lise and the boys are still in school then. Lise is trying to persuade Duncan to take the boys to Scotland. She would like them to meet their father's family. Raised in a large poor family, Duncan left Scotland twenty years ago and shows little interest in visiting the land of his birth. His present family provides all the warmth and happiness he expects from his life now.

6:30. Mark's alarm goes off, and the family's syncopated routine begins. Lise crawls out of bed when she hears her son turn off the shower. She likes to have breakfast with Mark. This time has become a special one for both of them. Fifteen-year-old Mark's future has become very important to him, and Lise always takes time to listen to

him. The posters that cover every square inch of his bedroom walls proclaim his dream. He wants to become a truck driver. He has been driving on back roads since he was twelve and can't wait until next year when he'll finally get his driving permit. Although she is an educator, Lise does not pressure her sons to be anything other than what they want to be.

7:20. Mark leaves the house as the bus appears around the bend in the country road. His high school is thirty-five kilometers away. Ian still has another hour; he attends a small primary school in Goulais River. Lise cleans up the kitchen while Ian eats breakfast. The boys make their own lunch, so Lise doesn't have to hear any complaints.

The Jamiesons buy their food in bulk, and their basement pantry looks like a grocery store, with enough food to last the family at least nine months. Once a week, Lise shops in the city for fruits, vegetables, and dairy products. Every two weeks she bakes bread and freezes the baked loaves. "My men are spoiled," she says with a smile. Early in their marriage, she promised Duncan homemade bread for the rest of his life in return for a washing machine and a dryer. Even so, there are times when Duncan finds himself kneading the dough.

8:00. As Lise leaves the house, she remembers at the last minute to take pork chops out of the freezer for dinner. She reminds Ian that she'll pick him up after his volleyball game after school and kisses him goodbye. He will lock up the house after his mother leaves, as he has another quarter of an hour to wait for his bus.

The news is beginning just as Lise starts the engine of her Toyota. The first part of her journey is relaxing. The road follows the lakeshore, and the maples offer spectacular colors that change with the seasons. The fall colors will reach their peak next week when the red of the maples predominates. Once she is past the lake, though, Lise cannot help thinking about her work. Her school is one of many in English-speaking Canada that are emphasizing bilingual education. One quarter of Canadians are French-speaking, and all Canadian laws, products, and labels are written in both languages. To get any kind of a national government position, Canadians must now be bilingual. Lise specializes in teaching exceptional children, both learning disabled and gifted.

12:00. Lise leaves the school to have lunch with her father, who lives close by. Her brothers and sisters are scattered all over the country, and her father lives alone in his old clapboard house. The seventy-year-old man is determined to fend for himself. He doesn't want his family to send him to a home for the aged like so many other old people in Canada. So far, he is taking good care of himself. He swims, goes bowling, and is out a lot with friends. Since her mother died, Lise has made a point of visiting her father regularly and making sure he is involved with his grandsons. She has added a room in the basement so he can feel free to come anytime.

He serves his daughter a delicious lunch in his large old-fashioned kitchen: soup, steak with mashed potatoes, green salad, and homemade cake. They talk about Ian, his favorite card-playing companion, and his enthusiasm for sports. Tonight Grandfather will attend his grandson's hockey game, as much to cheer Ian on as to get out and see some people.

3:45. Mark is the first one home and begins preparations for dinner. He browns the pork chops and puts them in the oven to braise. This done, he hesitates between playing video games on his computer and joining his friends to ride their motorized Honda tricycles. He opts for cruising through the woods with the other boys.

4:20. The volleyball game has already begun when Lise arrives at Ian's school. An avid competitor, Ian plays to win. Unfortunately, even Ian's energy isn't enough to win today. Lise drives him home to take comfort in a home-cooked meal. The only thing left for her to do is to put the potatoes and carrots on. Mark has baked dessert: chocolate cookies made from a mix.

6:00. After dinner, Lise cleans off the table so that the boys can do their homework. Then she goes down to the basement with a handful of dirty clothes to fill the washing machine. As soon as she hears Duncan's truck in the driveway, she reheats his meal in the microwave oven. It is ready in a minute, and Duncan can sit down at the table as soon as he walks in the door. "This is one invention that really makes women's lives easier," Lise remarks.

When the family is in the living room, the television is always switched on, although no one really watches it. Everyone talks about the day's events. Lise knits, the dog asleep at her feet. The telephone rings. It's Grandfather wanting to know what time Ian's hockey game starts. This evening it's Duncan's turn to drive the thirty-five kilometers into Sault Ste. Marie. Yesterday, Lise drove Mark to the arena for his hockey game.

9:30. Mark has gone to bed. His room is a disaster area, but Lise no longer cleans up after him. If he wants clean clothes, he'll have to pick them up off the floor and put them in the hamper. Lise puts down her knitting. At the speed she's going, she's not sure whether she will finish her sweater in time for winter, which starts next month. She relaxes in a bath and then puts the dishwasher on before she goes to bed. The noise doesn't carry as far as the bedrooms at the end of the hall.

11:00. Duncan and Ian return. Judging by the noise they make, Ian's team must have won.

*The carport they
are building will
allow Lise to get
into her car
without having to
sweep the snow off
on winter
mornings*

*Early in their
marriage, Lise
promised Duncan
homemade bread
in exchange for a
washing machine
and a dryer. Even
so, there are times
when Duncan
finds himself
kneading the
dough*

CANADA

THE VANASSE FAMILY

André Vanasse, age 32 (1)
Monique Vanasse, 30 (2)
Philippe Vanasse, 8 (3)
Jean-François, 7 (4)
Véronique, 1 (5)

TROIS-RIVIÈRES
March 15

Jean-François climbs down from the bunk bed that he shares with his brother and marches out to the dining room to inspect the clothes his mother has laid out for him on the table. He is very particular about his appearance and the latest fashions and checks to make sure his mother has properly matched the colors of the clean socks, sweater, and pants. Meanwhile his older brother, Philippe, already dressed, makes a beeline to the basement. François follows quickly; the two boys can't miss their morning dose of children's cartoons.

Their father, André, has refinished the whole basement, creating a laundry, pantry, playroom, shower, and guest bedroom, all painted in warm, bright colors. The playroom, where the boys sit squashed together in an armchair with a blanket over their knees, is equipped with a full home entertainment system: color television with cable, VCR, and piles of videocassettes.

7:15. Véronique has had enough of sleeping and expresses at full volume her desire to get up. Monique slips on her robe and enters her daughter's room, where her prompt response is rewarded with a broad smile.

From her high chair in the kitchen, Véro supervises her mother's breakfast preparations. Monique calms her impatience with a slice of buttered bread as she concentrates on the boys' hot chocolate and toast.

Two years ago, Monique faced an important decision: either to go back to her secretarial job or to have a third child and stay home. Fewer and fewer women in North America have that option. Most women choose to work to supplement their families' incomes. Monique's husband, whose family owns two automotive garages, earns enough to provide a good living. André supported Monique's decision. He likes doing things with children and, like her, would like eventually to have four. Monique has nine brothers and sisters. Though they are a modern couple, the Vanasses'

idea of a family is a traditional large one. Next year, they hope, Véro will have a baby sister.

8:00. Jean-François will not stop grumbling. The zipper on his pants pocket doesn't close and he refuses to go out like that. There is no end to the complaints from Monique's sons this morning. They've had enough of winter and want to wear parkas instead of snowsuits for the short walk to school. Their mother remains firm. It is March and it's 3° F. In addition, a flu epidemic is raging. "Do you want to be sick like your father?" she asks. André is in bed with a high fever. The boys grumble but obey. Just one more month until spring. Monique quickly closes the door behind them to keep the cold air out. Their brick bungalow, on the outskirts of the small city of Trois-Rivières, lies on the flat plain that stretches from Montreal to Quebec. The landscape offers little refuge from the strong winter winds.

Véro is busy emptying her toy box and André is still asleep, so Monique sips her scalding coffee while reading the newspaper that one of the neighborhood children has delivered. From time to time she glances up from the end of the table toward the bay window. The world outside is white. Monique is glad to be inside her cozy warm house. She spends a lot of time redecorating, and every so often, in an urgent desire to transform her surroundings, she slaps on a new coat of paint.

Véro has gotten into the kitchen cupboard, but even turning over pots and pans a thousand times does not amuse her. She begins to fret. "When you don't know what to do with yourself, little one, it's time for a nap." Mother is right. Véro falls asleep immediately, and Monique seizes the opportunity to take a shower and fill the washing machine.

10:00. The milkman rings the doorbell. Monique buys nine liters, which should be enough for the week. Then the butcher arrives and fills her order from the back of his truck: a small roast beef, four thick steaks, and some pork chops. The rest of her shopping—groceries, vegetables, and fruits—Monique buys on her weekly trip to the supermarket. The kitchen has large food cupboards, and in the basement there is a huge freezer for the meat and frozen food. Snowstorms can block the roads for several days, but there is no danger of starvation at the Vanasses'.

11:30. The vegetable soup is simmering on the electric stove. The family always eats a light lunch and the main meal in the evening. The boys enter with a blast of cold air, peeling off their boots at the door and throwing their snowsuits over a chair. Their shouts and laughter wake Véro and rouse André from his drowsiness. Father and sons take their positions on one side of the counter, with Véro and her mother on the other. Monique serves the hot soup with buttered crackers.

1:15. After tidying the house and stacking the dishes in the dishwasher, Monique bundles Véro up to her eyes, straps her into her car seat, and drives off to the mall, the only outing possible in these Siberian temperatures. The well-heated shopping center contains a wide variety of stores and boutiques, but Monique goes there mostly to get out and meet her neighborhood girlfriends. Véro is comfortably installed in her stroller and is not too impatient when her mother stops for her daily cup of coffee.

Despite his illness, André has some business to take care of. The furnace has broken at the garage where he works and the entire system must be replaced. As the youngest of the owners, André cannot approve the work without consulting his father and brother. Like many retired people, his parents spend their winters in Miami and his brother is there on vacation. He will try to phone in the evening when the rates go down.

3:15. Monique welcomes her sons back from school but insists they do their homework before they go out to play. The boys finish in a hurry and are about to race out the door when their mother notices that their boots are wet and makes them change to dry pairs. She orders them to stay in the backyard so she can keep an eye on them. Monique has read too many articles about child abduction.

The boys prepare for battle with their friends. War seems to be their preferred game. The combatants have snowballs and wooden swords and defend themselves by building snow barricades and climbing trees. When darkness falls, the boys return wet and hungry, their cheeks reddened by the cold. They warm their feet in slippers knitted by their grandmother and sit down at the table.

6:30. André does not feel well enough to join in his boys' antics. Usually away all day, André normally takes advantage of suppertime to talk and joke with his sons. This evening, the absence of André's usual cheerfulness is contagious, and the family doesn't linger at the table. Philippe has a bath with Véro, then wraps her warmly in her pajamas before Monique puts her to sleep. Now the boys have to play quietly. In the living room, André sits with his eyes closed; on the sofa, Jean-François and Philippe turn the pages of a book of fairy tales while they listen to the story read aloud on a cassette. There is little resistance when their parents send them to bed an hour later, but Philippe can still summon up enough strength to protest that it is his turn to sleep in the upper bunk.

9:00. After sleeping almost all day, André is now wide awake. Monique lights the wood stove in the basement to reduce the humidity and sits beside her husband, pulling a blanket up over them. Just as they did when they were teenagers in love, they snuggle together and watch a late movie.

*The Vanasses'
brick bungalow
lies on a
flat plain
that offers
little refuge
from the strong
winter winds*

*Snowstorms can
block the roads for
several days. With
the pantry and the
huge freezer in the
basement to stock
all her groceries,
Monique will still
have plenty to feed
her family*

CANADA

THE ALLEN FAMILY

Charlotte Vale Allen, age 45 (1)
Kimberly Allen, 14 (2)

TORONTO
April 25

7:00. Kim emerges silently from her own bathroom. She leaves her school uniform on its hanger and rummages frantically through her closet. The entire room is knee deep in slacks and pullovers. Today is "grub day," a day when the students at her school can wear whatever they want, and Kim wants to wear her newest clothes yet look as casual as can be. She can count on stiff competition from her friends. Finally, she settles on baggy slacks pleated at the waist, a T-shirt, and a large shirt that comes down to the thighs, thus obscuring entirely her slim figure.

Before she leaves her room, Kim switches on her telephone answering machine. This way she saves her mother from running dozens of times a day to answer its strident summons. She passes through the kitchen and tosses a banana into her rucksack with her school books. As usual, she wakes her mother at the last minute. Charlotte's eyes are barely open as she gets up to kiss her daughter goodbye. After picking up the newspaper, which is delivered to the door every morning, Charlotte closes the apartment door behind Kim and goes back to sleep under the fluffy white quilt that covers her enormous bed.

Kim leaves their apartment building and walks down the still quiet city streets. The spring air is cool, and the bright morning sun washes over the skyscrapers of Toronto, a city renowned for its modern beauty and cleanliness. According to the weather report, today will be a warm day. Kim might even be able to put on shorts after school. One of life's most delicious pleasures for a Canadian girl is to be able to dress lightly again at the end of the interminable winter. After fifteen minutes' walk through the downtown streets, Kim enters an old English mansion that houses the private girls' high school she has attended for the past two years. Like most other teenagers, Kim attended public school before her mother's success as a writer. There's still an hour to go before classes begin, but this morning Kim has to finish

the homework left half finished the day before, a prospect that she finds less than enchanting. Kim does not like school. "It's like prison," she says. She takes out her books, but one friend and then another join her. At fourteen, there are all sorts of things more important than math and science.

8:30. Charlotte makes herself some coffee and sits in the kitchen reading the newspaper. She has no reason to rush. The manuscript of her last novel went to the publisher only a couple of days ago. Last week she was still putting in ten- to twelve-hour days making the final corrections. Charlotte writes commercial women's fiction and her first book was a best-seller. Before that she was a woman who wore many different hats: as a singer, an actress, a secretary, and an insurance saleswoman, to name a few. Charlotte has made it after a difficult poverty-stricken childhood and two marriages that ended in divorce. "The important thing is to keep reaching further," Charlotte says. "A woman can only satisfy her needs when she is truly independent." Since she became a successful author, Charlotte's economic struggle as a single parent is over.

Charlotte goes to draw a bath, selecting oils from an imposing array of jars alongside her spacious tub. Afterward she pulls on a pair of fashionable knit tights and a long shirt, looking very much like her young daughter. Then she relaxes in front of the mirror and delves into a basket of cosmetics.

10:00. Since she doesn't want to get out of practice, Charlotte sits down for an hour at her electric piano and plays some popular nightclub songs. Then she begins her long-postponed project of putting her collection of travel photographs into an album. Over the last three years, Charlotte has traveled to England, then to Thailand. This summer she will accompany her daughter to see her father in the United States. The couple have remained good friends since their divorce, and try to give their daughter as complete a family life as they can. For Charlotte, however, there is no question of Kim going to school anywhere but Toronto. Violence and drugs are still not as much of a danger here as in other North American cities.

12:00. Charlotte drops in at her health club in the center of Yorkville before going to lunch with a group of her writer friends who gather every Friday in a pub to exchange the latest literary gossip. Today the conversation turns to politics, and there is a lively discussion of acid rain, a contentious subject in Canada's relations with its southern neighbors, and one which arouses strong passions in Canada.

4:30. Charlotte strolls home at a leisurely pace, lingering in front of the attractive windows of boutiques along the way. When she returns, the apartment seems transformed into a country club for the daughters of well-to-do families. A dozen girls, all blond and pretty, plunder the refrigerator's store of soda, to be consumed in front of the television. The Allens' home is the favorite hangout of the group, and this weekend, as always, there is an open invitation for anyone to spend the night. Charlotte is very tolerant of Kim's life and treats her as much like a roommate as a daughter. The girls all talk at once. It's not the soap opera that interests them, but the commentaries to which it gives rise. The more heartrending the love stories, the more sarcastic their comments, and their wild laughter is interrupted only by the constant ringing of Kim's telephone. There's a dance in a week's time, and the pairing-off process takes place via the telephone. Even if love stories make them laugh, choosing a partner is a serious affair. The burning question is "What am I going to wear?" Kim has decided to shock the

world and will wear a revealing tight-fitting black dress. Charlotte is delighted by her little girl's sudden emergence into womanhood and cannot resist having Kim model her new dress, and shape, in front of family friends.

6:00. The television evening news is over, and Charlotte goes to take a shower and touch up her makeup. This evening she is going to the theater with a girlfriend to see a musical comedy. Before the show they will go out for pizza. Kim and the girls are also going out. They will use their weekly allowances and eat hamburgers at McDonald's. "The day comes when you have to trust them," says Charlotte. "In any case, Kim is very responsible and never stays out late." Charlotte leaves the uproar in Kim's room, as excited girls vie with one another while instructing Kim on what to wear. She takes the elevator directly to the garage where she parks her gleaming Mercedes. She doesn't use the car much and prefers living downtown instead of commuting from the large suburbs, as does more than half the population.

12:00. When Charlotte gets home from the theater, the lights are out in the apartment. Kim and her friends lie sprawled on cushions on the living-room floor, illuminated only by the neon lights of downtown. The evening was disappointing. After cruising the streets for excitement they came back to the Allens' apartment. Charlotte's reminder to her daughter that she has to research a paper in the library tomorrow causes the little band to scatter. Kim makes up a bed in her room, since one girlfriend will sleep over. Charlotte closes her bedroom door and settles herself comfortably among her pillows and reaches for the book that is always at her bed table. Reading before bed is a ritual pleasure that has become Charlotte's prerequisite for a good night's sleep.

Kim can walk to school; Charlotte to the shops and health club. They both prefer living downtown to commuting from Toronto's large suburbs

Every afternoon the apartment is transformed by a dozen girls, all blond and pretty, who plunder the refrigerator's store of soda, to be consumed in front of the television

CANADA

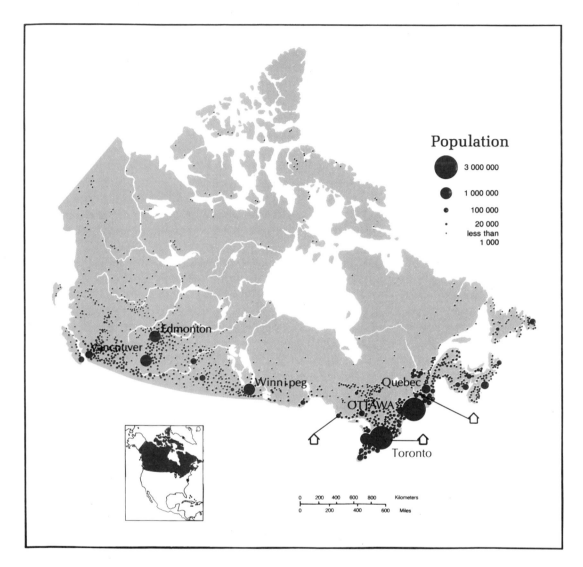

Population

- 3 000 000
- 1 000 000
- 100 000
- 20 000
- less than 1 000

Edmonton
Vancouver
Winnipeg
Quebec
OTTAWA
Toronto

| 0 | 200 | 400 | 600 | 800 | Kilometers |
| 0 | 200 | 400 | 600 | Miles |

THE NAME: From Huron and Iroquois *kanata*, meaning "village, settlement"

THE PEOPLE: The Canadians

GEOGRAPHY
From the Pacific to the Atlantic:
    Rocky Mountains in the west
    Western plains in the center
    Mountainous regions of Quebec and Labrador
    Maritime Provinces: lowlands in the east
    Max. altitude: 6,050 m. (19,524 ft.) (Mount Logan)
Area: 9,922,330 sq. km. (3,831,033 sq. mi.)
Density: 2.5 pers./sq. km. (6.6 pers./sq. mi.) (1986)
Arable land: 5% (1987)

Forest: 33%
Climate: Arctic in the north; subarctic in the center; maritime on the Pacific coast. From west to east it changes from mountain climate to moderate, semi-dry, and moderately wet.

CAPITAL: Ottawa, pop. 769,900 (metropolitan area) (1985)

LANGUAGE: English and French (official)

RELIGION
    Christian: 90%
    Other: 2%
    No religion: 7%

POPULATION: Total—25,400,000 (1985)
  Annual growth: 1.1% (279,400) (1980–85)
  Doubling time: 91 yrs.
  Urban: 76% (1985) (est. for year 2000: 79%)
  Rural: 24%

AGE GROUPS: (1980)
  7% less than 5 yrs.
  22% less than 15
  31% less than 20
  35% from 20 to 39
  21% from 40 to 59
  14% 60 yrs. and over

ETHNIC GROUPS: (1981)
  The majority is white, of European descent.
  Indigenous Indians: 2%

HISTORY
  20,000 B.C.: Arrival of Asian tribes across the
    Bering Strait
  1497: Exploration by John Cabot
  1524: Exploration by Giovanni da Verrazano
  1534: French claim by Jacques Cartier
  1663: Becomes a French province
  1713: Treaty of Utrecht: Acadia, Newfoundland,
    and Hudson Bay become British
  1763: France grants its possessions to England
  1791: Division between Upper and Lower Canada
  July 3, 1840: Union between Upper and Lower
    Canada
  July 1, 1867: Becomes a Dominion
  1982: Gains total control over its constitution

FAMILY
Marital status, for population 15 yrs. and older: (1980)
  Single: 26%
  Married: 61%
  Widowed: 10%
  Divorced: 3%
Single-parent families: 11% (female: 83%; male: 17%)
  (1980)
Fertility rate: 1.7 (1985)
Births out of wedlock: no data
Teenage births: 8% (1982)
Contraception: 73% (1985)
Abortions: 18/100 live births (1980)
Government's position on family planning: Has no
  national population policy deliberately aimed at
  influencing the population growth rate. No attempt
  has yet been made to influence fertility, since it is
  considered a matter of individual choice; the
  country has never had a national fertility survey.

SOCIAL INDICATORS
Life expectancy: 76 yrs. (male: 72; female: 79) (1980–
  85)
Infant mortality: 9/1,000 births (1980–85)
Crude birth rate: 15/1,000 pop. (1980–85)

Crude death rate: 7/1,000
Health:
  Access to health services: no data, but it can be
    assumed that almost all Canadians have access to
    medical care.
  Births attended by trained health personnel: 100%
    (1984)

HOUSING
Persons per household: 2.9 (1981)
Electricity: No data, but it can be assumed that almost
  all Canadians have access to electricity.
Access to safe water: No data, but it can be assumed
  that almost all Canadians have access to safe water.
Source of water: (1981)
  Piped inside: 99.5%
  Not piped: 0.5%
Toilet facilities: (1981)
  Flush: 98%
  Other: 2%
Building materials: No data. The majority of houses are
  made of a mixture of wood and brick and are
  insulated against the cold weather.

EDUCATION
Literacy: 99%
Gross enrollment ratio: (1983)
  First level: 106% (completing in 1980–84: 98%)
  Second: 102%
  Third: 44%
Educational attainment, for population 15 yrs. +:
  (1981)
  None: 2%
  First level: 19%
  Second: 50% (incomplete and complete)
  Third: 32%

ECONOMIC ACTIVITY
Economically active population: 65% (male: 77%;
  female: 54%) (1985)
Agriculture: 5.5% act. pop.; 4% of GDP
Mines: 8.5% act. pop.; 10% of GDP
Industry: 17% act. pop.; 19% of GDP
Services: 69% act. pop.; 67% of GDP
Per capita GNP: 13,680 U.S.$ (1985)
Population in absolute poverty: no data
National currency/per U.S.$: 1.37 Canadian dollar
  (1985)
Principal resources:
  Wheat, barley
  Petroleum, natural gas, coal, uranium

COMMUNICATIONS
Radio:
  Transmitters: 1,540 (1983)
  Receivers: 20,551,000—825/1,000 pop. (1983)
Television:
  Transmitters: 2,131 (1983)
  Receivers: 11,976,000—481/1,000 pop. (1983)

UNITED STATES OF AMERICA

THE LOVE FAMILY

Lillie Love, age 42 (1)
Mark Manley, 24 (2)
Edward Manley, 23 (absent from photo)
Sandra Love, 21 (absent)
Emma Love, 20 (absent)
Deon Love, 13 (3)

CHICAGO
August 28

7:30. Lillie Love leaves her bedroom, and as she walks along the corridor to the bathroom, she sees her son Edward Manley already sprawled daydreaming in a chair by the window in the room he shares with his brother Mark. Edward's seat overlooks the rest of Chicago's Robert Taylor Homes—a cement island of high rises separated from the main city by a massive expressway whose deafening roar is the backdrop to the everyday lives of the families who live in the housing project. This is Chicago's biggest black ghetto.

An hour later, Lillie sits in the family room eating breakfast while her young son Deon lies on the couch trying to decide on his plans for the day. Deon has finished his summer courses in French and algebra and will start high school on September 4, if the teachers don't go on strike next week. He works hard at school and may even be a gifted child, which means he could get a scholarship to college. Lillie is very proud of her son. Perhaps he will be the one to make it out of the ghetto.

Out on the landing, a group of students, under a summer job program, are sweeping the cement floor clean of garbage thrown there by the tenants. The view of Chicago and of Lake Michigan would be magnificent from the fifteenth floor were it not for the iron grills covering the façade from the ground floor to the sixteenth. Grills that make the Taylor Homes look like a prison and "give you the feeling of being in one," as Mark would say. There are twenty-eight sixteen-story buildings, each housing 160 families, low-rent housing for tenants on welfare. Because of a lack of money, Lillie had no other choice but to move in and add her name to the project's list of unemployed single black mothers, the poorest group in the United States.

9:00. Edward goes outside on the balcony and leans against the grillwork to smoke a cigarette with a vacant look in his eyes. Lillie stands with him, waiting for the elevator, which always takes ages. Lillie does not have a job, but she is far from inactive. This morning she is on her way to a tenants' meeting in the building's community center, whose existence is due to women like Lillie, dynamic, energetic women who have learned how to lobby and fight to get what they need. Lillie never has a moment's rest. She is involved in the daily distribution of meals to preschoolers, clothing drives, and neighborhood crime-stopping groups. At No. 4331, the women have learned that the only way to improve their situation is to change it themselves.

Here, in contrast to the other buildings, people feel slightly safer. All the buildings have gangs, many of which are violent and aggressive, but the boys who hang around the front of No. 4331 day and night are more concerned with protecting their families. The women worry less when their children go out and they themselves are less afraid of being mugged and raped when using the badly lit staircase alone during the frequent periods when the elevator is out of order. This doesn't spare them some uneasy moments while crossing the courtyard, since there is always the possibility of a stray bullet from one of the many feuds between the gangs in the various buildings. "School starts next week. We should thank God for such a beautiful summer and for having spared the lives of all the children," says the chairperson to those present at the meeting.

There is only one man at the meeting. He sits at the back of the room, listening. Black men are often on the periphery of family life. The welfare system gives greater benefits to single mothers with children. If there is a man in the house, the benefits go down, and the rent goes up. "Our men are illegal," says the chairperson, explaining the presence of so few men. "Rejected by their women because of the system and by society because of racism, their frustrations build up from childhood and erupt in revolt at adolescence. When you have seven children at home and one of your sons goes out, you worry, but you can't leave the other six alone to go and look for him. There's nothing left but to pray to the Lord that he won't do anything stupid. One day, he comes home and gives you five hundred dollars, saying, 'Here, Mom, I found this.' You don't ask any questions. You don't really want to know where he got the money. How can you refuse five hundred dollars? You don't have a radio or a TV, and school's about to start. Then he comes home with a color TV, and later on, a gun, and that's the day it's too late, you've lost your son."

Lillie considers herself lucky. None of her sons is a gang member and, of her five children, she worries only about Edward. He is already on welfare and spends his days with his friends, but Lillie can count on Edward at home. He likes to cook, so he does the shopping and prepares the family's meals. In the outside world, Edward is a drifter, and even Lillie's strength cannot put him on course. Lillie's daughters have been gone only one year. Sandra has moved in with the father of her third child, and Emma has found an apartment. She will continue her nursing courses next year when her son goes to a day-care center. For these girls, the simplest way of fulfilling their dreams of independence, their own apartment, and a monthly check is often to have a baby and be a single mother. In other words, to follow in their mothers' footsteps.

12:30. The three brothers eat their lunch. Deon, the talkative one, jokes with Mark and lets himself be served by his silent but accommodating older brother. Unlike Edward, Mark has a steady job. He is an assistant ambulance man and hopes to go back to school next year to get his paramedic's certificate. Respectful of his mother's untiring efforts, Mark is proud to be able to contribute financially to his family. This week he is on vacation and spends much of it watching TV. After their meal, the boys retreat to their rooms, and friends who stop in disappear behind their closed doors.

2:00. Lillie returns, serves herself the lunch her sons have left for her, then spends the afternoon visiting needy neighbors. A woman on the third floor is sick, and another neighbor at the end of the landing was attacked last night by her boyfriend, who wanted her welfare check. The police had to intervene. The young woman is nervous and cries constantly. She is afraid the man will come back looking for revenge. Lillie listens and consoles her. Then she goes down to the ground floor, where charity organizations have delivered secondhand clothes. They have to be sorted and stacked so that people can choose what they want.

6:30. After a quick snack, Lillie leaves the boys to get their own dinner. She takes the bus to downtown Chicago to a meeting of the Black on Black Love Society, an organization working to promote the idea of nonviolence within the black community. Violence by blacks against other blacks is one of the gravest problems facing black American society.

9:00. On her way home, Lillie crosses the courtyard lined on three sides with buildings. A crowd of people has gathered to enjoy one of the last warm nights of summer, and she sees Edward among them. The music is earsplitting, and the "ghetto blasters" (radio–cassette players) create a party atmosphere. Lillie has hardly stepped inside the door when a neighbor comes over for a chat. Although tired, Lillie enthusiastically shares her plans for the apartment. By Christmas, she wants to repaint and buy a new red carpet to match her red velvet sofa and black velvet armchairs.

9:30. Lillie is alone; Mark and Deon are behind closed doors watching TV. Lillie gets ready for bed and stretches out to watch her own color television, enjoying this time to herself. She is asleep when Edward returns. He locks up and turns out the lights, leaving on the one in the bathroom. It keeps the cockroaches away.

There are twenty-eight sixteen-story buildings, each housing 160 families. Low-rent housing for black tenants on welfare

Lillie considers herself lucky. None of her sons is a gang member. She has always tried to convince her sons that without education no dreams are possible

UNITED STATES
OF AMERICA

THE PRYBIL FAMILY

Eldon Prybil, age 45 (1)
Linda Prybil, 42 (2)
Philip, 17 (3)
Karie, 15 (4)
Errin, 11 (5)

700 pigs
12 cats

JOHNSON COUNTY
September 1

6:30. It's Saturday, but habit drives Errin out of bed anyway. His daughter's steps on the old house's wooden staircase is Eldon's daily signal to do the same. His wife, Linda, needs a few extra minutes and extra determination before she crawls out from under the covers.

Before he drinks his cup of coffee, Eldon hurries over to the building in which the sows give birth. In addition to growing soybeans and corn, Eldon maintains a herd of 700 pigs on his farm at all times. At this time of the year, twenty or thirty pigs are born each night. Eldon checks that all is well with the mothers and the new arrivals. He will come back later to vaccinate the newborn piglets.

7:30. Philip and Karie appear in the kitchen, dragging their feet. Last night the high school students had a dance to celebrate the beginning of the school year, and even at their age it can be difficult to recover from a party night. Silently they each prepare their breakfast as Linda readies the kitchen for a day of baking and preserving. For the past week, Karie and Philip have been living at their grandfather's, where they will spend the school year. Linda accepted this early separation so that the children would be able to enroll in a good high school in Iowa City. Grandfather, who lives alone, is delighted. He has arranged everything; it keeps him active to have young people in the house.

Over coffee, Eldon rattles off the chores for the day. There's no question of loafing around. Farm children have only a limited amount of leisure time, especially in the harvest months. On weekends their assistance is crucial. The Prybil children follow their parents' orders without complaint. Respect and discipline, hard work and affection have all been part of their traditional family environment. It's very unlikely that these adolescents will ever rebel against their family's values.

8:30. Errin is perched on top of the lawn mower. It takes her the whole morning to cut the lawn surrounding their turn-of-the-century farmhouse. Philip's job is to feed the pigs. He goes to the corncrib, where the ears are dried and stored, and fills a trailer hooked up to a tractor. When he has filled the mangers, he rejoins his father in the heavy-equipment shed. Here they keep a combine, a rain wagon, two trucks, a tractor for plowing, a disc harrow, a planter, a manure loader, and two small tractors. Harvesting will begin in two weeks, and all the machinery has to be in good working order.

The farm's outbuildings are enormous. They must be to contain all this equipment. The family house is no less imposing than the barns, with its three thousand square feet of space. The house has changed since the arrival of Eldon's grandfather from Czechoslovakia. The most recent addition dates from 1980, when the Prybils added on an immense family room and an office for Eldon. He needed it; the management of a thousand acres requires many hours of clerical work.

Eldon is a good businessman and a prudent farmer. He has never indulged in wild expenditures and he invested wisely during prosperous years. The last years have been very lean, but Eldon hasn't had to put his farm on the auction block like so many of his neighbors. Nevertheless, last year the Prybils made no profit and even had some losses. The sale of their grain was not enough to cover their expenses, which totaled $750,000. This includes payments to the bank to pay back the equipment loans and outlays for taxes, fertilizer, seeds, pesticides, and protein for the animals, not counting the cost of storage for the grain. This year the local silos are still overflowing with the grain that remained unsold from the year before, and the Prybils do not know what will become of the next harvest.

Already, to prevent himself from suffocating

under the burden of debt, Eldon has had to sell three hundred acres of his land. He refuses to consider stopping production, even though there is no hope of a profit at the end of the year. That would merely cause the machinery to deteriorate, resulting in even greater losses.

10:30. Karie and her mother spend the morning in the kitchen baking cakes and pies for their annual Labor Day barbecue. The two chatter incessantly while they work. Karie considers herself lucky to have such a calm, understanding mother, and there are no secrets between them. Eldon and Linda's friends will come from the city to celebrate with them. Eldon always finds opportunities to socialize. His natural, charming personality makes all their get-togethers a success.

Linda loves the country, but farm activities are not enough to keep her happy. She came from Chicago and went to college in Iowa City. She is an active woman and frequently make the half-hour trip to town to attend lectures, plays, and films. She is also a member of the school board and the PTA and is a former president of the University Women's Club. Linda works in the city as a part-time intensive-care nurse in the cardiology department of the university hospital. Her income covers the family's monthly expenses, especially their vital medical insurance premiums. Without this insurance, Linda would be haunted by the fear that one of the family might fall sick, and as a nurse, she knows only too well what this can cost. Before the economic situation became so critical, she used to take time from work to help with the harvest, but this year that is out of the question. Her salary is the only thing that gives Linda a sense of security.

12:00. Lunch break for everyone. At this time of the year, the sweet, tender ears of fresh corn are irresistible, delicious with butter and salt. Eldon issues a fresh set of instructions: there is still a lot of work to be done before nightfall.

Errin practices on the piano for an hour and then gets back on her mower to finish cutting the grass. Karie and Linda will devote the afternoon to preserving the fruits and vegetables overflowing from the garden. Karie brings her mother some beautiful ripe grapes to make juice and jams. At the very least the Prybils will always have enough food. The pantry shelves in the basement are lined with hundreds of jars. This winter, when the ground is covered with snow, the Prybils will enjoy the taste of fresh fruit and vegetables. Eldon accompanies Philip to the hog shed, where the boy will clean up the manure. Philip plans to study agriculture and maybe take over the family farm. But Eldon believes that a farmer must be a good businessman as well and has taken it upon himself to give his son and a group of neighboring farm boys a crash course in investment. Each parent contributed a small sum of money for the boys to pool and invest with a stockbroker. So far, the young men are doing quite well.

2:00. Eldon goes off with the truck to repair a well at one end of the farm. As he drives, he surveys his vast fields of soybeans and corn. It looks like the harvest will be good. Eldon is an experienced farmer. In previous years he has won many prizes, including that of Iowa's Champion Corn Producer. That year he harvested 300 bushels to the acre.

6:30. Eldon is the last to take a shower; then the family sits down to dinner. A large roast beef is in the center of the table, surrounded by vegetables from the garden. Linda serves out generous helpings to her starving crew.

The children clear away the dishes and stack them in the dishwasher. The sooner the job is finished, the sooner they can watch the cassette that they have rented from the video club. The VCR, however, is not abused in the Prybil household. Eldon and Linda prefer board games that let them maintain a close relationship with their children. As the sun starts to set, the family gathers in the old living room.

9:30. *The Karate Kid* was a great success. Philip and Karie still haven't had enough, so they fetch themselves a box of cookies and a glass of milk and watch another film. Errin, the early riser, goes upstairs to her room, and Linda finds a magazine to read. At eleven, when Linda prepares to go to bed, she wakes up her husband. It's always the same. Eldon wants to watch the late night news but can never stay awake long enough.

A wing has been added at the back. Eldon needed an office; the management of a thousand acres requires many hours of clerical work

At this time of the year, the tender, sweet ears of fresh corn are irresistible, delicious with butter and salt

UNITED STATES
OF AMERICA

THE ESGATE FAMILY

Dick Esgate, age 43 (1)
Margaret Esgate (Mimi), 37 (2)
Rachel Borelli, 17 (3)
Michael Borelli, 12 (4)
Ryan Esgate, 5 (5)

SAN DIEGO
September 12

6:30. A ray of sunlight slants through the tinted windows, and its reflection on the cedar-paneled walls fills the Esgate house with a gentle warmth. Mimi goes silently down the thickly carpeted stairs to the second story to awaken her children. She shakes twelve-year-old Mike first. Every morning he spends a great deal of time thinking about his appearance and thus monopolizes one of the bathrooms. Even though there are three in the house, this gives rise to constant conflicts between him and his sister Rachel. Mimi proceeds down to the ground floor to start the washing machine, then back up to the kitchen on the second floor to make breakfast. The children have a choice of chocolate milk, muffins, yogurt, granola, or fruit.

In front of the house the first exercisers have appeared on the bayfront promenade, which follows the shoreline around to the Pacific Ocean. The cool autumn mornings will soon force the joggers and cyclists to cover their tanned bodies with brightly colored sweat suits.

7:15. Mimi hears no signs of life from Ryan, and sure enough, he has gone back to sleep. "Quick, Ryan, we'll be late!" Mimi helps the five-year-old dress and searches the house, wondering where he could have left his shoes. As often happens in the morning, the boys race to the garage. The first one to reach Mimi's Mercedes gets to sit in the front. Rachel considers herself too old for these games.

Every other morning, Mimi picks up Brad, a friend of Ryan's. Tomorrow Brad's mother will drive the children. Mimi makes the twenty-minute drive to the elementary school just in time for Mike to catch the shuttle bus to the junior high school. Then she drops Rachel off at her high school. Dick and Mimi believe that the public schools are too crowded and undisciplined and have decided to send their children to private schools. "We can afford it now," says Dick. Dick recently formed an engineering consulting firm

that advises construction companies, who must comply with state specifications regarding modifications for the handicapped.

9:00. Mimi is back home in time for the arrival of Carmela, an old Mexican woman who was the Esgates' only cleaning lady until very recently. Now her back trouble prevents her from doing heavy work, so Mimi lets her do the ironing, which provides a small income for Carmela, who, as a domestic, will not receive a pension.

Mimi goes up to the third floor, where she has created a world of her own, a huge room that serves as bedroom, office, and hideaway with its own fireplace. It is off-limits to the children. Mimi has always been quite a homebody and has become more so since moving into this house a year ago. Dick bought it at a bargain price when its former owner went bankrupt. Mimi appreciates the quiet of the fall days. The summer people have gone. In the bay, the sailboats swing gently at their moorings. A lone woman is stretched out on the beach reading under an umbrella, while her two children play beside her in the white sand. Not a sound except the slap of ropes on the sailboat masts and the aircraft taking off at regular intervals from San Diego International Airport.

Mimi sits down on the balcony outside her room to finish typing a paper. She hopes to finish her Ph.D. in a new field of psychology called psychoenergetic therapy next May after six years of study. Mimi continued her college education despite numerous interruptions. Her family was not well off, and she had to start work very young. She married her first husband at twenty and took courses while raising Rachel and Michael. Now that Ryan is in school, and her second husband can afford it, she has been able to devote herself full-time to her studies.

Mimi came out to the West Coast ten years ago from New York State to teach learning-disabled children. Her husband was supposed to join her and their children later, but their work conflicts were too great, and Mimi finally asked for a divorce. When she met Dick, she decided to try again. "The second marriage is easier," she says. "It's based on greater maturity and experience; each partner makes a greater effort to keep the relationship healthy and stimulating."

2:30. Mimi paces the floor. She can't concentrate anymore and is impatient to see the children again. Several times in the course of the summer she longed for quiet and looked forward to school starting again. Now, after two days of classes, the silence of her big house seems a little oppressive, and although it is a bit early, she leaves to pick up the kids.

Mimi has a hard time finding a parking spot in front of the school. She is not the only parent who has to taxi her children wherever they want to go. It is virtually impossible to live without a car in San Diego. Public transportation is not very efficient, and the city sprawls for miles along the coast. While Mike stays in the library doing his homework, Mimi drives Rachel and Ryan to the park. Mimi has organized a football team for young children, and Rachel is the coach. The teenager has played on a girls' football team for the past five years and is a good teacher. After a warm-up period, the players get to kick the ball. Ryan clearly does not appreciate taking orders from his sister. On the way home there is a tense silence in the car. Mimi has let Rachel drive. She just got her learner's permit and can only drive under her mother's anxious supervision.

5:00. To keep the children happy, Mimi offers them a mango, but tortilla chips in hot sauce are more successful. Mexican cooking is a West Coast tradition, due to the nearness of the border and the large number of Californians of Mexican descent.

No sooner has Rachel arrived home than her friend Jeff appears on his bicycle. As on every afternoon, Rachel rides with him, perched on the handlebars of his bike, down to the ocean beach for a game of volleyball with the neighborhood

surfer boys. The beachfront is once again swarming with joggers, cyclists, and walkers seeking physical perfection and relaxation after a day at work. To enhance his own muscle tone, Mike heads straight for the exercise room in the basement. He works out on his weights and then spends a few minutes on the chest expander and the trampoline. There is also a sauna and a whirlpool, and next to the ground-floor kitchenette and living room there is a pool. Mike can swim his laps under Mimi's watchful eye as she makes Chinese food.

The sound of the station wagon in the driveway causes Ryan to forsake the cartoons on television and run into his father's arms, closely followed by Mike and Mimi. Dick appreciates the reception all the more because he is going through a difficult period at present. He has some important decisions to make. His firm has become so successful that his associates are pressuring him to open additional offices in major cities across the country. Dick is reluctant to do so. The larger his business becomes, the less time he will have to spend with his family. After the failure of his first marriage, his family time is very important to him. He readily accepts the suggestion of a swim to take his mind off the problem. Ryan quickly peels off his clothes and jumps into the water with his father.

6:00. As if she smelled dinner cooking, Rachel appears at the very moment when Mimi finishes setting the places at the ceramic table in the garden. Unfortunately they can't linger, for the evenings are growing cool. Rachel disappears as quickly as she arrived. She stretches out on the carpet in her room talking to her boyfriend on her private telephone. Her major preoccupation at the moment is her choice of a college for next year. Like all her friends, she looks forward to leaving San Diego and living away from her family. "It's time to grow up," she says.

9:00. Ryan has fallen asleep in Dick's arms and is put to bed. According to their mother's dictum, everyone now goes to his or her own room. Mimi believes that time for oneself is essential, that silence and space foster personal freedom and independence.

Mimi is working on the balcony outside her room. As soon as the sun rises, the first joggers appear on the bayfront promenade

This is the main kitchen. But in the summer the family uses the kitchenette on the ground floor for cooking and serving meals in the garden

UNITED STATES OF AMERICA

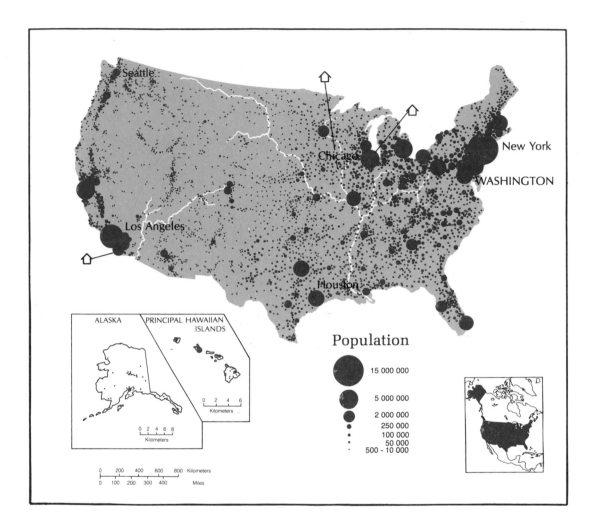

Population

- 15 000 000
- 5 000 000
- 2 000 000
- 250 000
- 100 000
- 50 000
- 500 - 10 000

THE NAME: America: given by a German geographer in recognition of the voyages of Amerigo Vespucci

THE PEOPLE: The Americans

GEOGRAPHY
Two belts of highlands with a vast lowland between them:
Appalachians in the east
Rocky Mountains in the west
Max. altitude: 4,417 m. (14,494 ft.) (Mt. Whitney)
Area: 9,529,200 sq. km. (3,679,245 sq. mi.)
Density: 25 pers./sq. km. (65 pers./sq. mi.) (1986)
Arable land: 20% (1987)
Forest: 28%

Climate: Ranges from tropical in Hawaii to subtropical in extreme southern Florida and along the Gulf coast; highly variable mid-latitude climate in most of the mainland: subarctic climate in Alaska and the mountain ranges; temperate maritime climate on the Atlantic coast.

CAPITAL: Washington, pop. 3,369,600 (metropolitan area) (1984)

LANGUAGE: English
More than one American in ten does not speak English at home.

RELIGION: (1983)
Protestant: 55%   Jewish: 4%
Catholic: 37%   Eastern churches: 4%

POPULATION: Total—238,000,000 (1985)
 Annual growth: 0.9% (2,142,000) (1980–85)
 Doubling time: 102 yrs.
 Urban: 74% (est. for year 2000: 83%)
 Rural: 26%

AGE GROUPS: (1984)
 8% less than 5 yrs.
 22% less than 15
 30% less than 20
 34% from 20 to 39
 20% from 40 to 59
 17% 60 yrs. and over

ETHNIC GROUPS
 White: 83% (including pop. of Hispanic origin)
 Black: 12%
 Asian and Pacific Islander: 1.5%
 American Indian and Eskimo: 0.6%

HISTORY
 From 986: Discovery of northeast coast (Vinland) by Scandinavians and Icelanders
 1513: Discovery of Florida by the Spanish
 1530: Giovanni da Verrazano explores Carolina and North Florida for France
 1607–1733: Settlement of 13 colonies by the British
 1619: Arrival of first slave cargo
 1763: Treaty of Paris ends French control; Florida ceded by Spain in return for Cuba
 1775–83: Revolutionary War
 July 4, 1776: Declaration of Independence
 1788: Constitution ratified
 1861–65: Civil War
 1929: Wall Street crash, followed by the Great Depression
 1941: U.S. entry into World War II
 1950–53: Korean War
 1960s: Civil Rights Movement
 1961–73: Vietnam War

FAMILY
 Marital status, for population 18 yrs. and older: (1980)
  Married: 61%
  Widowed: 18%
  Single: 18%
  Divorced: 8%
  Young adults marrying today have a 50% chance of ending their first marriage in divorce. 80% of all divorced people remarry.
 Female head of household: 31% (whites: 11%; blacks: 38%) (1984)
 Fertility rate: 1.9 (1985)
 Births out of wedlock: 19% (white: 12%; black: 57%) (1982)
 Teenage births: 15% (1981)
 Contraception: 68% (1984)
 Government's position on family planning: Has not adopted any formal goals for population growth or fertility levevls. Direct and indirect support is provided to ensure the availability of family-planning services and counseling to all individuals who desire those services.

SOCIAL INDICATORS
Life expectancy: 75 yrs. (male: 71; female: 78) (1985)
Infant mortality: 11/1,000 births (1985)
Crude birth rate: 16/1,000 pop. (1985)
Crude death rate: 9/1,000
Health:
 Access to health services: no data
 Births attended by trained health personnel: It can be assumed that almost all Americans have access to trained health personnel.

HOUSING
Persons per household: 2.7 (1985)
 Most households contain only 1 or 2 people.
Electricity: No data. It can be assumed that almost all Americans have access to electricity.
Access to safe water: No data. It can be assumed that almost all Americans have access to safe water.
Source of water: (1980)
 Public system or private company: 84%
 Well: 15%
 Other: 1%
Toilet facilities: (1980)
 One or more complete bathrooms: 95%
 Other: 5%
Building materials: (1980)
 Wood, brick, and cement

EDUCATION
Literacy: 99.5% (1979)
Gross enrollment ratio: (1984)
 First level: 101%
 Second: 95%
 Third: 57%
Educational attainment, for population 25 yrs. +: (1985)
 None: less than 1% Second: 74%
 First level: 93% Third: 19%

ECONOMIC ACTIVITY
Economically active population: 49% (male: 57%; female: 42%) (1985)
Agriculture: 3% act. pop.; 3% of GDP
Mines: 4% act. pop.; 5% of GDP
Industry: 24% act. pop.; 5% of GDP
Services: 68% act. pop.; 64% of GDP
Per capita GNP: 16,690 U.S.$ (1985)
Population in absolute poverty: (1982)
 12% of persons and 10% of families had income below poverty level (black families: 33%).
National currency: U.S. dollar
Principal resources:
 Agriculture: soybeans, wheat, corn
 Mines and industries: petroleum, natural gas, coal, uranium

COMMUNICATIONS
Radio:
 Transmitters: 8,359 (1977)
 Receivers: 479,000,000—2,043/1,000 pop. (1983)
Television:
 Transmitters: 972 (1977)
 Receivers: 185,300,000—790/1,000 pop. (1983)

Author's Note

THE FAMILIES in this book were chosen from detailed statistical profiles and accurately reflect the characteristics of each country. If the majority of a country's population is rural, the family chosen to represent it is rural. The family earns the average national income and has the average number of children. I have tried to choose couples in similar age groups (late twenties to early forties) because the changes between generations are extreme in many countries. A single-parent family is portrayed if, as is frequently the case in the Caribbean, this is a widespread feature of the society.

The family's home had to be representative of the country's architecture and the predominant standard of living. I also considered factors such as the availability of electricity and water, as well as the materials used to construct the house.

It was not always easy to identify a representative family. The personnel of the United Nations Development Programme (UNDP) and the United Nations Children's Fund (UNICEF) assisted me greatly in my search. They put me in contact with local professionals working at the grass-roots level. Group sessions were often required to define the family's main features and to locate someone who knew the community intimately enough to knock on a family's door and introduce me. Finding a guide to accompany me on a six-hour trek across rivers and mountains was an added difficulty; fortunately, it often ended up in one more friendship.

I must have seemed demanding to those who were kind enough to help me in my search. I often insisted that the family have one more or one fewer child in order to correspond to the ideal statistical profile; a larger or smaller house; or that the head of the household have a different oc-

cupation. Indeed, no concessions were made on major features. The essays are as faithful a depiction of each country as possible, so that the readers who are a part of the majority in their own country can say, "If I had been born there, that is how I would live."

I have made a few exceptions to my criteria which I would like to explain. In order to avoid repetition of identical material, I sometimes had to make difficult choices. To represent the majority in Peru, I should have chosen an Andes Indian family, but they would have looked and lived just like the family in Bolivia. Since thirty percent of Peru's city population consists of peasants who have migrated from the mountains with more doing so every day, I felt it was important to represent them instead.

In Trinidad, blacks and East Indians are nearly equal in number. Rather than choose between the two groups, I opted for a "mixed" family, which represents a growing population trend.

In Suriname, it should have been, as in Guyana, an East Indian family. But since Suriname is the most ethnically diverse country in Latin America, I chose a family from one of the minority groups.

The Amazonia region borders nine of the eleven countries of South America; it is inhabited by hundreds of Indian tribes. It is not a country, but I felt it essential to represent a primitive way of life which continues to flourish at the gateway to the most modern continent in the world.

In large countries, such as Brazil, Canada, and the United States, no representative family exists. However, the standard of living and the problems of everyday life are very similar in Canada and the United States. I therefore chose to portray six families who represent a cross section of predominant lifestyles in North America.

Sources

Key to Source Notes

1. **Area**
2. **Density**
3. **Arable land**—The percentage of land planted with crops, meadows for mowing or pasture, land devoted to market and kitchen gardens (including cultivation under glass), and land lying fallow. The datum is obtained by dividing arable land by the total area of a country, excluding land under inland bodies of water.
3a. **Forest**
4. **Total population**
5. **Annual growth**—The rate at which a population is increasing (or decreasing) in a given year due to natural increase and net migration, expressed as a percentage of the base population.
6. **Doubling time**—The number of years it would take for a country to double its population size, assuming that the current growth rate is constant.
7. **Urban/rural**
8. **Estimate for year 2000**
9. **Age groups**
10. **Ethnic groups**
11. **Marital status**—The personal status of women in relation to the marriage laws or customs of the country.

    A visiting union is one in which a woman has given birth during the previous year and was neither married nor in a common-law union at that time.

    The percentage of women who have never had a husband or common-law partner includes those who have never been married or been in a common-law relationship. It also includes women who consider themselves to be in a visiting union but who did not give birth during the previous year.
12. **Female head of household**
13. **Fertility rate**—The average number of children that would be born per woman during her lifetime if she were to live to the end of her childbearing years and bear children at each age in accordance with the prevailing age-specific fertility rates of a given year. A rate of 2.1 children is necessary for a population to replace itself.
14. **Births out of wedlock**

15. **Teenage births**—The number of live births for mothers aged 19 years and under as a percentage of live births for women of all ages in a given year.
16. **Contraception**—The percentage of currently married women of childbearing age using contraception. It generally refers to women between the ages of 15 and 49 who are practicing or whose husbands are practicing any form of birth control. The methods of contraception usually comprise male and female sterilization, intrauterine device (IUD), condom, injectable and oral contraceptives, spermicides, diaphragm, rhythm, withdrawal, and abstinence.
17. **Government's position on family planning**
18. **Life expectancy**—The number of years a newborn baby can be expected to live if subject to the mortality risks prevailing for the general population at the time of its birth.
19. **Infant mortality**—The number of deaths of infants under one year of age per 1,000 live births in a given year.
20. **Crude birth and death rates**—The number of live births and deaths per 1,000 population in a given year.
21. **Health**
22. **Persons per household**—The average size of a household or the number of persons living in households divided by the total number of households.
23. **Electricity**
24. **Access to safe water**—The percentage of the population obtaining water that does not contain chemical substances and microorganisms in concentrations that could cause illness in any form. Such water is considered adequate if obtainable from a facility situated near to or within the household.
25. **Source of water**—Piped water refers to water provided within housing units from community-wide systems or from individual installations such as pressure tanks and pumps. Housing units with piped water more than 100 meters from the house are defined as being without piped water.
26. **Toilet facilities**
27. **Building materials**—The predominant materials

used in building the outer walls of houses.

28. **Literacy**—The percentage of the population 15 years of age and over who are able to read and write. Unless otherwise specified, data are UNESCO estimates based on information provided or approved by each country.

29. **Gross enrollment ratio**—The gross enrollment ratio is the total enrollment of all ages divided by the population of the specific age groups which correspond to the age groups of primary and secondary schooling. At the third level, the figures for the population aged 20 to 24 years have been used throughout. All ratios are expressed as percentages.

    Since the gross enrollment ratio at the first and second levels includes pupils of all possible ages whereas the population is limited to the range of official school ages, countries with almost universal education among the school-age population at the first level will have a ratio exceeding 100, if the actual age distribution of pupils goes beyond the official school ages.

30. **First level**—completing primary school

31. **Educational attainment**—The percentage of the distribution of the highest educational attainment of the population expressed in levels defined by each country but closely corresponding to the following categories: none, primary, secondary, and university levels.

32. **Economically active population**—Comprises all persons who provide the supply of labor for the production of economic goods and services, as defined by the United Nations systems of national accounts and balances, during a specified time-reference period.

33. **GDP**—Gross domestic product. Measures the total final output of goods and services produced by an economy.

34. **Per capita GNP**—The gross national product (GNP) measures the total domestic and foreign output claimed by residents and is calculated without making deductions for depreciation. The GNP, converted to U.S. dollars, is divided by the mid-year population to derive the 1985 per capita GNP.

35. **Population in absolute poverty**—The percentage of the population found at an income level below which a minimum nutritionally adequate diet plus essential non-food requirements are not affordable.

36. **National currency**—Exchange rates which are expressed in terms of the number of units of national currency corresponding to one United States dollar as of 1985.

37. **Communications**

    Radio transmitters—The total number of radio transmitters in service used for domestic broadcasting to the general public, excluding transmitters primarily used for external broadcasting.

    Radio receivers—The total number of receivers of all types for radio broadcasts to the general public, including those connected to a cable distribution system (wired receivers). The datum includes such individual private receivers as car radios, portable radio sets, and private sets installed in public places as well as communal receivers. The datum on receivers is an estimate of the number of receivers in use.

    Television transmitters—The total number of television transmitters operating on a regular basis and used for broadcasting to the general public, regardless of whether the responsibility for them lies with the broadcasting institution or with other institutions such as Posts and Telecommunications. The datum relates to both main and relay transmitters.

    Television receivers—The total number of television receivers representing the estimated total number of receivers in use. Also given is the number of television receivers per 1,000 inhabitants.

Sources

South America

AMAZONIA

38. Roger D. Stone, *Dreams of Amazonia* (New York: Viking, 1985), p. 41.

39. Leandro Tocanting, "The World of the Amazon Region," *Man in the Amazon*. C. Wagley, ed. (Gainesville: University of Florida Press, 1974), pp. 21–32.

40. Emilio Moran, "Growth without Development: Past and Present Development Efforts in Amazonia," *The Dilemma of Amazonian Development*. E. Moran, ed. (Boulder, Colo.: Westview Press, 1983), pp. 5–23.

41. Jean Dorst, *South America and Central America: A Natural History* (New York: Random House, 1967), p. 76.

42. Susanna Hecht, "Cattle Ranching in the Eastern Amazon," *The Dilemma of Amazonian Development*. E. Moran, ed. (Boulder, Colo.: Westview Press, 1983), pp. 156–88.

J. J. Nicholaides, III et al., "Crop Production Systems in the Amazon Basin," *The Dilemma of Amazonian Development*. E. Moran, ed. (Boulder, Colo.: Westview Press, 1983), pp. 156–88.

43. Betty J. Meggers, *Amazonia: Man and Culture in a Counterfeit Paradise* (Chicago: Aldine, 1971), p. 9–10.

J. J. Nicholaides, III et al., "Crop Production Systems in the Amazon Basin."

44. *Bovo Indígenas do Brasil, 1984* (São Paulo: Sagarana Editora, Centro Ecumênico de Documentação e Informação).

45. James C. Jones, "Native Peoples in Lowland Bolivia," *Frontier Expansion in Amazonia*. M. Schmink and C. H. Wood, eds. (Gainesville: University of Florida Press, 1984), pp. 62–82.

46. *Anuário Estatístico do Brasil*, Fundaçao Instituto Brasileiro de Geografia e Estatistica, 1982.

Bovo Indígenas do Brasil, 1984.

47. *Encyclopedia Americana* (Danbury, Conn.: Grolier, Inc., 1985), p. 271.

48. William T. Vickers, "Indian Policy in Amazonian Ecuador," *Frontier Expansion in Amazonia*. M. Schmink and C. H. Wood, eds. (Gainesville: University of Florida Press, 1984), pp. 8–32.

49. Walter F. Edwards, ed. *Focus on Amerindians* (Georgetown: University of Guyana Press, 1980).

Peter Riviere, *Individual and Society in Guiana* (Cambridge: Cambridge University Press, 1984), p. 3.

50. Peter Riviere, *Individual and Society in Guiana*.

51. Anthony Stocks, "Indian Policy in Eastern Peru," *Frontier Expansion in Amazonia*, M. Schmink and C. H. Wood, eds. (Gainesville: University of Florida Press, 1974), pp. 33–61.

52. Peter Riviere, *Individual and Society in Guiana*.

53. Paul Henley, *The Panare: Tradition and Change on the Amazonian Frontier* (New Haven: Yale University Press, 1982).

Johannes Wilbert, *Survivors of Eldorado* (New York: Praeger, 1972), pp. 6–9.

54. S. S. Panagides and V. L. Magalhaes, "Amazon Economic Policy and Prospects," *Man in the Amazon*. C. Wagley, ed.

(Gainesville: University of Florida Press, 1974), p. 247.

55. *The Yanomami Indian Park: A Call for Action*. Special Publication of the Anthropology Resource Center, 1981.

N. Chagon, *Yanomamo: The Fierce People* (New York: Holt, Rinehart and Winston, 1968).

Antropología. La Reserva de Biosfera Yanomami: Una Auténtica Estrategia para el Desarrollo. Instituto Venezolano de Investigaciones, Departamento de Antropología.

J. V. Larisse Neel, and F. Salzano, "21.7% Census on 1,400 Men and 1,200 Women in 20 Villages."

ARGENTINA

1. *The New International Atlas* (Chicago: Rand McNally, 1986) Tables I–10 to I–13. Estimates for January 1, 1985, based on official data, United Nations estimates, and other available information.

2. Ibid.

3. *1987 World Population Data Sheet*, Population Reference Bureau (Washington, D.C.). Source: FAO and U.S. Department of State.

3a. Ibid.

4. *United Nations World Population Chart 1985*, Population Division, United Nations.

5. *Demographic Indicators by Countries as Assessed in 1984*, Population Division, United Nations (November 1985).

6. *1987 World Population Data Sheet*.

7. *The Prospects of World Urbanization*, Population Division, United Nations (rev. ed., 1984–85).

8. Ibid.

9. *Demographic Yearbook 1983*, United Nations.

10. George Thomas Kurian, *Encyclopedia of the Third World* (3rd ed.; New York: Facts on File, Inc., 1987), Vol. I, p. 92.

11. *Censo Nacional de Población y Vivienda 1980*, Instituto Nacional de Estadística y Censos, República Argentina, Serie D Población, p. 8.

12. Instituto Nacional de Estadística y Censos.

13. *State of the World Children 1987*, UNICEF (New York: Oxford University Press, 1987), annex tables.

14. *Anuario Estadístico de la República Argentina 1981–1982*, Instituto Nacional de Estadística y Censos, p. 195.

15. *Demographic Yearbook 1983*, United Nations. Data tabulated by year of registration rather than occurrence.

16. *World Development Report 1987*, World Bank (New York: Oxford University Press, 1987).

17. *Population Policy Briefs: The Current Situation in Developing Countries, 1985*, United Nations.

18. *State of the World Children 1987*.

19. Ibid.

20. Ibid.

21. Ibid.

22. *Censo Nacional de Población y Vivienda 1980*, Serie C Vivienda, p. 1.

23. Ibid.

24. *State of the World Children 1987*.

25. *Censo Nacional de Población y Vivienda 1980*. Serie C p. 14.

26. Ibid.

27. Ibid.

28. *Statistical Yearbook 1986*, UNESCO.

29. Ibid.

30. *State of the World Children 1987*.

31. *Statistical Yearbook 1986*, UNESCO.

32. *Yearbook of Labour Statistics 1986*, International Labour Office, Geneva, Chapter 1, Table 1, p. 13.

33. *Atlaseco de Poche, Atlas Economique Mondial* (Paris: Les éditions S.G.P., 1985). Data taken from World Bank sources.

34. *World Development Report 1987*.

35. *State of the World Children 1987*.

36. *Statistical Yearbook 1986*, UNESCO.

37. *Statistical Yearbook 1984*, UNESCO; *Statistical Yearbook 1986*.

BOLIVIA

1. *The New International Atlas* (Chicago: Rand McNally, 1986), Tables I–10 to I–13. Estimates for January 1, 1985, based on official data, United Nations estimates, and other available information.

2. Ibid.

3. *1987 World Population Data Sheet*, Population Reference Bureau (Washington, D.C.). Source: FAO and U.S. Department of State.

3a. Ibid.

4. *United Nations World Population Chart 1985*, Population Division, United Nations.

5. *Demographic Indicators by Countries as Assessed in 1984*, Population Division, United Nations (November 1985).

6. *1987 World Population Data Sheet*.

7. *The Prospects of World Urbanization*, Population Division, United Nations (rev. ed., 1984–85).

8. Ibid.

9. *Demographic Yearbook 1983*, United Nations. Estimates which are less reliable. Data adjusted for underenumeration.

10. George Thomas Kurian, *Encyclopedia of the Third World* (3rd ed., New York: Facts on File, Inc., 1987), Vol. I, p. 206.

11. *Demographic Yearbook 1982*, United Nations. Data exclude adjustment for underenumeration, estimated at 6.99%.

12. No data.

13. *State of the World Children 1987*, UNICEF (New York: Oxford University Press, 1987), annex tables.

14. No data.

15. *Demographic Yearbook 1983*, United Nations. Data from civil registers which are incomplete or of unknown completeness.

16. *World Development Report 1987*, World Bank (New York: Oxford University Press, 1987).

17. *Population Policy Briefs: The Current Situation in Developing Countries, 1985*, United Nations.

18. *State of the World Children 1987*.

19. Ibid.

20. Ibid.

21. Ibid.

22. *Compendium of Human Settlements Statistics 1983*, United Nations.

23. Ibid.

24. *State of the World Children 1987*.

25. *Compendium of Human Settlements Statistics 1983*, United Nations.

26. Ibid.

27. Instituto Nacional de Estadística, Bolivia, 1983.

28. *Statistical Yearbook 1986*, UNESCO.

29. Ibid.

30. *State of the World Children 1987*.

31. *Statistical Yearbook 1986*, UNESCO.

32. *Yearbook of Labour Statistics 1986*, International Labour Office, Geneva, Chapter 1, Table 1, p. 13.

33. *Atlaseco de Poche, Atlas Economique Mondial* (Paris: Les éditions S.G.P., 1985). Data taken from World Bank sources.

34. *World Development Report 1987*.

35. *State of the World Children 1987*.

36. *Statistical Yearbook 1986*, UNESCO.

37. *Statistical Yearbook 1984*, UNESCO; *Statistical Yearbook 1986*.

BRAZIL

1. *The New International Atlas* (Chicago: Rand McNally, 1986), Tables I–10 to I–13. Estimates for January 1, 1985, based on official data, United Nations estimates, and other available information.

2. Ibid.

3. *1987 World Population Data Sheet*, Population Reference Bureau (Washington, D.C.). Source: FAO and U.S. Department of State.

3a. Ibid.

4. *United Nations World Population Chart 1985*, Population Division, United Nations.

5. *Demographic Indicators by Countries as Assessed in 1984*, Population Division, United Nations (November 1985).

6. *1987 World Population Data Sheet*.

7. *The Prospects of World Urbanization*, Population Division, United Nations (rev. ed., 1984–85).

8. Ibid.

9. *Demographic Yearbook 1983*, United Nations. Estimates which are less reliable. Excluding Indian jungle population.

10. George Thomas Kurian, *Encyclopedia of the Third World*, (3rd ed.; New York: Facts on File, Inc., 1987), Vol. I, p. 244.

11. *Demographic Yearbook 1982*, United Nations. Data exclude adjustment for underenumeration, estimated at 6.99%.

12. No data.

13. *State of the World Children 1987*. UNICEF (New York: Oxford University Press, 1987), annex tables.

14. No data.

15. *Demographic Yearbook 1983*, United Nations. Data from civil registers which are incomplete or of unknown completeness.

16. *World Development Report 1987*, World Bank (New York: Oxford University Press, 1987).

17. *Population Policy Briefs: The Current Situation in Developing Countries, 1985*, United Nations.

18. *State of the World Children 1987*.

19. Ibid.

20. Ibid.

21. Ibid.

22. *Compendium of Human Settlements Statistics 1983*, United Nations. Data are provisional.

23. Ibid.

24. *State of the World Children 1987*.

25. *Compendium of Human Settlements Statistics 1983*, United Nations.

26. Ibid.

27. *Anuário Estatístico do Brasil 1984*, Fundação Instituto Brasileiro de Geografia e Estatística.

28. *Statistical Yearbook 1986*, UNESCO.

29. Ibid.

30. *State of the World Children 1987*.

31. *Anuário Estatístico do Brasil 1983*, Fundação Instituto Brasileiro de Geografia e Estatística (Rio de Janeiro, 1984), p. 236. *Statistical Yearbook 1986*, UNESCO.

32. *Yearbook of Labour Statistics 1986*, International Labour Office, Geneva, Chapter 1, Table 1, p. 13. For population 10 years and older.

33. *Atlaseco de Poche, Atlas Economique Mondial* (Paris: Les éditions S.G.P., 1985). Data taken from World Bank sources.

34. *World Development Report 1987*.

35. *State of the World Children 1987*.

36. *Statistical Yearbook 1986*, UNESCO.

37. *Statistical Yearbook 1984*, UNESCO; *Statistical Yearbook 1986*.

CHILE

1. *The New International Atlas* (Chicago: Rand McNally, 1986), Tables I–10 to I–13. Estimates for January 1, 1985, based on official data, United Nations estimates, and other available information.

2. Ibid.

3. *1987 World Population Data Sheet*, Population Reference Bureau (Washington D.C.). Source: FAO and U.S. Department of State.

3a. Ibid.

4. *United Nations World Population Chart 1985*, Population Division, United Nations.

5. Ibid.

6. *1987 World Population Data Sheet*.

7. *The Prospects of World Urbanization*, Population Division, United Nations (rev. ed., 1984–85).

8. Ibid.

9. *Demographic Yearbook 1983*, United Nations. Provisional. Adjusted for underenumeration.

10. George Thomas Kurian, *Encyclopedia of the Third World* (3rd ed.; New York: Facts on File, Inc., 1987), Vol. I, p. 413.

11. *Demographic Yearbook 1982*, United Nations. Including adjustment for underenumeration.

12. No data.

13. *State of the World Children 1987*, UNICEF (New York: Oxford University Press, 1987), annex tables.

14. No data.

15. *Demographic Yearbook 1983*, United Nations. Excluding adjustment for underenumeration.

16. *World Development Report 1987*, World Bank (New York: Oxford University Press, 1987).

17. *Population Policy Briefs: The Current Situation in Developing Countries, 1985*, United Nations.

18. *State of the World Children 1987*.

19. Ibid.

20. Ibid.

21. Ibid.

22. *Encyclopedia of the Third World*, p. 413.

23. *Compendium of Human Settlements Statistics 1983*, United Nations.

24. *State of the World Children 1987*.

25. *Compendium of Human Settlements Statistics 1983*.

26. Ibid.

27. *Viviendas, Hogares y Familias*, Censo 1970, Departamento Geografía y Censos.

28. *Statistical Yearbook 1986*, UNESCO.

29. Ibid.

30. No data.

31. Instituto Nacional de Estadística, República de Chile.

32. *Yearbook of Labour Statistics 1986*, International Labour Office, Geneva, Chapter 1, Table 1, p. 13.

33. *Atlaseco de Poche, Atlas Economique Mondial* (Paris: Les éditions S.G.P. 1985). Data taken from World Bank sources.

34. *World Development Report 1987*.

35. *Statistics on Children in*

UNICEF Assisted Countries,
UNICEF, April 1987.
   36. *Statistical Yearbook 1986,*
UNESCO.
   37. Ibid.

COLOMBIA

   1. *The New International Atlas*
(Chicago: Rand McNally, 1986),
Tables I–10 to I–13. Estimates for
January 1, 1985, based on official
data, United Nations estimates, and
other available information.
   2. Ibid.
   3. *1987 World Population Data
Sheet,* Population Reference Bureau
(Washington, D.C.). Source: FAO
and U.S. Department of State.
   3a. Ibid.
   4. *United Nations World
Population Chart 1985,* Population
Division, United Nations.
   5. Ibid.
   6. *1987 World Population Data
Sheet.*
   7. *The Prospects of World
Urbanization,* Population Division,
United Nations (rev. ed., 1984–85).
   8. Ibid.
   9. *Demographic Indicators:
Estimates and Projections 1980,*
United Nations.
   10. George Thomas Kurian,
Encyclopedia of the Third World
(3rd ed.; New York: Facts on File,
Inc., 1987), Vol. I, p. 440.
   11. Instituto Colombiano de
Bienestar Familial.
   12. Ibid. Estimate.
   13. *State of the World Children
1987.* UNICEF (New York: Oxford
University Press, 1987), annex
tables.
   14. No data.
   15. No data.
   16. *World Development Report
1987,* World Bank (New York:
Oxford University Press, 1987).
   17. *Population Policy Briefs: The
Current Situation in Developing
Countries, 1985,* United Nations.
   18. *State of the World Children
1987.*
   19. Ibid.
   20. Ibid.
   21. Ibid.

   22. *Encyclopedia of the Third
World,* p. 439.
   23. *XV Censo Nacional de
Población y IV de Vivienda,*
Departamento Administrativo
Nacional de Estadística, 1985.
   24. *State of the World Children
1987.*
   25. *XV Censo Nacional de
Población y IV de Vivienda.*
   26. Ibid.
   27. Ibid.
   28. *Statistical Yearbook 1986,*
UNESCO.
   29. Ibid.
   30. *State of the World Children
1987.*
   31. *Statistical Yearbook 1986,*
UNESCO.
   32. *Encyclopedia of the Third
World,* p. 451.
   33. *Atlaseco de Poche, Atlas
Economique Mondial* (Paris: Les
éditions S.G.P., 1985). Data taken
from World Bank sources.
   34. *World Development Report
1987,* World Bank (New York:
Oxford University Press, 1987).
   35. *State of the World Children
1987.*
   36. *Statistical Yearbook 1986,*
UNESCO.
   37. Ibid.

ECUADOR

   1. *The New International Atlas*
(Chicago: Rand McNally, 1986),
Tables I–10 to I–13. Estimates for
January 1, 1985, based on official
data, United Nations estimates, and
other available information.
   2. Ibid.
   3. *1987 World Population Data
Sheet,* Population Reference Bureau
(Washington, D.C.). Source: FAO
and U.S. Department of State.
   3a. Ibid.
   4. *United Nations World
Population Chart 1985.* Population
Division, United Nations.
   5. Ibid.
   6. *1987 World Population Data
Sheet.*
   7. *The Prospects of World
Urbanization,* Population Division,
United Nations (rev. ed., 1984–85).

   8. Ibid.
   9. *IV Censo de Población 111 de
Vivienda,* Instituto Nacional de
Estadística y Censos (INEC),
República del Ecuador. Resultados
Anticipados por Muestra. Ecuador.
November 1982. P. 4. Advance
sampling results.
   10. George Thomas Kurian,
Encyclopedia of the Third World
(3rd ed.; New York: Facts on File,
Inc., 1987), Vol. I, p. 579.
   11. *IV Censo de Población,* p. 15.
   12. No data.
   13. *State of the World Children
1987.* UNICEF (New York: Oxford
University Press, 1987), annex
tables.
   14. No data.
   15. *Demographic Yearbook 1983,*
United Nations. Excluding nomadic
Indian tribes. Data from civil
registers which are incomplete or of
unknown completeness.
   16. *World Development Report
1987,* World Bank (New York:
Oxford University Press, 1987).
   17. *Population Policy Briefs: The
Current Situation in Developing
Countries, 1985,* United Nations.
   18. *State of the World Children
1987.*
   19. Ibid.
   20. Ibid.
   21. Ibid.
   22. *Encyclopedia of the Third
World,* p. 579.
   23. *IV Censo de Población,* p. 64.
   24. *State of the World Children
1987.*
   25. *IV Censo de Población,* p. 61.
   26. Ibid., p. 64.
   27. Ibid.
   28. *Statistical Yearbook 1986,*
UNESCO.
   29. Ibid.
   30. *State of the World Children
1987.*
   31. *IV Censo de Población,* p. 25.
   32. *Yearbook of Labour Statistics
1986,* International Labour Office,
Geneva, Chapter 1, Table 1, p. 13.
   33. *Atlaseco de Poche, Atlas
Economique Mondial* (Paris: Les
éditions S.G.P., 1985). Data taken
from World Bank sources.
   34. *World Development Report
1987,* World Bank (New York:
Oxford University Press, 1987).

35. *State of the World Children 1987.*

36. *Statistical Yearbook 1986,* UNESCO.

37. Ibid.

GUYANA

1. *The New International Atlas* (Chicago: Rand McNally, 1986), Tables I–10 to I–13. Estimates for January 1, 1985, based on official data, United Nations estimates, and other available information.

2. Ibid.

3. *1987 World Population Data Sheet,* Population Reference Bureau (Washington, D.C.). Source: FAO and U.S. Department of State.

3a. Ibid.

4. *United Nations World Population Chart 1985.* Population Division, United Nations.

5. Ibid.

6. *1987 World Population Data Sheet.*

7. *The Prospects of World Urbanization,* Population Division, United Nations (rev. ed., 1984–85).

8. Ibid.

9. *1980–1981 Population Census,* Vol. I, p. 3.

10. Ibid., p. 172.

11. Ibid., p. 175. Where the respondent is more than 45 years old, the union status reported is that which existed at age 45.

12. Ibid., p. 345.

13. *State of the World Children 1987,* UNICEF (New York: Oxford University Press, 1987), annex tables.

14. No data.

15. No data.

16. Dorothy Nortman, *Population and Family Planning Programs: A Compendium of Data Through 1983* (12th ed.; New York: The Population Council, 1985), p. 56. Currently married women 15 to 49 years old using contraception.

17. *Population Policy Briefs: The Current Situation in Developing Countries, 1985,* United Nations.

18. *State of the World Children 1987.*

19. Ibid.

20. Ibid.

21. Ibid.

22. George Thomas Kurian, *Encyclopedia of the Third World* (3rd ed.; New York: Facts on File, Inc., 1987), Vol. II, p. 814.

23. *1980–1981 Population Census,* Vol. I, p. 300.

24. *State of the World Children 1987.*

25. *1980–1981 Population Census.*

26. Ibid.

27. Ibid.

28. *Statistical Yearbook 1986,* UNESCO.

29. Ibid.

30. *State of the World Children 1987.*

31. *1980–1981 Population Census,* Vol. I, p. 154.

32. *Yearbook of Labour Statistics 1986,* International Labour Office, Geneva, Chapter 1, Table 1, p. 13.

33. *Atlaseco de Poche, Atlas Economique Mondial* (Paris: Les éditions S.G.P., 1985). Data taken from World Bank sources.

34. *World Development Report 1987,* World Bank (New York: Oxford University Press, 1987).

35. No data.

36. *Statistical Yearbook 1986,* UNESCO.

37. Ibid.

PARAGUAY

1. *The New International Atlas* (Chicago: Rand McNally, 1986), Tables I–10 to I–13. Estimates for January 1, 1985, based on official data, United Nations estimates, and other available information.

2. Ibid.

3. *1987 World Population Data Sheet,* Population Reference Bureau (Washington, D.C.). Source: FAO and U.S. Department of State.

3a. Ibid.

4. *United Nations World Population Chart 1985,* Population Division, United Nations.

5. Ibid.

6. *1987 World Population Data Sheet.*

7. *The Prospects of World Urbanization,* Population Division, United Nations (rev. ed., 1984–85).

8. Ibid.

9. *Censo Nacional de Población y Viviendas 1982.* Avance de Resultados Muestra del 10%. República del Paraguay. Dirección General de Estadística y Censos. Asunción. September 1984. P. 20. Ten percent census sample.

10. George Thomas Kurian, *Encyclopedia of the Third World* (3rd ed.; New York: Facts on File, Inc., 1987), Vol. II, p. 1569.

11. *Censo Nacional de Población y Viviendas 1982,* p. 25. Ten percent census sample.

12. No data.

13. *State of the World Children 1987,* UNICEF (New York: Oxford University Press, 1987), annex tables.

14. No data.

15. *Censo Nacional de Población y Viviendas 1982,* p. 92.

16. *World Development Report 1987,* World Bank (New York: Oxford University Press, 1987).

17. *Population Policy Briefs: The Current Situation in Developing Countries, 1985,* United Nations.

18. *State of the World Children 1987.*

19. Ibid.

20. Ibid.

21. Ibid.

22. *Censo Nacional de Población y Viviendas 1982,* p. 105. Ten percent census sample.

23. Secretaría Técnica de Planificación, Asunción, Paraguay.

24. *State of the World Children 1987.*

25. Secretaría Técnica de Planificación, Asunción, Paraguay.

26. *Censo Nacional de Población y Viviendas 1982,* p. 102. Ten percent census sample. No information includes losses due to floods.

27. Ibid., p. 100. Ten percent census sample. No information includes losses due to floods.

28. *Statistical Yearbook 1986,* UNESCO.

29. Ibid.

30. *State of the World Children.*

31. *Censo Nacional de Población*

y *Viviendas 1982*, p. 37. Ten percent census sample.

32. *Yearbook of Labour Statistics 1986*, International Labour Office, Geneva, Chapter 1, Table 1, p. 13.

33. *Atlaseco de Poche, Atlas Economique Mondial* (Paris: Les éditions S.G.P., 1985). Data taken from World Bank sources.

34. *World Development Report 1987*, World Bank (New York: Oxford University Press, 1987).

35. *Statistics on Children in UNICEF Assisted Countries*, UNICEF, April 1987.

36. *Statistical Yearbook 1986*, UNESCO.

37. Ibid.

PERU

1. *The New International Atlas* (Chicago: Rand McNally, 1986), Tables I–10 to I–13. Estimates for January 1, 1985, based on official data, United Nations estimates, and other available information.

2. Ibid.

3. *1987 World Population Data Sheet*, Population Reference Bureau (Washington, D.C.). Source: FAO and U.S. Department of State.

3a. Ibid.

4. *United Nations World Population Chart 1985*, Population Division, United Nations.

5. Ibid.

6. *1987 World Population Data Sheet*.

7. *The Prospects of World Urbanization*, Population Division, United Nations (rev. ed., 1984–85).

8. Ibid.

9. *Censos 1981*, Volumen A, Tomo I, pp. 1–2.

10. George Thomas Kurian, *Encyclopedia of the Third World* (3rd ed.; New York: Facts on File, Inc., 1987), Vol. II, p. 1580.

11. *Censos 1981*, Volumen A, Tomo I, p. 164.

12. *Censos 1981*, Volumen A, Tomo II. Características Económicas (2da Parte), Características de los Miembros del Hogar, Censo de Vivienda, p. 1153.

13. *State of the World Children 1987*, UNICEF (New York: Oxford University Press, 1987), annex tables.

14. No data.

15. *Demographic Yearbook 1983*, United Nations. Data tabulated by date of registration rather than occurrence. Data from civil registers which are incomplete or of unknown completeness. Excluding Indian jungle population, estimated at 100,830 in 1961.

16. *World Development Report 1987*, World Bank (New York: Oxford University Press, 1987).

17. *Population Policy Briefs: The Current Situation in Developing Countries, 1985*, United Nations.

18. *State of the World Children 1987*.

19. Ibid.

20. Ibid.

21. Ibid.

22. *Censos 1981*, Volumen A, Tomo II, p. 1171.

23. Ibid., p. 1218.

24. *State of the World Children 1987*.

25. *Censos 1981*, Volumen A, Tomo II, p. 1227.

26. *Compendium of Human Settlements Statistics 1983*, United Nations.

27. *Censos 1981*.

28. *Statistical Yearbook 1986*, UNESCO.

29. Ibid.

30. *State of the World Children 1987*.

31. *Statistical Yearbook 1986*, UNESCO.

32. *Yearbook of Labour Statistics 1986*, International Labour Office, Geneva, Chapter 1, Table 1, p. 13.

33. *Atlaseco de Poche, Atlas Economique Mondial* (Paris: Les éditions S.G.P., 1985). Data taken from World Bank sources.

34. *World Development Report 1987*.

35. *Statistics on Children in UNICEF Assisted Countries*, UNICEF, April 1987.

36. *International Financial Statistics*, September 1987, International Monetary Fund.

37. *Statistical Yearbook 1986*, UNESCO.

SURINAME

1. *The New International Atlas* (Chicago: Rand McNally, 1986), Tables I–10 to I–13. Estimates for January 1, 1985, based on official data, United Nations estimates, and other available information.

2. Ibid.

3. *1987 World Population Data Sheet*, Population Reference Bureau (Washington, D.C.). Source: FAO and U.S. Department of State.

3a. Ibid.

4. *United Nations World Population Chart 1985*, Population Division, United Nations. Provisional.

5. Ibid.

6. *1987 World Population Data Sheet*.

7. *The Prospects of World Urbanization*, Population Division, United Nations (rev. ed., 1984–85).

8. Ibid.

9. *Demographic Indicators: Estimates and Projections 1980*, United Nations. Estimate.

10. George Thomas Kurian, *Encyclopedia of the Third World* (3rd ed.; New York: Facts on File, Inc., 1987), Vol. II, p. 1854.

11. National Economic Profile, National Planning Office of Suriname.

12. No data.

13. *United Nations World Population Chart 1985*.

14. No data.

15. No data.

16. No data.

17. *Population Policy Briefs: The Current Situation in Developing Countries, 1985*, United Nations.

18. *State of the World Children 1987*.

19. Ibid.

20. *Statistics on Children in UNICEF Assisted Countries*, UNICEF, April 1987.

21. *State of the World Children 1987*.

22. *Encyclopedia of the Third World*, p. 1668.

23. National Planning Office of Suriname.

24. No data.

25. National Planning Office of Suriname.

26. Ibid.

27. Ibid.

28. *Statistical Yearbook 1986*, UNESCO.

29. Ibid.

30. No data.

31. No data.

32. No data.

33. No data.

34. *World Development Report 1987*, World Bank (New York: Oxford University Press, 1987).

35. No data.

36. *Statistical Yearbook 1986*, UNESCO.

37. Ibid.

URUGUAY

1. *The New International Atlas* (Chicago: Rand McNally, 1986), Tables I–10 to I–13. Estimates for January 1, 1985, based on official data, United Nations estimates, and other available information.

2. Ibid.

3. *1987 World Population Data Sheet*, Population Reference Bureau (Washington, D.C.). Source: FAO and U.S. Department of State.

3a. Ibid.

4. *United Nations World Population Chart 1985*, Population Division, United Nations.

5. Ibid.

6. *1987 World Population Data Sheet*.

7. *The Prospects of World Urbanization*, Population Division, United Nations (rev. ed., 1984–85).

8. Ibid.

9. *Demographic Yearbook 1983*, United Nations. Estimates which are less reliable.

10. George Thomas Kurian, *Encyclopedia of the Third World* (3rd ed.; New York: Facts on File, Inc., 1987), Vol. III, p. 2069.

11. No data.

12. General Office of Statistics (Census 1975).

13. *State of the World Children 1987*, UNICEF (New York: Oxford University Press, 1987), annex tables.

14. No data.

15. *Demographic Yearbook 1983*, United Nations. Data tabulated by date of registration rather than occurrence.

16. No data.

17. *Population Policy Briefs: The Current Situation in Developing Countries, 1985*, United Nations.

18. *State of the World Children 1987*.

19. Ibid.

20. Ibid.

21. Ibid.

22. *Compendium of Human Settlements Statistics 1983*, United Nations.

23. 1975 Population Census, Uruguay.

24. *State of the World Children 1987*.

25. No data.

26. 1975 Population Census.

27. Ibid.

28. *Statistical Yearbook 1986*, UNESCO.

29. Ibid.

30. *State of the World Children 1987*.

31. *Statistical Yearbook 1986*, UNESCO.

32. *Yearbook of Labour Statistics 1986*, International Labour Office, Geneva, Chapter 1, Table 1, p. 13.

33. *Atlaseco de Poche, Atlas Economique Mondial* (Paris: Les éditions S.G.P., 1985). Data taken from World Bank sources.

34. *World Development Report 1987*, World Bank (New York: Oxford University Press, 1987).

35. *Statistics on Children in UNICEF Assisted Countries*, UNICEF, April 1987.

36. *Statistical Yearbook 1986*, UNESCO.

37. Ibid.

VENEZUELA

1. *The New International Atlas* (Chicago: Rand McNally, 1986), Tables I–10 to I–13. Estimates for January 1, 1985, based on official data, United Nations estimates, and other available information.

2. Ibid.

3. *1987 World Population Data Sheet*, Population Reference Bureau (Washington, D.C.). Source: FAO and U.S. Department of State.

3a. Ibid.

4. *United Nations World Population Chart 1985*, Population Division, United Nations.

5. Ibid.

6. *1987 World Population Data Sheet*.

7. *The Prospects of World Urbanization*, Population Division, United Nations (rev. ed., 1984–85).

8. Ibid.

9. *Demographic Yearbook 1983*, United Nations. Excluding Indian jungle population.

10. George Thomas Kurian, *Encyclopedia of the Third World* (3rd ed.; New York: Facts on File, Inc., 1987), Vol. III, p. 2096.

11. *Anuario Estadístico 1982*.

12. *Anuario Estadístico 1982*, Tomo VII: *Situación Social*. República de Venezuela. Presidencia de la República. Oficina Central de Estadística e Información. Caracas, Venezuela. June 1984. P. 9.

13. *State of the World Children 1987*, UNICEF (New York: Oxford University Press, 1987), annex tables.

14. No data.

15. *Demographic Yearbook 1983*, United Nations. Data from civil registers which are incomplete or of unknown completeness. Excluding Indian jungle population, estimated at 31,800 in 1961.

16. *World Development Report 1987*, World Bank (New York: Oxford University Press, 1987).

17. *Population Policy Briefs: The Current Situation in Developing Countries, 1985*, United Nations.

18. *State of the World Children 1987*.

19. Ibid.

20. *State of the World Children 1987*.

21. Ibid.

22. *Encyclopedia of the Third World*, p. 2095.

23. *IX Censo Nacional de*

Población y Vivienda, 20 Oct. 1981. Oficina Central de Estadística e Información. Venezuela.

24. *State of the World Children 1987*.

25. *IX Censo Nacional de Población y Vivienda*, 1981.

26. Ibid.

27. Ibid.

28. *Statistical Yearbook 1986*, UNESCO.

29. Ibid.

30. *State of the World Children 1987*.

31. *Statistical Yearbook 1986*, UNESCO.

32. *Yearbook of Labour Statistics 1986*, International Labour Office, Geneva, Chapter 1, Table 1, p. 13.

33. *Atlaseco de Poche, Atlas Economique Mondial* (Paris: Les éditions S.G.P., 1985). Data taken from World Bank sources.

34. *World Development Report 1987*.

35. No data.

36. *Statistical Yearbook 1986*, UNESCO.

37. Ibid.

Central America

BELIZE

1. *The New International Atlas* (Chicago: Rand McNally, 1986), Tables I–10 to I–13. Estimates for January 1, 1985, based on official data, United Nations estimates, and other available information.

2. Ibid.

3. *1987 World Population Data Sheet*, Population Reference Bureau (Washington, D.C.). Source: FAO and U.S. Department of State.

3a. Ibid.

4. *United Nations World Population Chart 1985*, Population Division, United Nations.

5. United States Bureau of the Census, *Statistical Abstract of the United States, 1985* (105th ed.; Washington, D.C., 1984).

6. *1987 World Population Data Sheet*.

7. *Statistics on Children in UNICEF Assisted Countries*, UNICEF, April 1987.

8. No data.

9. *1980–1981 Population Census*, Vol. I, pp. 2–3.

10. Ibid., Summary Tables, Bulletin 1.

11. Ibid., Vol. I, p. 112. Where the respondent is more than 45 years old, the union status reported is that which existed at age 45.

12. *Women in Belize* (Belize City: Women's Bureau, 1984).

13. Ibid.

14. Ibid.

15. Ibid.

16. No data.

17. *Population Policy Briefs: The Current Situation in Developing Countries, 1985*, United Nations.

18. *Statistics on Children*, UNICEF.

19. *State of the World Children 1987*, UNICEF (New York: Oxford University Press, 1987), annex tables.

20. *Statistics on Children*, UNICEF.

21. Ministry of Health, Belmopan, Belize.

22. *Belize Shelter Factor Assessment*, Co-operative Housing Foundation, 1982.

23. Ibid.

24. *Statistics on Children*, UNICEF.

25. *1980–1981 Population Census*, Vol. I, p. 142.

26. *Belize Shelter Factor Assessment*.

27. Ibid.

28. *Statistical Yearbook 1986*, UNESCO.

29. *Statistics on Children*, UNICEF. Data on institutions providing secondary and/or sixth-form education, 1985.

30. No data.

31. *Statistical Yearbook 1986*, UNESCO.

32. *Yearbook of Labour Statistics 1986*, International Labour Office, Geneva, Chapter 1, Table 1, p. 13.

33. *Atlaseco de Poche, Atlas Economique Mondial* (Paris: Les éditions S.G.P., 1985). Data taken from World Bank sources.

34. *World Development Report 1987*, World Bank (New York: Oxford University Press, 1987).

35. No data.

36. *Statistical Yearbook 1986*, UNESCO.

37. Ibid. Television was introduced in 1985.

COSTA RICA

1. *The New International Atlas* (Chicago: Rand McNally, 1986), Tables I–10 to I–13. Estimates for January 1, 1985, based on official data, United Nations estimates, and other available information.

2. Ibid.

3. *1987 World Population Data Sheet*, Population Reference Bureau (Washington, D.C.). Source: FAO and U.S. Department of State.

3a. Ibid.

4. *United Nations World Population Chart 1985*, Population Division, United Nations.

5. Ibid.

6. *1987 World Population Data Sheet*.

7. *The Prospects of World Urbanization*, Population Division, United Nations (rev. ed., 1984–85).

8. Ibid.

9. *Demographic Yearbook 1983*, United Nations. De jure population.

10. George Thomas Kurian, *Encyclopedia of the Third World* (3rd ed.; New York: Facts on File, Inc., 1987), Vol. I, p. 495.

11. *1984 Population Census* (computer printout).

12. No data.

13. *State of the World Children 1987*, UNICEF (New York: Oxford University Press, 1987), annex tables.

14. No data.

15. *Demographic Yearbook 1983*, United Nations. Data tabulated by date of registration rather than occurrence.

16. *World Development Report 1987*, World Bank (New York: Oxford University Press, 1987).

17. *Population Policy Briefs: The Current Situation in Developing Countries, 1985*, United Nations.

18. *State of the World Children 1987*.

19. Ibid.

20. Ibid.

21. Ibid.

22. *Censo de Vivienda 1984.* República de Costa Rica, Ministerio de Economía, Industria y Comercio, Direccíon General de Estadística y Censos, San José, Costa Rica, 1987.

23. Ibid.

24. *State of the World Children 1987.*

25. *Censo de Vivienda 1984.*

26. Ibid.

27. Ibid.

28. *Statistical Yearbook 1986,* UNESCO.

29. Ibid.

30. *State of the World Children 1987.*

31. *Statistical Yearbook 1986,* UNESCO.

32. *Yearbook of Labour Statistics 1986,* International Labour Office, Geneva, Chapter 1, Table 1, p. 13.

33. *Atlaseco de Poche, Atlas Economique Mondial* (Paris: Les éditions S.G.P., 1985). Data taken from World Bank sources.

34. *World Development Report 1987,* World Bank (New York: Oxford University Press, 1987).

35. No data.

36. *Statistical Yearbook 1986,* UNESCO.

37. Ibid.

EL SALVADOR

1. *The New International Atlas,* (Chicago: Rand McNally, 1986), Tables I–10 to I–13. Estimates for January 1, 1985, based on official data, United Nations estimates, and other available information.

2. Ibid.

3. *1987 World Population Data Sheet,* Population Reference Bureau (Washington, D.C.). Source: FAO and U.S. Department of State.

3a. Ibid.

4. *United Nations World Population Chart 1985,* Population Division, United Nations.

5. Ibid.

6. *1987 World Population Data Sheet.*

7. *The Prospects of World Urbanization* (Population Division, United Nations (rev. ed., 1984–85).

8. Ibid.

9. *Demographic Indicators: Estimates and Projections 1980,* United Nations.

10. George Thomas Kurian, *Encyclopedia of the Third World* (3rd ed.; New York: Facts on File, Inc., 1987), Vol. I, p. 631.

11. MIPLAN (Ministry of Planning), San Salvador. Based on a survey of couples.

12. *Indicadores Económicos y Sociales Enero–Junio 1980.* Ministerio de Planificación y Coordinación del Desarrollo Económico y Social. D.P. No. 6. San Salvador, El Salvador. p. 31.

13. *State of the World Children 1987,* UNICEF (New York: Oxford University Press, 1987), annex tables.

14. *Indicadores Económicos y Sociales Enero–Junio 1980.* Preliminary figures. Excluding children of mothers living abroad.

15. *Demographic Yearbook 1983,* United Nations.

16. *World Development Report 1987,* World Bank (New York: Oxford University Press, 1987).

17. *Population Policy Briefs: The Current Situation in Developing Countries, 1985,* United Nations.

18. *State of the World Children 1987.*

19. Ibid.

20. Ibid.

21. Ibid.

22. *Compendium of Human Settlements Statistics 1983,* United Nations. Based on a sample survey.

23. MIPLAN.

24. *Statistics on Children in UNICEF Assisted Countries,* UNICEF, April 1987.

25. MIPLAN.

26. *Compendium 1983,* United Nations. Based on a sample survey.

27. MIPLAN.

28. *Statistical Yearbook 1986,* UNESCO.

29. Ibid.

30. *State of the World Children 1987.*

31. *Statistical Yearbook 1986,* UNESCO.

32. No data.

33. *Atlaseco de Poche, Atlas Economique Mondial* (Paris: Les éditions S.G.P., 1985). Data taken from World Bank sources.

34. *World Development Report 1987,* World Bank (New York: Oxford University Press, 1987).

35. No data.

36. *Statistical Yearbook 1986,* UNESCO.

37. Ibid.

GUATEMALA

1. *The New International Atlas* (Chicago: Rand McNally, 1986), Tables I–10 to I–13. Estimates for January 1, 1985, based on official data, United Nations estimates, and other available information.

2. Ibid.

3. *1987 World Population Data Sheet,* Population Reference Bureau (Washington, D.C.). Source: FAO and U.S. Department of State.

3a. Ibid.

4. *United Nations World Population Chart 1985,* Population Division, United Nations.

5. Ibid.

6. *1987 World Population Data Sheet.*

7. *The Prospects of World Urbanization,* Population Division, United Nations (rev. ed., 1984–85).

8. Ibid.

9. *Demographic Indicators: Estimates and Projections 1980,* United Nations.

10. George Thomas Kurian, *Encyclopedia of the Third World* (3rd ed.; New York: Facts on File, Inc., 1987), Vol. I, p. 763.

11. *Censos de 1981,* Tomo 1, p. 75.

12. Ibid., p. 424.

13. *State of the World Children 1987,* UNICEF (New York: Oxford University Press, 1987), annex tables.

14. *Censos de 1981,* Tomo 1, p. 255. Excludes live births to mothers of unknown marital status.

15. *Demographic Yearbook 1983,* United Nations.

16. *World Development Report 1987,* World Bank (New York: Oxford University Press, 1987).

17. *Population Policy Briefs: The Current Situation in Developing Countries, 1985,* United Nations.

18. *State of the World Children 1987.*

19. Ibid.

20. Ibid.

21. Ibid.

22. *Encyclopedia of the Third World*, p. 763.

23. Ministry of Planning, 1980.

24. *State of the World Children 1987.*

25. Ministry of Planning, 1980.

26. Ibid.

27. Ibid.

28. *Statistical Yearbook 1986,* UNESCO.

29. Ibid.

30. *State of the World Children 1987.*

31. *Statistical Yearbook 1986,* UNESCO.

32. *Yearbook of Labour Statistics 1986,* International Labour Office, Geneva, Chapter 1, Table 1, p. 13.

33. *Atlaseco de Poche, Atlas Economique Mondial* (Paris: Les éditions S.G.P., 1985). Data taken from World Bank sources.

34. *World Development Report 1987.*

35. *State of the World Children 1987.*

36. *Statistical Yearbook 1986,* UNESCO.

37. Ibid.

HONDURAS

1. *The New International Atlas* (Chicago: Rand McNally, 1986), Tables I–10 to I–13. Estimates for January 1, 1985, based on official data, United Nations estimates, and other available information.

2. Ibid.

3. *1987 World Population Data Sheet,* Population Reference Bureau (Washington, D.C.). Source: FAO and U.S. Department of State.

3a. Ibid.

4. *United Nations World Population Chart 1985,* Population Division, United Nations.

5. Ibid.

6. *1987 World Population Data Sheet.*

7. *The Prospects of World Urbanization,* Population Division, United Nations (rev. ed., 1984–85).

8. Ibid.

9. *Demographic Yearbook 1983,* United Nations.

10. George Thomas Kurian, Encyclopedia of the Third World (3rd ed.; New York: Facts on File, Inc., 1987), Vol. II, p. 849.

11. CONSUPLANE (Ministry of Planning, Coordination, and Budget), Tegucigalpa, Honduras.

12. Ibid.

13. *State of the World Children 1987,* UNICEF (New York: Oxford University Press, 1987), annex tables.

14. No data.

15. *Demographic Yearbook 1983,* United Nations. Data tabulated by date of registration rather than occurrence. Data from civil registers which are incomplete or of unknown completeness.

16. *World Development Report 1987,* World Bank (New York: Oxford University Press, 1987).

17. *Population Policy Briefs: The Current Situation in Developing Countries, 1985,* United Nations.

18. *State of the World Children 1987.*

19. Ibid.

20. Ibid.

21. Ibid.

22. *Encyclopedia of the Third World,* p. 848.

23. CONSUPLANE.

24. *State of the World Children 1987.*

25. CONSUPLANE.

26. Ibid.

27. Ibid.

28. *Statistical Yearbook 1986,* UNESCO.

29. Ibid.

30. *State of the World Children 1987.*

31. *Statistical Yearbook 1986,* UNESCO.

32. *Yearbook of Labour Statistics 1986,* International Labour Office, Geneva, Chapter 1, Table 1, p. 13.

33. *Atlaseco de Poche, Atlas Economique Mondial* (Paris: Les éditions S.G.P., 1985). Data taken from World Bank sources.

34. *World Development Report 1987.*

35. *State of the World Children 1987.*

36. *Statistical Yearbook 1986,* UNESCO.

37. Ibid.

MEXICO

1. *The New International Atlas* (Chicago: Rand McNally, 1986), Tables I–10 to I–13. Estimates for January 1, 1985, based on official data, United Nations estimates, and other available information.

2. Ibid.

3. *1987 World Population Data Sheet,* Population Reference Bureau (Washington, D.C.). Source: FAO and U.S. Department of State.

3a. Ibid.

4. *United Natons World Population Chart 1985,* Population Division, United Nations.

5. Ibid.

6. *1987 World Population Data Sheet.*

7. *The Prospects of World Urbanization,* Population Division, United Nations (rev. ed., 1984–85).

8. Ibid.

9. *Demographic Yearbook 1983,* United Nations. Estimates which are less reliable. De jure population.

10. George Thomas Kurian, *Encyclopedia of the Third World* (3rd ed.; New York: Facts on File, Inc., 1987), Vol. II, p. 1342.

11. *Demographic Yearbook 1982,* United Nations. Estimates which are less reliable. De jure population.

12. No data.

13. *State of the World Children 1987,* UNICEF (New York: Oxford University Press, 1987), annex tables.

14. No data.

15. *Demographic Yearbook 1983,* United Nations. Data from civil registers which are incomplete or of unknown completeness.

16. *World Development Report 1987,* World Bank (New York: Oxford University Press, 1987).

17. *Population Policy Briefs: The Current Situation in Developing Countries, 1985,* United Nations.

18. *State of the World Children 1987.*

19. Ibid.

20. Ibid.

21. Ibid.

22. *Compendium of Human Settlements Statistics 1983*, United Nations Provisional.

23. Ibid.

24. *State of the World Children 1987.*

25. *Compendium of Human Settlements Statistics 1983.*

26. Ibid.

27. Ibid.

28. *Statistical Yearbook 1986*, UNESCO.

29. Ibid.

30. *State of the World Children 1987.*

31. *Statistical Yearbook 1986*, UNESCO.

32. *Yearbook of Labour Statistics 1986*, International Labour Office, Geneva, Chapter 1, Table 1, p. 13.

33. *Atlaseco de Poche, Atlas Economique Mondial* (Paris: Les éditions S.G.P., 1985). Data taken from World Bank sources.

34. *World Development Report 1987.*

35. No data.

36. *Statistical Yearbook 1986*, UNESCO.

37. Ibid.

NICARAGUA

1. *The New International Atlas* (Chicago: Rand McNally, 1986), Tables I–10 to I–13. Estimates for January 1, 1985, based on official data, United Nations estimates, and other available information.

2. Ibid.

3. *1987 World Population Data Sheet*, Population Reference Bureau (Washington, D.C.). Source: FAO and U.S. Department of State.

3a. Ibid.

4. *United Nations World Population Chart 1985*, Population Division, United Nations.

5. Ibid.

6. *1987 World Population Data Sheet.*

7. *The Prospects of World Urbanization*, Population Division, United Nations (rev. ed., 1984–85).

8. Ibid.

9. *Demographic Yearbook 1983*, United Nations.

10. George Thomas Kurian, *Encyclopedia of the Third World* (3rd ed.; New York: Facts on File, Inc., 1987), Vol. II, p. 1435.

11. *1971 Censos Nacionales*, Vol. I, p. 106.

12. Instituto Nicaragüense de Seguridad Sociale y Bienestar.

13. *State of the World Children 1987*, UNICEF (New York: Oxford University Press, 1987), annex tables.

14. No data.

15. No data.

16. *World Development Report 1987*, World Bank (New York: Oxford University Press, 1987).

17. *Population Policy Briefs: The Current Situation in Developing Countries, 1985*, United Nations.

18. *State of the World Children 1987.*

19. Ibid.

20. Ibid.

21. Ibid.

22. *Encyclopedia of the Third World*, p. 1435.

23. *1971 Censos Nacionales.*

24. *State of the World Children 1987.*

25. *1971 Censos Nacionales.*

26. COPVIDU (Conferencia Centro America Permanente de Vivienda y Desarrollo Urbano).

27. Ibid.

28. *State of the World Children 1987.*

29. *Statistical Yearbook 1986*, UNESCO.

30. *State of the World Children 1987.*

31. *Statistical Yearbook 1986*, UNESCO.

32. *Yearbook of Labour Statistics 1986*, International Labour Office, Geneva, Chapter 1, Table 1, p. 13.

33. *Atlaseco de Poche, Atlas Economique Mondial* (Paris: Les éditions S.G.P., 1985). Data taken from World Bank sources.

34. *World Development Report 1987.*

35. *State of the World Children 1987.*

36. *Statistical Yearbook 1986*, UNESCO.

37. Ibid.

PANAMA

1. *The New International Atlas* (Chicago: Rand McNally, 1986), Tables I–10 to I–13. Estimates for January 1, 1985, based on official data, United Nations estimates, and other available information.

2. Ibid.

3. *1987 World Population Data Sheet*, Population Reference Bureau (Washington, D.C.). Source: FAO and U.S. Department of State.

3a. Ibid.

4. *United Nations World Population Chart 1985*, Population Division, United Nations.

5. Ibid.

6. *1987 World Population Data Sheet.*

7. *The Prospects of World Urbanization*, Population Division, United Nations (rev. ed., 1984–85).

8. Ibid.

9. *Censos de 1980*, Vol. XI, Panama, p. 19.

10. George Thomas Kurian, *Encyclopedia of the Third World* (3rd ed.; New York: Facts on File, Inc., 1987), Vol. II, p. 1531.

11. *Censos de 1980*, Vol. XI, p. 21.

12. *Población y Familia en Panamá: Primer Encuentro Anual de Trabajo Pastoral Familiar*, Ministerio de Planificación y Política Económica (January 1984).

13. *State of the World Children 1987*, UNICEF (New York: Oxford University Press, 1987), annex tables.

14. *Población y Familia en Panamá.*

15. *Demographic Yearbook 1983*, United Nations.

16. *World Development Report 1987*, World Bank (New York: Oxford University Press, 1987).

17. *Population Policy Briefs: The Current Situation in Developing Countries, 1985*, United Nations.

18. *State of the World Children 1987.*

19. Ibid.

20. Ibid.

21. Ibid.

22. *Encyclopedia of the Third World*, p. 1531.

23. *Compendium of Human Settlements Statistics 1983*, United Nations. Based on a sample tabulation of census returns.

24. *State of the World Children 1987*.

25. *Compendium of Human Settlements Statistics 1983*. Based on a sample tabulation of census returns.

26. Ibid.

27. *Censos de 1980*.

28. *State of the World Children 1987*.

29. *Statistical Yearbook 1986*, UNESCO.

30. *State of the World Children 1987*.

31. *Censos de 1980*, Vol. XI, pp. 36–37.

32. *Yearbook of Labour Statistics 1986*, International Labour Office, Geneva, Chapter 1, Table 1, p. 13.

33. *Atlaseco de Poche, Atlas Economique Mondial* (Paris: Les éditions S.G.P., 1985). Data taken from World Bank sources.

34. *World Development Report 1987*.

35. *State of the World Children 1987*.

36. *Statistical Yearbook 1986*, UNESCO.

37. *Statistical Yearbook 1984*, UNESCO; *Statistical Yearbook 1986*. 1977 data on radio and television transmitters exclude the former Canal Zone.

The Caribbean

ANTIGUA and BARBUDA

1. *The New International Atlas* (Chicago: Rand McNally, 1986), Tables I–10 to I–13. Estimates for January 1, 1985, based on official data, United Nations estimates, and other available information.

2. Ibid.

3. *1987 World Population Data Sheet*, Population Reference Bureau (Washington, D.C.). Source: FAO and U.S. Department of State.

3a. Ibid.

4. *United Nations World Population Chart 1985*, Population Division, United Nations.

5. Ibid.

6. *1987 World Population Data Sheet*.

7. Estimate based on the capital's population.

8. No data.

9. 1970 Population Census.

10. George Thomas Kurian, *Encyclopedia of the Third World* (3rd ed.; New York: Facts on File, Inc., 1987), Vol. I, pp. 81–82.

11. *A Study of Contraceptive Prevalence in the Eastern Caribbean*, Institute of Social and Economic Research, UWI St. Augustine, Trinidad, n.d.

12. No data.

13. *1985 World Population Data Sheet*, Population Reference Bureau (Washington, D.C.).

14. *A Study of Contraceptive Prevalence in the Eastern Caribbean*.

15. Ibid.

16. No data.

17. *Population Policy Briefs: The Current Situation in Developing Countries, 1985*, United Nations.

18. *World Development Report 1987*, World Bank (New York: Oxford University Press, 1987).

19. *State of the World Children 1987*, UNICEF (New York: Oxford University Press, 1987), annex tables.

20. *United Nations World Population Chart 1985*.

21. *State of the World Children 1987*.

22. *Censo Nacional de Población y Vivienda 1980*, Serie C Vivienda, p. 1.

23. Ibid.

24. *State of the World Children 1987*.

25. Statistics Division, Ministry of Finance.

26. Ibid.

27. Ibid.

28. *Statistics on Children in UNICEF Assisted Countries*, UNICEF, April 1987.

29. Ibid.

30. No data.

31. No data.

32. *Yearbook of Labour Statistics 1978*, International Labour Office, Geneva.

33. Ministry of Labour.

34. *World Development Report 1987*, World Bank (New York: Oxford University Press, 1987).

35. No data.

36. *Statistical Yearbook 1986*, UNESCO.

37. *Statistical Yearbook 1984*, UNESCO; *Statistical Yearbook 1986*.

BAHAMAS

1. *The New International Atlas* (Chicago: Rand McNally, 1986), Tables I–10 to I–13. Estimates for January 1, 1985, based on official data, United Nations estimates, and other available information.

2. Ibid.

3. *1987 World Population Data Sheet*, Population Reference Bureau (Washington, D.C.). Source: FAO and U.S. Department of State.

3a. Ibid.

4. *State of the World Children 1987*, UNICEF (New York, Oxford University Press, 1987), annex tables.

5. United States Bureau of the Census, *Statistical Abstract of the United States, 1985* (105th ed.; Washington, D.C., 1984).

6. *1987 World Population Data Sheet*.

7. *The Prospects of World Urbanization*, Population Division, United Nations (rev. ed., 1984–85).

8. No data.

9. *Demographic Yearbook 1983*, United Nations.

10. George Thomas Kurian, *Encyclopedia of the Third World* (3rd ed.; New York: Facts on File, Inc., 1987), Vol. I, p. 116.

11. *Report of the 1980 Census of Population*, Department of Statistics, Ministry of Finance, Nassau, Bahamas.

12. *Report of the 1980 Census of Housing*, Department of Statistics, Ministry of Finance, Nassau, Bahamas.

13. *United Nations World Population Chart 1985*, Population Division, United Nations.

14. *Statistical Abstract 1983,* Department of Statistics, Ministry of Finance, Nassau, Bahamas, p. 154.

15. *Demographic Yearbook 1983.*

16. No data.

17. *Population Policy Briefs: The Current Situation in Developing Countries, 1985,* United Nations.

18. *United Nations World Population Chart 1987*

19. Ibid.

20. *Demographic Yearbook 1983.*

21. *State of the World Children 1987.*

22. No data.

23. *Report of the 1980 Census of Housing,* p. 154.

24. No data.

25. *Report of the 1980 Census of Housing.*

26. Ibid.

27. Ibid.

28. *Encyclopedia of the Third World,* Vol. I, p. 121.

29. Data given by Bureau of Statistics.

30. No data.

31. No data.

32. *Yearbook of Labour Statistics 1986,* International Labour Office, Geneva, Chapter 1, Table 1, p. 13.

33. *Atlaseco de Poche, Atlas Economique Mondial* (Paris: Les éditions S.G.P., 1985). Data taken from World Bank sources.

34. *World Development Report 1987,* World Bank (New York: Oxford University Press, 1987).

35. *Report of the 1980 Census of Housing.*

36. *Statistical Yearbook 1986,* UNESCO.

37. Ibid.

BARBADOS

1. *The New International Atlas* (Chicago: Rand McNally, 1986), Tables I–10 to I–13. Estimates for January 1, 1985, based on official data, United Nations estimates, and other available information.

2. Ibid.

3. *1987 World Population Data Sheet,* Population Reference Bureau (Washington, D.C.). Source: FAO and U.S. Department of State.

3a. Ibid.

4. *United Nations World Population Chart 1985,* Population Division, United Nations.

5. Ibid.

6. *1987 World Population Data Sheet.*

7. *The Prospects of World Urbanization,* Population Division, United Nations (rev. ed., 1984–85).

8. Ibid.

9. *1980–1981 Population Census of the Commonwealth Caribbean,* Barbados.

10. George Thomas Kurian, *Encyclopedia of the Third World* (3rd ed.; New York: Facts on File, Inc., 1987), Vol. I, p. 160.

11. Ibid., Vol. III, p. 35.

12. Ibid.

13. *Demographic Indicators by Countries as Assessed in 1984,* United Nations Population Division computer printout, November 1985.

14. *Report of the National Commission on the Status of Women in Barbados.*

15. *Demographic Yearbook 1983,* United Nations. Data tabulated by date of registration rather than occurrence.

16. *World Development Report 1987,* World Bank (New York: Oxford University Press, 1987). Of currently married women between the ages of 5 and 49 (1980–81).

17. *Population Policy Briefs: The Current Situation in Developing Countries, 1985,* United Nations.

18. *State of the World Children 1987,* UNICEF (New York: Oxford University Press, 1987), annex tables.

19. Ibid.

20. *Statistics on Children in UNICEF Assisted Countries,* UNICEF, April 1987.

21. *State of the World Children 1987.*

22. *1980–81 Population Census.*

23. Ibid.

24. *State of the World Children 1987.*

25. *1980–81 Population Census.*

26. Ibid.

27. Ibid.

28. *Statistical Yearbook 1986,* UNESCO.

29. Ibid.

30. No data.

31. *Statistical Yearbook 1986,* UNESCO.

32. *Yearbook of Labour Statistics 1986,* International Labour Office, Geneva, Chapter 1, Table 1, p. 13.

33. *Atlaseco de Poche, Atlas Economique Mondial* (Paris: Les éditions S.G.P., 1985). Data taken from World Bank sources.

34. *World Development Report 1987.*

35. *Statistics on Children,* UNICEF.

36. *Statistical Yearbook 1986,* UNESCO.

37. Ibid.

CUBA

1. *The New International Atlas* (Chicago: Rand McNally, 1986), Tables I–10 to I–13. Estimates for January 1, 1985, based on official data, United Nations estimates, and other available information.

2. Ibid.

3. *1987 World Population Data Sheet,* Population Reference Bureau (Washington, D.C.). Source: FAO and U.S. Department of State.

3a. Ibid.

4. *United Nations World Population Chart 1985,* Population Division, United Nations.

5. *Demographic Indicators by Countries as Assessed in 1984,* computer printout, Population Division, United Nations, November 1985.

6. *1987 World Population Data Sheet.*

7. *The Prospects of World Urbanization,* Population Division, United Nations (rev. ed., 1984–85).

8. Ibid.

9. *Censo 1981,* Volumen 16, p. 7.

10. Ibid., p. 12

11. Ibid., p. 47.

12. Ibid., pp. 22–23.

13. *United Nations World Population Chart 1985.*

14. No data.

15. *Demographic Yearbook 1983,* United Nations. Data tabulated by date of registration rather than occurrence. Based on births

recorded in the National Register of Consumers.

16. *World Development Report 1987*, World Bank (New York: Oxford University Press, 1987). Abortion: Christopher Tietze, *Induced Abortion: A World Review 1983* (New York: The Population Council, 1983), p. 26. Live births six months later.

17. *Population Policy Briefs: The Current Situation in Developing Countries, 1985*, United Nations.

18. *State of the World Children 1987*, UNICEF (New York: Oxford University Press, 1987), annex tables.

19. Ibid.

20. Ibid.

21. *World Health Statistics*, World Health Organization, Geneva, 1986.

22. *Censo 1981*.

23. *Compendium of Human Settlements Statistics 1983*, United Nations.

24. No data.

25. *Censo 1981*, Volumen 16, p. 438.

26. Ibid., p. 442.

27. Ibid., p. 424.

28. *Statistical Yearbook 1986*, UNESCO. For population, pp. 15–49.

29. Ibid.

30. No data.

31. *Statistical Yearbook 1986*, UNESCO.

32. *Yearbook of Labour Statistics 1986*, International Labour Office, Geneva, Chapter 1, Table 1, p. 13.

33. *Atlaseco de Poche, Atlas Economique Mondial* (Paris: Les éditions S.G.P., 1985). Data taken from World Bank sources.

34. *Statistics on Children in UNICEF Assisted Countries*, UNICEF, April 1987.

35. No data.

36. *Statistical Yearbook 1986*, UNESCO. Non-commercial rate applied to tourism and remittances from outside the ruble area.

37. Ibid.

DOMINICA

1. *The New International Atlas* (Chicago: Rand McNally, 1986), Tables I–10 to I–13. Estimates for January 1, 1985, based on official data, United Nations estimates, and other available information.

2. Ibid.

3. *1987 World Population Data Sheet*, Population Reference Bureau (Washington, D.C.). Source: FAO and U.S. Department of State.

3a. Ibid.

4. *United Nations World Population Chart 1985*, Population Division, United Nations.

5. Ibid.

6. *1987 World Population Data Sheet*.

7. *1980–1981 Population Census of the Commonwealth Caribbean*.

8. No data

9. *1980–1981 Population Census*, Vol. I, pp. 2–3.

10. Ibid.

11. *Facts about Women in Dominica*, Women's Bureau, Ministry of Home Affairs.

12. Ibid.

13. *1987 World Population Data Sheet*.

14. No data.

15. *Facts about Women in Dominica*.

16. No data.

17. *Population Policy Briefs: The Current Situation in Developing Countries, 1985*, United Nations.

18. *1987 World Population Data Sheet*.

19. Ibid.

20. *Demographic Yearbook 1983*, United Nations.

21. *State of the World Children 1987*, UNICEF (New York: Oxford University Press, 1987), annex tables.

22. *1980–1981 Population Census*.

23. Ibid., Vol. I, p. 130.

24. No data.

25. *1980–1981 Population Census*, Vol. I, p. 124.

26. Ibid.

27. Ibid.

28. *Statistical Yearbook 1986*, UNESCO.

29. No data.

30. No data.

31. *Statistical Yearbook 1986*, UNESCO. Population 15 years and over not attending primary or secondary school full-time.

32. *Yearbook of Labour Statistics 1986*, International Labour Office, Geneva, Chapter 1, Table 1, p. 13.

33. *Atlaseco de Poche, Atlas Economique Mondial* (Paris: Les éditions S.G.P., 1985). Data taken from World Bank sources.

34. *World Development Report 1987*, World Bank (New York: Oxford University Press, 1987).

35. No data.

36. *Statistical Yearbook 1986*, UNESCO.

37. Ibid.

DOMINICAN REPUBLIC

1. *The New International Atlas* (Chicago: Rand McNally, 1986), Tables I–10 to I–13. Estimates for January 1, 1985, based on official data, United Nations estimates, and other available information.

2. Ibid.

3. *1987 World Population Data Sheet*, Population Reference Bureau (Washington, D.C.). Source: FAO and U.S. Department of State.

3a. Ibid.

4. *United Nations World Population Chart 1985*, Population Division, United Nations.

5. Ibid.

6. *1987 World Population Data Sheet*.

7. *The Prospects of World Urbanization*, Population Division, United Nations (rev. ed., 1984–85).

8. Ibid.

9. *Demographic Yearbook 1983*, United Nations. Estimates which are less reliable.

10. George Thomas Kurian, *Encyclopedia of the Third World* (3rd ed.; New York: Facts on File, Inc., 1987), Vol. I, p. 559.

11. *Plan Trienal 1985–1987*, Asociación Dominicana pro Bienestar de la Familia, Santo Domingo.

12. No data.

13. *State of the World Children 1987*, UNICEF (New York: Oxford University Press, 1987), annex tables.

14. No data.

15. *Demographic Yearbook 1983*,

United Nations. Data tabulated by date of registration rather than occurrence. Data from civil registers which are incomplete or of unknown completeness.

16. *World Development Report 1987*, World Bank (New York: Oxford University Press, 1987).

17. *Population Policy Briefs: The Current Situation in Developing Countries, 1985*, United Nations.

18. *State of the World Children 1987*.

19. Ibid.

20. Ibid.

21. Ibid.

22. *VI Censo Nacional de Población 1981*.

23. La Situación de la Vivienda in 1981 Según Datos de las Encuestas Nacionales Urbana y Rural.

24. *State of the World Children 1987*.

25. *Compendium of Human Settlements Statistics 1983*, United Nations.

26. *Compendium of Human Settlements Statistics 1983*.

27. La Situación de la Vivienda in 1981 Según Datos de las Encuestas Nacionales Urbana y Rural.

28. *Statistical Yearbook 1986*, UNESCO. For population 5 years and over.

29. Ibid.

30. *State of the World Children 1987*.

31. *Statistical Yearbook 1986*, UNESCO.

32. *Yearbook of Labour Statistics 1986*, International Labour Office, Geneva, Chapter 1, Table 1, p. 13.

33. *Atlaseco de Poche, Atlas Economique Mondial* (Paris: Les éditions S.G.P., 1985). Data taken from World Bank sources.

34. *World Development Report 1987*.

35. *State of the World Children 1987*.

36. *Statistical Yearbook 1986*, UNESCO.

37. Ibid.

GRENADA

1. *The New International Atlas* (Chicago: Rand McNally, 1986),

Tables I–10 to I–13. Estimates for January 1, 1985, based on official data, United Nations estimates, and other available information.

2. Ibid.

3. *1987 World Population Data Sheet*, Population Reference Bureau (Washington, D.C.). Source: FAO and U.S. Department of State.

3a. Ibid.

4. *United Nations World Population Chart 1985*, Population Division, United Nations.

5. Ibid.

6. *1987 World Population Data Sheet*.

7. Population Census. Only the Parish of St. George is considered urban.

8. No data.

9. *1980–1981 Population Census of the Commonwealth Caribbean*, Vol. I, pp. 2–3.

10. *1980–1981 Population Census*.

11. Ibid., Vol. I, p. 119. For population 14 years and over (not attending school). Where the respondent is over 45 years old, the union status reported is that which existed at age 45.

12. *1980–1981 Population Census*.

13. Ibid.

14. Ibid.

15. *Demographic Yearbook 1983*, United Nations. Data tabulated by date of registration rather than occurrence.

16. No data.

17. *Population Policy Briefs: The Current Situation in Developing Countries, 1985*, United Nations.

18. *1987 World Population Data Sheet*.

19. Ibid.

20. *Statistics on Children in UNICEF Assisted Countries*, UNICEF, April 1986.

21. *State of the World Children 1987*, UNICEF (New York: Oxford University Press, 1987), annex tables.

22. George Thomas Kurian, *Encyclopedia of the Third World* (3rd ed.; New York: Facts on File, Inc., 1987), Vol. I, p. 750.

23. *1980–1981 Population Census*.

24. No data.

25. *1980–1981 Population Census*.

26. Ibid., Vol. I, p. 151.

27. *1980–1981 Population Census*.

28. *Statistical Yearbook 1986*, UNESCO.

29. Ibid.

30. No data.

31. *Statistical Yearbook 1986*, UNESCO. Population 15 years and over not attending primary or secondary school full-time.

32. *Yearbook of Labour Statistics 1986*, International Labour Office, Geneva, Chapter 1, Table 1, p. 13.

33. *Atlaseco de Poche, Atlas Economique Mondial* (Paris: Les éditions S.G.P., 1985). Data taken from World Bank sources.

34. *World Development Report 1987*.

35. No data.

36. *Statistical Yearbook 1986*, UNESCO.

37. Ibid.

HAITI

1. *The New International Atlas* (Chicago: Rand McNally, 1986), Tables I-10 to I-13. Estimates for January 1, 1985, based on official data, United Nations estimates, and other available information.

2. Ibid.

3. *1987 World Population Data Sheet, Population Reference Bureau* (Washington, D.C.). Source: FAO and U.S. Department of State.

3a. Ibid.

4. *United Nations World Population Chart 1985*, Population Division, United Nations.

5. Ibid.

6. *1987 World Population Data Sheet*.

7. *The Prospects of World Urbanization*, Population Division, United Nations (rev. ed., 1984–85).

8. Ibid.

9. *Demographic Yearbook 1983*, United Nations. De jure population. Estimates which are less reliable.

10. George Thomas Kurian, *Encyclopedia of the Third World* (3rd ed.; New York: Facts on File, Inc., 1987), Vol. I, p. 833.

11. *Recensement Général 1982 Population et Logement*, Résultats Anticipés du Recensement Général, Echantillon 2.5% Extrapolé, Institut Haïtien de Statistique et d'Informatique, Port-au-Prince, Haiti, 1982, p. 14. Results from a 2.5% sample. Subject to revision.

12. *Aid Housing in Haiti*, Doc. 08040.

13. *State of the World Children 1987*, UNICEF (New York: Oxford University Press, 1987), annex tables.

14. No data.

15. No data.

16. *World Development Report 1987*, World Bank (New York: Oxford University Press, 1987).

17. *Population Policy Briefs: The Current Situation in Developing Countries, 1985*, United Nations.

18. *State of the World Children 1987*.

19. Ibid.

20. Ibid.

21. Ibid.

22. *Recensement Général 1982 Population et Logement.*

23. Habitat Conference, Vancouver 1976.

24. *State of the World Children 1987*.

25. *Recensement Général 1982 Population et Logement*. Preliminary Data.

26. Ibid.

27. No data.

28. *Statistical Yearbook 1986*, UNESCO.

29. Ibid.

30. *State of the World Children 1987*.

31. *Statistical Yearbook 1986*, UNESCO.

32. *Yearbook of Labour Statistics 1986*, International Labour Office, Geneva, Chapter 1, Table 1, p. 13.

33. *Atlaseco de Poche, Atlas Economique Mondial* (Paris: Les éditions S.G.P., 1985). Data taken from World Bank sources.

34. *World Development Report 1987*.

35. *State of the World Children 1987*.

36. *Statistical Yearbook 1986*, UNESCO.

37. Ibid.

JAMAICA

1. *The New International Atlas* (Chicago: Rand McNally, 1986), Tables I–10 to I–13. Estimates for January 1, 1985, based on official data, United Nations estimates, and other available information.

2. Ibid.

3. *1987 World Population Data Sheet*, Population Reference Bureau (Washington, D.C.). Source: FAO and U.S. Department of State.

3a. Ibid.

4. *United Nations World Population Chart 1985*, Population Division, United Nations.

5. Ibid.

6. *1987 World Population Data Sheet*.

7. *The Prospects of World Urbanization*, Population Division, United Nations (rev. ed., 1984–85).

8. Ibid.

9. *Demographic Yearbook 1983*, United Nations.

10. George Thomas Kurian, *Encyclopedia of the Third World* (3rd ed.; New York: Facts on File, Inc., 1987), Vol. I, p. 1003.

11. *Population Census 1982*, Statistical Institute of Jamaica, Vol. I, p. 11. Population 14 years and over not attending primary or secondary school full-time in private and selected non-private households.

12. *Population Census 1982*.

13. *State of the World Children 1987*, UNICEF (New York: Oxford University Press, 1987), annex tables.

14. No data.

15. *Demographic Yearbook 1983*, United Nations. Data tabulated by date of registration rather than occurrence.

16. *World Development Report 1987*, World Bank (New York: Oxford University Press, 1987).

17. *Population Policy Briefs: The Current Situation in Developing Countries, 1985*, United Nations.

18. *State of the World Children 1987*.

19. Ibid.

20. Ibid.

21. Ibid.

22. *Encyclopedia of the Third World*, p. 1002.

23. *Population Census 1982*.

24. *State of the World Children 1987*.

25. *Population Census 1982*, Vol. I, p. 22.

26. Ibid., p. 24.

27. Ibid., p. 18.

28. *Statistical Yearbook 1986*, UNESCO.

29. Ibid.

30. *State of the World Children 1987*.

31. *Statistical Yearbook 1986*, UNESCO. For population 14 years and over.

32. *Yearbook of Labour Statistics 1986*, International Labour Office, Geneva, Chapter 1, Table 1, p. 13.

33. *Atlaseco de Poche, Atlas Economique Mondial* (Paris: Les éditions S.G.P., 1985). Data taken from World Bank sources.

34. *World Development Report 1987*.

35. *State of the World Children 1987*.

36. *Statistical Yearbook 1986*, UNESCO.

37. Ibid.

ST. KITTS and NEVIS

1. *The New International Atlas*, (Chicago: Rand McNally, 1986), Tables I-10 to I-13. Estimates for January 1, 1985, based on official data, United Nations estimates, and other available information.

2. Ibid.

3. *1987 World Population Data Sheet*, Population Reference Bureau (Washington, D.C.). Source: FAO and U.S. Department of State.

3a. Ibid.

4. *United Nations World Population Chart 1985*, Population Division, United Nations.

5. Ibid.

6. *1987 World Population Data Sheet*.

7. *United Nations World Population Chart 1985*.

8. No data.

9. *1980–1981 Population Census of the Commonwealth Caribbean*.

10. Ibid.

11. Ibid., Vol. I, p. 124. Females 14 years and over not attending

primary or secondary school full-time. Where the respondent is over 45 years old, the union status reported is that which existed at age 45.

12. Ibid., Vol. I, p. 168.

13. *1987 World Population Data Sheet*.

14. No data.

15. *Demographic Yearbook 1983*, United Nations. Data tabulated by date of registration rather than occurrence.

16. No data.

17. No data.

18. *World Development Report 1987*, World Bank (New York: Oxford University Press, 1987).

19. *State of the World Children 1987*, UNICEF (New York: Oxford University Press, 1987), annex tables.

20. *Demographic Yearbook 1983*, United Nations.

21. *State of the World Children 1987*.

22. *1980–1981 Population Census*. Total population divided by the number of households. Estimate.

23. Ibid.

24. No data.

25. *1980–1981 Population Census*.

26. Ibid.

27. Ibid.

28. *Statistical Yearbook 1986*, UNESCO.

29. No data.

30. No data.

31. *Statistical Yearbook 1986*, UNESCO.

32. *Yearbook of Labour Statistics 1986*, International Labour Office, Geneva, Chapter 1, Table 1, p. 13.

33. *Atlaseco de Poche, Atlas Economique Mondial* (Paris: Les éditions S.G.P., 1985). Data taken from World Bank sources.

34. *World Development Report 1987*.

35. No data.

36. *Statistical Yearbook 1986*, UNESCO.

37. Ibid.

ST. LUCIA

1. *The New International Atlas* (Chicago: Rand McNally, 1986),

Tables I–10 to I–13. Estimates for January 1, 1985, based on official data, United Nations estimates, and other available information.

2. Ibid.

3. *1987 World Population Data Sheet*, Population Reference Bureau (Washington, D.C.). Source: FAO and U.S. Department of State.

3a. Ibid.

4. *United Nations World Population Chart 1985*, Population Division, United Nations.

5. Ibid.

6. *1987 World Population Data Sheet*.

7. *1980–1981 Census of the Commonwealth Caribbean*.

8. No data.

9. *1980–1981 Population Census*, Vol. I, pp. 2–3.

10. Ibid., p. 106.

11. Ibid., p. 109. Females 14 years and over not attending primary or secondary school full-time. Where the respondent is over 45 years old, the union status reported is that which existed at age 45.

12. Ibid., p. 143

13. *1987 World Population Data Sheet*.

14. Ministry of Social Services Community Development, Castries.

15. *Demographic Yearbook 1983*, United Nations.

16. No data.

17. *Population Policy Briefs: The Current Situation in Developing Countries, 1985*, United Nations.

18. Total: *United Nations World Population Chart 1985*. By sex: *Statistics on Children in UNICEF Assisted Countries*, UNICEF, April 1987.

19. *State of the World Children 1987*, UNICEF (New York: Oxford University Press, 1987), annex tables.

20. *Statistics on Children in UNICEF Assisted Countries*.

21. *State of the World Children 1987*.

22. *1980–1981 Population Census*, Vol. I, p. 140.

23. Ibid., p. 132.

24. No data.

25. *1980–1981 Population Census*, Vol. I, p. 126.

26. Ibid., Vol. II, p. 441.

27. Ibid., Vol. I, p. 121.

28. *Statistical Yearbook 1986*, UNESCO. Population 10 years and over.

29. Ibid.

30. No data.

31. *Statistical Yearbook 1986*, UNESCO. Population 15 years and over not attending primary or secondary school full-time.

32. *Yearbook of Labour Statistics 1986*, International Labour Office, Geneva, Chapter 1, Table 1, p. 13.

33. *Atlaseco de Poche, Atlas Economique Mondial* (Paris: Les éditions S.G.P., 1985). Data taken from World Bank sources.

30. *State of the World Children 1987*.

34. *World Development Report 1987*, World Bank (New York: Oxford University Press, 1987).

35. No data.

36. *Statistical Yearbook 1986*, UNESCO.

37. Ibid.

ST. VINCENT and THE GRENADINES

1. *The New International Atlas* (Chicago: Rand McNally, 1986), Tables I–10 to I–13. Estimates for January 1, 1985, based on official data, United Nations estimates, and other available information.

2. Ibid.

3. *1987 World Population Data Sheet*, Population Reference Bureau (Washington, D.C.). Source: FAO and U.S. Department of State.

3a. Ibid.

4. *United Nations World Population Chart 1985*, Population Division, United Nations.

5. Ibid.

6. *1987 World Population Data Sheet*.

7. *1980–1981 Population Census of the Commonwealth Caribbean*.

8. No data.

9. *1980–1981 Population Census*, Vol. I, pp. 2–3.

10. George Thomas Kurian, *Encyclopedia of the Third World* (3rd ed.; New York: Facts on File, Inc., 1987), Vol. III, p. 1678.

11. *1980–1981 Population Census*, Vol. I, p. 111. Females 14

years and over not attending primary or secondary school full-time. Where the respondent is over 45 years old, the union status is that which existed at age 45.

12. Ibid., p. 161.
13. *1987 World Population Data Sheet.*
14. No data.
15. *Demographic Yearbook 1983*, United Nations. Data tabulated by date of registration rather than occurrence.
16. No data.
17. *Population Policy Briefs: The Current Situation in Developing Countries, 1985*, United Nations.
18. *1987 World Population Data Sheet* and *Encyclopedia of the Third World*, p. 1678.
19. *State of the World Children 1987*, UNICEF (New York: Oxford University Press, 1987), annex tables.
20. *Statistics on Children in UNICEF Assisted Countries*, UNICEF, April 1987.
21. *State of the World Children 1987.*
22. *1980–1981 Population Census.*
23. Ibid.
24. No data.
25. *1980–1981 Population Census*, Vol. I, p. 136.
26. Ibid.
27. Ibid.
28. *Statistics on Children.*
29. Ibid.
30. No data.
31. *Statistical Yearbook 1986*, UNESCO.
32. *Yearbook of Labour Statistics 1986*, International Labour Office, Geneva, Chapter 1, Table 1, p. 13.
33. *Atlaseco de Poche, Atlas Economique Mondial* (Paris: Les éditions S.G.P., 1985). Data taken from World Bank sources.
34. *World Development Report 1987*, World Bank (New York: Oxford University Press, 1987).
35. No data.
36. *Statistical Yearbook 1986*, UNESCO.
37. Ibid.

TRINIDAD and TOBAGO

1. *The New International Atlas* (Chicago: Rand McNally, 1986), Tables I–10 to I–13. Estimates for January 1, 1985, based on official data, United Nations estimates, and other available information.
2. Ibid.
3. *1987 World Population Data Sheet*, Population Reference Bureau (Washington, D.C.). Source: FAO and U.S. Department of State.
3a. Ibid.
4. *United Nations World Population Chart 1985*, Population Division, United Nations.
5. Ibid.
6. *1987 World Population Data Sheet.*
7. *The Prospects of World Urbanization*, Population Division, United Nations (rev. ed., 1984–85).
8. Ibid.
9. *Demographic Yearbook 1983*, United Nations.
10. *Population and Housing Census 1980*, Vol. II. Age Structure, Religion, Ethnic Group, Education, Administrative Areas. Republic of Trinidad and Tobago. Central Statistical Office, Ministry of Finance, 1983. Pp. 16, 28.
11. *Census 1980*, Vol. VI. Fertility, Union Status, Marriage. 1985. P. 37.
12. *Census 1980*, Vol. II, p. 3.
13. *1987 World Population Data Sheet.*
14. *Population and Vital Statistics Report 1980–1981*, Table 3, p. 6.
15. Ibid.
16. *World Development Report 1987*, World Bank (New York: Oxford University Press, 1987).
17. *Population Policy Briefs: The Current Situation in Developing Countries, 1985*, United Nations.
18. *State of the World Children 1987*, UNICEF (New York: Oxford University Press, 1987), annex tables.
19. Ibid.
20. Ibid.
21. Ibid.
22. *Census 1980*, Vol. VII, Households, 1985.
23. Ibid., p. 192.
24. *State of the World Children 1987.*
25. *Census 1980*, Vol. VII, p. 182.
26. Ibid., p. 202.
27. Ibid., p. 92.
28. *Statistical Yearbook 1986*, UNESCO.
29. Ibid.
30. *State of the World Children 1987.*
31. *Statistical Yearbook 1986*, UNESCO.
32. *Yearbook of Labour Statistics 1986*, International Labour Office, Geneva, Chapter 1, Table 1, p. 13.
33. *Atlaseco de Poche, Atlas Economique Mondial* (Paris: Les éditions S.G.P., 1985). Data taken from World Bank sources.
34. *World Development Report 1987.*
35. *State of the World Children 1987.*
36. *Statistical Yearbook 1986*, UNESCO.
37. Ibid.

North America

CANADA

1. *The New International Atlas* (Chicago: Rand McNally, 1986), Tables I–10 to I–13. Estimates for January 1, 1985, based on official data, United Nations estimates, and other available information.
2. Ibid.
3. *1987 World Population Data Sheet*, Population Reference Bureau (Washington, D.C.). Source: FAO and U.S. Department of State.
3a. Ibid.
4. *United Nations World Population Chart 1985*, Population Division, United Nations.
5. Ibid.
6. *1987 World Population Data Sheet.*
7. *The Prospects of World Urbanization*, Population Division, United Nations (rev. ed., 1984–85). De jure population.
8. Ibid.
9. *Demographic Yearbook 1983*, United Nations.
10. Ibid.
11. *Demographic Yearbook 1982*, United Nations. De jure population.
12. *Statistics Canada.*
13. *State of the World Children 1987*, UNICEF (New York: Oxford University Press, 1987), annex tables.

14. No data.

15. *Demographic Yearbook 1983*, United Nations. Excluding Newfoundland; including Canadian residents temporarily in the United States but excluding United States residents temporarily in Canada.

16. *World Development Report 1987*, World Bank (New York: Oxford University Press, 1987). Abortion: Christopher Tietze, *Induced Abortion: A World Review 1983* (New York: The Population Council, 1983), p. 26. Live births six months later. Excludes abortions in non-hospital clinics in Quebec.

17. *Population Policy Briefs: The Current Situation in Developing Countries, 1985*, United Nations.

18. *State of the World Children 1987*.

19. Ibid.

20. Ibid.

21. Ibid.

22. *Compendium of Human Settlements Statistics 1983*, United Nations.

23. No data.

24. No data.

25. *Compendium of Human Settlements Statistics 1983*. Data based on a sample survey.

26. Ibid. Data based on a sample survey.

27. No data.

28. "The World's Women: A Profile," 1985 chart, Population Reference Bureau.

29. *Statistical Yearbook 1986*, UNESCO.

30. *State of the World Children 1987*.

31. *Canada at a Glance*, Communication Division, Statistics Canada.

32. *Yearbook of Labour Statistics 1986*, International Labour Office, Geneva, Chapter 1, Table 1, p. 13. For population 15 years and over.

33. *Atlaseco de Poche, Atlas Economique Mondial* (Paris: Les éditions S.G.P., 1985). Data taken from World Bank sources.

34. *World Development Report 1987*.

35. Ibid.

36. *Statistical Yearbook 1986*, UNESCO.

37. Ibid.

UNITED STATES OF AMERICA

1. *The New International Atlas* (Chicago: Rand McNally, 1986), Tables I–10 to I–13. Estimates for January 1, 1985, based on official data, United Nations estimates, and other available information.

2. Ibid.

3. *1987 World Population Data Sheet*, Population Reference Bureau (Washington, D.C.). Source: FAO and U.S. Department of State.

3a. Ibid.

4. *United Nations World Population Chart 1985*, Population Division, United Nations.

5. Ibid.

6. *1987 World Population Data Sheet*.

7. *Demographic Yearbook 1983*, United Nations. De jure population, but excluding civilian citizens absent from the country for an extended period of time. Excluding armed forces overseas.

8. *Demographic Indicators of Countries: Estimates and Projections as Assessed in 1980*. Population Division, United Nations.

9. United States Bureau of the Census, *Statistical Abstract of the United States, 1986* (106th ed.; Washington, D.C., 1985), p. 26. Resident population excluding armed forces overseas. Estimate as of July 1, 1984.

10. *Demographic Yearbook 1983*, United Nations.

11. *Statistical Abstract, 1986*, p. 35. Females 18 years and over.

12. Ibid., p. 40.

13. *State of the World Children 1987*, UNICEF (New York: Oxford University Press, 1987), annex tables.

14. *Statistical Abstract, 1986*, p. 62.

15. *Demographic Yearbook 1983*.

16. *World Population Report 1987*, World Bank (New York: Oxford University Press, 1987).

17. *Population Policy Briefs: The Current Situation in Developing Countries, 1985*, United Nations.

18. *State of the World Children 1987*.

19. Ibid.

20. Ibid.

21. Ibid.

22. *Statistical Abstract, 1986*, p. 39.

23. No data.

24. No data.

25. *1980 Census of Housing*, Vol. I. Characteristics of Housing Units. Chapter B, Detailed Housing Characteristics. Part 1, United States Summary, HC80-1-B1. U.S. Department of Commerce, Bureau of the Census, December 1983. P. 66. Year-round housing units.

26. *1980 Census of Housing*, Vol. I, Chapter B, Part 1, p. 66. Year-round housing units.

27. No data.

28. *Statistical Yearbook 1986*, UNESCO. For population 14 years and over.

29. Ibid.

30. No data.

31. *Digest of Education Statistics*, 1987, Center for Education Statistics, Department of Education, Washington, D.C.

32. *Yearbook of Labour Statistics 1986*, International Labour Office, Geneva, Chapter 1, Table 1, p. 13.

33. *Atlaseco de Poche, Atlas Economique Mondial* (Paris: Les éditions S.G.P., 1985). Data taken from World Bank sources.

34. *World Development Report 1987*.

35. *1980 Census of Population*, Vol. I. Chapter C, General Social and Economic Characteristics. Part 1. PC80-1-C1. December 1983. P. 11.

36. *Statistical Yearbook 1986*.

37. Ibid. 1977 data do not include relay transmitters.